KU-255-280

The Mexican Petroleum Industry
in the Twentieth Century

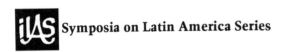 Symposia on Latin America Series

Institute of Latin American Studies
University of Texas at Austin

The Mexican Petroleum Industry
in the Twentieth Century

Edited by
Jonathan C. Brown and **Alan Knight**

University of Texas Press, Austin

Institute of Latin American Studies
31 Tavistock Square
London WC1H 9HA

D 338. 27282
MEX
M COLL 11696
-3. MAR. 1998

Copyright © 1992 by the University of Texas Press
All rights reserved
Printed in the United States of America

Requests for permission to reproduce material from this work should be sent to:
    Permissions
    University of Texas Press
    P.O. Box 7819
    Austin, Texas 78713-7819

♾ The paper used in this publication meets the minimum requirements of American National Standard for Information Sciences—Permanence of Paper for Printed Library Materials, ANSI Z39.48–1984.

Library of Congress Cataloging-in-Publication Data

The Mexican petroleum industry in the twentieth century / edited by
    Jonathan C. Brown and Alan Knight
        p.   cm. — (Symposia on Latin America series)
    Includes bibliographical references and index.
    ISBN 0-292-76533-9
    1. Petroleum industry and trade—Mexico—History—20th century—
Congresses. I. Brown, Jonathan C. (Jonathan Charles), 1942– .
II. Knight, Alan, 1946– . III. Series.
HD9574.M6M615 1992   92-30049
338.2'7282'09720904—dc20   CIP

Contents

.

Preface

The papers in this volume were presented at a conference organized at the University of Texas at Austin in February 1988. That conference was made possible by a generous grant from the C. B. Smith Sr. Chair for U.S.-Mexican Studies and by the support of the Department of History, the Institute of Latin American Studies, and the Mexican Center. In particular, Robert King, Dean of Liberal Arts, gave the project his full backing, while noting that there was a certain "delicious irony" in the fact that the University of Texas—an institution built on oil—should host a conference commemorating the fiftieth anniversary of the expropriation, by the Mexican government, of the Anglo-American petroleum companies.

Introduction

Alan Knight
Oxford University

In 1826, Captain George Lyon of the British Royal Navy came to Mexico as a representative of the celebrated Real del Monte mining company. His mission, like that of so many foreigners who had ventured to Mexico since Cortés's initial expedition of 1519, concerned precious metal, specifically silver, which, five years after Mexico's independence, still figured as the country's principal export and source of foreign exchange. Captain Lyon did not therefore feel any frisson of discovery when, amid the scattered cattle ranches inland from the port of Tampico, he came upon a "great lake," populated by crocodiles and turtles, upon whose surface floated large chunks of *chapopote*, "which is said to bubble up from the lakebed." Traders took the *chapopote* to Tampico, where it sold for 4 reales (about 13¢) a quintal, and was used as a form of varnish or to waterproof boat bottoms. Indeed, shortly after, as Lyon explored the hinterland, assailed by heat, bugs, and rainstorms, he availed himself of a ramshackle canoe that, newly caulked with *chapopote*, carried him back down the turbulent Pánuco River to Tampico.[1]

For Captain Lyon, *chapopote* was a local curiosity; for the fishermen and furniture-makers of Tampico it was a local resource. But, a hundred years later, petroleum had become a major item of international trade and investment, a crucial source of power (including naval power), and an object of bitter economic and political competition. With the second industrial revolution, which ushered in the era of cheap, precision-made machinery, development and production of the internal combustion engine forged ahead, generating a voracious demand for oil, rubber, copper, and other nonprecious minerals. Americans began to migrate from concentrated cities to new, sprawling suburbs; the navies of the major powers converted from coal to fuel oil; and in the Third World there began a new cycle of export boom and extractive investment. While the rubber interests ruthlessly plundered the Amazon and Congo basins, the oil companies looked to exploit new overseas resources in Persia, the Russian Caucasus, and Latin America, initially Mexico. The lumps of *chapopote* idly floating in the Tampico lagoons presaged the oil boom that, from the 1900s, would engulf the region, sucking in investment and labor, and turning Tampico from a sleepy port into bustling petroleum entrepôt, Mexico's version of Tsarist Baku.

In the Mexican case, as Jonathan Brown (chap. 1) shows, the oil companies first came to the country as sellers, not producers. Contrary to some common assumptions, the most bitter intercompany dispute— which pitted the rival pioneers Henry Clay Pierce of the United States and Weetman Pearson (later Lord Cowdray) of Great Britain against each other—occurred when Pearson challenged Pierce's effective monopoly on the sale of petroleum products in the Mexican market. Soon, however, Pearson switched to production, capitalizing on his close relationship with the long-standing Díaz government and sinking £5 million in oil exploration. In 1908 his company hit a gusher, Dos Bocas, in northern Veracruz. The well, however, caught fire and burned for eight weeks, with the loss of a £1 million and a million tons of oil. But a year later, when a second gusher, Potrero No. 4, burst from the soil of the Huasteca, Pearson's engineers, soaked in oil and almost asphixiated, improvised the technology required to tame the well: three million barrels of oil spewed into the surrounding countryside, devastating the fields; but Potrero No. 4 delivered another hundred million barrels during its eight-year lifetime.

Those eight years (1909–1917) coincided with the takeoff of the Mexican oil industry and, of course, with the Mexican Revolution. As Potrero No. 4 gushed, Francisco Madero was preparing and organizing his liberal democratic challenge to the Díaz regime, a personalist and authoritarian regime whose longevity belied its institutional frailty. By 1910, as Mexican oil production began a vertiginous rise, Madero was ready to challenge Díaz on the battlefield, enlisting the support of peasant forces whose socioeconomic—especially agrarian—grievances against the old regime differed from the political concerns of their educated Maderista allies. Díaz fell, to general surprise; Madero inaugurated a fragile liberal regime; and the oil continued to flow. Now, however, petroleum could not be insulated from politics. Conspiracy theorists (never wanting when revolutions occur) attributed the fall of Díaz to the displeasure of the U.S. oil interests, who resented Pearson/ Cowdray's close relationship with Díaz. In crude terms, Madero was an agent of Standard Oil. The charge, impossible either to substantiate or to refute, seems doubtful.[2] What is certainly clear is that the oil industry, now generating healthy returns on initial investment, was a resource that shaky governments could not ignore, especially when rumors of petroleum politicking came thick and fast. The state government of Veracruz and the national government of Madero imposed new taxes;

Mexican *políticos* and technocrats began to debate the status of the industry, the terms under which it should operate, and the degree of state regulation it should incur.[3] As Jonathan Brown argues, the subsequent history of the Mexican petroleum industry can be seen as a complex dialectic between companies and state, with respective powers and capabilities shifting according to the fortunes of internal political conflict and external economic conditions.

During the early years of the Revolution (1910–1914), governments and companies wrangled primarily over taxation. Thereafter, as production rose, as the stakes of the conflict grew, and as revolutionary administrations became both financially more desperate and politically more nationalist, so the disputes expanded to take in broader questions of control and sovereignty. Under the terms of the new 1917 Constitution, the Mexican state asserted the nation's ownership of subsoil deposits of hydrocarbons, thus rescinding the freehold rights acquired by the major oil companies under Díaz. The companies refused to accept the legitimacy of such retroactive legislation and the scene was set for protracted dispute, which stretched through the 1920s.

Meanwhile, the dyadic conflicts between government and companies soon acquired additional dimensions. Metropolitan government—chiefly Great Britain and the United States—backed their nationals in Mexico: first, out of a general and traditional imperialist concern for overseas assets, now threatened by an impudent Third World nationalism; second, out of a particular concern for petroleum resources, whose strategic value was emphasized by the First World War. Finally, with the dramatic increase in output (which peaked in 1921) and the concomitant growth of the port of Tampico, the oil region became a pioneer center of the Mexican labor movement. Here, as Lief Adleson (chap. 2) shows, migrants flocked to the oil fields and docks: the push factors of increasing landlessness, declining real wages, and, after 1910, revolutionary upheaval, combined with the pull factors of better wages and relative job security. However, life in the booming oil zone was harsh and unhealthy; it required rural migrants to adjust to new forms of work discipline, new modes of social organization and existence. Out of this emerged a working class community that was noted for its militancy and solidarity, which would become a key player in the oil politics of the 1920s and 1930s.

Mexico's first great oil boom peaked in 1921. Thereafter—for reasons that are open to debate—production declined and investment shifted elsewhere, chiefly to Venezuela.[4] Oil revenue tided over the precarious Carranza and Obregón administrations, but by the mid-1920s it had lost its previous importance, and President Calles, taking control of a more buoyant ship of state late in 1924, felt confident in enforcing the hitherto dormant provisions of the constitution in regard to both the oil industry and—that other revolutionary *bête noire*—the Catholic church. Calles, as his close collaborator Puig Casauranc put it, would be "master in his own house."[5] But on both fronts, Calles found he had a fight on his hands. The Catholics protested and rebelled; the oil companies—notwithstanding their diminishing Mexican returns—protested, lobbied, and invoked the support of a congenial Republican administration in Washington. These twin conflicts, which dominated Mexican politics and foreign relations during the later Calles presidency (1926–1928), could not be fought to a conclusion, however. Both resulted in stalemate and compromise. The Mexican government would not—could not—rescind the anticlerical and economic nationalist provisions of the constitution, which had now become shibboleths of revolutionary rectitude. But it could soft-pedal their implementation. The retroactive character of the Calles oil legislation was not enforced; companies were not required to exchange freehold property rights for concessionary leases.

The petroleum compromise (the Calles-Morrow agreement) of 1927 marked the end of a decade of wrangling initiated with the Constitution of 1917. It marked, too, a recognition that U.S. petroleum investments in Mexico were now less crucial, hence less capable of molding U.S. policy toward its southern neighbor. Ambassador Morrow, a banker with close ties to Mexico's major creditors, both epitomized and engineered this shift away from confrontation and in favor of detente. In addition, 1927 saw a downswing in the Mexican economy that paralleled similar retreats in many primary-producing countries in Latin America and elsewhere, and that foreshadowed the more sudden recession of 1929. As export prices fell and surpluses accumulated, the old development strategy of *desarrollo hacia afuera*—of export-led growth—was called into question. The crisis of global capitalism after 1929 gave further impetus to the formulation of new development strategies that emphasized greater state intervention, regulation, and concentration on the home market: *desarrollo hacia adentro*. In Mexico, these trends, nascent during the so-called Maximato (1928–1934), came to fruition with the Cárdenas administration of 1934–1940. The world depression, conspiring with powerful domestic forces, brought into being a radical reformist administration, friendly to organized labor, unimpressed by the virtue of the free market, and committed to a significant measure of *dirigisme* and state ownership.

As Mexico gradually withdrew from the global petroleum market, so oil production increasingly served domestic rather than foreign demand. It thus formed an important part of government plans for economic revival and industrial growth. But the foreign oil companies, which still controlled production, were hardly sympathetic to *dirigiste* policies, nor did they welcome the growing labor militancy of the oil workers. The latter, as Olvera (chap. 3) and Adler (chap. 5) show, followed national trends in successfully organizing, bargaining, and striking. They took advantage of—and in turn contributed to—the break-up of the old, dominant, *callista* labor confederation, the CROM, and the rise of the new, more militant, CTM, which supported (albeit conditionally) the reformist Cárdenas administration. The picture was further complicated by the revival in oil production brought about by the development of the new Poza Rica field by the Anglo-Dutch Mexican Eagle Co. (1932). Output now rose; the stakes—for companies, government, and unions alike—increased proportionately; and, not coincidentally, Poza Rica acquired one of the most militant and, according to Olvera, one of the most democratic union movements in the oil industry.

The sequence of events in the later 1930s, analyzed in several chapters in this volume, was rapid and dramatic. In 1936, the new petroleum workers union was established, grouping, for the first time, most of the workers in the industry. Its demand for a collective contract was resisted by the companies; arbitration failed to achieve a solution; and the Mexican Supreme Court, when it endorsed the arbitration award, incurred the defiance of the companies. Facing the threat of further unrest and economic dislocation, and angered by the intransigence of the oil companies, President Cárdenas nationalized the oil industry (March 1938). As Knight (chap. 4) argues, this was not the result of long-term calculation, but the product of immediate, unforeseen circumstances, in which companies, government, and workers all played autonomous roles.

The nationalization had a decisive impact on Mexico's foreign and domestic policies. It was, as George Philip (chap. 7) argues, an unprecedented action taken by a Third World power against First World corporate interests. It led to acrimonious wrangles between Mexico and the oil companies' metropolitan governments: that of the United States, which reacted with some circumspection, and that of Great Britain, which chose to make an issue of the expropriation, fearing its consequences elsewhere in the world. As a result, Lorenzo Meyer (chap. 6) shows, Anglo-Mexican relations reached a breaking point. The domestic impact of nationalization was also profound. Along with the railroads, the oil industry became a test case of the new relationship that had to be forged between government and unions in the wake of nationalization. This proved a tense relationship, Ruth Adler argues, since the oil workers—denied direct control of the industry—had to conform to the imperatives of national policy, which, after 1938, was increasingly conservative (or, at least, less radical). Policies of fiscal restraint and belt-tightening strained the government-union relationship and thus contributed to the fragmentation of the once impressive *cardenista* coalition. The 1940 presidential election both revealed the political disintegration of *cardenismo* and accelerated the government's shift to the center—and, later, the right—of the political spectrum.

In these changing circumstances, the role of Pemex also changed. First, as Barbosa (chap. 8) shows, the new nationalized industry faced severe problems, the result of international boycott and internal reorganization. Furthermore, Pemex now had to play its role within the emergent political economy of the 1940s: one in which *cardenista* collectivism increasingly gave way to *alemanista* individualism, and in which the public sector (be it *ejido*, Pemex, or Nafinsa [Nacional Financiera, S.A.]) increasingly served the interests of private capital accumulation. Isidro Morales's analyses (chaps. 9–10), covering the neglected years of Pemex from the 1940s through the 1970s, show how the company underwrote the industrial boom of the war years and the subsequent "economic miracle," supplying cheap fuel to a burgeoning industrial and urban society. Unspectacular (and hence relatively unresearched), Pemex's role in sustaining the growth rates of the 1940–1970 period was crucial, albeit it was a somewhat self-abnegating role, which deprived the company of needed investment capital. Meanwhile, within the company, a powerful union bureaucracy preserved lucrative jobs, perks, and a measure of industrial peace.

During the years of the "miracle," Mexico produced and consumed its own oil; after 1969 it became a net importer. With global oil prices rising, especially after the 1973–1974 crisis, it was vital for Mexico to expand its domestic output. Investment in Pemex rose, exploration was pushed ahead, and by the later 1970s rapid gains were being made. Mexico became a net exporter once again and, under the presidency of José López Portillo (1976–1982), the country experienced its second great oil boom, paralleling that of the 1910s and 1920s. Petroleum underwrote Mexico credit, facilitating lavish foreign loans; it financed increased public expenditure; it contributed to official graft; and, most important, it appeared to confer a new lease of life on the old import substitution model of development. Hard choices were postponed; petroleum would provide a painless means of economic modernization.

As Gabriel Székely's and George Baker's concluding chapters explain, the oil boom did not last: petroleum prices fell—in 1982 and again in 1986—and, as foreign exchange earnings slumped, the oil boom gave way to an oil bust. Mexico was left carrying a heavy burden of foreign debt and facing the overdue problems of economic restructuring. Since oil could no longer carry the burden of exports, alternatives had to be found and the later 1980s witnessed an aggressive drive toward export diversification. This in turn required a painful modernization of Mexican industry and (its proponents argued) an onslaught on the inherited bottlenecks and inefficiencies of the old political economy. Pemex had to be slimmed down and rationalized; to this end, the power of the entrenched union bureaucracy (whose resistance to rationalization had been clearly signaled during the 1988 presidential campaign) had to be broken. Within weeks of assuming the presidency, President Salinas de Gortari ordered a dramatic ouster of the de facto leader of the oil workers union, Joaquín Hernández Galicia, *La Quina*. The army surrounded his house, bazookaed his front door, and carried him off to jail. One of the most enduring symbols of the petroleum political economy was thus toppled.

It is a cliché that Mexico enters the 1990s in a state of rapid change and uncertainty. Economic liberalization proceeds apace; negotiations for a North American Free Trade Agreement (or Treaty) are under way; political reform is demanded, promised, and, at best, haltingly implemented. Analogies with Eastern Europe (often ill-conceived) raise the sense of expectation. Will the historic national political monopoly of the PRI be relinquished? Will the current policy of "state-shrinking" extend to that embodiment of revolutionary—especially *cardenista*—economic nationalism, Pemex? Although the current administration is prepared to concede greater foreign collaboration with Pemex, this clearly does not involve any thoroughgoing privatization. As regards the free trade negotiations, petroleum is a special and contentious case. Domestically, the privatization of airlines or telephones may be politically acceptable—even popular—but it is another thing altogether to put "revolutionary" items like the Cananea mines, or Pemex, on the auction block, especially when the leader of the leftist opposition is the son of Lázaro Cárdenas and when 18 March remains a hallowed day on the nationalist calendar. Even in these days of rampant technocracy, some political and historic landmarks command respect. For, as these essays demonstrate, the history of the oil industry closely interweaves with the grander story of Mexico's social-political and economic development during the twentieth century; the expropriation of 1938 represented the apotheosis of revolutionary nationalism; and the company born of that expropriation, Pemex, has played a major role in the building of a dynamic, modern, industrial Mexico. It will continue to play such a role as Mexico enters the 1990s, embarked upon a project of ambitious but arduous economic restructuring.

Notes

1. G. F. Lyon, *Residencia en México, 1826* (Mexico City: Fondo de Cultura Económica, 1984), pp. 31, 51.

2. Cf. P. A. R. Calvert, *The Mexican Revolution 1910–1914: The Diplomacy of Anglo-American Conflict* (Cambridge: Cambridge University Press, 1968),

pp.73–84; Friedrich Katz, *The Secret War in Mexico: Europe, the United States and the Mexican Revoution* (Chicago: University of Chicago Press, 1981), pp. 26–27, 37.

3. The classic study of the oil wrangle is Lorenzo Meyer, *México y Estados Unidos en el conflicto petrolero* (Mexico City: El Colegio de México, 1968).

4. Jonathan C. Brown, "Why Foreign Oil Companies Shifted Production from Mexico to Venezuela during the 1920s," *American Historical Review* 90 (April 1985), pp. 362–385.

5. Meyer, *México y Estados Unidos,* pp.183, 200–201, 234.

1. The Structure of the Foreign-Owned Petroleum Industry in Mexico, 1880–1938

Jonathan C. Brown
University of Texas at Austin

Any analysis of a foreign-owned economic asset in Latin America must address more than its exogenous determinants—especially, its relationship to the international economy. The analyst must also deal with the extent to which internal factors influence the industry. These subjects are by no means trivial. They go to the pith of debates among economists over development and dependency and among historians over modes of production and theories of foreign investment. Similarly, these concerns are ageless. In Latin America today, as at the turn of the century, politicians and intellectuals still argue over the proper role of foreign capital in their economies. Laborers continue to struggle for dignity and security in a fluid industrial society, set in motion decades ago by foreign entrepreneurs, in which employers still desire to maximize profits and the state seeks taxation and employment. The Mexican oil industry of today and yesterday illustrates the turbulence of these continuing debates. Foreign capitalists, the state, and labor continuously negotiate an elusive equilibrium.

This chapter proposes to investigate the structure of the Mexican oil industry roughly from its inception until its expropriation by the Mexican government. During this time, foreign companies controlled production and distribution of Mexico's oil, while Mexican workers became an industrial proletariat and the state benefited principally as a taxing agent. The crucial question is this: to what extent was the structure of Mexico's nascent petroleum industry determined by the foreign owners, by the native labor force, and by the state? This analysis assumes that a study of the structure of the Mexican oil industry prior to nationalization will be most revealing in terms of the relative autonomy of the foreign interests to carry on their operations without being restricted by other than market considerations. If growth and change in the early industry can be explained in terms of its connection to the international economy, then the entrepreneurs will be considered autonomous. At times, actions by labor and the state may disengage the industry somewhat from the economic environment. Changes in the international economic conditions, moreover, may indirectly affect the industry's autonomy insofar as they produce shifts in the activism of the state and labor.

The complexity of the nascent oil industry should not be surprising. In general terms, the domestic and international constraints on company autonomy varied dramatically during the first sixty years of Mexico's petroleum history. International prices and demand, the world business cycle, the relative political unity of the Mexican state, the ebb and flow of class struggle, the vitality of the domestic market, and the competition among the foreign interests—these factors worked in varying combinations at different periods of time, one set of factors sometimes acting as a countervailing force to others. Yet the long-term trend led to a reduced company autonomy.

In this respect, the expropriation of 1938 cannot be explained, as was the case at the time, as a short-term result of a Cárdenas government conspiracy (which was the company explanation). Nor did it result entirely from foreign capital's obstinacy (which was the Mexican government's interpretation).[1] Instead, Mexico's oil nationalization culminated a period in which the Mexicans themselves, because of the flux created by certain international and domestic factors, increasingly came to determine the fate of the foreign-owned petroleum industry. If there is one historical catalyst that differentiates Mexico's oil history from that of other Latin American nations, one would have to point to the 1921 oil bust. It appears to be the fulcrum on which all else balances.

Oil Pioneering during the Porfiriato

The birth of Mexico's modern oil industry is not marked by the dramatic Gulf Coast oil discoveries at the beginning of this century but by the growth of the Mexican market for petroleum at the end of the last. Railways, mining operations, domestic and export agriculture, industrial and artisan manufacturing, and internal consumption all expanded appreciably during the Porfiriato, from 1877 to 1911. The moving stock of railways needed petroleum-based lubricants, as did the agricultural processing equipment and the machinery in mining and textile plants. In the cities, increasingly prosperous and sophisticated consumers purchased imported lamps that burned kerosene. Even the Irish-made light buoys at the entrances of the nation's harbors burned petroleum fuel.[2]

At first, local production was not destined to supply this steadily rising demand. A number of foreign and domestic entrepreneurs attempted to exploit the commercial potential of numerous oil exudes, called *chapopotes*, that dotted the coastal plain along the Gulf of Mexico from Tampico to Ciudad del Cármen. Before 1900, oil pioneers suffered from a lack of capital and an insufficiently developed infrastructure. The small drilling and distilling operations at Sarlat, Cerro Viejo, and San José de Rusias between 1858 and 1896 were so isolated that the pioneer entrepreneurs had no way of delivering the petroleum to consumers in Mexico City, Guadalajara, and Monterrey.[3] Development of the Mexican market for petroleum products, a necessary precondition to domestic production, proved to be expensive. The petroleum seller needed capital, management skills, and technological expertise. These commodities, developed in more advanced capitalist economies, gave the advantage in Mexico to foreigners with prior experience in oil sales. Their success might have blocked forever any effective competition in petroleum on the part of private Mexican entrepreneurs.

In developing the market, the Waters-Pierce Oil Company of St. Louis came into monopoly control of petroleum sales within Mexico. Henry Clay Pierce was an experienced oil marketer in the United States. After affiliating his company with Standard Oil in 1878 (although Pierce jealously maintained management control), Waters-Pierce became Standard's major sales firm in the Lower Mississippi Valley. Mexico was but an extension of Waters-Pierce's U.S. market. The company marketed oil products exclusively produced and refined by other Standard Oil subsidiaries and affiliates. Waters-Pierce did not operate a single oil well or refinery of its own in the United States.[4] Very soon, the affiliate took advantage of tariff barriers by establishing three refineries, at Mexico City, Monterrey, and Tampico, importing crude oil via steam tanker from Standard Oil's Pennsylvania terminal. The Standard Oil connections accounted for the undisputed market position of Waters-Pierce in Mexico. As Henry Clay Pierce himself explained, "we shipped nearly everything that went into the upkeep of refineries in Mexico from New York, and the tin for the manufacture of cases went from there and iron for tanks, in fact everything that entered into the manufacture of oil down there was shipped from New York." At the height of its operations in 1902, Waters-Pierce maintained ten tank-distribution stations, sales agencies in the major cities, and more than 350 railway tank cars in Mexico.[5] The import of crude oil from the United States rose from an an annual average of 400 barrels between 1880 and 1884 to 670,000 barrels between 1905 and 1909.[6] More than anything, Waters-Pierce's access to U.S. petroleum production gave it a commanding position over potential Mexican competitors.

Waters-Pierce's monopoly in Mexico was ultimately broken for three reasons: its position in the U.S. market came under attack, competing foreign interests began to open up production in Mexico, and the government of Porfirio Díaz, fearful of the "Standard Oil Trust," promoted competition in the industry. Management friction between the affiliate and the parent company after the turn of the century weakened the ability of Waters-Pierce to fight new competition in Mexico. Having engaged blatantly in unfair practices throughout his marketing area, Henry Clay Pierce involved Standard Oil in lawsuits in Missouri, Kansas, and Texas. Standard Oil executives also resented the large dividends that Pierce declared, which sometimes amounted to 40 percent of the company's capitalization.[7] Moreover, the 1901 oil strike at Spindletop ended Waters-Pierce's dominance in Texas and Louisiana. Groups like Gulf Oil and the Texas Companies began to build marketing positions throughout the Southwest based on their growing production and refining capacities in East Texas.[8] Waters-Pierce's marketing clout in the United States was waning as the twentieth century began.

Concurrent with the Texas strike, foreign oilmen too began to move on Waters-Pierce's monopoly in Mexico by developing domestic production. Waters-Pierce came under siege—not from weak domestic entrepreneurs but from capable and well-financed foreigners. The Waters-Pierce monopoly could do nothing but await the inevitable. Edward L. Doheny entered Mexico after having opened up the Los Angeles oil fields in the 1890s.[9] North American railway builders, who had just laid a new rail line between San Luis Potosí and Tampico, invited Doheny to exploit some of the oil exudes along the right-of-way. They wanted a cheap and efficient domestic substitute for imported coal to fuel their locomotives. But Doheny's first production at El Ebano, discovered in 1902, was so heavy that trainmen refused to burn it. His agents in Mexico used it as paving asphalt. Finally, Mexican geologist Ezequiel Ordóñez brought in a larger well in 1904, and Doheny set up a small distillery at El Ebano to refine fuel oil.[10]

Up to 1906, nothing that Doheny had accomplished in Mexican production threatened very much the established sales monopoly of Waters-Pierce. He sold no lubricants or kerosene at all and had to develop his own markets for asphalt and fuel oil. All of this began to consume Doheny's capital. Already having laid out a good deal of his own fortune, Doheny raised additional capital in Pittsburgh and New York. The Standard Oil Company refused to help him, greatly annoying Doheny, but some Mexican bankers from San Luis Potosí may have invested in Doheny's endeavors. Doheny sank $6 million into the Mexican Petroleum Company in its first decade.[11] Nevertheless, he persisted. By 1905, he had acquired new properties in the Tuxpan district, hiring American and Mexican leasing agents to survey the territory on yachts, motor launches, canoes, horses, and donkeys, and by foot. Doheny created the Huasteca Petroleum Company to hold his Tuxpan properties.[12]

The persistence of this independent North American entrepreneur began to pay off in 1910. He finally drilled several producing wells at Casiano, and his men rushed to complete a pipeline and refinery at Pueblo Viejo, across the Pánuco River from Tampico. Faced with flush production, Doheny had no choice but to export, for another foreign entrepreneur was already capturing the Mexican market from Pierce. Therefore, in 1911, Doheny concluded an export contract with Standard Oil, which had just severed its connection to Waters-Pierce, that relieved him of two million barrels of Mexican crude per year for a period of five years.[13]

Doheny's relationship with the Mexican government at the time was correct but fraught with friction. Prominent members of the government's inner circle of *científicos*, Joaquín de Casasús and Pablo Martínez del Río, represented the Doheny interests, securing necessary building permits and duty-free import licenses. They arranged an interview between Doheny and President Díaz. The Díaz government wanted new industries and changed the property laws to encourage foreign investment in Mexico. Reversing centuries of Hispanic legal tradition that had vested ownership of the minerals to the state, the mining reform laws of 1884 and 1892 permitted owners of the land all the fee-simple rights to the subsurface wealth.[14] These private property provisions assured oilmen that they would be rewarded according to market mechanisms for their risk-taking, without government interference. Operating in Mexico was supposed to have been like operating in the United States.

Not all officials of the Díaz regime saw it this way, for many did not favor the success of Edward L. Doheny. The ruling faction was wary of North American domination of the economy; this was the reason why the government, fearing an American railroad trust in Mexico, began to buy railways in 1902. No one wanted an oil trust either. Díaz himself requested Doheny never to sell out to the Standard Oil Company, and his finance secretary, José Ives Limantour, was not above punishing those government officials who favored Doheny. He drove geologist Ezequiel Ordóñez, who was enthusiastic about the American's prospects, out of government service and into the employ of Doheny. As Doheny later reported, Limantour tried "to create an atmosphere of dislike, almost contempt, for our efforts," and many of the men around Díaz "considered our interests as being inimical to theirs."[15]

As yet, there was little that the powerful Díaz government could do to Doheny. His finances, technology, and management came from abroad. Even his skilled laborers were imported from the Pennsylvania and Texas oil fields. Certainly, the oil discoveries of 1910, which he exported to foreign markets, enhanced his bargaining position vis-à-vis the Mexican state, for many a Díaz bureaucrat knew full well that overt restrictions on the American oilmen threatened the continued foreign investment that had made them personally wealthy and politically powerful. The Díaz government did have one recourse: it raised their taxes. In 1910, the government increased the bar duties it collected at the port of Tampico to 50 centavos per ton of exported oil.[16] This was to be the first of many fiscal assessments levied on the foreign-owned petroleum industry.

Since Doheny's activities only indirectly impinged on the Waters-Pierce monopoly, it fell to an unlikely British businessman to stomp on the commercial instep of Henry Clay Pierce—"unlikely" because Sir Weetman Pearson was not an oilman at all but owner of an engineering firm that built railways, port complexes, electrical utilities, and drainage and water systems. But Sir Weetman presented the Mexican state with its one foil against the experienced and well-financed Americans. The Díaz government seized the opportunity.

Pearson's entry into Mexico's oil industry had come in a roundabout fashion. His engineering company at the time was rebuilding the Tehuantepec National Railway in partnership with the Díaz government, and oil exudes existed along its right-of-way as well. Spurred to action by the Spindletop strike, Pearson wired J. B. Body, his general manager in Mexico, to "secure option not only on oil land, but all land for miles around."[17] By 1905, Pearson's men had developed a modest production in a light crude that yielded valuable ends of kerosene, lubricants, and fuel oil. Yielding to optimism, the Pearson group constructed a refinery at Minatitlán, which was enlarged after a fire in 1908.[18] Yet, Pearson too was losing money, as the cost of buying American machinery, hiring skilled American and unskilled Mexican workers, and building pipelines and warehouses consumed more capital than the group was recouping in its initial sales of fuel oil to Mexican railways. Pearson did not even have enough Mexican production to operate his refinery. Like Waters-Pierce, he began buying American crude oil—not from Standard Oil but its new production competitors in Texas.[19]

Unlike Waters-Pierce, however, Pearson cultivated a relationship with the Mexican government that encouraged him to declare war on the Standard Oil affiliate. A government increase in oil import duties hurt Pierce, who still imported every barrel of petroleum he sold in Mexico. In 1906, Pearson received a fifty-year government concession to exploit the oil resources on all national lands and waterways in the state of Veracruz.[20] The government also brought Pearson together with another British entrepreneur, Percy Furber, who was unable to develop his oil field near Papantla for want of capital and expertise.[21] The acquisition of

Furber's property (on which the Poza Rica oil field later was to be discovered) directed Pearson's attention to the region around Tuxpan, where his agents soon confronted Doheny's buyers. In the spring of 1908, a 2,000 barrel per day (b/d) well came in at San Diego, the first of Pearson's oil production outside of the Isthmian region. What happened next confirmed his optimism. An exploratory well at Dos Bocas blew in at the rate of 100,000 b/d. Its column of oil and gas caught fire and burned uncontrollably for two months, reducing the exhausted well to a gapping, bubbling crater.[22] Pearson's men continued exploring the hinterland behind Tuxpan and prepared to move on the Waters-Pierce marketing monopoly—with some help from the government.

Mexican politicians considered it expedient to assist a British businessman against an American. For one thing, Limantour had feared that Standard Oil would absorb all the oil interests in Mexico. Pearson assuaged these fears by incorporating his Compañía Mexicana de Petróleo "El Aguila," S.A., in Mexico and by appointing prominent politicos to the board of directors. He also attempted (albeit unsuccessfully) to sell the company's stock to the Mexican public.[23] Friends in high places secured for El Aguila a contract to supply the National Railways with one-third of its lubricating oils, for which Waters-Pierce previously had been the sole supplier. Soon, El Aguila had bulk storage facilities in the National Railways train yards in ten Mexican states.[24] Henry Clay Pierce responded politically, launching a vicious and transparent press campaign in Mexico to smear the new "Mexican" company. (These press salvos continued during the Revolution, as Pierce attempted to link Pearson to the deposed and discredited Díaz clique.) Pearson's company responded by slashing its prices by 20 percent and recruiting many of Waters-Pierce's sales agents.[25] Because it lowered prices, the "great oil war" in Mexico simultaneously widened the consumption of petroleum products, from 9 million gallons per month in 1906 to 12 million in 1909.[26] Waters-Pierce's volume sales actually increased, although its profit margin declined.

The end of monopoly and beginning of oligopoly, control of the market by a few large companies, came with Pearson's giant oil discovery. In December 1910, at the Hacienda Potrero del Llano near Tuxpan, Pearson's crew of American geologists and drillers brought in the world's most prolific well. Once capped, it would yield 90 million barrels. El Aguila rushed its pipelines and new refinery at Tampico to completion, while Pearson was being elevated to the peerage in England as Lord Cowdray.[27] The supreme irony was yet to come. In May 1911, both Huasteca and El Aguila began to export Mexican petroleum, having successfully converted the Mexican oil industry from monopolistic to oligopolistic ownership and from an importer to an exporter—the very month in which the Díaz government that had contributed to this transition fell from power.

Growth during Revolution

Beginning in 1911, the foreign oil companies entered a decade in which their Mexican operations, benefiting from a confluence of several stimuli, renewed their structural autonomy. Mexican oil production rose spectacularly, international markets were buoyant, prices climbed, the external market gained precedence over the internal, labor remained pliant, and the government was weakened by political disorder and financial need. Cowdray and Doheny took advantage of the situation to expand their petroleum operations. They even developed significant transportation and marketing assets in American and European markets, heretofore dominated by Shell and Standard Oil. The Mexican oil boom attracted a large number of independent oil interests as well as the international giants, who now entered direct production in Mexico for the first time. Waters-Pierce withered. The Revolution further disrupted its large domestic marketing organization, while the newer production and exporting oil companies became dominant in the industry. One countervailing force tempered, however ineffectively, the structural power of the foreign oil companies during this period. That was the disruption of competing military forces and the outbreak of banditry in the oil region. Carranza's nationalistic program and the beginnings of labor organization in the industry caused these growing companies some problems, but they remained harbingers of future obstacles.

World oil prices began to rise gently beginning in 1911 and then steeply with the wartime demand in 1916. The oil interests in Mexico reaped the benefits. (See fig. 1.) This was a time in which navies and trading companies converted their ships from coal to fuel oil.[28] Mexican crude oil from the Golden Lane lent itself, with slight elaboration, to the manufacture of bunker fuel, and every major port along the Atlantic seaboard of the Western Hemisphere took on stocks of Mexican oil.

Price and production trends supported an unprecedented frenzy of exploration on Mexico's Gulf Coast. Of course, both Doheny's Mexican Petroleum and Cowdray's El Aguila retained the lion's share of properties. But now hundreds of independent oilmen, wildcatters, prospectors, and adventurers descended upon the Huasteca and Pánuco regions in search of oil seeps. Most secured contracts on worthless oil land, others sold their leases to bigger concerns, and a lucky minority became wealthy.[29] The confusion of an oil boom in a region where property lines were blurred and informal multifamily ownership was the norm, re-

Figure 1. Average U.S. Price per Barrel of Crude Oil at the Well, 1900–1940 (in U.S. $)

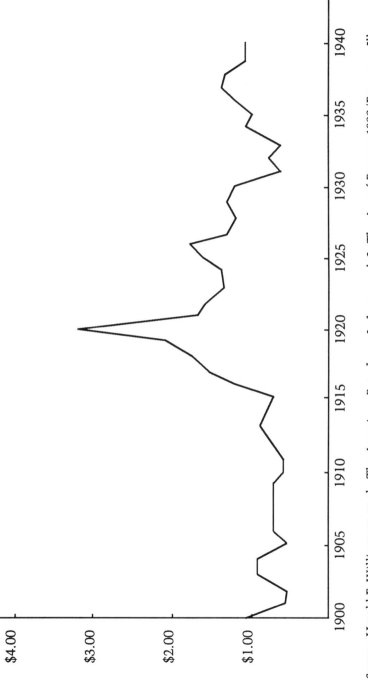

Source: Harold F. Williamson et al., *The American Petroleum Industry*, vol. 2, *The Age of Energy, 1899* (Evanston, Ill., 1963), pp. 39, 464, 539.

sulted in a great many leases' being suspect. If the land, by chance, yielded a flowing well, later litigation became endless, as was the case at Huasteca's Cerro Viejo field.[30]

The multinational oil companies, especially Shell and Standard Oil (New Jersey), whose world market share was eroded by the sudden infusion of Mexican oil, could not afford to stay out of Mexico. Shell organized La Corona Oil Company in 1912 to work a number of oil properties surrounding the town of Pánuco. The Gulf and the Texas Oil companies were among the larger U.S. oil firms to enter Mexico, where they acquired production for export.[31] Although it purchased crude from Doheny, Jersey Standard did not enter production directly until 1917. But Doheny's group was building refineries in New Orleans and Baltimore, and El Aguila was acquiring a sales organization in England and building storage plants in a dozen Latin American ports.[32] Jersey Standard and Shell had to move, if only to save their international dominance. In 1917, Jersey purchased Transcontinental, a company with only one well but with a drawer full of leases. Soon, Jersey Standard had veteran American managers in Mexico directing the work of foreign drilling crews, constructing pipelines, and putting in an oil terminal at Puerto Lobos, midway between Tuxpan and Tampico. By 1920, Transcontinental's production had surpassed 38,000 b/d, becoming the third largest oil concern in Mexico.[33]

The Mexico oil industry turned robust. Together the big and the little production concerns opened up field after field in the Faja de Oro: Ozuluama, San Gerómimo, Chinampa, Amatlán, Tantima, Tanhuijo, Alazán, Horcones, Naranjos. In the northern fields, as the heavy oil district west of Tampico was called, a number of companies worked the oil deposits at Chijol, Pánuco, Topila, beside Doheny's El Ebano. Ownership of the oil fields differed widely. Certain of the fields, such as Chijol in the north and Naranjos in the Golden Lane, were also flourishing agricultural areas, and property ownership had been distributed widely among Mexican smallholders. Each landowner leased to a different company. Thus, offset campaigns ensued in which an individual would take as much from his wells as possible before the neighboring well-owners drained the common reservoir. El Aguila and Mexican Petroleum, on the other hand, already had secured the larger properties, like El Ebano, in the north; Furbero and Cerro Azul in the Faja de Oro; and El Aguila's large holdings in Tabasco and the Isthmus of Tehuantepec.[34] The Cowdray and Doheny interests managed these larger oil fields in the interests of conservation.

Only Waters-Pierce did not seem to benefit greatly from the Mexican bonanza. Pierce's refinery at Tampico was obsolete in comparison to Cowdray's and Doheny's nearby. It was also dangerous. A fire broke out

Figure 2. Oil Production and Exports in Mexico, 1910–1940 (millions of barrels per year)

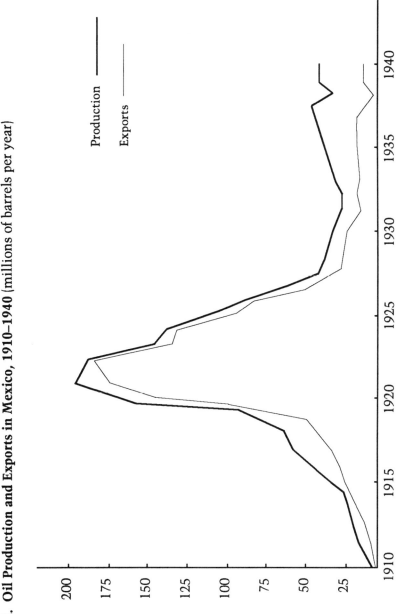

Source: American Petroleum Institute, *Petroleum: Facts and Figures.* 9th ed. (New York, 1951), pp. 444, 450.

at the refinery in 1912, destroying bulk storage tanks, damaging the stills, killing some workers, and forcing others to flee their homes nearby. Safety was to be one of the later demands of the Pierce workers.[35] More damaging was the destruction to Pierce's domestic market in Mexico. The Mexican Revolution devastated the railroad system, destroyed and stranded oil tank cars, and closed mines and businesses that had been buyers of Pierce's products. Of course, the same thing happened to El Aguila's domestic marketing apparatus, but El Aguila more than made up the loss by participating in the export boom. Pierce, on the other hand, drilled a few wells in the Chijol oil field without ever becoming a major producer.[36]

To conclude that labor presented little threat to the structural hegemony of the oil interests in Mexico is not to say that Mexican workers were entirely satisfied with their situation in the industry. The most important change in labor after 1911, which favored the employers, concerned recruitment. Revolution in the highlands disrupted mining and railroading sufficiently to free up Mexican carpenters, boilermakers, mechanics, blacksmiths, and machinery operators. These men readily found jobs in the growing oil industry. Unskilled laborers also migrated from agricultural areas suffering depredations, so much so that companies no longer needed the services of the *enganchadores*, labor contractors who had been recruited laborers during the Porfiriato.[37] Several problems confronted the worker in the great labor emporium of Tampico. The companies did not provide much housing even for the skilled Mexicans, let alone the larger mass of unskilled. On the other hand, American technicians and drilling crews stayed at specially built bachelor hotels. Foreign managers and their families inhabited company-built, single-family, hillside residences, with window screens and corrugated roofing. The Mexicans lived in settlements of tin-roofed *casuchas* and thatched-roofed *jacales* and jerry-built houses on the swamplands surrounding Tampico and the lowlands of oil camps.[38] Moreover, the American worker in Mexico was not the fittest ambassador of the "American way." Principally from Texas and the Old South, the white American workers demanded to live separately. They had their own mess halls, where Chinese cooks prepared the meals. Foreigners made twice as much as Mexicans who worked at similar tasks.[39]

This is not to say that the Mexican resented working for foreign companies, at least initially. Oil jobs were positions of relatively high pay and social status, preferable to working for Mexican enterprises and haciendas that paid much less. There was genuine opportunity to advance for the Mexican who worked hard. Those Mexicans who rose to supervise shops and work gangs received correspondingly higher pay and even company housing. The educated Mexican attorneys and accoun-

Map 1. Northern Veracruz Oil Zone, 1918

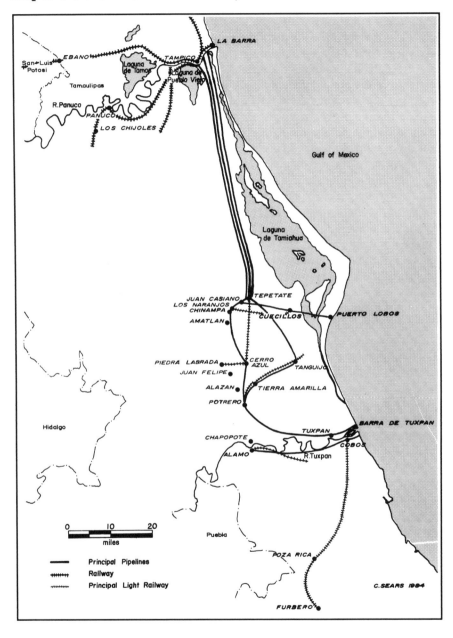

San Luis Potosi

EBANO

TAMPICO

LA BARRA

Laguna de Tamos

Laguna de Pueblo Viejo

Tamaulipas

R.Panuco

PANUCO

LOS CHIJOLES

Gulf of Mexico

Laguna de Tamiahua

JUAN CASIANO
LOS NARANJOS
CHINAMPA

TEPETATE

CUECILLOS

PUERTO LOBOS

AMATLAN

PIEDRA LABRADA

CERRO AZUL

TANGUIJO

JUAN FELIPE

ALAZAN

TIERRA AMARILLA

POTRERO

Hidalgo

BARRA DE TUXPAN

TUXPAN

CHAPOPOTE

COBOS

ALAMO

R.Tuxpan

0   10   20
miles

Puebla

POZA RICA

——— Principal Pipelines
+++++ Railway
++++ Principal Light Railway

C.SEARS 1984

FURBERO

tants who worked for salaries rather than hourly wages, of course, had superior employment situations, even though the foreign managers retained the authority.[40] These conditions redounded to the benefit of the companies, for morale among the native proletariat remained relatively high. When foreigners momentarily evacuated the oil zone following the 1914 Veracruz invasion and the 1916 Pershing expedition, Mexican workers stayed at their jobs, unpaid, protecting wells and pumping equipment.[41]

One thing, more than anything else, set the worker against the companies: job insecurity. Every worker in the industry worked under individual contracts, often verbal and informal agreements between the employer or contractor for a specific job. Unskilled workers dug foundations, mixed mortar, laid brick, carried building materials, lifted barrels, and cleared vegetation. Working from day-to-day at unskilled tasks, the peon had no guarantees of steady employment, if he wanted it, until the pipeline was in or the refinery built. Only the skilled Mexican enjoyed a modicum of security; the pool of skilled workers grew every day as a result of the revolutionary turmoil elsewhere.[42] Nevertheless, the Mexican industrial proletarians in the booming oil zone were not overtly dissatisfied—until 1915.

At the height of the military struggles between the constitutionalists and conventionists, food shortages and inflation became serious. Mexico City experienced a near famine, and commodity prices rose even in the oil zone, where, beginning in 1913, bands of *carrancistas* and *villistas* marauded through the oil camps.[43] The economic distress did not much affect levels of employment in the oil industry—for booming foreign markets maintained the strong demand for labor—but it did inflate the workers' cost of living. The value of the paper peso slipped, and prices of imported food, which increasingly replaced local production, rose accordingly. Foreign workers did not suffer at all: they were paid in U.S. currency. Because Mexican silver money was in short supply, employers paid Mexican workers in deteriorating Mexican script. Many workers at El Aguila's refineries and oil camps refused to work rather than accept lower real wages.[44]

Strikes broke out and workers succeeded in shutting down a refinery here and a topping plant there, yet only for isolated and short periods of time. The work stoppages that began in 1915 reached a crescendo in 1917 and continued up to 1920. The easing of the economic crisis and the victory of the constitutionalists—signaled by the 1917 Constitution, which outlined the worker's rights and the employer's responsibilities—encouraged Mexico's oil workers to press hard. The skilled workers organized trade unions among themselves. The boiler workers, boatmen, mechanics, and so forth sought to recover lost purchasing power and, not incidentally, to secure more job tenure by pushing for the collective contracts to replace individual ones. These craft unions then sought to organize the less skilled workers in the plants. Some coercion was involved, and scabs and free workers found themselves confronted and threatened by union men. Strikers also demanded that the companies get rid of the Chinese workers.[45] Few strikes lasted because many workers, frightened of losing already insecure jobs, quickly broke ranks.

Labor strength nonetheless increased. Some strikes did succeed in obtaining reluctant concessions from unenlightened employers. Then in 1918, strikes occurred with increasing frequency, as national labor organizers with ties to the defunct Casa del Obrero Mundial, the newly organized Confederación Regional Obrera Mexicana (CROM), and the infamous IWW proselytized among the workers. Foreign managers feared the "wobblies" and "bolshevists," and local military commanders feared public disorder. The constitutionalist generals alternated between negotiating on behalf of the workers and cracking down on their union rallies.[46] While the foreign interests in Mexican oil lost time and money to worker militancy, they did retain control over the workplace. But workers were building upon a base of grievances and organization with which to renew the struggle at a more opportune time.

By the same token, government taxation and regulation of the oil industry, although agitating the oilmen, did not seem to erode much of the owners' autonomy. The state was impoverished by the political and social struggles of the Revolution and grew jealous of a foreign-owned industry that was booming. Not satisfied merely to benefit at old tax rates from burgeoning production, the governments of Madero, Huerta, and Carranza sought to increase the share of revenues from the oil industry. Madero increased the Díaz-era tax rates, Huerta asked the oil companies for emergency loans, and Carranza sought to collect a production royalty. The oilmen saw Mexican officials as inept, confiscatory, and ungrateful. They resisted each new customs duty, bar tax, registration fee, export tax, extraordinary dredging fee, and tax stamp imposed upon them. They protested against Madero, refused to lend money to Huerta (and were happy when a misguided French banker did), and ignored Carranza's demands.[47] At one point, Carranza ordered his troops to cap wells that had not been registered with his government. Since constitutionalist troops were unable to occupy the oil zone permanently, the companies simply reopened the wells upon their departure. Carranza finally relented in 1920.[48]

The operations of the oil companies had been immune from the violence of the Revolution until 1914. In December, the *villistas* and *constitucionalistas* fought the only pitched battle in the oil zone at El Ebano, causing some damage to Doheny's oil field. Yet the aftermath of this struggle had a more telling effect. Constitutionalist bands roamed among the oil camps, appropriating cattle, horses, foodstuffs, and cash from the oilmen and the rural residents. The constitutionalist commander and Veracruz governor, Cándido Aguilar, initiated a series of regulations and extraordinary taxes on the companies operating in the Golden Lane.[49]

A regional reaction to this encroachment drew the oil companies further into the revolutionary ferment. Manuel Peláez gathered up a guerrilla movement in order to challenge the invaders for control of the Golden Lane. Among his partisans were Spanish landowners, hacienda peons, large and small holders who were lessors in oil contracts, farmers threatened by rural insecurity, and Mexican workers from the oil camps. Isolated and without arms, Peláez relied on the resources of the oil industry to fund his local rebellion. When Huasteca and El Aguila camp managers refused his demands for "tax revenues," Peláez ordered his followers to cut the water lines, incapacitating the boilers at pump stations and at drilling rigs. The oil companies in the Golden Lane paid up "under duress" after stiff protests to the State Department and the Carranza government.[50] Cleverly, Peláez denounced Article 27 of the 1917 Constitution and supported private property rights in the oil zone. After all, as owner of Tierra Amarilla hacienda and lessor to El Aguila, for whom his brother had once worked as an attorney, Peláez was protecting his own economic interests as well.[51] Still, he could not provide physical security to the oil companies, for constitutionalist troops still entered the Huasteca region at will, even if they could not hold it.

The oil companies suffered confiscations, payroll robberies, death of foreign managers and Mexican employees, and worker flight from the oil camps. Yet, the companies were able to absorb such disruptions because the major pipelines and pump stations already were constructed, their refineries and terminals continued untroubled, and drilling proceeded. Strong foreign demand and high international prices for Mexican crude more than offset the inconveniences that the oil companies suffered on account of worker unrest, revolutionary insecurity, and conflict with the government.

From Depression to Depression

The year 1920 was a watershed for the foreign oil companies in Mexico. Petroleum prices began to break, production commenced to decline, and the Carranza government fell to the rebellion of General Alvaro Obregón. Obregón consolidated political control of the state to a degree not enjoyed by a Mexican president since Porfirio Díaz, allowing him and his successor to impose new taxes and regulations upon the industry. The workers also contributed to the period of declining structural power of the companies by organizing larger unions and by fashioning an alliance with the state. Wage increases, improved benefits, and union recognition followed in due course during the recovery from 1923 to 1925. The concentration of ownership in the industry, aided and abetted by its decline, preserved a measure of the companies' former autonomy, although British oilmen often broke with their American counterparts on labor and governmental issues. In general, the period from depression to depression was not at all ambiguous. Labor and the state were making important inroads into the industry's autonomy.

Mexican oil production, having increased nearly fivefold between 1916 and 1920, began a decline, gradually at first, then more precipitately. Oilmen first noticed a geological problem in 1918 they had not encountered elsewhere: some of the largest producing wells the world has ever known started flowing to saltwater. In 1921 and 1922, whole fields within the famed Golden Lane, Naranjos, Amatlán, Alazán, Alamo, and Chinampa, declined in production.[52] The Golden Lane's production peaked in 1921, when 158 million barrels were produced there, then declined to a yearly rate of barely one-fifth that total by 1925. Some companies such as Transcontinental recovered losses by expanding production in the northern oil fields astride the Pánuco River. This region's production rose to more than 100 million barrels of heavier crude in 1925, before it too began a decline.[53] By the end of the decade, total Mexican production amounted to fewer than 40 million barrels, just 20 percent of what it had been in the peak year of 1920.

Mexico's adversity was compounded by an even steeper downturn in the international prices of crude petroleum as new fields in the United States and Latin America came on line. The high prices of 1920 dropped suddenly by 45 percent to $1.73 during the succeeding year and to $1.17 by 1928.[54] Shell and Jersey Standard were investing heavily in infrastructure and exploration in the Maracaibo region of Venezuela, while Jersey Standard abruptly moved men and matériel from its faltering Mexican fields to its subsidiaries in Peru and Colombia. As Mexican production declined, that of its competitors rose. In 1929, Venezuela had become the third largest producer of raw petroleum in the world, and Mexico dropped to seventh.[55]

The structure of ownership responded in a manner designed to minimize Mexico's weakness in an increasingly competitive international marketplace: it consolidated. Lord Cowdray began the process as early as 1919, selling management control of El Aguila, Mexico's largest oil firm, to the Royal Dutch Shell. Cowdray and his associates desired particularly to combine El Aguila's production with Shell's refineries and retail outlets throughout Europe.[56] The considerable assets of

Doheny in Mexico also went on the sales block. In 1925, the midwestern marketing giant, Standard Oil Company of Indiana acquired the Pan American Petroleum Corporation, including Doheny's refining and marketing properties on the East Coast of the United States, his Mexican assets, and the Lago concession in Venezuela.[57] Smaller companies now sold out or abandoned their Mexican properties. By the end of the decade, Sinclair bought out the Pierce refining and marketing group. Transcontinental shut down its terminal at Puerto Lobos and its topping plant at La Barra and turned its remaining oil fields over to the reorganized Huasteca. By 1930, when oil prices slipped once again, Jersey Standard seemed to have withdrawn from Mexico.[58] But not even Indiana Standard could withstand the falling prices. Toward the end of 1932, the beleaguered marketing giant reconstituted itself by selling off its Venezuelan and Mexican assets to Jersey Standard.[59] Now Huasteca passed under the control of the world's biggest oil company, despite Porfirio Díaz's plea of twenty-five years earlier.

These realignments within Mexico's oil industry, natural enough given the production and price trends of the 1920s, accompanied a readjustment in the final destination of Mexico's oil production. Still predominantly an oil exporter, Mexico experienced an economic resurgence following the 1920 crisis. El Aguila and Huasteca expanded their domestic marketing, diverting increasing proportions of their production to meet growing domestic demands. Indeed, by 1928, a narrow majority of El Aguila's gross sales receipts came from domestic as opposed to foreign sales.[60] Such an attractive sales opportunity invited competition. Erosion of Mexico's production, combined with the railway bottlenecks across the Sierra Occidental, induced the import of California oil products along the West Coast. California Standard built bulk stations at the major ports of Guaymas, Mazatlán, and Acapulco and penetrated inland as far as Guadalajara.[61] As in the United States, gasoline for cars and trucks proved to be the growth market. By 1933, the end of this period, the oil firms had parceled out the domestic market for gasoline in the following fashion: El Aguila, 33.7 percent; Huasteca, 24.3 percent; Sinclair-Pierce, 21.6 percent; and California Standard, 20.4 percent.[62]

These structural developments permitted the now reconstituted Mexican state to increase taxation and regulation of the oil companies. Obregón's neutralization of Peláez gave the national government physical control over the oil region, so that the state could exercise its prerogatives under Article 27 of the Constitution. It issued concessions on terrain the government defined as state lands but considered by the bigger companies to be their exclusive properties. For example, the National Railways secured drilling rights along its right-of-way adjacent to Huasteca's El Ebano camp. A small American producer, Agwi, received riverbed drilling sites right through Transcontinental's Amatlán oil field. When both the National Railways and Agwi drilled nearly risk-free wells on properties the companies had proven, paying 15 percent royalties to the government, company executives were livid.[63] Obregón and Calles also insisted on issuing "confirmatory drilling concessions" for new wells in the companies' older oil fields. With equal fervor but declining effect, the companies insisted that their pre-1917 property rights allowed them to drill without seeking government permission.[64] The most spectacular confrontation came in 1921. Obregón placed a tax on petroleum exports, which the oil executives claimed was contrary to their preconstitutional contracts. The American companies declared a boycott, shutting down half the petroleum industry in protest. Thousands of workers were put out of work and required government rail passes to return to their hometowns in the highlands. Nonetheless, the companies eventually relented, and the state's tax rates increased even as the oil industry declined.[65]

No doubt, the oilmen might have resisted more effectively had they been able to remain united. To counter the nationalist program, the companies formed the Association of Petroleum Producers and Exporters of Mexico. The Association kept up an incessant barrage of protests to the State Department, the Foreign Office, and the international press. However, the drilling permit crisis of 1920 weakened the Association. The British firm, El Aguila, feeling the pinch of government restrictions, withdrew from the Association in order to make a deal with the government over drilling rights. The American companies were outraged, doubtlessly giving El Aguila an added excuse not to participate in the Americans' 1921 oil embargo as well.[66] Other companies eventually compromised enough to renew their drilling programs, yet the wells they sank remained inside the Faja de Oro and Pánuco districts. Each new well produced increasingly insubstantial output. Only El Aguila had made enough of a compromise with the government; in the mid-1920s, it began exploring Poza Rica, which it had acquired together with the Furbero field in 1912. While their Venezuelan drilling programs were yielding spectacular results, the foreign oilmen discovered no other Mexican oil fields besides Poza Rica.[67]

Government pressure on the oil companies was unrelenting, yet a number of factors limited Obregón's commitments. He badly needed government revenues. At one point, his finance secretary met with the so-called Big Five, the chief executives of the biggest American firms, to negotiate a revision of the tax laws in exchange for the companies' aid in reducing the government's defaulted bonds. They obtained a tacit agreement from the strapped Mexican government to ease its onslaught on property rights. Nonetheless, the oilmen found themselves compromised by the diplomats and bankers and by the government's refusal to grant exploratory rights to new oil lands in Mexico until the companies gave up their private property rights to the oil fields they were already working.[68] The Obregón government played off the bankers and claims commissioners, who wanted to increase Mexico's tax revenues, against the oil managers, who wished to restrict taxation and regulation. Meanwhile, the Mexican president had to contend with a major domestic crisis—the de la Huerta rebellion.

Obregón's personal promise to ease the pressure on the oil firms, however, did not carry over to his successor, President Calles. The petroleum law of 1925 authorized the government to implement Article 27 of the Constitution. Once again, drilling permits were held up until the oil companies converted their private properties to government concessions.[69] Stalemate again ensued when Ambassador Dwight Morrow, who had had banking rather than oil connections, reached a broad settlement with the Mexican government. Faced with the Cristero rebellion and the need to prepare for a presidential successor, Calles in 1928 revised the petroleum law while obtaining the State Department's acceptance of the doctrine of "positive acts." By "positive acts," the oil companies gave up private property rights to their pre-1917 oil reserves on which they had made no improvements. The oil companies vigorously protested the Calles-Morrow agreement.[70] In all, the oil companies in the 1920s forfeited a portion of their autonomy.

Simultaneously, another internal constraint, labor militancy, encroached on the owners' command of the industry in the period between depressions. From 1920 to 1922, Mexican workers suffered untold hardships in the massive layoffs with which the companies responded to falling prices and production. The owners' boycott of 1921 further dislocated the work force.[71] As prices stabilized and the layoffs ceased, the workers organized to recoup lost income and to gain a measure of security in the industry. The old trade unions of skilled workers in the refineries and oil terminals organized workers at the plant and company level. The first strikes broke out at refineries in Tampico and Minatitlán in 1922, and the Obregón and Calles governments, which counted on the support of organized labor, showed sympathy. The newly appointed inspectors of the expanding Labor Department mediated the labor disputes.[72] There existed a specter of coercion to this militancy. As a government inspector wrote, "Most [of the workers] do not agree with the movement and on several occasions told us that if most of them did not return to work [during the strike], it was because they feared being victims of the violence of some of the other workers."[73]

In these efforts, unions were asking the companies to comply with the basic guarantees outlined in Article 123 of the 1917 Constitution. The 1924 El Aguila refinery strike in Tampico broke new ground for oil workers, and, much to the chagrin of the American companies, El Aguila gave in. Soon refinery and terminal unions of Huasteca, Pierce, La Corona, and El Aguila Minatitlán and Puerto México won pacts that were carbon copies of the 1924 El Aguila contract. Labor organizers won union recognition at the plant level, increases in pay, a wide range of benefits, an eight-hour day, and compensations for layoffs.[74] Labor successes had a ripple effect in the mid-1920s.

Huasteca's Mata Redonda refinery workers in 1924 scored yet another labor breakthrough, uniting the terminal and oil field workers into one companywide union. But the victory exacerbated rivalries among labor leaders, minority unions, and nonunion workers whose jobs were threatened by the dominant union's new influence in the workplace. After a scuffle that ended in death for one labor leader, the companywide union struck again to force Huasteca to dismiss members of the rival group. The government was reluctant to support blatant interunion rivalry. The company decided to hold out. When the strike collapsed, Huasteca managers rehired independent workers and union members who repudiated their leaders.[75] The disintegration of the Huasteca union was witnessed firsthand by Lázaro Cárdenas, who was zone military commander at the time.

Labor organization in the meanwhile had become involved in national politics in a way that accentuated the rivalries among workers for the declining number of jobs. The national leadership of CROM took umbrage at the rejection of the Tampico unions to its intervention in their labor disputes. Most Tampico workers affiliated themselves with regional confederations, the rival Confederación General de Trabajadores (CGT), and municipal and state politicos distrustful of CROM. Only La Corona in Pánuco and several El Aguila unions on the Isthmus willingly cooperated with CROM leadership.[76] But the appointment of CROM leader, Luis Morones, to the Calles cabinet tended to mute his inclination to support new labor demands. In the 1925 El Aguila refinery strike of CROM's own Minatitlán affiliate, the national leadership intervened directly with management in Mexico City. El Aguila paid CROM $125,000 that was supposed to have been distributed—but may not have been—among the Minatitlán affiliates.[77] There followed a period of squabbling among disillusioned labor leaders, compounded in 1926 by another break in oil prices.

Additional price shocks in 1930 further disorganized and crippled the labor movement. In order to cut expenses and remain viable in the international oil market, the oil companies further cut the work force. Layoffs continued throughout 1931 and 1932. There are no statistics suggesting the exact extent of layoffs during this time period. Clearly, the long-range statistics are grim. The industry employed upward of 50,000 Mexicans in 1920, perhaps 16,000 in 1922, and 15,000 in 1935, when companies were rehiring.[78] Struggling to survive a second depression, workers in the early 1930s forswore union militancy for the time being.

In summary, the period between depressions signaled the retrenchment of the companies before the onslaught of oil field exhaustion, international competition, growing domestic demand, the resurgent Mexican state, and incipient labor militancy. Private foreign capital was forced to concede some of its exclusive property rights and to yield to workers' demands for more security and reward. The government and the workers succeeded to a degree. For the first time since the Díaz era, the companies' exclusive command of the Mexican oil industry was constrained. If the depression and internal political turmoil of the early 1930s rendered labor and the state unable to capitalize on the industry's weakness, these precedents nevertheless remained to be acted upon later.

Resurgence of Labor and the State

In 1934, Mexico and the oil companies entered a new age, strengthening one and weakening the other. Both labor and the state renewed the centralization begun in the early 1920s, but now in ways even more mutually reinforcing. The proprietors of the oil companies in Mexico became increasingly marginalized on the international market. Venezuela continued its growth at the same time that international oil interests began to explore for oil in the Middle East. An early Mexican rebound from worldwide depression enhanced the domestic market for petroleum products, a factor that multiplied the ways in which labor and the state could impose new restrictions on the companies. For all of this, it remains difficult to state that the oil companies structurally were doomed in Mexico. When the period of resurgence of labor and the state began in 1934, no one could have predicted the oil expropriation.

International oil markets began to recover from a long period of declining prices in 1934, and prices rose gradually into the war years. Many economies of the world renewed the 1920s trend of rising consumption of gasoline in cars, trucks, tractors, and power machinery. Those international oil companies that retained their Mexican assets, like Jersey Standard and Shell, were expanding their production and refining capacity in other countries. (To do so in Venezuela, ironically, the large oil concerns worked under the types of concessionary contracts for which the Mexicans had been pressing since 1917.)[79] The spread of refining technology to "crack" crude petroleum under heat and pressure, yielding higher proportions of gasoline, valorized the heavier crudes of California and eastern Venezuela that competed with Mexican oil. The upshot of these developments was the continuing international marginalization of Mexican production. Mexico now produced just 2 percent of the world's total supplies of petroleum.[80]

Slippage of its world ranking, however, did not mean the continued decline of Mexican production. In fact, the companies had taken advantage of the Calles-Morrow agreement to increase the yields of their known fields, and El Aguila moved quickly to open up Poza Rica. El Aguila constructed a new refinery at Azcapotzalco outside Mexico City and built a pipeline from Poza Rica, pleasing the government, which for some time had desired new oil assets to serve the growing internal market. The nation's industrial production and exports by 1934 had recovered to their 1929 levels, and the numbers of cars and trucks multiplied. By 1937, domestic consumers were using 70 percent of total Mexican oil production.[81] These developments tended to secure for El Aguila, historically the more flexible of the foreign companies, nearly two-thirds of Mexico's total oil industry.

The state's encroachment into the industry as a taxing and pricing agent also grew with the domestic market. In an effort to stabilize the cost of living of workers who depended upon urban transportation to travel to and from work, the government fixed the prices of gasoline. A public furor had met El Aguila's gasoline price increases to 5.5¢ per liter in 1934, taxi drivers of the capital having gone on strike in protest. Thereafter, the state established the gasoline price at 4.9¢ per liter, of which it took 2.2¢ as tax, the latter having doubled since 1931.[82] Such federal powers tended to place a ceiling on the earnings of the oil companies.

Meanwhile, a political coalition was consolidating its control of the government, eliminating political rivalries that had prevented the full exercise of state power over the industry since the assassination of Obregón in 1928. Lázaro Cárdenas was to be the first postrevolutionary Mexican president to serve a six- rather than four-year term. Labor organizations at first were ambivalent about his candidacy. The national labor movement itself was in a state of flux. An internal rebellion within CROM in 1932 resulted in the purge of Vicente Lombardo Toledano, who subsequently united numerous anti-FROC unions in the CGOCM. In the meantime, Cárdenas's presidential campaign aimed to generate the active participation of urban and industrial workers. He urged receptive workers in Minatitlán to form industrywide unions to redress the grievances of the depression years. His message to laboring groups in Tampico was the same.[83]

President Rodríguez also moved to solidify labor support for the candidate. Taking a page from the 1931 labor law, he added the "exclusionary clause" to the Minatitlán refinery contract he was asked to mediate in 1934. That clause established a union shop, meaning that all newly hired laborers were to be from the contracting union. Also, workers expelled from that union were to lose their company jobs.[84] In quick succession, the Tampico refinery union of El Aguila organized the Poza Rica oil field workers, making the Tampico group the most hegemonic and powerful of the oil unions. Then the workers at the Azcapotzalco refinery were mobilized into a new union that also included the clerks at El Aguila's Mexico City headquarters. All won contracts with the exclusionary clause.[85] These resurgent but now mostly anti-CROM unions in 1935 and 1936 supported Cárdenas in his political showdown with the *callistas*. Eventually, Lombardo Toledano brought his trade unions together with the new industrial unions, especially the railway workers, and formed the Confederación de Trabajadores de México (CTM).

Even before Cárdenas had taken office, the companies once again came under pressure to conform to Article 27. They experienced delays in obtaining drilling permits and complained that the government was violating the Calles-Morrow agreement. However, the oilmen made the mistake in 1935 of sending a representative to pay a "courtesy call" on ex-President Calles,[86] confirming the *cardenistas'* impression of their meddlesomeness in Mexican politics. Furthermore, unqualified diplomatic support, always questionable, dissipated even more into the 1930s. Great Britain concerned itself with the ominous events in Europe, while the American ambassador, Josephus Daniels, upheld the Good Neighbor policy and absolutely loathed the American oilmen.[87]

Once again, the oilmen attempted to form a united front to resist further erosion of what remained of their private property rights. The American petroleum executives in particular did not wish to open Pandora's box by allowing the government to alter its contracts. Who knew where contract alteration might lead in the more important producing countries like Venezuela? But El Aguila's interest in Mexico had become greater than all the American companies combined. Moreover, 80 percent of its stockholders, represented by the late Lord Cowdray's Whitehall Securities, had few oil interests outside of Mexico. In November 1937, El Aguila signed an agreement with the Mexican state that converted its Poza Rica properties into a government concession. It agreed to pay royalties to the government ranging from 25 to 35 percent of production. Cárdenas let it be known that he desired to conclude an identical agreement covering Huasteca's properties.[88] Such a scenario was not to be, for the workers were making their own demands.

Formation of the national petroleum union brought great pressure on the companies. After an initial failure to amalgamate by the smaller oil unions, the El Aguila refinery unions of El Aguila–Tampico, Huasteca, and El Aguila–Minatitlán brought together some twenty-one separate unions representing seventeen different foreign interests to form the Sindicato de Trabajadores Petroleros de la República Mexicana (STPRM).[89] The STPRM subsequently joined the CTM and presented the companies a lengthy collective contract that would have equalized pay and benefits across the industry, bringing workers in the oil fields of smaller companies up to the standard of those in the refineries of the bigger concerns. Most important, the companies would lose a large number of management and supervisory positions to union control. For example, the contract would have allowed El Aguila only one confidential employee in its Azcapotzalco refinery, instead of the thirteen who then worked there.[90] Labor-management negotiations, hosted and mediated by Cárdenas's labor secretary over a six-month period, settled a mere 35 of 250 separate clauses of the contract. The stalemate, however, did provoke the intervention of Lombardo Toledano. Thereafter, as Lombardo fought the disintegration of the CTM—the railway workers withdrew in 1937, and *cromistas* were fighting *cetemistas* in the textile industry—he increasingly took up the cause of the STPRM.[91]

Labor's organizational drive climaxed the companies' gradual loss of control over the workplace. Many foreign workers had been laid off during the early 1930s and not replaced. More than any other program, the decline in the number of foreigners in the industry tended to speed the transfer of technology to Mexican workers. At the same time that the Mexican workers were gaining ascendancy in the workplace, the union was extending its control over them. By January 1938, only three thousand of the eighteen thousand laborers in the industry remained outside the STPRM.[92]

Having little room in which to maneuver, the companies made their position clear from the outset of the labor dispute. The executives said that any labor settlement that increased their operating costs, making them less competitive in the international market, merely contributed to the demise of the Mexico-based companies. Such warnings, hurled at every Mexican administration since Madero's, fell on disbelieving ears.[93] But the companies were serious about two things. They bristled at the idea of labor leaders' having any greater authority over management than they already had under the exclusionary clause. Moreover, Jersey Standard and other American executives did not want Mexico to establish a precedent that other countries would be tempted to emulate.[94] These considerations prompted the companies, which already considered the Mexicans incapable of running their own oil industry, to repudiate the mediated settlement of the Cárdenas administration and reject the Supreme Court decision of 1 March 1938.

These actions placed the companies on a collision course with government and labor in Mexico. The British and Dutch managers of El Aguila wished to reach a last-minute compromise but failed to convince the adamant Americans.[95] By 18 March 1938, the structural strength of the companies to resist domestic impositions had been greatly reduced from the autonomy they had enjoyed during the 1910s.

Conclusion

This structural analysis of the Mexican petroleum industry, in and of itself, does not explain the nationalization of 1938. It is intended to demonstrate the economic parameters within which the foreign interests operated and the variables that determined their degree of control over domestic constraints. Nevertheless, this examination helps explain why, at any given moment between 1880 and 1938, the foreign companies were either more or less susceptible to the influences of labor and the state. In general, the owners of the industry were stronger in the 1880s and 1890s, weaker in the 1900s, stronger in the 1910s, weaker in the 1920s, stronger in the early 1930s, and weakest of all in the mid-1930s. Specifically, these factors weighed most heavily:

1. The foreign interests were more responsive to labor and the state under oligopolistic rather than monopolistic ownership of the petroleum industry. Oligopoly enhanced competition, which Mexican labor and the state manipulated, despite the companies' attempts at forming a cartellike united front. The 1908 Mexican oil war, the 1921 taxation and drilling controversy, and the 1938 expropriation crisis serve as examples of how domestic interests exploited differences between foreign interests.

2. The structural autonomy of the industry was greater when either its supplies or its markets were overwhelmingly external. Thus, until 1905, Waters-Pierce as importer of North American oils enjoyed a major degree of freedom in its operations. All companies remained unfettered in their operations during the Revolution, partly because most Mexican petroleum was exported. Conversely, the domestic marketing of purely domestic production tended to reduce the autonomy of the operating companies, as in 1908, the 1920s, and the 1930s.

3. Politically unified Mexican governments also infringed upon the operating autonomy of the companies. During the height of their power, Díaz, Obregón, Calles, Rodríguez, and Cárdenas all were able to influence the structure of the oil industry. Conversely, domestic political conflict reinforced the structural power of the foreign interests. Con-

tinuing revolutionary upheaval weakened Carranza in his dispute with the companies in 1919, just as the political confusion following the assassination of Obregón also worked in the companies' favor. In addition, each Mexican president, with the possible exception of Abelardo Rodríguez, weakened considerably toward the end of his term.

4. The international business cycle affected the relative autonomy of the companies insofar as it motivated labor to organize during times of recovery from depression. For example, the economic crises of 1915, 1920, and 1930 clearly motivated the subsequent years of labor militancy. Repetition of the cycle strengthened labor's resolve and encouraged support from the state. Another structural phenomenon closely linked to the business cycle—that is, the tendency toward consolidation of ownership when prices were falling—in the long run did not protect the industry from labor militancy.

5. The relative weight of the Mexican industry in the world's supplies of crude oil made little difference to the operating autonomy of the companies. The industry was susceptible to internal manipulation—Díaz's favoritism toward Cowdray, taxation in 1921, and labor demands of 1923 and 1936, and El Aguila's concession of 1937—despite the fact that Mexico's world ranking varied greatly in those years.

Finally, one must ask whether this analysis indicates that the Mexican oil expropriation was structurally inevitable. The international oil companies in Colombia, Peru, Argentina, and Venezuela, after all, had experienced similar structural variations without having suffered denouement—except for Peru in 1968—in quite the same fashion as in Mexico. Moreover, the petroleum workers of these countries never made the same kinds of demands on the foreign interests as the STPRM. In the final analysis, the oil bust of 1921 makes the structural history of the Mexican oil industry unique. No other Latin American country, before or since, experienced the depth of depression in its petroleum industry that the simultaneous drop in oil prices and oil production produced in Mexico. The 1921 oil bust produced truly extraordinary tensions between foreign companies, the state, and labor. Yet, this examination of the structure of the foreign-owned industry cannot alone explain how the state and labor in Mexico have reacted to economic changes throughout the twentieth century and how they imposed their own demands on the oil sector. This is the task of the following chapters.

Notes

1. Standard interpretations can be found in Government of Mexico, *The True Facts about the Expropriation of the Oil Companies' Properties in Mexico* (Mexico City, 1940), p.13; Miguel Alemán Valdés, *La verdad del petróleo en*

México (Mexico City, 1977), pp. 41, 48; Jesús Silva Herzog, *Historia de la expropriación de las empresas petroleras* (Mexico City, 1964), p. 105; Antonio J. Bermúdez, *The Mexican National Petroleum Industry: A Case Study in Nationalization* (Stanford, Calif., 1963), pp. 19–20; Francisco Alonso González, *Historia y petróleo. México: el problema del petróleo* (Mexico City, 1972), p. 62; Francisco Colmenares, *Petróleo y lucha de clases en México, 1864–1982* (Mexico City, 1982), pp. 1, 98; Donald R. Richberg, *The Mexican Oil Seizure* (New York, n.d.), 18; William E. McMahon, *Two Strikes & Out* (Garden City, N.Y., 1939), p. 1; Standard Oil Company (New Jersey), *Present Status of the Mexican Oil Expropriation* (New York, 1940), p. 36; Standard Oil Company (New Jersey), *The Reply to Mexico* (New York, 1940), pp. iii, 31, 94–96.

2. Daniel Cosío Villegas et al., *Historia moderna de México*, 8 vols. (Mexico City, 1955–1972), vol. 7, pt. 1, *El Porfiriato: la vida económica:*, pp. 145, 256, 517, 624, 628, 695; Richard Guenther to Department of State, Mexico City, 11 Oct. 1890, no. 32, National Archives, Washington, D.C., Record Group 59, General Records of the Department of State, Dispatches of U.S. Consuls in Mexico City, 1822–1906 [hereafter cited as NADS, U.S. Consuls, Mexico City].

3. On nineteenth-century exploration, see Ezequiel Ordóñez, "El petróleo en México: bosquejo histórico," *Revista Mexicana de Ingeniería y Arquetectura* 10:3 (15 March 1932), pp. 135–144; Gabriel Antonio Menéndez, *Doheny El Cruel: episodios de la sangrienta lucha por el petróleo mexicano* (Mexico City, 1958), pp. 17–19; Alonso González, *Historia y petróleo*, p. 55.

4. See Ralph W. Hidy and Muriel E. Hidy, *Pioneering in Big Business, 1882–1911: History of the Standard Oil Company (New Jersey)* (New York, 1955), pp. 49, 122; Allen Nevins, *John D. Rockefeller: The Heroic Age of American Enterprise*, vol. 1 (New York, 1940), pp. 657–658; United States Supreme Court, *Transcript of Record: The Waters-Pierce Oil Company vs. the State of Texas*, Oct. term, 1908, no. 356 (Washington, D.C., 1909), p. 441.

5. United States Supreme Court, *Transcript of Record* (1908), pp. 466, 1108; and United States Supreme Court, *Transcript of Record: Standard Oil Company, et al. vs. the United States*, Oct. term, 1909, 221 U.S. 1, pp. 1095–1096.

6. Treasury Department, "Annual Report on the Foreign Commerce and Navigation of the United States" in *Executive Documents of the House of Representatives* (Washington, D.C., 1881–1912).

7. Bruce Bringhurst, *Antitrust and the Oil Monopoly: The Standard Oil Cases, 1890–1911* (Westport, Conn., 1979), p. 57; Hidy and Hidy, *Pioneering in Big Business*, pp. 609, 633; Nevins, *John D. Rockefeller*, vol. 1, p. 659; vol. 2, pp. 531–533, 571.

8. See Joseph A. Pratt, *The Growth of a Refining Region* (Greenwich, Conn., 1980), pp. 34–35; Martin V. Melosi, *Coping with Abundance: Energy and Environment in Industrial America* (Philadelphia, 1985), pp. 40–46.

9. Ward Ritchie, *The Dohenys of Los Angeles* (Los Angeles, 1974), pp. 15–18; Gerald T. White, *Formative Years in the Far West: A History of Standard Oil Company of California and Predecessors through 1919* (New York, 1962), pp. 152–153.

10. See Doheny's testimony in U.S. Congress, Senate, Committee on Foreign Relations [hereafter, Senate Committee on Foreign Relations], *Investigation of*

Mexican Affairs, 66th Cong., 1st sess. (1919), pp. 214, 216, 241, 269; Ordóñez, "El petróleo en México," pp. 154–161.

11. Senate Committee on Foreign Relations, *Investigation of Mexican Affairs*, pp. 115–116; [Mexican Petroleum Company], *Los impuestos sobre la industria de petróleo* (Mexico City, 1912), p. 1; and Clarence W. Barron, *The Mexican Problem* (Boston, 1917), p.131.

12. Mexican Oil Corporation, Ltd., *Mexico Today: The Mexican Petroleum Industry* (London, 1905), pp. 19–21; [Pan American Petroleum Corporation], *Mexican Petroleum* (New York, 1922), pp. 28–29; Senate Committee on Foreign Relations, *Investigation of Mexican Affairs*, pp. 226–227, 299.

13. [Mexican Petroleum], *The Oil Industry in Mexico*, pp. 35–38; and McMahan, *Two Strikes and Out*, p. 39.

14. Antonio J. Bermúdez, *The Mexican National Petroleum Industry: A Case Study in Nationalization* (Stanford, Calif., 1963), pp. 2–3; Merrill Rippy, *Oil and the Mexican Revolution* (Leiden, 1972), chaps. 1–4; José Colomo, *The Mexican Petroleum Law: Its Basis and Its Aims* (Mexico City, 1927), pp. 8–10.

15. Martin R. Ansell, "Pouring Oil on Troubled Waters: Edward L. Doheny and the Mexican Revolution," Master's thesis, University of Oregon, 1985, pp. 33, 49; Senate Committee on Foreign Relations, *Investigation of Mexican Affairs*, pp. 212, 218–219, 225; Ordóñez, "El petróleo en México," p. 158; Friedrich Katz, *The Secret War in Mexico: Europe, the United States and the Mexican Revolution* (Chicago, 1981), p. 22.

16. Ronald Macleay to Foreign Office, Mexico City, 18 March 1909, Public Record Office, London, Foreign Office Records [hereafter cited as FO], [document] 368-309, no. 12924; [Mexican Petroleum Company], *Los impuestos sobre la industria de petróleo*, p. 4.

17. As quoted in J. A. Spender, *Weetman Pearson: First Viscount Cowdray, 1856–1927* (London, 1930 [Reprint: New York, 1977]), pp. 149–150.

18. Weetman Pearson to J. B. Body, London, 1 May 1906; Body to Pearson, Mexico City, 21 Jan. 1909; "History: The Mexican Eagle Oil company, Limited," n.p., n.d., British Science Museum Library, London, Records of S. Pearson and Sons [hereafter cited as Pearson Records], box A-4, box C-43, file 1.

19. Pearson to Body, London, 6 Oct. 1906; Pearson, "Memo for Mr. Body," New York, 21 April 1907, "History: The Mexican Eagle Oil Company, Limited," Pearson Records, box A-4, box C-43, file 1.

20. "Contrato entre Secretaría de Fomento y la Compañía S. Pearson & Son, Ltd.," 12 May 1906, National Archives, General Records of the Department of State, Record Group 59, Internal Affairs of Mexico, 1910–1929 [hereafter cited as NADS], 812.6363/126; and I. H. MacDonald to Major Cassius E. Gillette, Mexico City, 13 Oct. 1906, Pearson Records, box A-4.

21. Percy Norman Furber, *I Took Chances: From Windjammers to Jets* (Leicester, Eng., 1953), pp. 139–141; "Oil Fields of Mexico Co.," *Joint Stock Companies' Journal*, 14 Aug. 1912, Shell Press Clippings, Shell International Petroleum Company, London.

22. Merrill Griffith to assistant sec. of state, Tampico, 15 Aug. 1908; Griffith to Thompson, Tampico, 6 July 1908; NADS, Numerical and Minor Files, no. 14453; *The Pipe Line* 3:63 (23 May 1923), p. 126.

23. Robert Keith Middlemas, *The Master Builders: Thomas Brassey, Sir John Aird, Lord Cowdray, Sir John Norton-Griffiths* (London, 1963), p. 216; Ronald MacLeay to Sir Edmund Gray, Mexico City, 18 June 1909, FO 368-309, no. 25272.; "History: The Mexican Eagle Oil Company, Ltd.," Pearson Records, box C-3, file 1.

24. Pearson to Dr. M., 16 April 1909, in "Summary of Correspondence: Negotiations with W.P.O. Co."; contracts dated 26 Nov. 1908, Pearson Records, box C-44, file 7, box C-43, file 2.

25. F. C. Gerretson, *History of the Royal Dutch*, 4 vols. (Leiden, 1952), vol. 4, p. 261; Ezequiel Ordóñez, "El petróleo en México," p. 158, and *Revolutions in Mexico. Hearing before a Subcommittee of the Committee on Foreign Relations. United States Senate*. 62th Congress, 2d session (Washington, D.C., 1912), pp. 263–265; Benjamin Ridgely, "A Great Oil Fight in Mexico," 18 July 1908, NADS, Numerical and Minor Files, no. 11770/2-3.

26. "Extract from a letter to Señor Guillermo Landa," 30 July 1909, Pearson Records, box A-4.

27. Body to Cowdray, Mexico City, 28 June 1911, and "History: The Mexican Eagle Oil Company, Limited," Pearson Records, box A-4, box C-43, file 1; Young, *Member for Mexico*, p. 131; Jonathan C. Brown, "Domestic Politics and Foreign Investment: British Development of Mexican Petroleum, 1889–1911," *Business History Review* 61:3 (1987): 387–416.

28. Harold F. Williamson et al., *The American Petroleum Industry*, 2 vols. (Evanston, Ill., 1963), vol. 2, pp. 208, 449–455.

29. Swain to C. T. White, 26 March 1915, and "List of Leases Protocolized in Name of John Kee," 19 April 1917, Standard Oil Company (New Jersey), New York, Esso Standard Records, Legal Department, file 117. (These and other Standard Oil materials were given to the author by the late Henrietta M. Larson.) Invariably, the lease takers have a poor reputation for honesty and fair play. See Gene Z. Hanrahan, *The Bad Yankee: El Peligro Yankee: American Entrepreneurs and Financiers in Mexico*, 2 vols. (Chapel Hill, N.C., 1985); Francisco Martín Moreno, *México negro: una novela política* (Mexico City, 1986).

30. Body to Cowdray, 19 Dec. 1916, Pearson Papers, box A-3.

31. Gerretson, *History of the Royal Dutch* 4: 264–265.

32. "Reports on London & Pacific Properties and Lobitos," 22 April, 15 July 1913, Imperial Oil Company, Toronto, file 157; *Annual Reports of the Mexican Petroleum Company*, 1920, 1922, Huntington Library, San Marino, Calif.; *Pan American Record*, July 1917, pp. 3–8; and Lord Cowdray, "Memorandum re. the Aguila Co.," 13 Jan. 1919, Pearson Records, box C-44, file 3.

33. "Transcontinental Consolidated Oil Co.," Aug. 24 1917, no. 7, Production Department, and "Statistical Tables," Records, Coordination and Economics Department, Standard Oil Company (New Jersey), New York.

34. Teagle to Sadler et al., 2 March 1920, Sadler's old Mexican Files, SONJ; Interview with L. Philo Maier (former Jersey engineer in Mexico in 1920), Coral Gables, Fla., 30 Dec. 1982; *Carta de la zona petrolífera del Norte de Vera Cruz*, March 1919, American Geological Institute Map Collection, University of Wisconsin, Milwaukee.

35. Clarence Miller to sec. of state, Tampico, 25 May 1912, NADS 812.6363/

4; Dawson to sec. of state, Tampico, 25 Sept. 1917, National Archives, Washington, D.C. General Correspondence of the Department of State, Record Group 86, General Correspondence of the Tampico Consulate [hereafter cited as NADS Tampico Correspondence], decimal file 850.4.

36. H. C. Pierce to sec. of state, St. Louis, 2 Dec. 1913, NADS 812.6363/19; Robert S. Israel, "Deposits of Fuel Oil," Nogales, 4 Oct. 1919, National Archives, Military Intelligence Directorate, Mexico Files, 10640-1695/6.

37. Jesús Silva Herzog, *El petróleo de México* (Mexico City, 1940), p. 5.

38. Enrique S. Cerdán, "Informe," 9 Jan. 1920, Archivo General de la Nación, Departamento de Trabajo [hereafter cited as AGN DT], C. 224, E. 24; Lief Adleson, "Historia social de los obreros industriales de Tampico, 1906–1919," PhD diss., El Colegio de México, 1982.

39. "Tampico and Minatitlán refinery estimates," 1916, Pearson Records, C-45, file 4; Zamora to chief, 19 May 1927, AGN DT, C. 1209, E. 5.

40. Senate Committee on Foreign Relations, *Investigation of Mexican Affairs*, pp. 220, 235; document dated 10 Feb. 1932, Archivo General de la Nación, Mexico City, Junta Federal de Conciliación y Arbitraje, C. 70, E. 13.

41. W. A. Thompson to Robert Lansing, 29 May 1914, NADS 812.6363/85; Hohler to Foreign Office, 26 June 1916, FO 371-2701, no. 123687.

42. On the rest of the Mexican economy, see John Womack, Jr., "The Mexican Economy during the Revolution, 1910–1920," *Marxist Perspectives* 1:4 (1978); Alan Knight, *The Mexican Revolution*, 2 vols. (Cambridge, Eng., 1986), vol. 2, pp. 406–419.

43. Senate Committee on Foreign Relations, *Investigation of Mexican Affairs*, pp. 276–277; Peter Calvert, *The Mexican Revolution, 1910–1914: The Diplomacy of Anglo-American Conflict* (Cambridge, Eng, 1968), pp. 275, 282..

44. J. B. Body to Cowdray, Mexico City, 22 Dec. 1916; Vaughn to Anglo-Mexican, Tampico, 4 Dec., 1916, Pearson Records, box A-4.

45. John M. Hart, *Anarchism and the Working Class in Mexico, 1860–1931* (Austin, Tex., 1978), p. 139; Enrique S. Cerdán to chief, Mexico, 29 Jan. 1920, AGN DT, C. 224, E. 23; Inspector to Chief, Minatitlan, 11 July 1920, AGN DT, C. 215, E. 4, Fs. 40-43; J. C. Evans to Thomas H. Bevan, Tampico, 14 June 1915, NADS, Tampico Consulate, 850.4/242.

46. James D. McLachlan, "Report on Bolshevism in Mexico," Mexico City, 20 May 1919, FO 371-3830, no. 83812; W. F. Buckley et al., to Woodrow Wilson, Tampico, 22 May 1916, Pearson Records, box A-3; W. F. Pulford to Norman King, Tampico, 17 June 1919, FO 371-3831, no. 10305; Knight, *The Mexican Revolution*, vol. 2, p. 431.

47. Cowdray to Limantour, London, 10 April 1913, Pearson Records, box A-3; [Mexican Petroleum Company], *Los impuestos sobre la industria petrolera*, 4; Knight, *The Mexican Revolution*, vol.2, p. 507; Lorenzo Meyer, *Mexico and the United States in the Oil Controversy, 1916–1942* (Austin, Tex., 1977); Calvert, *The Mexican Revolution*, p. 183.

48. Carranza to Foreign Oil Producers, Mexico City, 22 Jan. 1920, NADS 812.6363/6289; Antonio J. Bermúdez, *The Mexican National Petroleum Industry: A Case Study in Nationalization* (Stanford, Calif., 1963), p. 7; Meyer, *Mexico and the United States*; Jonathan C. Brown, "Why Foreign Oil Companies Shifted

Their Production from Mexico to Venezuela during the 1920s," *American Historical Review* 90:2 (April 1985): 362–385.

49. Ciro R. de la Garza, *La Revolución Mexicana en el Estado de Tamaulipas*, 2 vols. (Mexico, 1975), vol. 2, pp. 119–120; Body to Cowdray, Tampico, 3 March 1916, Pearson Records, box A-4.

50. J. A. Brown to E. J. Sadler, April 29, 1929, SONJ, Sadler's Mexican files, Meyer, *Mexico and the United States*, pp. 50–51; Stewart to Maurice De Bunsen, 6 April 1918, FO 371-3243/63332; Senate Committee on Foreign Relations, *Investigation of Mexican Affairs*, pp. 281, 301–303, 553; Peter S. Linder, "Every Region for Itself: The Manuel Peláez Movement, 1914–1923" (Master's thesis, University of New Mexico, 1983); Heather Fowler Salamini, "Caciquismo and the Mexican Revolution: The Case of Manuel Peláez," unpub. ms. (1981).

51. Manuel Peláez, "To the Mexican People," translation, 31 Dec. 1917, Pearson Papers, box A-3; M. Cervantes, "Relación de las compañías petroleras," Mexico City, 5 Nov. 1920, Archivo General de la Nación, Mexico City, Papeles Presidenciales, Fondo Calles-Obregón [hereafter cited as AGN FOC], 101-P-6.

52. Claude I. Dawson, "Development in Tampico Oil Fields, " Tampico, 7 Dec. 1921, NADS 812.6363/1054.

53. Charles A. Bay, "Review of the Petroleum Industry in Tampico, 1924"; "Review of the Petroleum Industry in Tampico, 1925," NADS 812.6363/1558 and /1760.

54. Harold F. Williamson et al., *The American Petroleum Industry*, 2 vols. (Evanston, Ill., 1963), vol.2, p. 539; American Petroleum Institute, *Petroleum Facts and Figures*, 9th ed. (New York, 1950), p.170.

55. American Petroleum Institute, *Petroleum Facts and Figures*, pp. 444–445.

56. "Scheme for the Amalgamation of the UK Organization of the Shell Marketing Co. and the Anglo-Mexican Petroleum Co.," 16 April 1920, Pearson Records, C44, file 9.

57. Paul H. Giddens, *Standard Oil Company (Indiana): Oil Pioneer in the Middle West* (New York, 1955), pp. 240–242.

58. Robert Herndan, "Changes in Administration of the Petroleum Companies," 25 July 1929, NADS 812.6363/2655; "World Petroleum in Review," *Oil Weekly* 58:11 (29 Aug. 1930): 64.

59. Giddens, *Standard Oil Company (Indiana)*, pp. 489–493; Mira Wilkins, *The Maturing of Multinational Enterprise: American Business Abroad from 1914 to 1970* (Cambridge, Mass., 1974), p. 210.

60. Assheton, "Results for Year 1932 and Comparison with Prior Years," Pearson Papers, box C43, file 7.

61. Dudley G. Dwyre, "Refined Products (Gasoline)," Guadalajara, 7 Nov. 1924, NADS 812.6363/1539.

62. Silva Herzog, *El petróleo de México*, p. 46; Philip, *Oil and Politics in Latin America*, p. 80.

63. Summerlin to sec. of state, Mexico City, 7 Sept. 1920; C. O. Swain to sec. of state, 15 Nov. 1920; Guy Stevens to sec. of state, 23 May 1921, NADS 812.6363/724, /742, and /833.

64. Dawson, "New Rules for Oil Exploration on Federal Lands," Tampico, 6

April 1922, NADS 812.6363/1093; Alfred Northrop to Obregón, Mexico City, 22 March 1922; "Minutes," 4 Nov. 1922, AGN FOC 104-P1-P-13.

65. Dawson, "Tampico Oil Report for September 1921," 15 Oct. 1921, NADS 812.6363/1017; Meyer, *Mexico and the United States*, p. 16, and Philip, *Oil and Politics*, p.17.

66. Foreign Office to Sir A. Geddes, London, 24 Dec. 1920, FO 371–4499, no. A9015.

67. Assheton to Body, 27 Oct. 1924, Shell International Petroleum Company, London, Group History, Country Series, Mexico Management [hereafter, Shell GHC/MEX], D29/1/1; *Royal Dutch Petroleum Company, 1890-1950: Diamond Jubilee Book* (The Hague, 1950), pp. 34–35, 38; Jonathan C. Brown, "Why Foreign Oil Companies Shifted Their Production."

68. Cardin to Foreign Office, Mexico City, 23 Oct. 1921, FO 371-5580, no. A7814; Lloyd Burlingham to sec. of state, Salina Cruz, 5 Sept. 1921; C. O. Swain, "Presentation of Committee," 22 Sept. 1924, NADS 812.6363/960, and /1529; Stephen Kane, "Bankers and Diplomats: The Diplomacy of the Dollar in Mexico, 1921–1924," *Business History Review* 47 (1973): 334–352.

69. Departamento de Petróleo, "Relación de títulos de concesión petrolera que fueron autorizados," 26 Dec. 1925 to 10 April 1936, Archivo Histórico "Genaro Estrada" del Secretaría de Relaciones Exteriores, Mexico City, Expropiación de la Industria del Petróleo Mexicana, L-E-56.

70. Standard Oil Company (New Jersey) to sec. of state, 27 April 1928, DS 812.6363/2558; and Dwight W. Morrow to sec. of state, Mexico City, 12 Sept. 1930, NADS 812.6363/2698.

71. Tagle, "Informe sobre emigración obrera," Tampico, 23 July 1921, AGN DT, C. 329, E. 30; Andrés Barrientos to Obregón, Tampico, 27 Sept. 1921, AGN FOC, 104-H-10, Leg. 1.

72. Andrés Araujo to chief, Tampico, 4 July 1925, AGN DT, C. 728, E. 3.

73. "La mayor parte de [los trabajadores] no están conformes con el movimiento y en varias ocasiones nos manifestaron que si no vuelve la mayor parte de ellos al trabajo es por temor a ser víctimas de las violencias cometidas en las personas de algunos trabajadores." H. R. Márquez, "Memorandum al C. Presidente," 27 Oct. 1924, AGN FOC, 407-T-13, appendix 2.

74. Leif Adleson, "Coyuntura y conciencia: factores convergentes en la fundación de los sindicatos petroleros de Tampico durante la década de 1920," in Elsa Cecilia Frost et al. (eds.), *El trabajo y los trabajadores en la historia de México* (Mexico City and Tucson, 1979), pp. 632–660.

75. Araujo to chief, Tampico, 13 May 1925, 30 July 1925, AGN DT, C. 725, E. 2; Bay to sec. of state, Tampico, 26 May 1925, NADS, Tampico Correspondence, 850.4.

76. Luis Morones to sec. of industry, Tampico, 15 June 1924, AGN DT, C. 772, E. 5; H. K. V. Tompkins to Peter Flood, 29 Jan. 1925, NADS Tampico Correspondence, 850.4.

77. See correspondence in "Conflicto: la Cía. de Petróleo 'El Aguila' y sus empleados, 1925-1926," AGN DT, C. 977, E. 1; John W. F. Dulles, *Yesterday in Mexico: A Chronicle of the Revolution, 1919–1936* (Austin, Tex., 1972), p. 393;

Barry Carr, *El movimiento obrero y la política en México* (Mexico City, 1976).

78. C. E. Macy to sec. of state, 2 Sept. 1931, NADS 812.00-Tamaulipas/44; Adleson, "Coyuntura y conciencia," p. 643; Jonathan C. Brown, "Foreign Oil Companies, Oil Workers, and the Mexican Revolutionary State," in *Multinational Enterprise in Historical Perspective* (Cambridge, Eng., 1986), pp. 257–269.

79. Willis C. Cook, "Petroleum Industry in Venezuela, 1921," National Archives, General Correspondence of the Department of State, Record Group 59, Internal Affairs of Venezuela, 1910–1929, 831.6363/105; Jonathan C. Brown, "Jersey Standard and the Politics of Latin American Oil Production, 1911–30," in *Latin American Oil Companies and the Politics of Energy*, edited by John D. Wirth (Lincoln, Neb., 1985), pp. 35–39.

80. Huasteca Petroleum Company and Standard Oil Company of California, *Expropriation* (New York, 1938), p. 3; and Williamson, *The American Petroleum Industry*, vol.2, p. 728.

81. E. V. F. Fitzgerald, "Restructuring through the Depression: The State and Capital Accumulation in Mexico, 1925–40," in *Latin America in the 1930s: The Role of the Periphery in World Crisis*, edited by Rosemary Thorp (New York, 1984), pp. 253–254; *Latin American Oil Companies*, p. 263.

82. Edward P. Bordon, "Automobile Touring in Mexico," 9 March 1932; Daniels to sec. of state, 17 July 1934, 18 March 1938, NADS 812.111/347, 812.3/2785, 812.45/704.

83. Julio Valdivieso Castillo, *Historia del movimiento sindical petrolero en Minatitlán* (Mexico City, 1963); Dulles, *Yesterday in Mexico;* Alan Knight, "Cambridge History of Latin America: Mexico, c. 1929–49," unpub. ms. (ca. 1986), pp. 7–8.

84. J. Rennow to Luis I. Rodríguez, 15 Dec. 1934, Archivo General de la Nación, Mexico City, Papeles Presidenciales, Fondo Lázaro Cárdenas [hereafter cited as AGN FC] 432.2/8, E. 1.

85. Armando T. Vázquez to Cárdenas, Mexico City, 20 Dec. 1934, AGN FC 432.2/8, E. 1; Alberto J. Olvera R., "La acción obrera después de la nacionalización petrolera: el caso de Poza Rica, 1937–1940," unpub. ms. (ca. 1987), p. 3.

86. R. C. Tanis, "Memorandum," Washington, D.C., 21 Sept. 1934; A. Madrazo to H. N. Branch, Mexico City, 23 May 1935; R. Henry Norweb to sec. of state, 11 June 1935, NADS. 812.6363/2791, /2847, /2851.

87. Edward L. Reed, "Memo of Conversation with Mr. Vanderwoude," Washington, D.C., 4 March 1935, NADS 812. 6363/2823; Josephus Daniels, *Shirt-Sleeve Diplomat* (Chapel Hill, N.C., 1947).

88. Owen St. Clair O'Malley to Foreign Office, Mexico City, 18 Nov. 1937, FO 371-20636/A8692/132/26; Daniels to sec. of state, 6 Jan. 1938, NADS 812.6363/3064.

89. "Extractos," 14 Aug. to 3 Sept. 1935, AGN FC 437.1/37

90. 1 July 1937, AGN, Archivo Histórico de Hacienda [Records Commission of Experts], 1844-3, F. 25.

91. Daniels to sec. of state, 14 May 1937; S. Roger Tyler, Jr., "Development in the Petroleum Labor Code in Mexico," Mexico City, 21 May 1937, NADS 812.504/1650, /1658.

92. For example, La Corona's men at Pánuco belonged to a CROM union, although the Minatitlán workers had repudiated CROM leaders. "Extracto," 3 July 1937, AGN FC 432/634.

93. *El Universal*, 16 March 1938; Alan Knight, *U.S.-Mexican Relations, 1910–1940: An Interpretation*, Monograph Series 28, Center for U.S.-Mexican Studies, UCSD (1987), pp. 78–79.

94. See *The Mexican Oil Strike of 1937: The Economic Issue* (Mexico City, 1937), p. 25; also, the comments of Jersey Standard's W. S. Farish, *New York Times*, 20 March 1938.

95. O'Malley to Foreign Office, Mexico City, 16 March 1938, FO 371-20640/ A2066. On the expropriation, see Philip, *Oil and Politics in Latin America*.

2. The Cultural Roots of the Oil Workers' Unions in Tampico, 1910–1925

S. Lief Adleson
Instituto Nacional de Antropología e Historia, Mexico City

The petroleum industry in Mexico developed rapidly in the period from 1910 to 1925. This occurred in a country whose population was fundamentally rural and agrarian in composition. At the outset, scant local working-class labor tradition existed because the industrialization process had barely begun. Consequently, many of those who labored under factory conditions constituted the first generation of industrial workers. Nevertheless, by the end of the first quarter of the century a significant segment of Mexican oil workers showed signs of having adopted the traits of an industrial labor force.

These wage earners had assimilated to a large degree a frame of reference compatible with industrial discipline: they were increasingly concerned with issues of job security and safety, they and their families were dependent on wages as a means of survival, and most were members of labor unions. They identified themselves as workers and conceived of their common interests as class interests.

This chapter is concerned with describing and explaining how Mexican oil workers in the petroleum port town and refining center of Tampico, Tamaulipas, carried out and participated in this course of change. It attempts to portray and to analyze the process by which working men and women made a transition from relating to one another and to their superiors in ways reflective of an agrarian-dominated world, to relating with behavior patterns influenced by values associated with urban, working-class experiences. This chapter deals primarily with the experience of Mexican oil workers through references to their cultural background and to the social and labor conditions they encountered in Tampico during the industrialization process. It does not focus on the varied political situations generated by the relations between the foreign oil companies and the Mexican government, nor to any great degree on the relations between the latter and the oil workers. These undoubtedly swayed the complex Tampico social equation. Nevertheless, the intent of this chapter is to fathom the process of social change from the point of view of the workers. Hence, political considerations are taken into account only to the degree they had a direct and lasting effect on the mode of Tampico working-class formation. In addition, I have taken certain liberties with generalizations. I have expressed them as though they were absolute, notwithstanding certain variations that naturally occurred. For example, in many instances I have lumped worker and management attitudes into broad generalizations. Obviously, there were many deviations and discrepancies among people. Nonetheless, I feel that I have accurately portrayed dominant motivations and perceptions behind human action.

Oil and Migrants

Worker migration was associated with the initial era of Mexican petroleum production because the oil fields were located in sparsely populated zones. A vast infrastructure for the exploration, exploitation, and export of oil had to be built. Thousands of workers were needed to handle the jobs of laying out roads and railway lines and of constructing buildings, docks, refineries, storage tanks, pumping facilities, warehouses, shops, and pipelines. Available workers came from more densely populated areas of Mexico. In addition, the period of oil labor demand coincided with the outbreak of the Mexican Revolution. The nascent oil industry thus offered a potential alternative for many people whose traditional forms of subsistence had been challenged by civil and military unrest.

Tampico became the major administrative, refining, and export center for the petroleum business in Mexico due to its proximity to the producing zones. Located near the mouth of the Pánuco River on the Gulf of Mexico, it was already an important port by 1910, thanks to the completion two decades earlier of a pair of river jetties and of two different railroad lines. The former linked the city to the rest of the world by sea, and the latter linked it to the interior of the country by land. In 1910, Tampico was a moderately sized provincial commercial city. It had about 23,500 inhabitants. Moreover, the heavy influx of migrants in response to the labor demands of the oil industry provoked a demographic avalanche. It is estimated that by 1921 roughly 150,000 people resided in Tampico and environs.[1]

Migrants, then, accounted for a significant part of the labor force. They brought with them patterns of work and norms of behavior often forged during generations of social interaction on haciendas, and in the countryside, pueblos, towns, and cities. These traditions and customs typically framed their social conduct and expectations. Such cultural baggage frequently was the point of departure from whence the newcomers interpreted and dealt with the new conditions they found in Tampico. Therefore, individual and collective actions during the first oil boom period can be more fully understood by taking into account the social origins of the migratory population.

Three general kinds of migrants made up the influx of people who converged on Tampico between 1910 and 1925. The vast majority were campesinos. Some were artisans and craftsworkers, and a few were industrial workers. Campesinos came from a broad area of North-Central Mexico formed by an geographic band running from Michoacán, Colina, and Jalisco to Aguascalientes, Guanajuato, Querétaro, and San Luis Potosí.[2] These were people whose outlook had been conditioned to a large degree by their relation to the land. Their world was one of natural cycles: of tilling, sowing, and harvesting; of sunrise and sunset; of wet and dry seasons. Work still entailed a great deal of personal involvement in the determination of daily rhythms and the manner in which it was carried out. Tools frequently were the property of the users or, if not, users were responsible for their care and repair.[3]

The family was at the center of campesino life. Structured as a unit of production, it formed the basic social component to whose maintenance the members contributed and from which they received support and orientation vis-à-vis the rest of the society. As such, it could integrate into one household parents, children, in-laws, cousins, uncles, aunts, and grandparents around the family plot or communal agricultural activity. The confluence of labor patterns and family ties often resulted in a division of labor in which work was not a separate activity, but rather an integral part of daily endeavors in which the development and preservation of social relations was a key undertaking.

Beyond the extended family, the symbolic relationships of *compadrazgo* and *padrinazgo* further served to structure the campesino social world. Individuals were laced into complex networks of personal allegiances and mutually convenient associations by means of formal ritualistic arrangements with other members of the community. In addition, local social hierarchy was often determined on the basis of canons of moral authority. These ranged from the precepts of deference to age and wisdom still prevalent in more traditional settings, to sentiments influenced by the reign of political and economic power, as was increasingly seen on haciendas.

Campesino attitudes reflected social and economic changes in their social relations. There still existed to some degree notions concerning mutual obligations of protection and service between the powerful and the weak. The fulfillment of those obligations legitimized the unequal relations between them. In addition, to varying degrees the concept of "justice" prevailed, according to which individuals had the right to live in peace if they fulfilled their obligations and did not infringe upon the rights of others.

Nevertheless, the foundations of traditional behavior patterns were changing. During the second half of the nineteenth century, arable land for family cultivation became increasingly harder to come by. Hacienda encroachment on communal lands accelerated. Family plots were frequently bequeathed to surviving sons, thus dividing individual patrimony into continually smaller portions with each generation. In addition, in some instances the land itself became exhausted after centuries of cultivation.

Social relations were also transformed. More and more hacienda owners and administrators thought of their land and those who worked it as components of production and less and less as elements of social prestige. Concurrently, the institutions of *compadrazgo* and *padrinazgo* more frequently assumed horizontal instead of vertical dimensions. That is, they served more to link people of the same social status than those of differing rank. Hacendados tended to establish ritual social relationships with other hacendados and those of similar standing, while campesinos tended to develop ritual relationships with other campesinos.

These and other factors modified the bonds that tied numerous individuals to the land and to their villages. Many of them sought alternatives by hiring themselves out to distant landowners, by apprenticing themselves to learn a trade with a relative, by looking for other kinds of employment such as becoming traveling peddlers, or by a combination of these, through emigration. In sum, campesino attitudes were frequently based on experiences in a context dominated by what can be called a moral economy in transition.

Artisans and craftsworkers were a second type of worker who made up the petroleum industry labor force. Most came from cities such as Monterrey, San Luis Potosí, Aguascalientes, Querétaro, Mexico City, and Guadalajara, as well as from towns throughout the region from which the campesinos originated. Others had lived or worked in places requiring their specialized skills, such as El Oro, Estado de México; La Luz, Guanajuato; or Real del Catorce, San Luis Potosí.[4] Their labor experience was most often associated with small-scale workshop production. These skilled workers participated in fairly structured social environments. Crafts and trades in Mexico, although no longer formally organized into guilds at the end of the nineteenth century, still maintained many of the traditions and customs developed generations before.

Entry into and mastery of a skilled trade usually followed prescribed patterns and conditions of apprenticeship. Seven years were not an unusual term for the training period. Sometimes only family members were among the select few accepted to learn the arts and secrets of the craft. The discipline of apprenticeship reinforced careful and accurate conveyance of skills and a respect for the social hierarchy of the craft system. For the most part, artisans were owners of their tools, occasionally working for master craftsworkers who had set up shops. Not exceptionally, they had a direct relationship with the person for whom the finished product was intended.

Such association with the means of production and with consumers contributed to the maintenance of a special place in society for artisans. Not only could they determine the rhythms and execution of their work, but they could decide what they produced and for whom. Also, for the most part, artisans were literate persons. Their independence and authority created an aura of prestige and stature, not only among their colleagues in the workshops, but also in the rest of laboring society. The master and journeyman were often looked up to as teachers and natural leaders by other working people.[5]

Notwithstanding the artisans' heritage, during the last quarter of the nineteenth century and the first decade of the twentieth newer forces were also active in transforming artisan work and, ultimately, their place in society. Industrial machines yielded greater quantities of manufactured goods previously elaborated by craft labor, undercutting prices and displacing independent producers.[6] In some places, and most notably in the textile industry, artisans were incorporated into large-scale production operations in great numbers with their tools, equipment, and machines.[7]

Thus, many artisans who immigrated to Tampico around the first decade of this century may already have experienced the erosion of their independence in the workplace. But the impact of status modification in the labor sphere appears to have affected their general social standing more slowly. Many of the skilled craftsworkers who went to Tampico still retained an air of superiority and leadership frequently associated with persons of their group.[8]

The third type of worker to join the labor ranks in Tampico was factory operatives. They undoubtedly were the least numerous, as Mexico still did not have much of an industrial tradition. Their presence in the oil region is hard to detect because they either blended into the labor scenery or they were not conspicuous in their opposition to the requirements of the industrial system. They were familiar with the nature of the work discipline and with factory production routines. Wage labor dependency was not new to them. In addition, the industrial workers who turned up in Tampico probably were of several types and skill levels.

At least two types of industrial workers stand out. First, there were those who possessed craft skills and who applied them to the company's tools and machinery. They established and controlled the pace and quality of the work they performed.[9] Second, semi- or unskilled machine operators and/or general laborers represented a new breed of industrial workers. They had internalized the rules of management expectations and accepted them as the framework within which labor relations were to occur. These workers sometimes identified with company interests and occasionally defended them against encroachment by outside interests. Not surprisingly, they were frequently selected by company administrators for training and promotion to low-level supervisory posts.[10]

These, then, were the three principal kinds of origins and labor backgrounds of the Mexicans who made up the petroleum industry work force during the first oil boom period. What most of them encountered in Tampico was a marked contrast to their previous experiences. The ways in which they tried to make sense of and deal with the new social, economic, and labor realities help explain the peculiar process by which working-class identification and solidarity evolved.

New Realities

Although final judgment has still to be rendered, historical evidence indicates that many laboring migrants who went to Tampico were young, single men.[11] They often arrived without customary kinship support structures. This meant that key facets of the traditional social apparatus that individuals used to define themselves with respect to the rest of the community, and that aided their integration into local society, were not present or had been left behind on the arduous trip to the coastal lowlands of the petroleum zone. For example, few immigrants had a network of relatives or kinfolk living in Tampico on whom they could depend for help in obtaining a place to stay, a good job, or other assistance in dealing with boomtown reality. As a result, such reference points as family ties and *compadrazgo* bonds for coping with people and situations were either absent or weakly structured in the novel context.

This did not mean that traditional methods for confronting problems were abandoned. Rather, it meant that new associative bonds, especially in the arena of ritual relationships, had to be forged and defined in the context of the Tampico experience. For example, people previously unknown to one another established new *compadrazgo* relationships as they tried to come to terms with problems arising from the unique material conditions of the oil center. They thus constructed fresh patterns of social interaction.

One particular situation exemplified this process. Housing conditions affected nearly every immigrant. The difficult circumstances derived in part from the fact that the city was hemmed in on almost all sides by water. As a result, for years the geographic area in the city center available for working-class occupancy was a little more than half of a square mile.[12] The nearly fivefold population increase in the ten years after 1910 put severe pressure on the housing market. Property owners, for their part, paid scant attention to the physical conditions of existing structures when it came to renting to laboring people. In contrast, renovation and new construction centered on providing offices for such high-paying occupants as the petroleum enterprises, as well as for making available luxurious accommodations for high-level foreign managers and technicians.

Consequently, rent prices consumed an increasing percentage of working people's income. In addition, human density per square meter of interior space increased uncomfortably, and the material state of the buildings they occupied deteriorated. It was not unusual by 1917 to have reports stating that "said tenement [*vecindad*] has 30 rooms [in] which more than 200 people live."[13] The wooden floors, walls, and roof of many were so rotten that numerous occupants had at one time or another fallen to the smelly mud below, had suffered from cold winter air blowing through the cracks, or had been rained upon due to copious leaks overhead. The densely packed housing units surrounding a common courtyard also tended to stink. Running water and drainage, when existent, were often deficient. On average, only one to four toilets, not necessarily functional, served scores of inhabitants.[14]

Tenants adapted customs and traditions from other contexts to try to resolve these problems. What began as individual complaints to repre-sentatives of the local health department against negligent landlords developed into organized collective actions. The property owners usu-ally reacted to isolated protests with threats of eviction. But renters soon realized that cooperative action and mutual defense, similar to organi-zational procedures used by communal villages against encroaching hacendados, could give them protection of numbers. They also utilized group action to organize themselves into work units responsible for cleaning common areas such as central patios, showers, and toilets.[15]

Concurrent with these kinds of actions, other immigrants reacted in different ways to try to deal with the bleak housing situation. Clandes-tinely and collectively, they organized nocturnal invasions of malodor-ous swamplands that were owned by the national railroad company. The encroachers organized group actions in order to stake out plots and to pursue rudimentary housing construction before the first rays of dawn revealed their presence. In the absence of extensive family networks and symbolic relations, it was not unusual for the intruders to organize and plan their activities on the basis of association in the workplace. Subsequently, they became neighbors.[16] This kind of organizational and cooperative effort reflected the inertia of past traditions. For most immigrants, this type of response seemed more coherent and natural than those based on solitary efforts to cope with the situation. Nevertheless, the pressures of individualization abounded.

Restaurants, eating houses, lunchrooms, and sidewalk tables proliferated. They offered, in exchange for money, meals to thousands of men in Tampico who arrived without the women who, in other circumstances, cooked and tended house for them. Traditional white cotton campesino pants and shirts, as well as leather *huaraches*, were swapped via the medium of currency, for denim overalls, khaki shirts, and manufactured shoes. Even after-hours socialization became subject to the availability of revenue. The principal meeting and entertainment places available to friends and acquaintances were bars, cabarets, brothels, and dance halls.[17] The commercialization of these activities was predicated on the conversion of the population into individualized elements of consumption.

The contrasts between this situation and accustomed forms of daily existence reflected dissimilarities between Tampico and other social environments. As suggested above, the absence of articulated familial and symbolic relationships weakened and altered one of the traditional mechanisms of social defense at the disposal of the individual. The family was no longer physically a point of reference and identification with respect to the rest of society. In addition, other social and ethical guideposts had also been transformed.

The bonds of at least two time-honored elements of moral authority had been loosened. First, in Tampico the Catholic church played a relatively minor role in sanctioning and condoning patterns of local social behavior. Its presence in the Gulf of Mexico region was historically limited. Further, for years there was only one Catholic church in the city, even after the population had grown precipitously. Attempts to establish rural chapels in two worker neighborhoods met with scant enthusiasm, due not only to the general anticlerical mood prevalent during the revolution, but also to the insufficiency of local donations to cover the cost of renting a house in which to conduct services. Symptomatic of its limited influence was the fact that in 1918, when the population presumably exceeded one hundred thousand people, daily attendance in the main square church was no more than fifty to one hundred faithful.[18]

Second, other key elements of traditional Mexican society were missing. Not infrequently, communities had local patriarchs and/or social elites who played a prominent role in the social, economic, and political life of the towns. These were people whose authority epitomized Porfirian social structure. Sometimes these were religious leaders, other times they were landowners or merchants. They were agents of local economic forces and frequently represented the underpinnings of political power.[19]

In Tampico, soon after the petroleum bonanza began, the principal members of the social and economic elite affiliated themselves with the oil companies, foreign technical and supervisory personnel, and with the new rich who had profited from oil lands speculation. Some became lawyers and highly paid accountants for the local operations of the petroleum consortiums. They sent their sons and daughters to the United States or England to be educated and spent their vacations in Europe. Almost without exception, they turned their backs on lower social strata, for whom they had alternately either been objects of awe and deference or by whom they had been despised and hated. At any rate, they were points of reference and their actions and life-styles had been the beacons of Tampico society. This change of social orientation was exemplified by the fact that they no longer offered to be, nor allowed themselves to be, inducted as honorary presidents of the mutual aid societies of workers.[20]

Such abdication of social and political leadership roles cast doubt on the coherence of the local social structure, especially to newcomers. The absence of traditional patriarchs projected an aura of incertitude on the legitimacy of the social hierarchy, which in the circumstances of many of the immigrants' previous experience had offered a context in which to explain and justify the public inequalities among citizens. The pull of the economic tide of the petroleum industry left a political and cultural vacuum in the oil boomtown. The most visible agents of social validation and political integrity ceased to serve as guideposts for behavior in a new and different environment. This portended a breakdown in social cohesion that left an open field for exploring alternatives.

This situation was exacerbated by the Revolution. In 1914 the triumphant revolutionary officials initiated a campaign of persecution in Tampico against former political elites whom they associated with the "forces of reaction." Inasmuch as there had been a high correlation between political, economic, and social dominance in the port during the late Porfirian era, the Constitutionalist offensive amounted to a further disaccreditation of those who had been established representatives of social status.[21]

Enfeeblement of civil authority accompanied the debilitation of traditional agents of social authority. The torrents of immigrants to Tampico soon proved to be greater than the authorities could handle. Oil companies paid wages higher than the going rate in order to attract workers. Many local policemen abandoned their jobs for better pay in the oil industry. The train station, where most of the thousands of newcomers arrived, became a notorious hunting ground for pickpockets and thieves.[22] Unrest increased as time and again rumors of revolution swept the city. Madero's victory and Porfirio Díaz's departure resulted in the unexpected disintegration of the local law enforcement and political apparatus. The *jefe político* resigned, as did the *rurales*, the local constabulary, and many other municipal public officials. Notwithstanding the fact that the local political bureaucracy was reinstalled a fortnight later, the façade of political and civil control had been shown to be in shambles. People began to openly resist and disobey the dictates of municipal authorities.[23]

By the time the next phase of the civil war approached the city in 1913 and early 1914, Tampico had become a strategic port in General Huerta's scheme of defense. Military considerations took precedence over civil necessities. In the eyes of the working public, this further diminished the stature and legitimacy of local leaders as they bowed to the dictates of martial priorities. Severe water shortages went unattended, the municipal drainage system soon deteriorated, and small pox and typhoid epidemics ensued.[24]

Nor did the Constitutionalists have the wherewithal to reestablish coherent social and political parameters when they took control of the city in 1914. For almost three years, regional and local military commanders exercised political authority parallel to and, at times, in lieu of the local civilian government. However, the officials discharging those duties changed frequently, as did the circumstances that determined the way civil problems were handled.

Senior military officers had different styles and distinct personal and political interests to pursue. Not infrequently, Tampico commanders had to perform an about-face when dealing with community affairs. Parties affected negatively by their policies often appealed to higher authority, and at times succeeded in persuading superior officers to countermand the orders of their subordinates. This portrayed a varied and unstable image of what the worker population could expect from the local authorities. For example, in December 1914, corn suddenly disappeared from many stores. The local chief of arms, Col. Francisco A. Espinosa, sent troops to inspect warehouses and ordered merchants to present proof of the price they paid for grains found. These he forcibly purchased at cost and sold to the general public for the same price. Shortly afterward, the state military command changed. Gen. Luis Caballero took over and immediately issued a decree guaranteeing free and unhindered commerce of cereals and grains in the state. Prices skyrocketed and supplies continued to fluctuate erratically.[25]

The attitude and actions of the military commanders with respect to the numerous worker movements portrayed a similar fickleness. For example, in April 1916 the local military commander, Gen. Emiliano P.

Nafarrate, used a cavalry detachment to arrest labor leaders and to break up a popular demonstration that supported a general strike over the issues of hours and wages. He ordered workers and management to negotiate a solution to the conflict. However, he stipulated that they do so on the basis of terms unacceptable to either of them. While he insisted on his unsatisfactory conditions, representatives of the two sides worked out an arrangement behind his back. A few weeks later, Nafarrate's disposition seemed to have changed radically, as he gave what seemed to be unequivocal support to workers striking against U.S. oil companies.[26] Time and again military forces repressed worker demonstrations that, from the wage earners' perspective, sought to oblige oil companies to treat them fairly. On other occasions, the commanders turned a blind eye or even aided strikers. More often than not, military actions hinged on considerations beyond the arena of worker-management relations, a fact not always apparent to the local labor participants. Consequently, many workers grew to distrust and repudiate military authority, because they did not know what to expect from it.[27]

In the administrative realm, local officials also presented an image of ineptitude and ineffectiveness. From the time of their arrival in May 1914, Constitutionalist politicians had spoken loudly in public forums and had written in the local press about the need to defend popular interests. One specific action they attempted in this regard had to do with price controls for basic necessities such as food. Between 1914 and 1916, in the face of rampant inflation, numerous local officials attempted to implement price limitations for certain commodities. This was a period of continual conflict between local commercial concerns and the authorities. Businesses took advantage of divergent positions among competing political actors to protect their interests. Similarly, they tried to manipulate popular pressure by causing artificial shortages and by closing their establishments in protest. In the long run, the economically powerful prevailed, but not until after they exacerbated a famine in mid-1916 in an attempt to force the administration's hand.[28]

These and other factors served to illustrate ways in which, from the viewpoint of laboring immigrants, the local government lacked power to do much for them. This perception added to the seeming lack of respect for recognizable moral archetypes. In the material and social context of Tampico, this translated into the image of a world out of control. Many ethical precepts that had structured pre-Tampico existence no longer functioned. Basic notions of justice had been distorted. Evidence suggested that the individual could no longer count on the belief that one had the right to live in peace if one fulfilled one's obligations and did not infringe on the rights of others. Furthermore, one's obligations with respect to the community were no longer clear.

There seemed to be little or no reciprocity in the Tampico experience. Inhabitants did what was demanded of them: they worked. But in return they did not feel as though they had been inducted into a society in which they had a place. They hadn't been incorporated into a network of relations that guaranteed social security. Housing circumstances threatened to become worse month by month. Living quarters became more crowded as time went by. Monetary devaluation and price inflation brought personal economic instability, and the cost of basic goods varied wildly from one week to the next.[29] Moreover, there appeared to be no authority at hand to whom to appeal, nor any familiar mechanisn that would help laboring inhabitants to define the situation. Working people also perceived threats to social coherence in their common experience at work.

The Labor Experience

For a great number of wage earners in the Tampico petroleum industry, work also had many strange elements. Supervisory personnel insisted on doing things in an alien fashion. Notwithstanding certain modifications to adapt their operations to local labor market conditions, by and large the foreign oil companies imported contemporary U.S. and English managerial ideas for organizing the labor processes. Work activities were subjected to a rigorous division of labor. Productive procedures, whether they had to do with digging ditches, laying pipe, or milling specialized pieces, were broken down into their constituent parts and treated as separate sequences. Not infrequently foreign bosses oversaw the work of the Mexican subordinates.[30]

For the uninitiated, the novelty of these arrangements resided in the fact that they hardly made sense. They deprived work of its customary meanings. Management stipulated and tried to control workers' labor patterns and rhythms. The overseers defined how to perform tasks and almost never accepted deviations from those formulas. As a result, many job holders did not have a complete picture of what it was they were doing. In addition, supervisors insisted that the wage earners apply themselves incessantly to their jobs during the entire day. If prescribed tasks were completed before the whistle sounded, the laborers were not allowed to relax their pace or to hand in their tools, even if it was only five minutes before the end of the shift.[31]

Not only were time and work controlled by company representatives, but so was space. Refineries were blocked off into areas according to the productive processes carried out in each. Wage workers were prohibited from leaving their assigned employment location without permission from the boss, even if only to use the toilet facilities.[32]

These conditions tended to redefine not only what work was, but how and where it was to be carried out. In addition, the oil companies developed novel criteria concerning the value of workers' labor. This they did by establishing homogeneous professional categories according to their particular requirements. Specialized workers were classified either as first-, second-, or third-class craftsworkers. No distinction was made among the different kinds of skills required for different professions. Hence, a second-class mechanic received the same pay as a second-class welder, a second-class boilermaker, or a second-class machine operator. Such categorization offered little respect for the relative difficulty or dissimilitude in the knowledge and length of experience required to become proficient in different skills.

This, however, was a secondary consideration for the petroleum enterprises. They were not necessarily interested in employing artisans with vast knowledge and competence in their respective fields. Inasmuch as they defined the jobs to be done, provided the materials to be used, and decided how the parts would create the whole, they needed only welders who could weld, carpenters who could swing a hammer, electricians who could string wires and place insulators, and lathe operators who could operate lathes.[33] Their definition of what constituted a skilled worker was in marked contrast to traditional notions associated with lengthy and rigorous apprenticeship practices.

Furthermore, the oil companies tended to place a higher value on supervisory talents than on skill abilities. Workers who internalized management priorities were treated with greater deference than others. Those who, in addition to identifying with company interests, possessed foremanship abilities, were rewarded with more promotions and higher pay than their counterparts of equal seniority who lacked leadership qualities.[34] Consequently, many workers received a twisted version of reality, because it appeared that those who worked less, the bosses, were paid more. The global effect of this compensation scheme was to reformulate the process by which workers' skills and abilities were evaluated. Previously, master artisans judged the quality, scope, and preparedness of their peers and of juniors aspiring to professional status. Now, however, the oil company employment practices and payment systems placed these prerogatives in the hands of personnel departments and supervisory staffs who employed distinct criteria in measuring the competence of their subordinates.

These contrasts with traditional practices were framed in the context of overall relations between workers and management. Employers considered that the payment of wages discharged their obligations to the workers. Except in the case of a limited number of key upper-level employees, there were few written contracts between the petroleum enterprises and their Mexican employees. The wage earners toiled on a daily basis with a tacit understanding that, if the foreman or section head judged them reliable, they could normally count on engagement for the duration of the project or until their services were no longer needed. However, in practice, such unexpected factors as fluctuations in the international petroleum market or inclement weather could alter employment prospects from one day to the next.[35]

Furthermore, the Mexican workers discovered that entering oil company properties was like going into another world. Once inside the main gate, the bosses ordered them about and treated them as though their sole function was to obey and perform duties. But when they were on the other side of the wall, management acted as though they did not exist. Not only did the bosses usually live in separate parts of the city in their own exclusive neighborhoods, they also seldom established nonprofessional association with the Mexican employees. There was not even any kind of paternalistic or client-patron relationship between the former and the latter. It was as though management was unconcerned with the nonlabor aspects of the workers' existence.[36] In this context, the possibility was remote, at best, for developing extended social relationships between the two.

Mexican employees also felt victimized by two kinds of discrimination. Supervisory personnel was composed overwhelmingly of foreign individuals. Rampant among them was both latent and overt racial bias against non-English speakers. Their attitudes ranged from condescending to hostile. Second, with noticeable frequency, Mexican employees received lower salaries for the same kind of work than non-Mexican employees.[37]

These combined labor conditions affected different kinds of workers in different ways. For individuals with a campesino experience, petroleum industry activity seemed unnatural, inhuman, strange, and humiliating. Work lacked social meaning. It had been divorced from other human endeavors. Frequently, laborers were required to perform tasks for unknown reasons. What they did was detached from why they did it. Work seemed to have no intrinsic binding function between them and those for whom they performed it. Further, it was disjointed and no longer had natural rhythms that related it to the rest of existence. Finally, work no longer provided any guarantee of a stable place in the community.

The Tampico petroleum labor regime affected artisans in slightly different ways. It degraded their professional attributes. Specialized abilities were identified with the use of tools and not with the knowledge and implementation of skills. Artisans were stripped of control over the rhythm and pace of their work. Their labor status was defined by salary level, not by the quality and specialty of their work or by consumer satisfaction. In addition, professional pride was often trampled by boorish supervisors who had less expertise in the trade than workers did.[38] In sum, the artisans were humiliated as skilled human beings and treated as though they were an extension of the machinery.

For their part, factory operatives saw the Tampico labor environment as a prolongation of what they had known previously. It offered to some the opportunity to ingratiate themselves with bosses and to progress through the ranks of factory hierarchy. Additionally, their experience, combined with the daily social conditions, impressed upon some of them the need for workers to act collectively in order to define and defend their group interests.

Responses and Options

Migrant laborers, then, had reason to perceive the sum of Tampico experience as different from and hostile to the reality they knew before arriving there. It left many feeling as though they were without a secure place in society. The rules for getting along and developing a niche in the social structure were almost unrecognizable. The usual signposts that legitimized the uneven distribution of wealth, power, and prestige in communities had been replaced by topsy-turvy explanations that seemed to have little basis for comprehension according to past experience. This left laborers with two realizations. First, they felt that in Tampico they were on the bottom of an unjust and barely rational scheme of things. This found expression in the growing sense of identification that, as workers, they were the victims of a society that favored some people, but not them. As they complained to the mayor:

> all of this radius is completely surrounded by dwellings, even
> though they are miserable shacks; we who live in them are workers
> who do not have sufficient means to occupy places in the center of
> the city and we believe that we have just as much right to exist-
> ence as those who live in opulence in elegant houses located in the
> center of the city.[39]

And, second, the kind of work, treatment, and pay they received at the hands of the oil companies deprived them of their sense of worth as working people:

> with profound indignation we have seen the villainous tyranny
> with which the companies treat us, and in particular the "El
> Aguila" company and the Huasteca Petroleum Company and

others, who impose laws on us which [make it] seem that we are in a Babylon, and there doesn't appear to be anyone who can put an end to this evil.[40]

Many of the working-class inhabitants' individual and collective activities in Tampico from 1910 to 1925 took place in the context of this socioeconomic environment and within the framework of the immigrants' cultural heritage. Their actions can be understood not only as attempts to mitigate the adversities they experienced, but as efforts to offer coherent and reasonable alternatives to unnatural and incomprehensible social values foisted upon them by landlords, managers, and others in the community. The inhabitants' responses to crowded tenements and unhealthy living conditions illustrate the dual nature of their quest. To deal with sanitary problems and deteriorating structures, they organized cleaning brigades and stimulated collective defense against landlords who did not maintain buildings in good repair. This kind of initiative also helped give them a sense of control over their own lives, as well as to provide them with a forum for the beginnings of communal action. Similarly, invasions of land once considered uninhabitable brought together men and women in a common enterprise. The sense of cooperation and mutual defense fostered during the nighttime endeavors was in sharp contrast to the forces of individualization that hammered at them on all sides in the oil city. For many, it provided an alternative to high rents and arrogant landlords.

By 1917, land invasions had become a major response to one aspect of what capital-intensive Tampico represented. They became a partial answer to the commercial housing monopoly that thrived on maintaining a general scarcity in order to drive up the price of rents. The self-help and group-protection structures that grew out of spontaneous, clandestine colonization actions were another antidote to isolated consumerism, which the widespread monetization of the local economy imposed on the inhabitants. These activities also represented an option to the social isolation of not having a family, group, clan, or community with which to identify.

In 1917 up to five thousand people had participated in the extralegal occupation of the swamp area known as Llanos del Golfo. They organized themselves into their own governing body, laying out streets, assigning lots for future school construction, planning and installing their own water supply, and defining the local code of conduct. They also established participatory mechanisms for venting and resolving disputes among inhabitants of their area.[41] Such enterprises provided the opportunity for people to take some control of their life and to build an organization that represented their interests and responded to their needs. As such, it was a welcome alternative to the formal political institutions that daily discredited themselves in the eyes of many Tampico residents.

In addition to these types of measures to address material problems, working people also created new social and cultural institutions. As time progressed, they founded more workplace-based associations. These contributed to the task of constructing alternative interpretations of the industrial format of social relations. As labor unions began to proliferate (see below), they also played a role in implementing their contrasting perspective of how men and women should relate to one another. Specifically, labor unions were frequently organized on the basis of participatory democracy. They often rotated leadership functions on a biannual basis, and encouraged lively, thorough, and, at times, prolonged debate concerning most matters. Significantly, the guiding principle of unions stipulated that the assembly of members had the final word and was the authority of last appeal. Thus, workers could consider and analyze among themselves proposals and courses of action. This was a distinct alternative to how people could organize their affairs that contrasted with the authoritarian environment they experienced on oil company properties.[42]

Workers also created other cultural options for interpreting and redefining the industrial world around them. As early as 1915, one of the few social activities available at no cost was the Sunday morning popular meeting in the main commercial plaza. Every week orators would lecture passionately on the nature of class society, highlighting its exploitative elements, and calling on workers to struggle, "against the bourgeoisie who are not concerned with even minimally assuaging the needs of the people; rather, like buzzards they exploit us iniquitously, without paying heed to our tears and sufferings." In addition, wage earners established numerous theater groups. These performed works by leftist playwrights such as Emilio Solm , Ricardo Flores Magón, Maxim Gorki, and Joaquín Dicenta. Several radical newspapers circulated freely, providing stimulating and revolutionary interpretations of events in which local, national, and international workers participated.[43] These forums undoubtedly created an environment of discussion that workers pursued in the many cantinas and bars throughout the city. These also were worker cultural sanctuaries into which men from other classes entered only by mistake. Elements such as these helped to forge and propagate among workers a radical interpretation of industrial society. In the absence of cohesive alternative interpretations, usually sanctioned by the principal social and econonic elite and subtly woven into the dominant value construct, this view of the world had a persuasive influence in Tampico. Thus, workers could build a competing frame of reference with which to order and understand the meaning of industrial social relations in terms that made sense to them.

Organizational and job actions conveyed similar messages. Short-term goals often dealt with current problems, while the sum of collective experiences yielded viable methods of opposition to the harsh and unnatural conditions of industrial work. More often than not, workers were trying to redress specific situations that created material hardship, as well as attempting to find alternatives to conditions that provoked moral tension. They formed organizations whose goals, as stated in the words of one of them, were "to get together some capital and to provide ourselves with mutual aid and to struggle eternally for a state of peaceful union for assembling order in the [realm of] social obligations."[44]

Thus, certain kinds of mutual aid societies founded in Tampico between 1910 and 1915 were, on one level, efforts to confront the effects of not having access to customary social support in the form of family and ritual social relations. The funds each member regularly contributed aided the needy during moments of distress: unemployment, sickness, or death. Also, these types of mutual aid societies organized dances, parties, and musical and literary social events.[45] Other mutual support associations restricted membership to skilled persons of the name trade. One of their aims was to continue a long-established practice of strengthening and protecting professional group identity. This was important because the structure of industrial work constituted an attack on the integrity of many manual arts. Moreover, in Tampico these organizations served as natural starting points for strangers from diverse regions to associate and to develop a sense of fraternity in a hostile environment. Not only did it provide the chance to share tips concerning better employment opportunities, but it afforded the occasion to comment on places to eat, housing situations, and social activities.[46]

Increasingly, Tampico inhabitants formed organizations from the starting point of what they had in common: their work experience. Individuals in guildlike occupations such as stevedores, carpenters, river boat sailors, and sheet metal builders founded associations that grouped many, if not all, of the people engaged in similar activities. It was not uncommon for these associations to retain many of the social functions of the mutual aid societies.[47] However, their creation signaled a change in the way many inhabitants assessed their situation and sought to defend their interests. More and more it became clear to them that the labor front was an important arena in which to address the problems of their status in Tampico.

By early 1915, wage earners began to form numerous labor unions. While still performing important community social roles, these organizations' principal sphere of action was promoting worker interests against bosses, management, and other representatives of capital. They took shape along craft lines, thus preserving time-tested organizational practices. Workers without trade alliances could join the general laborers union (Sindicato de Jornaleros). The Labor Union Federation (Federación de Sindicatos) coordinated solidarity activities and often spoke on behalf of the Tampico labor movement in general.[48]

From the beginning, just and sufficient compensation was one of the principal concerns with which the unions dealt. Tampico inhabitants had been thrust into a monetized economy in which they could survive only by selling their labor power. Many traditional structures and mechanisms for getting along without becoming a wage slave were absent. However, some cultural notions attendant to other life-styles lingered. Specifically, an unspoken belief prevailed that reciprocity was the norm that guided relations among people. Thus, workers assumed that they would receive satisfactory remuneration for their work.

Labor unions, in turn, strove to secure this for their members. As the boomtown economy pushed prices and rents higher, strikes demanding that wages be increased were frequent. Further, beginning in 1916, workers began to insist that payment be made in gold coin or foreign currency instead of Mexican paper bills.[49] These attempts to provide greater monetary security for workers were couched in moral terms. Points of reference based on traditional social relations showed up in the terminology employed to justify strike actions. One labor group closed its statement of demands with the words, "if you do not accept our JUST claim, you will be responsible for the consequences."[50]

Workers also used their unions to defend and protect what they considered to be their prerogatives in the productive processes. Here, too, they sought to preserve attributes reminiscent of preindustrial situations. They called strikes because they considered certain supervisors to be either incompetent, despotic, or lacking the necessary skills to judge their work. Further, some job actions centered around worker demands that bosses be fired, that unacceptable security guards be sent away, and that foremen be Mexicans citizens. In addition, there were numerous complaints that the companies were arbitrary and unfair in the way they assigned tasks or laid off employees. While workers made such statements on the basis of moral indignation, superintendents repudiated their claims as unwarranted interference in management affairs.[51]

Such protests illustrated that many workers continued to struggle against the rules of industrial discipline and to resist the new social relations of production on the basis of past experience. Nevertheless, there were indications of change. Unions and strikes were working-class tactics aimed against capitalists. As wage earners realized that more and more elements of moral economy had less and less relevance in Tampico, they modified and adapted behavior patterns in order to better deal with current realities. Slowly, haltingly, and on a piecemeal basis, workers made attempts to confront portions of industrial existence on its terms.

Worker reaction to the 1917 Mexican Constitution was illustrative of this process. Certain provisions of the new Magna Carta offered potential benefits to Tampico wage earners. However, the mechanisms that had to be pursued for their implementation implied recognition of the government as a legitimate arbitrator. Similarly, acceptance of the legal guidelines implied acknowledgment of new parameters in the arena of worker-management relations. Initial worker experimentation in such matters yielded frustrating results for laborers. Therefore, the umbrella Tampico labor organization rejected the process as inexpedient. Nevertheless, the experience did open up the possibility of third-party intervention in labor-management affairs. Within two years, workers were seeking aid and arbitration from government officials.[52]

A substantial alteration of organizing practices in 1919 was more indicative of the changes in jobholder attitudes. After years of confrontation and mobilization on the basis of craft lines, working people began to establish company-based unions. The transformation of artisans' work, the treatment of common laborers by oil companies, and the similitude of their nonwork expriences brought the two together. Wage earners in the same place of work, irrespective of their skills and job classifications, had more in common than journeymen and craftsworkers of the same trade in different companies. This stimulated the creation of industrial unions such as the United Workers of the Transcontinental Oil Company, the United Workers of the Texas Oil Company, the United Workers of the Pierce Oil Company, the United Workers of Main Depot, and the United Workers of El Aguila Refinery. In time, these horizontal unions supplanted the craft-oriented organizations.[53]

The willingness to organize and struggle from the common ground of being employed by the same company signaled an important transformation. New values were crystallizing. Men and women began to accept the fact that as workers they were sellers of their labor power. Overwhelmingly, they began to equate that fact with the understanding that their interests and those of the industrialists were antagonistic. In this context, the workers saw the need to define and defend their rights. They realized that if they did not, no one else would do it for them, and capitalists would impose their criteria on them.

The consequences of this reality were further revealed in 1921. In that year, the Mexican oil boom hit its apogee and began to decline. Saltwater seeped into several key oil-producing fields and yields dropped precipitously. Tens of thousands of oil workers were laid off. For the first time,

Tampico experienced massive emigration. The wage earners who remained felt compelled to accept job and salary restructuring for fear of joining the ranks of those already fired.[54] The year 1921 was a turning point in the life of many of them; they had to make a decision as to whether they wanted to stay in the oil industry labor force or to return to their place of origin. Those who continued in Tampico had made their decision on the basis of being industrial workers.

Once this watershed was passed, workers' perspectives changed. The issues of safety, job security, seniority rights, and work and retirement benefits took on new meaning. Wage earners had thrown in their lot on a long-term basis as employees of the petroleum consortiums. Only by securing guarantees of continuity could they feel assured about the future. This perception implied an acceptance of the framework of the rules of industrial work. The struggle that ensued was one to spell out and define the specifics of those rules and the mechanisms by which workers and management would struggle within that framework to earmark and defend their interests.

In 1924, after a protracted strike, the oil workers of El Aguila oil company won management recognition of the union as their legal representative. The victory included the first collective labor contract in the petroleum industry. With it came a realization by both workers and management in the Tampico oil region that the petroleum industry labor force had assimilated the logic of industrial work. The wage earners were neither docile nor passive. However, capitalists knew that they could count on them to struggle within the rules of the game, since they had left behind ways reflective of an agrarian-dominated world of relating to one another and to their superiors.

Conclusion

The people who immigrated to Tampico from 1910 to 1925 came to a region dominated by the oil industry. Many elements that defined and structured traditional social relations were either absent or distorted in the petroleum boomtown. Immigrants, therefore, adopted customs and time-tested ways of identifying with their peers to the novel circumstances. They established new associative relationships to overcome hostile situations in the monetized commercial environment. Workers also utilized long-standing values concerning group participation to structure labor unions in their search to affirm a positive rationality in their workplace relations.

Parallel to these efforts to secure and maintain material benefits from their labor situation, the Tampico workers developed a sense of class identification. They validated and ratified this recognition by developing a range of cultural activities that offered a coherent interpretation of capitalist society and of their place in it. The development, assimilation, and evolution of new values drew the laboring population farther away from previous cultural and social reference points and led it to adopt new modes of relating to peers and superiors.

This process was spurred on in part by the fact that a technologically advanced industrial activity established an enclave in a predominantly agrarian and rural setting. This occurred during moments of Mexican social and political upheaval. The historical juncture added a special impetus to the process by setting up conditions that illustrated in especially stark terms the antagonistic nature of class relations.

Notes

1. Concerning the construction of Tampico's maritime infrastructure, see Elmer Lawrence Corthell, "The Tampico Harbour Workes, Mexico," in *Minutes of Proceedings of the Institution of Civil Engineers, with Selected and Abstracted Papers*, London, CXXV (1895–1896), part 3, pp. 123–181. Population figures and estimates can be found, among other places, in the 1910 national census and in Ezequiel Ordóñez, "El petróleo en México, bosquejo histórico," *Revista mexicana de ingeniería y arquitectura* 3:3 (15 Dec. 1932).

2. The geographic origins of Tampico immigrants for this period have been ascertained through indirect evidence. There does not appear to exist a systematic inventory of their birthplace, so nonrepresentative information such as a list of facility occupants during epidemics and records of train ticket destinations have been used to construct an approximation. Examples of quarantine registry can be found in Head of the Municipal Sanitary Brigade to mayor, 31 Oct., 30 Nov., and 1 Dec. 1915. Tampico Municipal Historical Archives (henceforth, AHT), file 27-1915. AHT, file 83-1921 contains an enumeration of approximately two thousand train station destinations of unemployed oil workers during a government-sponsored program to provide free railway transportation to destitute workers in order to alleviate social tensions in the Tampico area.

3. These and the following observations about the nature of life, work, and social relationships in the Mexican countryside are based upon Friedrich Katz, *La servidumbre agraria en México en la época porfiriana* (Mexico City, 1980); John Foster, *Tzintzuntzan: los campesinos mexicanos en un mundo de cambio* (Mexico City, 1976); Paul Friedrich, *Agrarian Revolt in a Mexican Village* (Chicago, 1977); Karl Kaerger, *Agricultura y colonización en México en 1900* (Mexico City, 1986); and Eric R. Wolf, *Peasants* (Englewood Cliffs, N.J., 1966).

4. These were mining towns. In addition to miners, men from other specialized trades, such as electricians, carpenters, and blacksmiths, worked there. Information on the origin of skilled workers is scattered and scarce at best. Occasional references appear in historical documentation housed in the Tampico municipal archives, especially among papers concerning petitions by individuals for municipal services, claims against third parties, or requests for grants of municipal land for house construction purposes. For example, see T. Meza

Moreno et al. to mayor, 12 Jan. 1917, AHT, file 14-1917, unnumbered; Hilario Pezaña et al. to mayor, 29 Sept. 1917, AHT, file 122-1917, no. 802. Other information on the origins of artisans was gathered from oral interviews with retired workers. See "Entrevista al señor Francisco Bega Soria, realizada por S. Lief Adleson," Naucalpan de Juárez, 31 March, 2, 7 April 1978; "Severo Paredes Rosales, Poza Rica, 10, 11 April 1976; "Tito Durán y Huerta," Tampico, 23, 27 Aug., 10 Sept. 1976; "Aurelio Castillo Trujillo," Ciudad Madero, 18, 25 April 1978, in Dirección de Estudios Históricos, Instituto Nacional de Antropología e Historia (henceforth, DEH-INAH), PHO/4/49, /51, /54, /88.

5. See Ann Craig, *The First Agraristas: An Oral History of the Mexican Agrarian Reform Movement* (Berkeley, Calif., 1983).

6. Rodney D. Anderson, *Outcasts in Their Own Land: Mexican Industrial Workers, 1906–1911* (DeKalb, Ill., 1976), pp. 46–50.

7. Luis Gerardo Morales, "Máquinas y huaraches: la fábrica textil 'El Mayorazgo,' Puebla, 1906–1920" (Mexico City: Universidad Autónoma Metropolitana, 1981), licenciate thesis.

8. "Entrevista al señor Filogonio Olguín Rojo, realizada por María Ruiz Hernández y S. Lief Adleson," Tampico, 4, 5 May 1976; "Francisco Ruiz Hernández," Tampico, 8, 9, 16, 18 Sept. 1976; "Francisco Vega Soria," Naucalpan de Juárez, 31 March, 2, 7 April 1976; "Gonzalo Ruiz Carrillo," 11, 17 March 1975, DEH-INAH, PHO/4/46, /57, /49, /38.

9. For a lucid account of this phenomenon in the United States, see David Montgomery, *Workers' Control in America: Studies in the History of Work, Technology, and Labor Struggles* (Cambridge, 1979), especially chap. 1. Related circumstances in Mexico are documented in Mario Camarena, "Fábricas rurales en la industria textil mexicana, segunda mitad del siglo 19," unpublished paper presented at Coloquio Sobre Estudios Históricos Regionales, Puebla, 21–23 Oct. 1987; and "Entrevista al señor Alejo Calvillo Uvalle," Tampico, 17, 19, 21 Oct., 25 Nov. 1978, DEH-INAH, PHO/4/90.

10. For an example of worker defense of company interests, see Compañía de Petróleo "La Corona" to mayor, 15 May 1917, AHT, file 164-1917, no. 347.

11. A preliminary analysis of a municipal census carried out in 1917 suggests that there were approximately 117 men for every 100 women. See AHT, file 132-1917. In addition, it is probable that up to another 10 percent of the male population was underregistered due to the manner in which the head count was performed. See S. Lief Adleson, "Historia social de los obreros industriales de Tampico, 1906–1919," PhD diss. (Mexico City: El Colegio de México, 1981), appendix 1. The 1921 national census enumerated 44,307 women and 50,360 men in the municipality of Tampico (Estados Unidos Mexicanos, Departamento de la Estadística Nacional, Censo general de habitantes, 30 Nov. 1921, Estado de Tamaulipas, Mexico City, 1928, p. 125.) Notwithstanding, the local census takers reported numerous difficulties and deficiencies in the count procedure that led them to suggest that the percentage of underreporting of men was probably even greater than that experienced four years earlier. See José F. Montesinos to mayor, 24 Nov. 1921, AHT, file 77-1921, unnumbered document.

12. Clarkson Jones, "Report on the City of Tampico—Electric Light, Power, and Tramways," Feb. 1912, S. Pearson & Son, Ltd., Historical Records, British Science Museum, London (henceforth, SP&S), box B-2.

13. Head of the Sanitary Brigade to mayor, 26 May 1917, AHT, file 1-1917, no. 374.

14. For years, the municipal Sanitary Brigade diligently made frequent rounds of the many *vecindades*, leaving abundant testimony of living conditions, inhabitant density, and individual and collective complaints concerning rents, renters, and landlords. For samples of the daily reports, see AHT, files 12-1914, 21-1914, 23-1914, 4-1915, 8-1915, 13-1915, unnumbered, 1915, 9-1916, 1-1917, 2-1918, 3-1918, 31-1918.

15. For examples of complaints against landlord threats, see Head of Special Sanitary Brigade to mayor, 25 Nov. 1915; Macario Hernández to mayor, undated (1916); AHT, 3-1915, unnumbered, 1916, unnumbered.

16. "Entrevista al señor Horacio Sierra Aguilar," Tampico, 28 Feb., 2 March 1979, DEH-INAH, PHO/4/94; author's interview with Andrés Araujo Araujo [*sic*], Tampico, 26 Nov. 1978; mayor to Eduardo C. Piñeiro, 19 Aug., 5 Sept. 1918, AHT, file 169-1918; eight signatories to mayor, 5 Sept. 1918, AHT, 280-1918, unnumbered document.

17. Extensive description of the social conditions of Tampico working-class life during this period can be found in Adleson, "Historia social," pp. 324–381.

18. M. P. Viramontes to mayor, 29 June 1918; municipal medical health inspector to mayor, 28 Oct. 1918, AHT, file 276-1918, unnumbered, file 163-1918, no. 316.

19. See Luis González y González, *Pueblo en vilo* (Mexico City, 1984), pp. 48–57, 88, 98–100; Friedrich, *Agrarian Revolution*.

20. Author's interview with Camilo Román Cota, Poza Rica, 8 Nov. 1987; Miller to State Department, Tampico, 16 March 1912, National Archives, Washington, D.C., Records of the Department of State Relating to the Internal Affairs of Mexico, 1910–1929, Record Group 59 (henceforth cited as Na/SDR), 812.00/3337; history of mutual aid society, "Hermanos del Trabajo," 10 March 1914, Archivo General de la Nación, Ramo de Trabajo (henceforth cited as AGN-RT), file 1913-8(115:800), bundle 4, file 9; and Jorge García Granados, *Los veneros del diablo* (Mexico City, 1941), pp. 61–62, 64, 83, 154.

21. Consul to British chargé d'affaires in Mexico City, Tampico, 14 June 1914, Public Records Office, London, Foreign Office Records (henceforth cited as PRO), FO 371/2131, file 4757.

22. Tamaulipas state governor to Department of Labor, Ciudad Victoria, 6 May 1913, AGN-RT, file 5-1913, no. 931; superintendent of Compañía de los Ferrocarriles Nacionales de México to mayor, 27 May 1913, AGN-RT, file 14–1913, no. 23-bis; police chief to mayor, 19 Aug. 1913, AHT, file 53-1913.

23. Ciro de la Garza Treviño, *La revolución mexicana en el estado de Tamaulipas: cronología, 1885–1973*, 2 vols. (Mexico City, 1974), vol. 1, pp. 68, 71, 73; superintendent of Ferrocarriles Nacionales to mayor, 12 Aug. 1912, AHT, file 236-1912, no. 1131; Consul Wilson to consul general, Tampico, 27 Feb. 1912, PRO, FO 371/1392, no. 11270.

24. City civil engineer to city council, 17 March 1944, AHT, file 28-1914, unnumbered; consul to British chargé d'affaires, Tampico, 25 March, 13 April 1914, FO 371/2027, file no. 107075, /2029, file no. 23192; M. Ortega Elorza to labor department, Tampico, 25 March 1914, AGN-RT, 1914-8 (043.1-24-3), no. 4797.

25. Mayor to chief of arms, 18 Dec. 1914, AHT, file 134-1914; mayor to several merchants, 22 Dec. 1914, AHT, file 134-1914, no. 719; fourth officer of local military detachment to mayor, 24 Dec. 1914, AHT, file 134-1914; public notice issued by governor and state military commander, Ciudad Victoria, 5 Feb. 1915, AHT, unnumbered file.

26. Consul to State Department, Tampico, 6 April 1916, NA/SDR, 812.504/46; Evaristo Tejeda to Labor Department, Tampico, 11 Aug. 1916, AGN-RT, 1916-8 (220-24-1), folder 30, file 276, no. 150. Nafarrate's attitude reversal a few weeks later appears to have been strongly influenced by the fact that the United States had recently launched its "punitive expedition" in Chihuahua against Francisco Villa. This was popularly construed in Mexico to be an invasion of national sovereignty. See consul to State Department, 10 May 1916, and consul to special representative of the U.S. government in Mexico, 11 May 1916, National Archives, Washington, D.C., Tampico Post Records, Record Group 84, "General Correspondence" (hereafter cited as NA/TPR/GC), 1916, file 800.

27. Consul to State Department, 26 April 1917, NA/TPR/GC, 1917, file 350; consul to State Department, Tampico, 30 July 1915, NA/SDR, 812.504/9; consul to State Department, Tampico, 3 Aug. 1915, NA/SDR, 812.00/15628; Adleson, "Historia social," pp. 271–282.

28. An unnumbered 1916 file in AHT contains ample documentation of the tactics and pressures that local merchants applied against civil and military authorities. Almost all of the major personages of Tampico commercial enterprises appear in the correspondence. Famine conditions and the resulting death rate were certified by Dr. Gregorio Gutierres of the U.S. Public Health Service, who had been sent to Tampico to investigate health conditions. According to the U.S. consul, Dr. Gutierres had told him that "he had never before seen such frightful conditions; and he had more than sufficient opportunity to find out that the victims died because the price of food and fuel and medicines were beyond their reach." See consul to State Department, 15 Nov. 1916, NA/TPR/GC, 1916, file 800.

29. For descriptions of weekly price fluctuations, see Commerce Department inspector to mayor, 27, 31 Jan.,1, 16 Feb. 1917, AHT, unnumbered file-1917; *La Prensa* (Tampico), 18 Dec. 1917. The U.S. consul relayed information about local merchants' speculative practices in consult to State Department, 18 June 1918, NA/TPR/GC, 1918, file 850.

30. Ramón G. Garza to jail warden, 9 Feb. 1913, AHT, file 17-1913; "Entrevista al Mario Ortega Infante," Tampico, 18, 19 Feb. 1974, DEH-INAH, PHO/4/28; "Reference Notebook—Oil (General)—Lord Cowdray," n.d., SP&S, box A-1; Francisco, González Alonso, *Historia y petróleo* (Mexico City, 1972), p. 144.

31. Author's interview with Febronio Martínez Sánchez, Mata Redonda, 8 May 1973; "Entrevista al Mario Ortega Infante," Tampico, 18, 19 Feb. 1974, DEH-INAH, PHO/4/28.

32. Andrés Araujo to mayor, 11 May 1917, AHT, file 247-1917; "Entrevista al Gonzalo Bada Ramírez," Cerro Azul, 30 Sept., 1, 22 Oct., 5 Nov. 1978, DEH-INAH, PHO/4/91.

33. J. B. Body, "Report on accounts for year ended 30th June 1916," Mexico City, July 1916, SP&S, box C-43; "Entrevista al Gonzalo Bada Ramírez"; W. J. Archer, *Mexican Petroleum* (New York, 1922), pp. 102-103.

34. "Entrevista al León Vargas Domínguez"; "Entrevista al Teodoro Rabishkin Masloff," Mexico City, 27 Sept. 1974, "Entrevista al Masloff," Ciudad Madero, 21 March 1978, DEH-INAH, PHO/4/58, /4/87.

35. Correspondence between Enrique S. Cerdán and Labor Department, 15 Sept., 16 Oct. 1919, AGN-RT, 1919-8(022-24-1), dossier 20-135.

36. Notwithstanding an interest in keeping the professional relationship with their subordinates undiluted by elements of nonlabor activities, the oil companies at times had to forego this principle when it impinged on their immediate interests. In the Tampico region, the most noticeable examples of deviation from normal practice were the construction of worker housing on refinery property, free medical service for workers and their families living in company-owned housing (during times of extreme crisis—the 1919 epidemic of Spanish influenza), and the provision for minimal social infrastructure for workers' families in the early days of oil production at El Ebano, San Luis Potosí. These activities were initiated by the Huasteca Petroleum Company. Its director, Edward L. Doheny, also paid for the reconstruction in 1922 of the Tampico Catholic church after it had collapsed. The Compañía Mexicana de Petróleo "El Aguila" also provided living quarters for some single skilled workers in the unmarried men's hotel. See "Interview with Herbert H. Wylie," May 1918, in the Edward L. Doheny Collection, Special Collections Department, Occidental College, Eagle Rock, Calif. (henceforth cited as Doheny Collection), box I, 252-1308; "Entrevista al Gonzalo Ruiz Carrillo," Ciudad Madero, 11, 17 March 1975, "Entrevista al Cecil Knight Montiel," Ciudad Madero, 18, 22 April 1974, DEH-INAH, PHO/4/38, /4/35; Carlos González Salas, *Del reloj en vela* (Mexico City, 1983), pp. 88–89.

37. United States Senate, 66 Congress, 2d session, Committee on Foreign Relations, *Investigation of Mexican Affairs*, 2 vols. (Washington, D.C., 1919), vol. 1, p. 234; Frederick R. Kellogg," "The World Petroleum Problem—Mexico," *Bulletin of the American Petroleum Institute*, no. 132 (10 Dec. 1920), p. 13; Warren C. Platt, "Oil Industry Providing Work, Giving Peon First Real Chance," *National Petroleum News* (8 March 1922), pp. 65–71.

38. J. B. Body, "Report on accounts for year ended 30 June 1916," July 1916, SP&S, box C-43; "Entrevista al Gonzalo Bada Ramírez."

39. Mateo Cantú et al. to mayor, 28 Jan. 1918, AHT, file 2-bis-1918, no. 124.

40. As quoted in Garza Treviño, *La revolución mexicana*, vol.2, p. 240.

41. Liga Pro-Defensa de Poseedores de Terreno en Pequeño del Ejido de Tampico to mayor, 28 Jan., 27 Dec. 1919, 28 Jan., 4 Sept. 1920, AHT, file 23-1919, file 84-1920, no. 2693; author's interview with Andrés Araujo Araujo, Tampico, 26 Nov. 1978.

42. Enrique S. Cerdán, report, Tampico, 29 Jan. 1916, AGN-RT, card 84, unnumbered dossier; *Tribuna Roja* (Tampico), 16 Aug. 1916.

43. *Tribuna Roja*, 1 April, 3 May 1916; *El Luchador* (Tampico, 21 March 1915); Cerdán, report, 29 Jan. 1920, AGN-RT, 1920, card 84, unnumbered dossier; "Entrevista al Mario Ortega Infante."

44. Sociedad Recreativa Mutualista "Unión y Progreso" to mayor, 27 July 1914, AHT, file 162-1914.

45. Ibid.; statistical questionnaire on associations, Tampico, March 1914, AGN-RT, 1913-8 (115-800), file 9; meeting minutes book no. 1, 21 July 1911,

Historical Archives of the Gremio Unido de Alijadores, Tampico (henceforth cited as AHGUA).

46. "Entrevista al Camilo Román Cotá," Poza Rica, 23 Dec. 1975, 29 Feb. 1976, DEH-INAH, PHO/4/46; "Hermanos del Trabajo" to Labor Department, Tampico, 10 March 1914, AGN-RT, 1913-8 (115:800), dossier 4, file 9.

47. Unión Moralizadora de Carpinteros to Labor Department, Tampico, 31 March 1912, AGN-RT, 1912, "Statistics-societies," dossier 4, file 1, no. 10; Gremio Marítimo Fluvial to mayor, 5 Feb. 1913; Sociedad Mutualista de Constructores en Fierro Laminado to mayor, Doña Cecilia, 15 July 1914, AHT, file 37-1913, file 128-1914; meeting minutes book no. 1, 28 June 1911, AHGUA.

48. Cerdán, report, 29 Jan. 1920; Mariano Benítez et al. to mayor, 1, 2 May 1920, AHT, file 127-1917.

49. Superintendent of Standard Oil Company to vice consul, 27 May 1915, vice consul to State Department, 16 April 1916, NA/TPR/GC, 1915, file 850.4, 1916, file 850; Tampico garrison commander to strike representatives of Pierce Oil Company, AGN-RT, 1919, 8.820 (24-3); Centro de Estudios Sobre la Historia del Movimiento Obrero, *Historia obrera*, 5 vols. (Mexico City, 1981), pp. 2–5.

50. Consul to State Department, 15 Aug. 1917, NA/TPR/GC, 1917, file 800.

51. *El Luchador*, 19 June 1915; Garza Treviño, *La revolución en Tamaulipas*, vol. 2, p. 240; British consul to British ambassador, Tampico, 4 May 1915, PRO, FO 371/2400-73441; strike committee to Huasteca Petroleum Company, 15 June 1917, AHT, file 127-1917. AHT file number 164-1917 is full of complaints concerning arbitrary employment practices.

52. Pérez Arce to Andrés Osuna, Tampico, 25 July 1919, AGN-RT, 1919-8.820 (24-3).

53. Transcontinental Oil Company strike committee to mayor, 16 April 1919, AHT, file 24-1919; Cerdán report, 29 Jan. 1919, AGN-RT, 1920, 8 (206-14-3); *El Popular* (Tampico), 24 March 1919.

54. Wendell C. Gordon, *The Expropriation of Foreign-Owned Property in Mexico* (Westport, Conn., 1975), pp. 53–54; Jesús Silva Herzog, *Historia de la expropiación de las empresas petroleras* (Mexico City, 1964), pp. 63–66.

3. The Rise and Fall of Union Democracy at Poza Rica, 1932–1940

Alberto J. Olvera
Centro de Investigaciones Históricas, Universidad Veracruzana

The objective of this chapter is the analysis of the social practices, ideas, and values by which Poza Rican oil workers lived and which shaped their understanding of the first years of the industry's nationalization. In other words, it examines the workers' actions during that period, taking as a starting point the culture and institutions created by them in previous years, in order to understand the changes wrought by the expropriation. The Poza Rica oil field was chosen as the object of study because it was the most important in Mexico for nearly three decades. Also, its workers developed a radical political culture, whose democratic and independent practices permitted them to take a critical stance when faced with the nationalized industry's management. Furthermore, they were able to intervene directly in the control of their work process from 1938 to 1940.

The chapter is made up of three parts. The first discusses the social origins of the workers who arrived at Poza Rica, the formation of the workers' culture, and the effects that the foundation of a trade union had upon the oil field. The second part explains the specific actions taken by the workers during the year prior to expropriation. Finally, the third section analyzes the workers' practices, struggles, and ideas during the first three years of the nationalized oil industry.

Background

At the beginning of the 1930s, the Mexican oil industry was slowly recuperating from the deep crisis it had suffered since the mid-1920s. The fall in crude oil production was stopped, and a modest but unsteady recovery set in. This was accompanied by profound changes in the industry's profile. While the traditional productive areas (the northern Huasteca in Veracruz, the Golden Lane or *Faja de Oro*, and the extreme south of Veracruz) continued to register falling production levels, two new fields accounted for the rise in national output: Las Choapas (known as El Plan) and Poza Rica. Both of these fields belonged to the Companía

Mexicana de Petróleo El Aguila, part of one of the most powerful transnational enterprises of the time: Royal Dutch Shell. These fields permitted El Aguila to oust the North American companies from the dominant position they had occupied up until the end of the 1920s. Thanks also to the expansion of its crude oil refining capacity, El Aguila was able to control the internal supply and export of refined products.

It must be emphasized that in this process, Poza Rica played a crucial part. In 1934, this field produced almost four million barrels of oil, that is, nearly 10 percent of national production, while by 1936 the respective figures were almost fourteen million barrels and one-third of national production. If we add to this last percentage, the crude produced in nearby Papantla (the Tajín field) by the Standard Oil Company (just 2.5 million barrels), we find that this new productive zone accounted for nearly half of the national crude output.[1] By 1937, Poza Rica was unofficially considered the second most important field in production in the world, after Richfield in Texas, and also the only real long-term reserve in the country.[2]

The Poza Rica field was opened only in 1932.[3] Groups of workers from very different social origins came together for this task. They included oil workers, old hands who arrived from other fields, workers with industrial backgrounds but in other productive sectors, and, finally, laborers who came directly from the countryside. To begin with, their different cultures coexisted in a hostile environment, socially empty and lacking a culture of its own. Each worker subgroup took refuge within itself and could not establish links with the others. It is worth noting that qualified workers, and in general those with an urban background, looked down upon those of rural extraction.

Consequently, they formed their own local groups and institutions that excluded those who had recently arrived from the countryside. For example, in 1934 a masonic lodge was formed by five workers who previously had been members of similar organizations in Tampico and Mexico City. This lodge was to be of great importance for the future of Poza Rica, because it brought together those workers with more political knowledge and experience, as shown later on. However, the reduced space in which the field developed and the formation of squads that lived and worked together fostered relationships among different types of workers and made for a slow but sure exchange of experiences. At the same time, difficult living and working conditions, exacerbated by the field's isolation, a shortage of housing, and the bosses' despotism, all contributed to the development of solidarity among the workers.

Furthermore, social life in brothels, bars, and pool halls permitted a progressive socialization of experiences, ideas, and values among the workers. However, it was only with the foundation of the local trade union that workers with political or trade union experience and knowledge had a medium through which to transmit to their colleagues the elements for a new working-class culture, which in that region had been fundamentally nurtured in the anarcho-syndicalist tradition, still alive in the great Mexican oil center in Tampico. This culture also drew upon the discourse of the Mexican Revolution, whose embers still glowed, even if its basic postulates remained unfulfilled.

In August 1934, a group of workers on the pumping line, many of whom had a certain degree of union experience, took the initiative and formed Delegation 2 of Local 1 of the Sindicato de Obreros y Empleados de la Compañía Mexicana de Petróleo El Aguila in Poza Rica. The local had its headquarters in Ciudad Madero, Tamaulipas, and was the strongest oil union at that time.

The initiative to form the union came from urban-based workers, for whom this type of institution was known and accepted as a mechanism for the defense of working-class rights. The idea of turning to the local in Ciudad Madero is equally understandable when taken in the context of the times. The Ciudad Madero union was founded in 1924 as a result of a large-scale and prolonged struggle; it became the most advanced group of oil workers with respect to joint contract terms, union organization and practices, and political principles. The radical anarcho-syndicalist tradition, inherited from the workers' policy that the Casa del Obrero Mundial (House of the World Worker) had upheld since 1915 and that had guided and formed this and other unions in the Tampico region, was to play an important part in the elaboration of the political and unionist discourse and practice among the Poza Rica group.[4]

Although unionism in Tampico had become less forceful toward the end of the 1920s and the beginning of the 1930s and although it shed its doctrinaire radicalism of the first years, its political cultural legacy could still be felt among the workers. This meant an independent union (from the government), democratic procedure concerning union affairs (frequent meetings, periodic changes of executive committees, collective decisions made in assemblies, and so forth), as well as the sense of belonging to a class that had certain common interests.

The establishment of the union involved a series of complex actions to be undertaken by Delegation 2. In the first place, it was necessary to retabulate and reclassify jobs in order to apply Local 1's contract in Poza Rica, a problem that arose from the fact that the latter referred to a refinery and not to an oil field. Given that the Poza Rican workers lacked experience, the Local 1 leaders took on the job, although several commissions from the delegation took an active part in the reforms. This forged a new practice that was to become very important: the holding of departmental assemblies, that is, those held by each division of the oil industry: workshops, drilling, security, refining, administration, and so forth. It was in such assemblies that the classification of each job and the structuring of the wage scale and promotions were to be discussed.

The pressing need to adapt the collective contract to the conditions prevalent in Poza Rica forced the workers with previous experience in unionism to leave reclassification open to free discussion. They also wanted to teach new members the meaning of unionism and how a union should be run. These workers understood quite well that their active participation might bring about financial advantages. It could stop the bosses from arbitrarily promoting a certain worker. That is why many decided to join the new union.

The immediate gains made during this process, as well as the fact that the delegation held the monopoly over the hiring of workers, even for contractor companies, quickly attracted members and caught the interest of a growing number of qualified workers. Little by little, the union became a real power factor in Poza Rica, and also a means of cultural unification of the first order.

In effect, the union quickly began to play the role of political mentor to the oil field workers. By means of the discussion of labor problems, the experienced workers clearly defined the separate interests of workers, company, and government. For example, in 1935 and 1936, several complaints were made against the bosses' authoritarianism at the same time pointing out the prevailing favoritism toward foreigners. This included the complaint that the payment of overtime was not always fair. In May 1935, the assembly elected a committee to sort out the question of experienced drillers, which in turn demanded that the company give the Mexican workers the category of assistant driller, claiming that "several gringos are drillers in spite of not knowing anything; back home they are vegetable sellers."[5] At the same time, they avoided giving support to the goverment concerning publication of the minimum salary decree "because the workers should remain independent of the government," and thus side-stepped being judged "ignorant of socialism."[6]

The leaders also informed their comrades of the struggles that other workers were sustaining in different parts of the country. From 1934, work stoppages took place to support other oil company unions. It was also agreed to stand by the teachers of the state of Tamaulipas in demand of higher wages. Very soon, they received calls from the peasants near Poza Rica asking for aid and solidarity. Little by little, the oil workers of this field assumed a critical vision of the world that surrounded them, and they began to understand that they were part of a distinct working class with its own specific interests. A veteran worker of this period has reminisced:

After attending weekly meetings for several months, I began to understand what the leaders meant when they referred to us as members of a separate class: the boss was after more profit, while we, the exploited, got less; we had the support of the government but we had to keep our distance. Of course I understood that the peasants had other troubles. We had to negotiate salaries and work conditions, and prevent the bosses from taking us for a ride.[7]

The union had created a powerful link among all the workers, through which they could feel a collective identity. For the first time, the qualified worker and the unskilled laborer shared interests and reasons to act together. From this point on, relations among the workers showed a marked improvement.

The union became the promoter of a workers' culture. New symbols arose before their eyes, such as the delegation's banner, while a novel type of language came into use through union discussions. Concepts such as democracy, class struggle, proletarianism, socialism, and many others began to take on meaning for the workers. Up until then, these were words never before heard or understood in their full sense: "Most of us didn't know about socialism and class struggle," says another worker. "We learned about it little by little and not always all that well, after listening in the meetings to the old timers or those who were better informed."[8] Furthermore, the increasing awareness that labor and capital had opposing interests, plus the togetherness implicit in the constant holding of assemblies, led to the development of relationships of solidarity among the workers.

Solidarity was expressed on two levels. Inside the union, the workers were supportive at all times. Many workers who fell sick asked the assembly for financial help to pay medical bills or to support their family until they got better. It was always granted, being a practice somewhat similar to the first mutual organizations.[9]

On the other hand, the workers of a given department (whether drilling or mechanical workshop) had the backing of the rest when fighting against the unfair dismissal of a member or when dealing with internal problems where the company wanted to assert itself. During these years, a great many telegrams were sent by the local union to back different workers' struggles in other parts of the oil industry as well as in other industries, including cooperatives: this practice became more frequent in later years.[10]

The union also spread and confirmed a national culture. It held solemn memorial services on the country's relevant historical days (5 May, 16 September, and 20 November), whose significance was unknown to the majority of workers at that time. A veteran workers recalls:

On my arrival in Poza Rica, I, the same as many others, could neither read nor write. I had heard my parents tell about our independence and the revolution, but only as tradition. To tell the truth, I really didn't know what such dates as the 5th of May or the 16th of September meant. But here on those days the leaders gave speeches and organized events where the teachers spoke as well. That's where we learned a little bit more about our history.[11]

The union channeled the message contained in the discourse of President Cárdenas; in assemblies the workers were informed of the far-reaching measures taken by the government. For example, at a meeting held in April 1936, Plutarco Elías Calles's expulsion from the country was announced. At another meeting, the members were informed of the good news that the Confederación de Trabajadores de México (CTM) had been formed "with the support of a government that wanted justice for the workers."[12] Finally, the union gave an impulse to education, both for children and adults. For this reason, it arranged for Poza Rica to have teachers, who in turn brought with them the discourse and spirit of the socialist educational policy.[13]

In 1935, those who had founded the union in Poza Rica were ousted. David Cano was elected general secretary by those who sympathized with the Communist party, with which the early leaders did not see eye to eye. This result was obtained because the executive committee was elected in an open assembly; it was also due to Cano's solid leadership. This event represented the birth of one of the Poza Rica union's characteristics: the formation of a hegemonic group or the existence of a single strongman was prevented by the presence of different and opposing currents of opinion (a relative state of equilibrium between groups was to last at least until the mid-1940s).

It should be pointed out that differences among unionist currents in other locals of the oil union usually led to deep and prolonged conflict, resulting at times in violence. From 1929 to 1934, there were frequent fights in Ciudad Madero among rival groups within the refinery union of El Aguila, with a cost of several lives. Also during those years, in Minatitlán there were two unions within the refinery due to political differences. In 1935, once the Sindicato de Trabajadores Petroleros de la República Mexicana (STPRM) came to the fore, widespread differences were put aside in favor of the creation of a strong union. However, in Minatitlán a new directive group was formed that had no counterweight or rank-and-file control. From this point onward, dominant groups were formed in the great majority of the STPRM locals, which controlled union life and frequently eliminated internal democracy.[14]

The founding of the STPRM at the end of 1935 gave greater force and legitimacy to the delegation. Thanks to this development, employees and more qualified workers began to join; they understood that given the growing local power of the delegation, it would be a mistake to stay out in the cold.

In 1936, the leaders of Local 1 of the STPRM in Ciudad Madero were called upon to discuss and draw up a national collective contract to be presented to all the oil companies. In November of the same year, the STPRM called for a general strike to force the companies to sign this general contract. These activities kept the union leaders busy, distracting them from their usual affairs in Poza Rica.

Under these conditions, employees and qualified workers took direct control of Delegation 2, because they were the better prepared to understand and assimilate the nature of the labor-capital negotiations that affected the oil field. However, they did not have a free hand, because the participation of the mass of workers implied a degree of control over their leaders. This control was felt in more than one way. The executive committee was changed every six months and, from 1937 on, every year. Nevertheless, all union officers could be demoted at any time—something that happened quite frequently—if the assembly thought that they were not carrying out their work properly.[15] Furthermore, commissioned officers had to hand in a report as well as a precise expense account. If the assembly thought him to be extravagant, such as having stopped to eat at a fancy restaurant, the officer would be severely reprimanded.[16]

In this process, the local Masonic lodge played a decisive role due to the fact that the main unionists, such as David Cano and Cosme Pantín, met there. Cosme Pantín was at that time (1937) the leader of the STPRM in Poza Rica. Among other prominent union leaders, Constantino Casanova and Vérulo de la Cruz were also present. All of them had previously been active members of their hometown lodges. At a time of fierce anticlericalism and rising nationalism, Masonic lodges were rather popular. Several leaders had accrued experience in union affairs while in Ciudad Madero, where the local proletariat was all for liberalism and democracy. Nevertheless, they could not be considered a politically unified group: Cano considered himself a communist, Pantín a "liberal," and de la Cruz a *cardenista*.

At the start of 1937, Delegation 2 became Local 30 of the STPRM, and its leaders assumed the fight against their employers, a struggle that had been defined since the previous year in terms of the national union versus the united front of foreign companies. It is worth remembering that in November 1936 the STPRM threatened all the companies with a strike for the national contract. The reply from the companies and the government was that a convention should be held between labor and management, at which a contract law applicable to the whole industry was to be drawn up. This phase of the dispute lasted until May 1937, and was characterized by the concentration of decision making in the hands of the national and sectional leaders of the union and also by the creation of many study and negotiation commissions. Local chapter leaders learned the secrets of high politics; they rubbed elbows with the leaders of the CTM and acquired a more complete vision of the industry. This apprenticeship was transmitted to their companions by various means: weekly reports to their locals, which were usually very wide-reaching and explicit; daily circulars sent to the locals by the General Executive Committee; and the presence in local assemblies of commission members. From 1935 to 1937, an average of 70 local assemblies per year were held in Poza Rica, of which 52 were ordinary sessions and 18 of a special character. This intense union activity helped disseminate union and political culture, shared by all the Poza Rican workers, who by 1937 numbered 800 permanent and 400 temporary laborers. Although the latter were not formally members of the union, which demanded that a worker be permanent to obtain membership, they participated fully in union life.

The Fifty-seven Day Strike and the Government

The labor negotiations between the union and the oil companies ended in the strike of May–June 1937, by which means the STPRM tried to force the oil companies to sign the contract, which even after six months of sessions could not be agreed upon. The strike ended after nine days, when the union leadership presented the oil companies with a demand *(conflicto de orden económico)*[17] following the advice of the government. This particular course of action was taken under the provisions of Article 572 of the Federal Labor Law. It meant that the Federal Conciliation and Arbitration Board, having carried out a careful study, had to decide whether the companies were in a position to pay an increase in salaries and benefits as demanded by the union. In the meantime, the strike had to be lifted, and both workers and bosses would have to accept the board's decision. As the government held a predominant position on the board, the decision was really that of the executive. It should be pointed out that as a negotiating body interposed in labor-management conflicts, the Conciliation and Arbitration Board is made up of three parts: government, bosses, and unions. Usually, it is the government that tilts the balance one way or the other. In this case, the government wanted control over the companies, to be able to look into their bookkeeping, and, through an alliance with the STPRM, to arrive at a solution favorable both to the workers and to the country.

This event caught Local 30 midway in its negotiations with El Aguila to bring Local 1's contract in line with conditions at Poza Rica. Since Local 30 was formed in January 1937, it needed to sign its own contract with the company, according to its new legal status. However, El Aguila took advantage of the stalemate created by the economic demand to leave the Poza Rica problem pending, arguing that it was best to await the outcome of the STPRM's conflict. Local 30 did not accept this point of view, on the grounds that it was not trying to negotiate a new contract but rather was modifying one already in force. Confronted by the company's stance, which was a deliberate tactic taken in the context of the conflict between the companies and the government, Local 30 called a strike at the end of July 1937, even though it went against the wishes of the government as well as the national union leadership.[18] After presenting a list of seventy-six demands, the Poza Rican workers went out on a strike that was to last fifty-seven days. This caused another national shortage of petrol and derivatives, given that in that year the Poza Rica field alone produced 40 percent of national crude oil.

The effect of the strike was to create a stronger identity among the men of Local 30 and to elicit sympathetic support from the Poza Rican community. During the strike, the workers controlled the field. Because of the strike's duration and the drastic effect it had on the nation, the workers concluded that the best way to resolve the problem was to propose the expropiation of the field and the setting up of a workers' cooperative.[19] Behind this initiative was the fact that the government (during the 1930s) firmly pushed the creation of cooperatives as a way to open more jobs as well as to provide a better living for the workers. Besides, the workers were well aware that cooperatives meant that they were the bosses of the enterprise, and not mere employees as in the case of a government company.

At the end of August, this proposal was delivered to Cárdenas by the Local 30 leaders, with the General Executive Committee's blessings. The president replied that this was unacceptable, because the national conflict was moving toward resolution.[20] Finally, in September, a presidential ultimatum put an end to the strike. Up to that point only twenty of the seventy-six demands had been agreed upon.[21] The Poza Rican workers had to accept a promise that negotiations would continue under the auspices of the Labor Department. However, the radical Poza Rican workers did not back down. While negotiations continued in Mexico City, Local 30 mounted labor stoppages to force the company to acquiesce. This scandalized both the government and El Aguila, which at that moment were negotiating an agreement without precedent, the importance of which was greater than any particular workers' interest. In November 1937, El Aguila and the federal government signed an agreement whereby the company renewed its concession to exploit the Poza Rica field during the next fifty years in exchange for 35 percent of the production to be delivered to the Agencia General del Petróleo Nacional (AGPN), the state oil company, formerly Petróleos de México (Petromex).[22] The idea behind the agreement was to break the common front of the oil trust and thus start new relations between the companies and the state, guaranteeing growing government participation in the control of production.

Under these circumstances, the radicalism of the Poza Rican workers constituted a real obstacle. The government did not understand the cause of their "agitation," and in desperation committed an act that illustrated perfectly its vision of workers' politics. Eduardo Pérez Castañeda, the prime delegate for Local 30 in the conflict with El Aguila, was ordered not to return to Poza Rica under any circumstances. One way or another, all the other sectional leaders were threatened and held responsible for the illegal stoppages. This was a mistake. It was the mass of Poza Rican workers who during assemblies had decided on the stoppages, at times against the advice of their leaders.[23] However, the government did not believe the workers capable of thinking for themselves.

During this period of national workers' mobilization and the rise of oil unionism, the Poza Rican workers enjoyed an interval of autonomy during which they asserted their own culture, independent of the state. Union assemblies were permeated by an atmosphere of frank and open discussion of every problem. A permanent union bureaucracy was not formed, because the entire executive committee was changed, initially every six months, and later, each year.

From 1934 to 1939 about forty workers served on the executive committee of the local union. Only a few were reelected but never occupied the same office. It was not until 1940 that David Cano was to serve as general secretary for a second term. Thus, during that period, a large number of workers had the opportunity of gaining experience in union affairs. There were some twelve or fifteen workers who stood out in assemblies because of their political experience and gifts. However, they were neither a tight-knit group, nor did they have control of the executive, and therefore they were unable to set themselves up as a clique capable of manipulating their comrades. Nor did any group or current of opinion direct the assemblies. On a small scale, political parties were to be found in the area, but they had no control over the working masses. All this explains the workers' actions in Poza Rica in these years, especially during 1937.

The Workers Face the Nationalization

Since the beginning of February 1938, the STPRM General Executive Committee (GEC) took precautions in case the foreign companies should defy Mexican law. At a board meeting held during the first three days of February, the GEC and the leaders of the thirty-one locals agreed that, in the case of an expropriation, each local would form a Local Administrative Council, made up of a local general secretary, the labor secretary, and the president of the local vigilance council. The objective was to guarantee continued production in the face of an emergency.[24] The expropriation of the foreign oil companies was decreed on 18 March 1938. Apparently, it was caused by the oil companies' refusal to accept the ruling made by the Conciliation Board on 18 December 1937. The board's decision had granted to the oil workers a total wage increase of 26 million pesos ($7.2 million) per year, including fringe benefits. The oil trust alleged that it was unable to pay this sum to its workers, if it were to avoid bankruptcy. Therefore, it appealed to the National Supreme Court of Justice. On 1 March 1938, the court upheld the board's ruling, but the companies refused to abide by this decision, and virtually declared themselves in a state of rebellion. Faced with this situation, the government had no alternative other than to expropriate. The real cause of this historical event was the companies' opposition to a greater degree of state control over their operations and wider government participation in the national oil market.

Once the nationalization had been decreed, the plan agreed upon by the union leaders was put into effect. At the national level, an Oil Administration Council was set up, with five government representatives and four from the STPRM, which was to take charge of the central direction of the industry. This was a temporary organ, later to be modified according to federal government decisions.

The formation of the local administrative councils meant that the union took control of crude and refined oil production, but not of the central administrative apparatus. The impact of the expropriation upon the levels of central administration and operation-production in the field and refineries must be explained. The possibility of greater workers' control over the productive process in the fields was based upon the very nature of the work process of the industry at that level, and may be broken down into six points:

1. Repair and maintenance work based upon artisan skills and practical knowledge. This applied to the mechanical and electrical workshops, the repair of wells, and the maintenance of tracks and roads.

2. Maintenance and control of continuous flow processes, such as the pumping of oil and gas, the care of separators, conduction lines and the

elemental processing of crude in absorption plants. In this sphere of action, the workers' experience was basic.

3. Well-drilling, which was a basic task in the industry. This represented an important sphere for artisan skills, both of the driller and of his gang, even though the basic decision as to where to drill and to what depth, was still the responsibility of the engineers.

4. Exploration required high technical skills and modern measuring instruments.

5. Infrastructure. This included laying railway tracks, opening roads, laying pipelines, installing drilling equipment, and building houses and workshops. In this part of the work process, the crew worked as a team, but the division of labor and the skills needed were minimal, except in the case of welders and crane operators.

6. Administrative work. This included the payroll, estimates, materials, accounting, labor affairs, and so forth, all of which required experience.

With the exception of exploration, for which the nationalized industry lacked both technicians and equipment, all the other stages of the work process in the oil fields were known and controlled by the workers, thanks to their experience and/or craftsmanship. This applied also to drilling, although in this field of operations know-how was hard to come by given that the foreign companies had always avoided the hiring of Mexican drillers. However, there were nationals who had been drillers' mates, and in many cases they acquired sufficient experience to take charge of this activity. As long as the technology in use did not change, qualified workers could control the entire productive process without the assistance of technicians, excepting exploration, where specialists were required before drilling could be started.

On the other hand, regarding central administrative activities, there were several aspects concerning the administration of the enterprise that demanded centralized decision making and for which there was little experience at all levels: (1) international sales, whose mechanisms were a close secret of the foreign companies; (2) the global administration of material resources, especially the acquisition of machinery and spare parts; and (3) the hiring, maintenance, and administration of transport (oil tankers, railway tanks, etc.).

In these three spheres, the workers had no previous experience, not even the administrative workers who stayed on. Also, the newly assigned directors were unaccustomed to these practices. Furthermore, the boycott declared by the companies caused tremendous difficulty in the export of oil and the import of spare parts. Consequently, the central administration became chaotic and faced serious problems. Other administrative aspects, such as national sales and payroll control, the payment of benefits, and labor management, posed problems for the new directors; the many different systems employed by the foreign companies made immediate centralization impossible. All this caused a "directive vacuum" immediately after the nationalization. Such was not the case at the production level in the oil fields, where the problem was reduced to a shortage of spare parts and equipment. To a certain degree, this was overcome thanks to the qualified workers who repaired drills, pumps, and other equipment. They put their artisan skills and political will at the service of the nation.[25]

In addition to the real possibility of taking control of the work process, the Poza Rican workers decided to elect their own bosses.[26] On 19 March 1938, the STPRM sent a circular to all the locals, in which the local administrative councils were given a free hand to name security and directive personnel in the industry. In a meeting held at the beginning of April, Eduardo Pérez Castañeda read out his own list of new directors.[27] However, the workers ignored his proposal, deciding that the following day each department would democratically elect its own bosses. Furthermore, the Consejo de Administración del Petróleo had issued instructions concerning promotions to fill those vacancies left by foreign personnel; only a worker's skills were to be taken into account and not the rung one occupied on the job ladder. However, the Poza Rican workers decided to uphold the latter principle, in order to avoid internal conflict as well as favoritism by the local administrative council.[28] This procedure resulted in the virtual disappearance of all intermediate directive personnel, who used to be hired by the bosses and thus were directly responsible to them.[29]

These decisions showed that the mass of workers held considerable power over their leaders. Furthermore, the fact that local leader Pérez Castañeda had not been active in union affairs for long (having joined Local 30 at the beginning of 1937) and that the other union leaders in Poza Rica had little confidence in him favored a balance of forces between the company's new administration and the workers. It also stopped the leader of Local 30 from taking advantage of his dual power (as union leader and as head of the administration) to impose his own criteria and decisions. Therefore, the incompetence of the central administration during the first months created suitable conditions for the workers in the oil fields and refineries to decide more or less freely what to do next. Also, the absence of foreign technicians, a shortage of spare parts, plus the need to carry on working created the necessary conditions for workers to assume responsibility for their own work.

The immediate impact of the expropriation amounted to a political motivation for the workers, who considered it a historical achievement of such importance that they were more than willing to make sacrifices in order to save the industry. They also believed that, if the government had decided the companies were in a position to pay higher wages now that they had been expropriated, there was a greater likelihood that the ruling of 18 December 1937 would be put into effect. In this sense, the workers were at best thinking in terms of temporary sacrifices. It was believed that the disappearance of the foreign companies would reduce administrative costs and rationalize operations, and also that the profits taken by the magnates could now be shared among the workers.

However, far from falling, administrative costs in the nationalized industry rose gradually but constantly. The centralization process was met by the immediate resistance of the union leaders and, in part, of labor as a whole. There were several reasons that justified this attitude. In the first place, centralization meant the loss of local power, which was concentrated in the hands of Mexico City bureaucrats. The labor leaders were afraid of losing their autonomy over decision making as well as control over the workers, who operated via favoritism (filling new vacancies with members and friends) or via concessions given to their sections. On the other hand, workers who had taken steps to control the productive process would have no say in organizing their daily tasks.

It should be stressed that this opposition to centralization not only afforded a front for the leaders' interests, but also represented the workers' idea that in order to guarantee their own position in their respective locals, via their representatives, they should occupy a leading place in the new administration of the industry. This idea encouraged the workers of each local to participate willingly in the fight for national positions, a struggle they could not let other locals win. The defense of local interests, and even more of their department's interests, reflected the oil workers' localism. There was not only an intersectional struggle for high-level central or crucial regional positions, such as the post of superintendent in Tampico, fights also took place over which departmental representatives would occupy local directive positions.[30]

Another powerful factor encouraged union leaders to fight for posts. The central administration decided that the industry's new bosses would get the same salary as the foreign employees before them. Thus, the general manager would receive a monthly income of $531, which was more than a state minister's salary. The numerous departmental chiefs were to earn $398 a month.[31] Initially, Pérez Castañeda was an office clerk on $121 a month; as a superintendent, he was paid $332. Gonzalo Herrera had been a deputy production chief on $117 a month, but on his promotion to chief, he got $265.[32] By comparison, a federal government department head received $155 a month, and a university professor, approximately $55.[33]

This functional and salary differentiation between union leaders–

cum–public officials and their fellow workers clearly showed that the overall operation of the industry had not changed; the gaps left by foreign personnel had simply been filled. This also implied that the nationalized company reproduced well-known methods within its overall management.

None of the new administrators, or any of the active union leaders, thought that this state of affairs could be changed. The workers also believed that the existing administrative structure and working conditions were the norm. However, they fought against despotism in the daily routine, without being able to suggest alternative forms of work and productive organization. Nobody thought that this system could be radically changed. By the end of July 1938, President Cárdenas ordered the elimination of the local administrative councils on the grounds that the state of emergency was over. He gave powers to the administration councils of the recently founded Petróleos Mexicanos and the Distribuidora de Petróleos Mexicanos to name all directive personnel in the industry.[34] The Poza Rican workers refused to accept this order, and they demanded the fulfillment of the 18 December 1937 resolution, which had been suspended. The idea behind this attitude, which was not shared by all the locals, was that the elimination of the councils nullified workers' power in the field's administration.[35]

The government tried to soften workers' opposition in two ways. On the one hand, it ordered the fulfillment of the wage tables fixed in the above mentioned resolution, even though they suffered an 8 to 15 percent reduction depending on the amount of salary.[36] In spite of the discount, the new rates meant a real rise in salaries, given that the majority of oil workers had not received an increase since 1936.[37] On the other hand, in most cases, the government named major local union leaders as superintendents, who, in turn, had to answer to the nationalized company's general manager.

In the short-term, however, this did not mean that the union leaders ceased to be such, because they could now operate legally by means of a union commission. But very soon their work load as administrative bosses became so demanding that they had to take leaves of absence from their union posts.[38] De facto, the duality of functions began to disappear; the leaders became public officials, even though they owed their positions to their previous union posts.

From July onward, discontent spread among the workers over the course that the industry was beginning to take. Above all, they wanted a clear definition of their role in the administration of the nationalized company. In an assembly, Pérez Castañeda said that it was urgent that the oil workers should know what they were: "government employees, cooperative partners, co-owners of the company or new paupers."[39]

Local 30 voted to call a special convention of the STPRM, and proposed a guideline document, in which the principle of "workers' administration" was upheld, and criticism was voiced of the government's refusal to contemplate labor management of the industry.[40]

The new labor offensive faced certain restraints, among others, the great strength of the dominating ideology at a time of confrontation with imperialism. All social struggle was judged by the govenment and by the people in the light of national interest, leaving aside class interests. Furthermore, because of the lack of previous experience similar to the nationalization of the oil companies, the workers had no point of reference or any ideas of their own to shed light on their present situation. The government, the CTM, and the mass media maintained that Pemex was the property of the whole nation; therefore, there were no longer any conflicts between workers and bosses, only cooperation between workers and the government. Therefore, the union struggle within Pemex was to be understood as an attack on the nation. The Mexican Communist party leadership upheld this view, which also held sway within the oil union executive body. In this light, the workers' struggle was declared "treason," "a conspiracy of the foreign companies," and the like. Facing hostile public opinion, a government desperate to escape a serious financial predicament caused by the boycott of the foreign companies, and a rising right-wing tide in the country as a whole, the oil union could not orient its conflicts in a manner politically appropriate to the dramatic circumstances of late 1938. For this reason, and under government pressure, the STPRM leadership systematically refused to hold the special convention, fearing that it would lose control and be pushed into a head-on conflict with the state.[41]

Meanwhile, in the area of production, there were various facts that indicated the Mexican government's lack of confidence in the workers' capacity to control the oil industry. To begin with, believing that the absence of foreign technicians could cause an immediate collapse of the industry, the Pemex management began to look for engineers wherever it could: in other industries, within the bureaucracy, and among recently graduated university students. The great majority of recruits had no experience in the oil industry, and therefore had to be taught by the qualified workers. In spite of being novices, these technicians occupied supervisory posts, which outraged the workers, because little by little they were being pushed to one side.[42]

It was in the oil fields that Pemex's doubts concerning the ability of Mexican drillers to carry out their tasks came to the fore. In 1938, only a few wells were drilled, partly because of the lack of exploration plans. Of those wells that had already been located, the relevant data had been carried off by the foreign companies. The shortage of drills and other equipment contributed to the problem, but mistrust of the drillers' ability was also an important factor. The General National Petroleum Administration (AGPN), however, continued to be independent of Pemex, and drilled wells using contractors that employed foreign drillers.[43] This policy shows the mentality of the government and of the industry's management alike: a deep mistrust of the workers' skills and a cult of technical knowledge. Underlying this reductionist conception of workers' know-how was a political position: the "too radical" working culture of the period was thought dangerous. Radicalism led to "indiscipline and low productivity" among the workers, and, therefore, another type of employer was required to control them.

This conception did not reflect reality. As far as we know, Mexican drillers, particularly those in Poza Rica, did a good job under the circumstances. According to the report that Vicente Cortés Herrera delivered in March 1940, Pemex and AGPN had since the expropriation and up to January of 1940 drilled 32 wells, of which 9 were in Poza Rica, 13 on the Isthmus of Tehuantepec, and 10 in the neighborhood of Tampico. Of the 118,319 feet drilled, 70,322 were in Poza Rica, where the deposits were much deeper than elsewhere.[44]

The number of wells drilled as well as their total depth, remained almost stable compared with those figures registered by the company over the last two years,[45] but production and sales dropped because of the international boycott. In Poza Rica, before the expropriation, only 22 wells had been drilled over a period of 6 years (3.6 per year). Two were drilled in 1938 and 7 in 1939.[46] Production rose considerably in this field. From 18,664,773 barrels in 1937, it rose to 28,440,399 barrels in 1940.[47] In the remaining oil regions, there was a severe drop in production. At the national level, production amounted to 46,803,584 barrels in 1937, 38,462,127 in 1938, and 44,169,346 in 1940.[48]

In fact, the holdup in drilling activities had causes other than the supposed inability of national drillers. The matter was much simpler: because of the boycott, there was no one to whom to sell production. Cortés Herrera stated in the same report that drilling continued in the North and South only to keep the permanent workers busy. Another example of the government's attitude toward the workers came in mid-1939, when it tried to push through a contract between Pemex and the W. R. Davis Company to drill 10 wells in Poza Rica. By means of detailed studies, Local 30 blocked the contract, showing that it was unjustified from a technical, economic, and political point of view. The GEC seconded Local 30's position, and, finally, the contract was canceled.[49]

In desperation, Pemex attempted to negotiate new drilling contracts to get out of the ever deeper economic crisis caused by two basic factors: the fall in export sales due to the boycott and the increase in personnel.

The first factor was external and out of Pemex's control; the second was internal and the only one over which it could exercise some influence. In April 1938, there were 14,368 permanent and 1,527 temporary workers employed in the oil industry. By October 1939, the figures had risen to 16,141 and 6,932, respectively.[50] This increase was totally unjustifiable given that the operational level had fallen. In Poza Rica, the number of permanent workers had risen from 1,232 to 1,410, and temporary workers from 500 to 1,000.[51] This was the basic cause of the conflict between the STPRM and the Cárdenas government, essentially a struggle for control over the oil industry.

The government laid all the blame for the increase in personnel on the STPRM, stating that the leaders' commitments to their specific groups forced them to create more jobs. Therefore, as long as the union maintained its influence in management, the problem would continue.

For those new union leaders who had not been able to fit themselves into the administration, and for the mass of workers, the problem was caused by a lack of control over Pemex's directors, which resulted in inefficiency, corruption, and abuse of power for clientelistic ends. The only way to stop these abuses was to turn over the direction of the industry to the workers by means of a "workers' administration," as had been done in the case of the Mexican National Railway Company.

The problem of real power in the industry was most acute at the intermediate management level, precisely where control was closest to the productive process, that is, with the superintendents. They managed refineries and oil fields, and were usually ex-union leaders. In order not to lose sway with the workers, they created jobs. They also used other clientelistic methods in collusion with their superiors in the Labor Department, who in turn were ex-leaders, or they simply took advantage of the chaotic central administration, which had lost control over what went on.

The dual power of union leaders would not have been a problem had the mass of workers been able to keep an eye on them. However, the majority of locals did not follow democratic union practices; instead, hierarchies and bossism ruled. Even in places where the power of the rank and file was implanted, such as Poza Rica, there was a certain consensus that viewed job creation as a means to help the needy, as well as an expression of "humanitarianism." In Poza Rica, unlike the other fields, the process was controlled by the workers' assemblies; although this represented an important political difference compared with other locals, it contributed in the long run to the same outcome: an unnecessary increase in personnel.

Faced with this situation, the government acted accordingly and, in August 1939, issued details for implementation of the decree that had given life to Pemex the previous year. In the first place, the category of *personal de confianza* was reinstated, a measure that would affect all top and middle executives, as well as the drillers and even some shorthand typists. But also, all labor leaders in management posts automatically had to give up their union positions.[52]

The STPRM finally held its second special convention in mid-1939 (a year after the original call made by Local 30). The situation of the industry was fully discussed, and the most important chapters—1 (Tampico), 10 (Minatitlán), and 30 (Poza Rica)—proposed a "workers' administration," which received the CTM's blessings.[53]

This did not mean that the CTM had changed its critical position concerning the STPRM because of the latter's extreme radicalism toward the government. "Workers' administration" was considered the highest level that could be achieved by means of an alliance of government and workers. This form of organization would also avoid a worsening of the differences between the two parties, because if the workers were to take control of management, they would have to exercise self-control and became aware of the financial situation of Pemex, which did not allow for the payment of higher salaries and fringe benefits. However, in the end the political impossibility of gaining this objective was recognized, given the unfavorable national and international conditions. At that time, the right wing in Mexico was on the march, external pressure had grown because of the expropriation, and fascism was spreading across Europe. Therefore, there was no alternative to direct control by the government, which was now under way.[54]

In spite of the legal changes instituted, the problem of excess personnel was not resolved; on the contrary, it worsened. Even though the ex-leaders were now *personal de confianza*, they still controlled their union groups and tried to control the local leaders in order to guarantee their influence and power in the locals. Thus, the legal reforms changed nothing. For their part, the workers in many locals still looked up to these leaders-cum-managers as genuine representatives who at a previous stage had been real social fighters. Without them, there was no direction.

Such was not the case in Poza Rica. Only two or three of the twenty-odd prominent leaders of the unions formed in the time of the foreign companies took *confianza* jobs. The problem that the remaining leaders caused was that during 1939 they left their local unattended; they were away most of the year on union business in Mexico City, dealing with questions such as job equivalences, drilling, analysis of the application of the Board of Arbitration's decision, and administrative centralization, not to mention their intervention in the second special convention. This absence allowed Pérez Castañeda to form his own power base in Poza

Rica and to begin imposing his decisions upon the workers of the country's most important oil field. However, the workers resisted. Throughout 1939, Local 30 was extremely unstable, which led to a constant turnover of leaders. Inevitably, this situation ended in the formation of two opposing union groups: one headed by the superintendent, Pérez Castañeda, and the other by the Masons and the radical leaders.[55]

During the election of a new local executive committee in 1940, this split widened. David Cano, Communist party member and sworn enemy of Pérez, was elected general secretary of Local 30. The local superintendent immediately tried to discredit Cano in government and in the eyes of the STPRM. He counted on the help of several Pemex secret agents, who made up the story that Cano and other members of his group were hatching a series of attacks of sabotage in Poza Rica, in collusion with the foreign companies. Another of the traditional Poza Rican leaders, Rafael Suárez, had just been elected national general secretary of the STPRM. He was also an enemy of Pérez, and his name was blackened with the same accusations.[56] Investigations carried out by government and army agents proved the charges to be false. The situation reached dangerous heights, threatening political stability in Poza Rica, so the government decided to remove Pérez from his post.

Meanwhile, at the national level, the face-off between the government and the STPRM reached crisis proportions. Since late 1939, President Cárdenas had asked the union to present a reorganization plan for the industry, aimed at saving it from bankruptcy. In the absence of specific proposals, Cárdenas delivered a memorandum on 28 February 1940 to a plenary session of STPRM leaders, which enumerated fourteen points for the company's reorganization.

The president blamed the union for the industry's crisis, which, according to Cárdenas, was to be explained almost exclusively by the increase in the number of workers employed. Therefore, Cárdenas proposed a reduction of full-time personnel to the level of 18 March 1938. This meant a drastic drop in the number of temporary workers and of positions in general. He also wanted a reduction in administrative salaries and the appointment of supervisory personnel on the basis of their abilities rather than of union pressure. He had the idea of further centralizing authority and extending the decision-making capacity of managers and superintendents.[57]

The STPRM did not know how to react when faced with this government attack, mainly because public opinion and the whole state apparatus were against the union. The indignation of the main union locals was overwhelming, because the permanent workers considered the crisis to have been caused by the industry's directors. In Ciudad

Madero, the workers proposed that "all the so-called technicians" should leave Pemex, while in Minatitlán, complaints were heard about the luxury and ostentation in which the directors lived at company expense.[58] In Poza Rica, there were thirty-five engineers, whereas in the times of El Aguila, there were only five engineers employed.[59] However, the press did not feed this type of information to the public; it printed only the deluge of opinions voiced against the STPRM by groups of every political persuasion.

The GEC was caught in a cross fire coming, on the one side, from the government attack seconded by the CTM, and, on the other, from the pressure of the mass of workers, who still expressed the radical culture that had been so useful to the union leadership in the past. Also, the leaders of Local 1 and several others in the center of the country felt that they were being ousted by the executive committee headed by Suárez.

The GEC tried to negotiate the company's reorganization with the government, but reached no significant agreement. Under these circumstances, on 25 July 1940, Pemex, the Distribution Company, and the AGPN managements laid before the Central Arbitration and Conciliation Board a demand for an economic measure against the STPRM. This document demanded that the board impose a collective work contract, without the participation of the interested parties. To crown it all, the board received another demand that was to take effect until the original petition was resolved. This second demand required that the above-mentioned companies be allowed to apply a series of emergency measures, which included the suspension of the payment of savings and of house rents and the right to fire workers. Acting with unprecedented speed, the board gave its decision on the same day: it ruled against the union. Consequently, the union now had no legal right to strike, and its hands were tied against the government.[60]

The locals immediately threatened work stoppages, and the GEC decided to stage a national slowdown (not a legal strike) for 30 July.[61] The situation was such that the government had to accept negotiations with the union leadership in order to prevent the rank and file from taking the initiative. Thus, on 4 August, an "emergency agreement" was signed, in which two-party commissions were set up to study alternatives to the suspension of benefit payments. A thirty-day suspension of the board's 25 July decision was also agreed upon.[62] The commissions worked hard but could not reach an agreement. The union representatives presented statistical evidence proving serious errors made by the Pemex management, arguing that there were financial alternatives to the suspension of benefit payments. The union documents were frankly devastating.[63]

Faced with union opposition, Cárdenas took the offensive again. On 12 September 1940, he broke the emergency agreement and the Conciliation Board prepared to "put into (immediate) effect the contents of the oil industry reorganization plan." The locals' indignation was without bounds. At a mass meeting held in Mexico City on 13 September, the workers voted for a general strike and a break with the CTM, which was considered an accomplice of the government and no more than an official organ.[64]

The government's response to the STPRM did not take long. The CTM leadership took the GEC by force, which, under tremendous pressure, was obliged to accept the president's decision. The only concession was that the union could intervene in the selection of who was to be fired. Faced with this situation, several locals tried to fight. A labor stoppage in Atzcapotzalco was broken up by the army toward the end of September.[65] It was evident that the union alone could not fight against the state. The workers had not expected so drastic a response from the government. However, it is not surprising if we take into account the existence of two distinct sets of objectives. The workers basically sought to protect their salaries and retain their influence within the company. The government, however, gave priority to stable labor relations, the raising of production to previous levels, and operational control. As things stood from 1938 to 1940, there could be no compatibility between these two groups of objectives. Labor leaders were well aware of the contradiction, but not so the rank and file. Their world was restricted by immediate reality: work, salaries, and power struggles among local leaders. At the national level, the general picture could not be worse. The right-wing Almazán opposition was riding high, and the North American government returned to its offensive against Mexico.[66] Under these conditions, there was no hope for workers' power.

However, such macropolitical factors were irrelevant, and even incomprehensible, to the workers in the remote oil fields. They saw and felt that the management was enforcing the same way of life and work methods as the old foreign bosses. They also understood that their influence over the company's actions was declining day by day, and that their material conditions were rapidly deteriorating. What they could not understand was how the same government that just two years before had given them all its support, now assumed an openly entrepreneurial attitude. And furthermore, those who had been their companions, as radical as themselves, were now bosses trying to impose a capitalist logic and bringing about the loss of what had been gained in labor rights. The oil workers suffered a head-on collision with reality, in which all the terms and conditions of the fight were changing.

In the first half of 1940, the Poza Rican workers had regained control that they had originally possessed over the company: when Pérez Castañeda left, the sphere of union action in the company grew, while the workers recovered their ability to elect their bosses, with the exception of the general superintendent. Furthermore, David Cano staged an important ethics campaign in Poza Rica, which included a systematic attack on the centers of vice. During his administration, the supply of the cooperative store improved, as did the quality of the hospital service, and once again education received attention.[67] At the local level, the offensive of the right against Cárdenas's government was not to be seen, nor were the effects of a fascist Europe. What went on in the higher circles of national and union politics, on the one hand, and in the daily life in Poza Rica, on the other, were like two mostly parallel routes that converged only at critical moments, before parting company again. In this context, we can understand not only the radicalism of the workers' stance, but also its limits; at such a distance from the center of power, they could not alter national policy.

The Poza Rican workers' autonomy was based upon their strong local tradition of democratic participation in assemblies, where decisions were made collectivly and where they were fully conscious of their rights and capabilities. For example, between 25 July and 2 August 1940, Local 30 held six general assemblies, all of which had a quorum. From 1938 to 1940, there was an average of seventy-five assemblies per year.[68]

On the other hand, Local 30 took to heart Cárdenas's proposal that the union should design its own reorganization plan. In mid-March of 1940, a commission was named with this express objective. On 6 May, it presented a full report of proposals, department by department. It even included the question of the superintendency, and the suggestion that five employees should be fired. An assembly approved the proposed reorganization, and also agreed that Vicente Cortés Herrera, Juan Gray, and Gutiérrez Bustamante should be fired from their supervisory posts, because they were inept and inefficient.[69] Obviously, these proposals had little echo higher up.

Later, on 25 July 1940, Poza Rica's local executive committee was ousted, on the grounds that its lukewarm attitude had allowed Cárdenas to present his demand for an economic battle with the union. The workers even clamored for Suárez's resignation. Passions ran so high that they were directed against the workers' own leaders, occasionally with no reason whatsoever. The workers' stance at this point was symptomatic of their desperation in the face of imminent defeat at the hands of the government. Outraged, the workers attributed their predicament to the incapacity of their leaders and not to the political realities of the times, which were the real cause of the debacle. The demand for the leaders' heads also reflected the influence of opposing special interest groups within the union. Each of these groups hoped to extend its sphere of control in its respective local. The STPRM was the scene of the main struggle for power within the oil industry. In the majority of cases, the struggle was between personal and group interests, and ideological reasons took second place. Less than a month later, David Cano died in a mysterious accident while carrying out his work in Palma Sola. Many blamed Pérez for his death.

The workers were taken by surprise by the magnitude of the state's attack. Union minutes for the month of September show that the Poza Rican workers were ready to fight, but they also demonstrate the workers' confusion over what to do. In mid-crisis, the loss of David Cano and the absence of other leaders in Mexico City compounded their lack of direction. In the end, Local 30 had to accept the fait accompli, and through Suárez had to seek the best way to prevent the mass firing of Poza Rican workers. In order to oppose readjustments, the local executive committee alleged that Poza Rica was a special case, given that it was an expanding field. As a contingent plan, the committee considered placing a stay of law writ *(amparo)* against the decision of the Board of Conciliation and Arbitration, which was expected in November of 1940. This last line of action did not work, because the *amparo* would have meant the suspension of contractual benefit payments that were reestablished in the board's decision. The only advantage of the *amparo* would have been a temporary holdup of the inevitable readjustment.[70]

The defeat of the workers in 1940 had a strategic character. From that time on, the workers in the nationalized industry progressively lost their power. This was a long and silent struggle, which was to have further critical bouts. The workers could no longer intervene in the industry's management; their role was reduced to carrying out central bureaucratic instructions. The Mexican government was recognized as a substitute boss in place of the foreign companies. In that capacity, the government signed the first national contract with the STPRM in mid-1942, having started discussions at the beginning of 1941.

However, for many years to come, the tradition of struggle and the working-class culture in Poza Rica allowed the workers of this field to maintain their local resistance to the policy that was trying to crush labor power. But, that is another story.

Notes

The author would like to thank David Skerritt, without whose help there would be no English version of this text.

1. Gobierno de México, *El petróleo de México* (Mexico City, 1940), chap. 4, pp. 131–142.

2. Author interview with Eduardo Pérez, Ciudad Victoria, Tamps., 10 Nov. 1984.

3. For the following, see A. Olvera,"Origen social, condiciones de vida y

organización sindical de los trabajadores petroleros de Poza Rica, 1932–1935," in *Anuario IV* (Xalapa: Centro de Investigaciones Históricas, Universidad Veracruzana, 1986.)

4. Lief Adleson, "Casualidad y conciencia: factores convergentes en la fundación de los sindicatos petroleros de Tampico durante la década de los veinte," in *El trabajo y los trabajadores en la historia de México* (Mexico City: COLMEX, 1979). See also Adleson, "Historia social de los obreros industriales de Tampico," PhD. diss., Colegio de México, 1982, chaps. 7 and 8.

5. Archive of Section (Local) 30–STPRM (hereafter A. S. 30), file 003-2 (minutes), minutes 12 May 1935.

6. Ibid., minutes 30 Aug. 1934.

7. Author interview with Teodoro Tapia, Poza Rica, Ver., 23 Aug. 1986.

8. Author interview with Herminio Govea, Poza Rica, Ver., 15 June 1987.

9. In almost all the union's assemblies, there were requests for help. Cases of tuberculosis, accidents in the workplace, malaria, and even alcoholism were discussed; the workers as a whole took care of the families of their sick brothers. A. S. 30, file 003-2, minutes 12 Jan., 24 May 1935, 30 Jan. 1936.

10. Ibid., minutes 5 Sept. 1935, 1 Feb., 3 May, 8 July 1936, 2 Jan. 1937, and so on. The solidarity shown toward the strikes of the Tampico workers was notable.

11. Author interview with Raúl Noriega, Poza Rica, Ver., 2 Nov. 1984.

12. A. S. 30, file 003-2, minutes 28 Feb. and 30 April 1936.

13. Ibid., minutes 13 Dec. 1934, 3 Jan. 1935, 26 Aug. 1936, and so on.

14. Tampico: Author interview with Severo Paredes, Poza Rica, Ver., 18 June 1983. Minatitlán: Julio Valdivieso, *Historia del movimiento sindical petrolero en Minatitlán* (Mexico City: Ed. del Autor, 1963). Unfortunately, no detailed studies of other oil unions in the early 1930s are available or even of other locals of the STPRM since its inception. One of the few exceptions is to be found in Rodolfo Zavala, "El sindicato petrolero y la nacionalización en Las Choapas," in *El petróleo de Veracruz* (Mexico City: Pemex, 1988).

15. In November 1934, the first general secretary of Delegation 2 was ousted from his post after only three months in office. In 1935, two treasurers, two officers in charge of conflicts, and a secretary of minutes were substituted. In the years that followed, these changes came about with greater frequency.

16. A. S. 30, file 003-2, minutes 13 Dec. 1934, 5 Feb., 12 Oct. 1935, 13 Feb. 1936, and so on.

17. Gobierno de México, *El petróleo*, chap. 9, pp. 519–536, where an explanation of the *conflicto de orden económico* and the results of the labor-management convention are to be found.

18. Mario Román and Rosario Segura, "La huelga de los 57 días en Poza Rica," in *Anuario V* (Xalapa: Centro de Investigaciones Históricas, Universidad Veracruzana, 1988).

19. On this point, see chap. 5 by Ruth Adler.

20. Sinesio Capitanachi, *Palma Sola, Furbero y Poza Rica*, published by the author, Xalapa, Ver., 1983, pp. 268–271; author interview with Eduardo Pérez, 11 Oct. 1984.

21. *El Nacional*, 13 and 14 Sept. 1938.

22. Convenio Ejecutivo Federal–Compañía Mexicana de Petróleo El Aguila, 11 Nov. 1937, in Capitanachi, *Palma Sola*, pp. 204–221.

23. A. S. 30, file 003-2, minutes for Nov. and Dec. 1937.

24. A. S. 30, file 041-2, GEC report on its work in 1938–1939.

25. Author interview with Rafael Suárez, Poza Rica, Ver., 2 May 1982.

26. At the beginning of 1938, Eduardo Pérez Castañeda rose to the general secretaryship of Local 30, thanks to the prestige he had acquired during his persecution. However, the majority of the other local leaders mistrusted him, and from the outset of his leadership they maintained a critical distance.

27. A. S. 30, file 003-2, minutes 30 March 1938.

28. Ibid., minutes 6, 10 April 1938.

29. In Spanish: A particular form of labor contracting known as *personal de confianza.*

30. A. S. 30, file 003-2, various minutes, 1938.

31. Jesus Silva Herzog, *Petróleo mexicano* (Mexico City: F. C. E. 1941), pp. 230–231.

32. A. S. 30, file 003-2, minutes 1 June 1938.

33. Silva Herzog, *Petróleo mexicano*, p. 233.

34. Juan García Hernández, *El cuchillito de palo* (Mexico City: Ed. del Autor, 1967).

35. A. S. 30, file 003-2, minutes 24 July 1938.

36. Ibid., file 013-2, circular 15 Feb. 1937.

37. Ibid.

38. Ibid., file 003-3, minutes 30 July 1938.

39. Ibid., minutes 28 July 1938.

40. Ibid., minutes 7 and 14 Sept. 1938.

41. Ibid., circular 10 Dec. 1938.

42. Valdivieso, *Historia del movimiento sindical*, pp. 111–113.

43. A. S. 30, file 003-3, minutes 3 Nov. 1938.

44. Pemex, *Los veinte años de la industria petrolera nacional. Informes del 18 de marzo (1938–1958)* (Mexico City, 1958), p. 28.

45. Gobierno de México, *El petróleo*, chap. 3, pp. 108–112.

46. Fabio Barbosa Cano, "La situación de la industria petrolera en 1938," en *Anuario V*, p. 98.

47. Ibid.

48. Ibid., p. 101.

49. A. G. N. Ramo Presidentes, Fondo Lázaro Cárdenas, file 527/2.

50. Silva Herzog, *Petróleo mexicano*, p. 233.

51. A. S. 30, file 041-2.

52. García Hernández, *El cuchillito*, p. 82.

53. On this point, see Ruth Adler, chap. 5.

54. Fabio Barbosa Cano, "El movimiento petrolero en 1938–1940," in Javier Aguilar, coord., *Los sindicatos nacionales: petroleros* (Mexico City: G. V. Editores, 1986), pp. 63–65.

55. A. S. 30, file 003-3, minutes, 1939.

56. A. G. N. Ramo Presidentes, Fondo L. Cárdenas, file 432.2/ 253.32; archive of David Cano, Informe de Labores del Primer Semestre de 1940, CIH-U. V.

57. Barbosa "El movimiento," pp. 66–70.

58. Valdivieso, *Historia del movimiento*, p. 125.

59. A. S. 30, file 003-3, minutes 4 April 1939.

60. Barbosa, "El movimiento," pp. 69–71.

61. A. S. 30, file 003-4, minutes 28 July 1939.

62. Barbosa, "El movimiento," pp. 69–71.

63. A. S. 30, file 013-3, circular 105. This is the result of the deliberations of the commission that studies possible savings in Pemex, with the objective of avoiding the suspension of benefit payments.

64. Barbosa, "El movimiento,"pp. 72–73.

65. Ibid.

66. On this point, see chap. 4 by Alan Knight.

67. A. S. 30, file 003-3, minutes 1940; archive of David Cano.

68. A. S. 30, file 003-3, minutes 1938–1940.

69. Ibid., minutes 6 May 1940.

70. Ibid., minutes 11 Oct., 30 Nov., 7 Dec. 1940.

4. The Politics of the Expropriation

Alan Knight
Oxford University

The Mexican Revolution had two principal effects on the nascent petroleum industry. First, it accelerated working-class organization in the petroleum sector. This process—expertly analyzed in several other chapters in this volume—culminated in the creation of the national union, the STPRM, in 1936. Second, the Revolution brought to power a regime committed to the redefinition of the status of the petroleum industry, a commitment formally vested in Article 27 of the 1917 Constitution and practically reinforced by the revolutionary state's pressing fiscal needs. The result was a series of well-known controversies, as successive administrations—Carranza's, Obregón's, Calles's—sought to increase state control of the industry, in the face of dogged company opposition.[1] The stakes were high, certainly in the early 1920s, when Mexico figured as a major oil exporter, and when petroleum-derived revenues made up a large slice of government income.[2] Thus, while U.S. policy toward Mexico did not and could not simply reflect the narrow interests of the oil companies, the oil controversy was certainly the major source of tension in U.S.-Mexican relations during the decade following the promulgation of the new constitution. At times, the controversy seemed capable of producing U.S. intervention.[3]

The late 1920s and early 1930s, however, witnessed a distinct shift in what might be termed the political economy of Mexican oil. Production, which had peaked at 193 million barrels in 1921, reached a low of 33 million in 1932; the petroleum sector's contribution to GNP fell from 7 percent to 2 percent; its contribution to governmental revenue fell from 22 percent (a freak 34 percent in 1932) to 11 percent (a low of 6 percent in 1928). The stakes of the old conflict thus diminished, and the U.S. oil companies increasingly transferred their attention and investment elsewhere, notably to Venezuela.[4] As the petroleum issue lost some of its salience in U.S.-Mexican relations, the chances for détente increased. During 1927–1928, Dwight Morrow negotiated an agreement with the Calles administration, whereby the old, vexed question of the oil industry's status was—for the time being—resolved, largely in the companies' favor: where "positive acts" had been performed prior to 1917, the companies received confirmatory concessions of indefinite duration. The companies caviled at the term *concession* but, in practice, the Morrow-Calles agreement basically guaranteed their position in Mexico.[5]

Meanwhile, even as it shrank, the Mexican petroleum industry underwent a degree of involution. Exports—which had constituted around 90 percent of production during the early 1920s—fell to 62 percent (1932) and lower thereafter.[6] Following 1932, production began to rise again, chiefly on the strength of the aptly named Poza Rica field. Thus, by the mid-1930s, petroleum figured not only as a source of foreign exchange and tax revenue but also as a source of energy for Mexico's domestic economy, which was now shifting from a phase of postrevolutionary reconstruction (still premised on the old model of *desarrollo hacia afuera*) to one of depression-induced industrialization and state intervention (*desarrollo hacia adentro*). Though this new "project" achieved its clearest form under Cárdenas, it was signaled well in advance: by the initial downswing in foreign trade in 1927, compounded by the subsequent world depression; and by the reformist and interventionist policies heralded in the Six Year Plan (published in 1934, but the product of discussions going back to 1932).

As part of this project, the Rodríguez administration established Petróleos Mexicanos (Petromex), a state company designed to compete with the foreign companies and to supply the growing domestic market. Petromex, however, was responsible for less than 2 percent of total Mexican output; it remained, in Luis González's words, *un bebé enclenque*, a sickly babe.[7]

The Cárdenas administration, which from the start expressed its desire to extend state regulation of the oil industry, thus built upon existing precedents. But it did so in a context of mounting industrial conflict. As other chapters in this volume show—with more insight and erudition than I can muster—the 1934–1938 period was one of marked syndical mobilization: the Aguila Co. was hit by strikes in 1934 and 1935; 1936 saw the creation of the national union which, representing eighteen thousand oil workers, at once demanded a collective contract whose terms were variously deemed "patently absurd" or "unreasonable and fantastic."[8] The subsequent story is well known. With a national strike in the offing, the government intervened and obliged the two parties to negotiate. Negotiations broke down in May 1937, with the two parties still far apart, not least on the basic question of pay. The union then struck, appealing to the Federal Board of Conciliation and Arbitration. After a brief but serious stoppage (whose consequences we will note later), the Board accepted the appeal and appointed a commission of experts, who, in August, delivered a report highly critical of the companies and broadly (though not exclusively) favorable to the union. Through the fall of 1937—as tempers rose, the companies politicked and propagandized, and wildcat strikes continued to affect the industry—the Arbitration Board pondered its decision. Finally, on 18 December, it broadly endorsed the experts' recommendation. The companies appealed to the Supreme Court (a resort that had produced last-minute compromises in previous disputes). This time it was not to be. On 1 March, the Court ruled against the companies; on 15 March, with the companies still refusing to obey the board ruling, they were declared to be *en rebeldía*; on 18 March, they were expropriated.[9]

Then and later, the companies—and not just the companies—maintained that this elaborate sequence had been choreographed by the regime; that, all along, expropriation had been the objective. "Developments from early 1935 . . . all indicated that the Mexican government was driving toward the expropriation of the oil companies," Frank Kluckhohn wrote. At the time, the U.S. ambassador reported, "some oil representatives told me . . . that they believed the intent all along was to expropriate the oil fields."[10] The British Foreign Office considered the labor dispute a "pretext" used to justify the state's "desire to acquire valuable properties"; although, it further believed, "such acquisitions will not, in fact, in the circumstances, in any way redound to the benefit of the state."[11] Such a plot, of course, required a villain. The London *Times* pointed its finger at Lombardo Toledano and his "political clique."[12] Another candidate was Francisco Múgica who—according to a particularly imaginative version—"is said to have been working toward the expropriation of the oil companies and for the benefit of himself and (the) Japanese since 1934."[13]

Was there any truth in this kind of conspiracy theory? We will use this question as a point of entry to our subject, the politics of the expropriation, and begin by considering the decision to expropriate. Then we will analyze the immediate context of the expropriation—how it took place, what response it elicited. Finally, we will hazard a somewhat longer-term evaluation of its consequences. In general, conspiracy theories are to be avoided. In this case, the evidence for a concerted drive to expropriation is weak (though, like any conspiracy theory, this one can be rescued by alleging that every deviation and equivocation on the part of the conspirators is, in fact, a subtle dissimulation). It is certainly true that Cárdenas—and some of his close political allies, like Lombardo and Múgica—looked to a progressive Mexicanization of the petroleum industry. But the evidence suggests that most economic nationalist opinion precisely saw this as a progressive trend, not a precipitate measure; there was no need for a *golpe teatral*, as one critic termed the expropriation; a useful analogy might be the gradual (and unspectacular) Mexicanization of the electrical energy sector, as analyzed by Miguel Wionczek.[14]

Pre-1934 policy had been geared to this end, and post-1934 policy did not represent a decisive break. Cárdenas had repeatedly stressed his desire to encourage productive foreign investment in Mexico. Petromex, he asserted, posed no conceivable threat to the foreign companies (it was a minnow among whales anyway); his government, he reiterated in his 1938 New Year's message, "had no desire to monopolise the exploitation of the oil fields."[15] Nor did the president's espousal of the union's cause imply any commitment to expropriation. Government intervention in the labor dispute was—like government interventions in the past—designed to achieve a "stable composition [*sic*] of the rights and interests of the workers *and of the employers* so that labor conflicts might be reduced as far as possible."[16] This was neither airy rhetoric nor subtle dissimulation. The Cárdenas administration was ready to crack the whip over the workers when they appeared to step out of line; conversely, the administration was ready to enter a major collaborative agreement with the Aguila Company in November 1937, looking to joint exploitation of the Poza Rica field.

Of course, Cárdenas went further than his predecessors in abetting unions in labor disputes; the equilibrium he sought, in other words, was located somewhat to the left of that previously sought by the Sonorans. And the Poza Rica agreement was a breakthrough in that it facilitated the state's active role in the petroleum sector, while promising handsome returns. The British Legation and Aguila management in Mexico believed that the agreement—though far from ideal—was "probably as good as anything they could have got in the circumstances," since "the pooling of profits on Poza Rica lines . . . is the only basis on which the continued operation of foreign oil companies in Mexico will be possible." It should be noted, too, that a comparable deal was offered the American Huasteca Company.[17] The very novelty and—from the Mexican point of view—the success of the Poza Rica agreement must cast doubt on the notion that it was a deliberate preamble to expropriation. At the time, it seemed a significant forward step in the long march of Mexicanization; proof, as the far from friendly London *Times* later put it, that Cárdenas "has shown himself anxious for the introduction of foreign capital, engineering and organising ability."[18] Similar conclusions could be drawn from *cardenista* policy in sectors other than oil: in mining, for example, where the expropriation of going concerns was expressly ruled out; in manufacturing, where foreign investment was positively encouraged.[19] Given his ambitious programs of social betterment and national development, Cárdenas could hardly afford to adopt "Boxerish" policies of xenophobic extremism.

Yet it was Cárdenas himself who individually decided upon and decreed the expropriation. That, at any rate, seems the likely truth. Of course, the decision-making process remained shrouded in uncertainty, hence open to speculation. Contemporaries were baffled: "a kind of oriental fog of secrecy and intrigue and misrepresentation covers the struggle going on all the time between the President, his advisers, the syndicates, the Generals and so on," observed the British Minister in December 1937.[20] But, as the crisis came and went and the fog somewhat dissipated, the consensus of contemporary opinion was that the president had individually resolved on the dramatic policy of expropriation. Lombardo certainly approved; Múgica was chosen to draw up the historic announcement (Cárdenas was no great speechwriter or speechmaker himself); but the decision was the president's. Indeed, close observers—convinced that "Cárdenas himself is the key to the situation"—described how, as Labor Department Chief Antonio Villalobos strove for a last-minute compromise, "Cárdenas himself went to Villalobos' office and told him to throw his work in the waste paper basket, since he had decided to expropriate the companies."[21]

To take this view is not to espouse some naive Great Man theory of historical causality. The circumstances of the 1938 crisis were not of Cárdenas's making: two of the principal participants—the oil workers' union and, to a greater extent, the oil companies—acted autonomously and dynamically. But the expropriation decision was the president's, and it represented a choice among several options. It is worth pointing out the options that existed, as well as the factors—internal and external, personal and political—that decided Cárdenas in favor of expropriation. Just as expropriation was not decided upon years, or even months, in advance, nor was it generally expected even when it happened. Of course, as the crisis developed and the options narrowed, outright expropriation was envisaged. The Poza Rica workers (Local 30 of the STPRM) had advocated it during their fifty-seven-day strike in the summer of 1937.[22] But, as Olvera's chapter shows, Local 30 was a particularly radical group, out of step with both the government and the national union leadership. Within the government, individuals like Suárez, Secretary of Hacienda, were considered to be moderates, and the signals they (and others) put out aroused hopes of a compromise settlement, even at the eleventh hour.[23]

The U.S. ambassador, at least, was convinced: he "does not believe that the Cárdenas government intends to take over the oil industry" (21 January 1938); on the contrary, he discerned "a willingness to compromise" on the part of the administration.[24] When two months later the expropriation occurred, it came, the ambassador said, like a "bolt from the blue."[25] This was hyperbole, but not wild hyperbole. In the interim, the crisis had deepened, such that some form of government takeover of the industry seemed more likely. Under Secretary of Foreign Relations Ramón Beteta had warned as much, as had the minister of labor, in conversation with Standard Oil's T. R. Armstrong.[26] However, the predicted outcome, at least that predicted by "most Americans," was that at worst the government "would . . . name a receiver or receivers to operate the fields," pending some conclusive settlement (this scheme was revived by the State Department in the wake of Cárdenas's "over-hasty" act of expropriation: that is, they sought, in vain, a lease-back arrangement).[27]

Ambassador Daniels was not simply victim of his own wishful thinking (a genuine sympathizer with the Cárdenas administration, he believed "it would be a calamity if no agreement could be reached," especially when the parties had "come so near to concord").[28] The *Boletín Financiero* considered the expropriation a "sensation." Radio listeners who tuned in to the famous broadcast of the evening of 18 March got a "lively surprise." Opinion in the provinces does not seem to have been prepared for expropriation: "up to the very time of the expropriations [*sic*] virtually everybody [in Sonora] was certain that an eleventh-hour solution would be found."[29] The companies, from their quite different perspective, agreed. They doubted that the government would dare expropriate, and they counted on another spatchcocked compromise on the lines of 1923 or 1927. Their "main idea of negotiation," an observer had commented in 1926, "appears to be bluff, with graft if bluff fails"; and, like the Bourbons, the companies had learned nothing and forgotten nothing in the intervening period.[30]

But during this period, the times had changed. Roosevelt was not Coolidge and, even more important, Cárdenas was not Calles. Furthermore, the structure of the oil industry itself had evolved, and a powerful national *sindicato* had established itself. In more general ways, too, the events of 1938 revealed that Mexican politics had changed and were still changing at a rapid pace, as we shall see. In this new context, bluff and graft were less effective, and even counterproductive. Convinced of their inherent bargaining strength, the companies doggedly resisted the wage award—which the arbitration board had trimmed down to 26 million pesos ($7,222,222), from the union's 65 million pesos ($18,055,555)—right to the end, protesting that it was impossible for them to pay. Weeks before, the British minister, aware of the perils of brinkmanship, had argued that the U.S. government must act "before legal remedies have been exhausted, *viz.*, before the President has got into a position from which . . . retreat would be very difficult."[31] But the brinkmanship continued. At the last minute, the companies conceded the $7.2 million, thus revealing the hollowness of their previous claim that it would entail bankruptcy. Now, it became clear, their chief concerns were to retain managerial prerogatives and, at the same time, to send a signal to other countries that government intervention in their business operations would be strenuously resisted. They "belatedly . . . came to the point of willingness to meet the increased payroll, provided labor would recede from demands which the oil company representatives said would take the control of the business out of their hands." On this basis, the U.S. ambassador conceived a "strong hope" that agreement would now ensue, and the press expected further talks.[32]

Cárdenas, however, was not impressed by the companies' eleventh-hour conversion. It was belated, grudging, and a tacit admission that previous indignant protestations had been tactical maneuvers. It offered no guarantee that a settlement could be swiftly achieved; yet political passions were on the rise and the economic stakes of the conflict were mounting.[33] At this point, as we approach the moment of decision, it is worth pondering the character of Cárdenas, as well as the immediate context of his decision. Cárdenas was resistant to bluff and impervious to graft. As military commander in the Huasteca in the 1920s, he had encountered the oil companies at first hand. He disdained their overtures when a "beautiful Packard sedan, brand-new and glistening, a fortune on four wheels" drew up outside Cárdenas's residence, alongside his "ancient and decrepit Hudson."[34] He witnessed the squalor and inequality of the oil camps—and did so in the company of Francisco Múgica, whose recollections of the *Africa Mexicana*, more poetic than anything Cárdenas himself ever penned, described not only the heat and the insects but also the poverty, *caciquismo*, violence, and backwardness, much of which could be attributed to the boom-and-bust oil industry, its enclave status, and its cynical disregard for the host population. Here, too, were fresh reminders of the "traitor" Peláez, who between 1915 and 1920 had helped convert an economic into a political and military enclave, defiant of the central government.[35]

These initial impressions of the oil companies did not easily fade. Graft remained a chief weapon in their armory, often exercised during Calles's era. But Cárdenas again spurned them: he was, said a company representative, "extremely innocent and did not properly understand business conventions as understood in Mexico."[36] The president harbored profound suspicions of oil company machinations (a staple of many a populist, Mexican or North American), and recent events served to confirm rather than to allay them. High-ranking members of the administration believed that "at the time of Calles' elimination Mexican Eagle had offered or supplied money to Calles' faction"; however,

Cárdenas—reacting to these stories with magnanimity rather than skepticism—was prepared to "let bygones be bygones."[37] In the immediate wake of the expropriation, of course, similar stories circulated concerning Cedillo's liaison with the oil companies.[38] There was also an international dimension to the suspicions aroused by the companies. In July 1937, Ortiz Rubio (ex-President, fellow-Michoacano, ex-head of Petromex, and an old ally of Cárdenas) sent the president a resumé of a French publication that, Ortiz Rubio alleged, "serves to confirm the various reports which I previously submitted to you"; the gist of the publication was that global political alignments—from the First World War to the rise of Nazism—were determined by the epic struggle of Deterding's Royal-Dutch Shell and Rockefeller's Standard Oil. Accordingly, Deterding—who was certainly sympathetic to fascism—channeled cash to Hitler ("thanks to English money Hitler conquered Germany"), in the hope that Hitler would revalidate Royal-Dutch's lost Caucasian concessions: "Such is the real basis of the conflict which threatens to cover the world in blood once again."[39] The theme is a familiar one;[40] what is arguably significant is that such themes agitated the minds of the Mexican elite in the 1930s.

These suspicions usually had some basis in fact. The oil companies *had* financed Peláez (though that did not make Peláez a simple mercenary); they *had* strongly influenced—though not controlled—U.S. policy toward Mexico; they *had* paid ample graft to the *callistas*; they *did* later receive overtures from Cedillo (though it seems unlikely that they responded to them positively). Company bookkeeping—another source of complaint and suspicion—was also genuinely suspect. In the past, allegedly "confiscatory" taxes had been paid, finally and grudgingly, without the companies' being bankrupted.[41] The recent episode of the 26 million pesos ($7.2 million) was only a further example of the companies' financial sleight of hand. Taken together, these several actions created an impression, also based in fact, of overmighty corporate subjects who, when they chose, flouted the sovereignty of the Mexican state. When, as we shall note, Mexican critics denounced the companies' colonialism and racism, they were possibly exaggerating but certainly not inventing these attributes. In their dealings with Mexico, the companies often appeared to entertain a notion of supersovereignty, of de facto extraterritoriality, which enabled them to insulate themselves from Mexican reality. They ran up large profits during the decade of revolution and hardship; they fiercely contested tax increases; they bought off collaborators, who connived at the companies' continued self-interested insulation. In the same spirit, they displayed a racist contempt for Mexicans: not only for their workers (the spatial segregation and salary differentials of the oil camps are well known), but also for the revolutionary authorities, the embodiments of the state. While this did not make them unique among foreign businessmen, the oil companies' power and position gave them an unparalleled capacity to offend. Deterding himself "was incapable of conceiving Mexico as anything but a Colonial Government to which you simply dictated orders"; subordinates who questioned this approach and advised greater flexibility and diplomacy were likely to be accused of Bolshevism.[42]

Deterding was something of a special case (after 1925 he became, as Philip puts it, rather charitably, "increasingly eccentric") but these sentiments ran deep, and they encouraged the companies in their defiance and brinkmanship. The revolutionaries would not dare "kill the goose that lays the golden eggs," Lord Cowdray had boasted during the armed revolution; twenty years later the illusion of indispensability remained, though with much less justification.[43] The companies did not believe the government would dare expropriate; hence, they pursued their policy of "passive unhelpfulness to[ward] the Mexican authorities."[44] They further believed that expropriation would prove disastrous to Mexico; hence, with perverse paternalism, they construed their policy of confrontation as ultimately serving Mexico's, and Latin America's, own best interest: "Mexico, we all know, does not have the trained population to manage a vast complex of publically-owned property. In our opinion, on a foundation of confiscation Mexico is heading towards disorder and revolution"; thus, since "confiscation is as corrosive to the confiscators themselves as it is unjust to the owners," the United States should take steps to deter it; for, were the United States to remain inactive, it would be "doing no service to the countries of Latin America."[45]

To a degree, therefore, the oil industry remained a mental as well as an economic and political enclave. And this enclave status—established under Díaz, defended with guns under Peláez, with bribes under Calles—remained a stain on Mexican sovereignty. Calles had confronted the companies in 1925, striving, as he put it, to be "master in his own house." Again, in 1937–1938, the issue of sovereignty became paramount: "The question of oil, to the Mexican people, was only partly an economic matter. It was also emotional, involving race and nationality."[46]

In this, a theme we will develop, Cárdenas took the lead. Cárdenas was no trained economist. Indeed, his education had been basic; his attitude toward intellectuals (I am aware it is risky to equate economists and intellectuals) was diffident. He does not appear to have espoused any grand ideological blueprints. He had come up through the military, and made a successful, orthodox career in the cut-and-thrust, sometimes the literal cut-and-thrust, of revolutionary politics. He had a good grasp of those politics (witness his outmaneuvering of Calles), but he lacked a

Institute of Latin American Studies

31 Tavistock Square

London WC1H 9HA

grand, encompassing intellectual vision; he was—to use the old but convenient cliché—a man of action, not of words. He was also a man of sentiment. He was fiercely patriotic: his infant imagination had been fired by stories of the French Intervention, in which his grandfather had fought; as an adolescent, he conceived of himself as a man of destiny and he dreamed of leading a triumphant army for "the liberation of the *patria.*"[47] Less intellectual than Mao Zedong, he nevertheless shared with Mao (his almost exact contemporary, also of petit-bourgeois provincial origins), a fierce patriotism, a hankering after military glory, and a voluntarist faith in the efficacy of action and will and in the essential goodness of the people, whose interests he embodied. He chafed at the restraint of bloodless laws—the laws of economics, the laws of evolutionary development—and he believed that individual energy and dedication could guarantee results. His early military exploits (and we should recall that Cárdenas, more than any president save Obregón, was a product of the revolutionary military) had been varied, extensive, and often dramatic, involving several defeats (Obregón had a low opinion of Cárdenas's military competence), a near-suicide, and a serious wound. Throughout, the young Cárdenas had displayed more aggression than prudence; he did not grasp, a biographer comments, "that caution in a commander is as necessary as valor."[48] Subsequently, on his tireless tours of the country, he exhausted his entourage, inspired his rustic listeners, and dispensed presidential patronage with abandon.[49] He was the kind of leader, military or political, who believed that Rubicons were there to be crossed.[50] He was, by the same token, stubborn, sometimes opinionated, even authoritarian: critics alleged that he surrounded himself with yes-men, spurned unwelcome advice, and maintained an unshakable belief in his own righteousness.[51]

In short, Cárdenas was not the kind of man likely to back off from a challenge. Of course, he was ready to concede a compromise that preserved national and presidential honor—hence the scaling down of the original *laudo.* But when the companies spurned this offer and appeared instead to stall, maneuver, obstruct and, finally, to defy Mexico's sovereignty, they ensured their own downfall. In these precarious moments, both the international political and the domestic economic contexts were fundamental considerations. Concerning the first, I will say little, since in Lorenzo Meyer we have the leading authority in the field. Suffice to say that Cárdenas and his advisers were well aware of the factors governing U.S. policy and inhibiting any aggressive response toward Mexico: fear of Axis expansion in Latin America; a desire to promote hemispheric collaboration under U.S. auspices; the unpopularity of the oil companies among the North American public; the hostile relationship between U.S. big business and FDR; the friendly attitude of U.S. Ambassador Josephus Daniels who, apart from evincing a genuine sympathy for *cardenista* reform, no doubt wished to rid his conscience of the stain of the (1914) Veracruz occupation.[52] The outcome—a Standard Oil executive lamented as the expropriation occurred—is that the "feeling in general in Mexico is that the Government of the United States will take no action on behalf of the oil companies."[53] Foreigners in Mexico therefore applauded the testy British note of April 1938, contrasting HMG's tough—but, as it turned out, entirely counterproductive—attitude with "what is considered [the] weakness of the U.S. Government."[54] Ex-President Abelardo Rodríguez, a spokesman of the probusiness revolutionary right, went further, blaming the United States for the whole deplorable business: "Rodríguez regretted very much [the] complete inaction [of the] State Department . . . which he considers largely responsible [for the] present situation and remarked [that the] policy of of taking action after [the] event instead of before [is] usually fatal in Mexico."[55]

If the United States—State Department and oil companies—indeed displayed complacency, underestimating Cárdenas's resolve, this was partly due to the current economic situation. Yet, arguably, economic factors also stiffened that resolve. After a sustained period of economic growth during 1932–1936, the Mexican economy began to falter in the course of 1937 (in the United States too, modest recovery gave way to renewed recession in that year). The Mexican trade balance fell, as did government revenue; the federal deficit jumped; inflation quickened. At the end of the year, the government felt compelled to seek a loan in the United States (which did not materialize) and to lobby for the maintenance of U.S. silver purchases; in January, Mexico was "within an ace of having to devalue."[56] While in North American eyes these accumulating problems should have induced caution or even deference south of the border, their actual effect on the Mexican administration, Cárdenas especially, was arguably different. True, Finance Minister Suárez was reckoned to be against expropriation.[57] Cárdenas, however, appears to have followed an old tradition in reacting against the pressures of dollar diplomacy.[58]

He may also have believed that the alternative to immediate expropriation—prolonged litigation, strikes, and paralysis in the oil industry—posed an even greater threat to the nation's economic well-being. The strikes of summer 1937 (the nine-day national stoppage followed by the fifty-seven-day Poza Rica strike) had had a severe impact, provoking protests and appeals throughout the republic. Coparmex complained that the national strike was "seriously affecting innumerable commercial and industrial interests quite unconnected with the conflict"; the

Jalisco Centro Patronal reported that, with transport interrupted, basic necessities were running short, prices were rising, and "the situation in this state is daily worsening, such that in a short time it will be intolerable."[59] Businessmen therefore wanted the strike halted (as, indeed, it was). But businessmen were not the only victims or plaintiffs. Tourism suffered; the textile factories ran short of fuel, as the port of Guaymas did of water; from the steamy Tuxtepec valley the members of a banana cooperative reported that, for want of fuel, "we have not been able to cut a single clutch of bananas and the fruit is rapidly spoiling."[60]

The government, too, already overcommitted with its ambitious agrarian policy, could not afford to lose further revenue and did not wish to see its social programs abruptly curtailed. There was also the threat of syndical militancy, violence, and even sabotage. The Poza Rica strike clearly revealed—company and other allegations notwithstanding—that the government did not exercise a tight control over the oil workers; the latter possessed a good deal of autonomy and their future actions were unpredictable, especially as the labor dispute became more prolonged and embittered. In June 1937 militant railway workers, sympathizers with the *petroleros*, allegedly advocated derailing trains bringing oil into Mexico from the United States.[61]

Fears of shortages, disruptions, and worse recurred early in 1938, as the dispute reached its climax. Meanwhile, the actions of the oil companies seemed, in many eyes, to verge upon sabotage. They stonewalled on the labor dispute, while repatriating their liquid assets. According to Frank Tannenbaum (a good source), Cárdenas was "indignant" and "disgusted" because the companies, by stopping credit sales and sending capital out of the country, had made an "inexcusable effort to influence the government to take a stand against labour." Indeed, Anderson, the choleric manager of the Huasteca Co., sought to go further: "he . . . suggested that the oil companies should not only refuse to accept the *fallo* but should take away essential working parts of their plant in order to make it impossible for agents of the Mexican Government to operate foreign plants themselves."[62] But the most provocative example of company "sabotage"—and a factor behind the expropriation that has perhaps been underestimated—concerns the alleged connivance of the oil companies and Asarco. Asarco dominated the Mexican mining industry and, in consequence, it exerted great influence within the Mexican economy. Its labor force alone exceeded that of the entire oil industry.[63] Like the oil companies, Asarco faced demands for a collective labor contract, which the company strenuously resisted. During 1937, there were recurrent strikes, but no complete stoppage. Precisely as the oil crisis came to a climax, however, Asarco's labor troubles also mounted, bringing the threat of paralysis. Facing recurrent one-hour stoppages at Monterrey and Chihuahua, the company began to discharge all such strikers; at Chihuahua the response was a walkout, followed by a workers' occupation of the smelter. The occupation was orderly but seemed to presage a long hard conflict. "Officials (of the company) emphatically state . . . that in the circumstances they have no intention of renewing operations."[64] At the moment when the petroleum companies were expropriated, Asarco's Monterrey and Chihuahua plants were both shut down.[65] A key sector of the economy, vital for exports, for earning foreign exchange, for maintaining the peso and bolstering government revenue, was thus jeopardized.

What is more, the government believed that Asarco was acting in connivance with the oil companies. When news of the Asarco conflict reached the capital, it was reported, "the Minister of Labor . . . hurried to the President in indignation and told him about the incident and that it was evidence that the oil companies and the smelting companies were in concert to compel the Mexican Government to accept dictation." The official press, too, denounced Asarco's conduct as "a display of capitalist solidarity with the petroleum companies against Mexico."[66] In the event, the oil expropriation soon eclipsed the Asarco dispute; but it also induced the government to put pressure on the miners and to offer firm guarantees to the company. No mining expropriation was contemplated, Cárdenas repeatedly stressed.[67] Nor was the collective contract achieved. Instead, an agreement was signed early in April 1938 that maintained the system of local labor contracts preferred by the company.[68] If there was collusion between Asarco and the oil companies, it was Asarco that emerged the winner. What seems clear, however, is that the perception of collusion existed, reinforcing the belief that the oil companies were engaged in a systematic campaign of obstruction and quasi-sabotage, which threatened the health of the economy and the viability of the *cardenista* reform project. As the president addressed the STPRM in February 1938:

in order that the forward movement of the Revolution may continue and that . . . its eminently constructive action be not retarded it is necessary that we be prepared at all times to resist, even at a cost of serious sacrifice, attacks by those who do not understand the justice of the Mexican cause and who seek to bring about its failure by creating a situation of uncertainty and alarm. Such seems to be the case with the Petroleum Companies in their recent attitude. . . . when they have hurriedly withdrawn their deposits and have carried on an intentional publicity campaign to create alarm among businessmen and to restrict or refuse further credit to industries. They have done this as if they were trying to use illegal coercion for the purpose of enforcing a definite decision to the benefit of their commercial interests.[69]

Cárdenas's allegation, therefore, was that now, as in the past, the oil companies were playing fast and loose with Mexican sovereignty, setting themselves above the law, defying the government, jeopardizing the economy, and obstructing the legitimate goals of the Revolution. These were the charges leveled in the celebrated address of 18 March—written by Múgica and read by Cárdenas over the radio: that the companies had, for months, sustained an "underhanded and able campaign" designed to "seriously injure the economic interests of the Nation"; in which they succeeded, raising the prospect of fuel shortages, threatening the paralysis of commerce and the banking system, the termination of public works, and, in short, "a crisis incompatible not only with our progress but with the very peace of the Nation," which further raised the possibility that "the existence of the Government itself would be greatly endangered, for if the economic power of the State were lost, political power would likewise be lost and chaos would ensue." Privately, too, Beteta explained that Cárdenas felt that "the responsibility for the break was due to the oil companies and he (Beteta) said that the financial situation was so acute Cárdenas felt that longer delay would be injurious."[70]

The companies, of course, denied such allegations; but they no more saw Cárdenas's point of view than he saw theirs (empathy had never been Cárdenas's strong point). The outcome, always potential if not inevitable, was a mutual flight from compromise, hence an outright confrontation. It was, as one observer, striving successfully for cliché, put it, the old collision between the irresistible force and the immovable object.[71]

The effects of the collision, of course, went far beyond the petroleum sector itself. March 1938 thus offers the example of a historical climacteric, within both the Cárdenas administration and the Revolution as a whole. Historians unanimously assert that it was a great event, evoking profound emotions, elevating presidential prestige, dealing a blow to imperialism, marking a fresh revolutionary conquest. Precisely because of its mythic status, however, the expropriation has remained wreathed in nebulosity. In the latter part of this chapter, I will try to dissipate some of the clouds; I will attempt this by looking, first and very rapidly, at the event, then, a little more analytically, at the rhetoric, the popular response, and the longer-term outcome.

In the short term, the expropriation proceeded remarkably smoothly (contingency plans had, of course, been made in the preceding days). Mexican personnel took charge of the company installations and, contrary to many predictions (made by those ignorant of the precedent of 1914), proved entirely capable of handling the day-to-day technical operation of the enterprises.[72] The problems that the newly nationalized industry faced—analyzed elsewhere by Adler, Barbosa, Olvera, and others—were of a different character, and reflected management failings, continued labor unrest, and, of course, the companies' boycott. Notwithstanding even these serious problems, it was the relative success, rather than the failure, of the newly nationalized industry that struck critics (certainly those who had initially and confidently expected disaster): "in a period of just over seven months," a long British Foreign Office resumé of December 1938 concluded, "it would appear that Mexico . . . had made considerable progress in the running of an industry which calls for much technical and specialised knowledge."[73]

What is more, the change of control—the first on such a scale in the global history of the oil industry—appears to have proceeded with relatively little rancor and virtually no violence. Foreign fears of persecution proved unfounded; apart from a few harmless rhetorical flourishes ("the ambition of the foreigner is now at an end," a gatekeeper at Minatitlán allegedly declared, barring the way to a "foreign official"), there was no xenophobic sentiment.[74] The best complaint the Aguila Company could muster came from their general manager, who protested the "discourteous and unceremonious eviction of himself and his foreign assistants from their offices by members of the sindicato." Reports to company headquarters in London, however, indicated "no disturbances anywhere and general syndical feeling not unfriendly." An alleged confrontation at the Tampico Terminal Building proved, on further investigation, to be greatly exaggerated. Conditions in Tampico remained "quiet" and "outwardly calm"; elsewhere, the turnover of the distribution network (which covered the bulk of the country) was similarly smooth, although gasoline supplies ran low in places.[75]

Subsequently, as patriotic demonstrations began to take place across the country, they were rarely if ever characterized by overt displays of anti-Americanism: demonstrators were never violent, and rarely even abusive.[76] In some cases, American spectators watched the proceedings with interest and impunity. A demonstration was held in a "very orderly manner" at Torreón, where "the banners and placards carried in the procession carried no special reference to the U.S. or its citizens"; there was "no evidence of anti-American feeling" at Guadalajara; at Matamoros, where the parade passed in front of the consulate, the consul described how "all of the marchers appeared to be in high good humor and seemed to be enjoying the opportunity of marching and reciting their pieces. No disorders of any kind were reported. I saw no placards directed against the U.S. or against Americans and heard no shouts in which either was mentioned." So, too, at other border towns: Nuevo Laredo ("most orderly and without any . . . manifestations of animosity or ill will towards anyone"), Piedras Negras, and Mexicali. Tampico witnessed "no anti-American demonstrations of any kind," while reports of anti-American outbreaks in Mexico City were publicly denied by Ambassador Daniels. At Monterrey, finally, despite references to foreign exploitation and demands of "Mexico for the Mexicans," "no insults to the American government were made nor have . . . any reports of American citizens being molested" come to light; indeed, there were "many American tourists on the streets during the parade who appeared to be enjoying the spectacle."[77]

It is worth stressing, therefore, that the expropriation was not accompanied by displays of outright hostility, still less violence. Now, as in the past, anti-American (not to mention anti-British) sentiment was somewhat cerebral, certainly very distinct from the popular xenophobia that had been vented against other foreign groups—Spaniards and Chinese—especially during the armed revolution.[78] How, then, should the popular mood be gauged? What did "the people" think of the expropriation? And how did the regime seek to win support for this act of "incredible temerity," whose consequences remained incalculable?[79] The received opinion is that Mexico was swept by a wave of patriotic jubilation, a national *ralliement* that united regions, creeds, and classes in an unprecedented display of nationalist cohesion. Cárdenas himself claimed a "surge of enthusiasm" that filled every corner of the country; "in a surge of national passion," a historian recounts, Cárdenas "was upheld by everyone."[80]

If this is true—and it is certainly broadly believed to be true—then historians and political scientists have somewhat neglected the significance of this event. After all, as recent scholarship stresses, independent Mexico remained, right through the nineteenth and well into the twentieth century, a politically and culturally fragmented country, torn by linguistic, ethnic, and regional divisions. Furthermore, I would add, the relatively recent experience of the armed revolution had revealed not the strength but the weakness of the country's coherence, of its "common culture," of its unifying sentiments of nationalism. How does 1938 fit this picture? Either national cohesion was older and greater than usually supposed; or it had advanced significantly in the twenty years since the Revolution; or the degree of cohesion displayed in 1938 was less than generally supposed. In my tentative view, the first explanation is the least satisfactory; the second and third have a good deal to recommend them, as I shall briefly suggest. In this final part of the chapter, therefore, I will be using 1938 as a kind of litmus test of Mexican national cohesion and consciousness.

First, a word about the rhetoric of 1938. Historians today pay more attention to rhetoric—verbal rhetoric, verbal and iconographic symbols—than they have in the past. It may be worth pausing to consider the kind of symbols and images evoked during the heady days of spring 1938. First, as might be expected, cold cost-benefit analysis did not figure very prominently. The expropriation was rarely justified by a careful appeal to economic benefit (on the contrary, we shall note, the economic *costs* were more often stressed; Mexicans were urged to tighten, not to loosen, their belts). Second, we may discern two distinct discourses at work: one radical and anti-imperialist, the other more mainstream traditional and patriotic. Symbolically, we may see them as represented by the red flag and the tricolor, respectively. At Guadalajara, both flew together; but, we should note, "although red banners were greatly in evidence . . . such banners were greatly outnumbered by Mexican flags which were carried for the most part by school children." This was not just a manifestation of *tapatío* conservatism. Elsewhere, too, the tricolor prevailed over the red flag, literally as well as figuratively: at Monterrey "many Mexicans of prominence were heard to remark that it was surprising to see the national colors being carried by labor groups who had heretofore only marched with their red and black flags."[81] Anti-imperialism, in other words, was a minor current, which fed into the grander patriotic mainstream.

The chief exponents of the radical, anti-imperialist discourse were the labor unions, the schoolteachers (in some respects, a distinct subsection of the labor movement of whom more anon), and, to a lesser degree, the organized peasantry. The ample presidential files are full of radical applause and exhortation, sometimes couched in popular front terminology and given a global gloss: "magnificent enthusiasm for the call you make to the people against imperialist enemies and (for) the united front of workers of the world against criminal aggressors . . . and incendiaries of (a) new world war." Recurrent images are: "the claws of yankee imperialism" (never "gringo"); the "octopus" of the oil companies; even, in one case, more graphic than zoologically correct, the "claws of the octopus."[82] The labor unions, who provided the backbone of the big 23 March demonstration in Mexico City carried placards reading: "against the imperialist mire (*sic*)—united oppressed people"; "Marx, Lenin, Cárdenas." Previously, students had carried giant coffins filled with old oil cans and labeled "imperialism U.S.A.," which they had burned in front of the National Palace. Some demonstrators demanded further expropriations—of the tramway company, for example (a few radicals like Adalberto Tejeda, concurred, but the government would have none of it).[83] Similarly, in San Luis, where the CTM confronted an old enemy, state boss Saturnino Cedillo, some radical banners were to be seen:

"yankee imperialismo is carrying off the wealth of the country"; "Cárdenas will free Mexico from the Foreign Capitalist Yoke"; and (another call for further expropriation?) "Asarco exploits Mexico. It doesn't repay the sacrifice of Mexicans."[84] And in Monterrey, another state where the CTM contested the power of local conservatives, "labor unions carried the national colors, followed by union black and red flags and banners with various inscriptions of adhesion to President Cárdenas in liberating the country from imperialistic capital, [and] Yankee control."[85]

Here, as in several cases, Mexico figured as a bulwark of Latin solidarity against Yankee imperialism; a gesture, no doubt, to Lombardo Toledano's new continental project (the CTAL), but also a resurrection of an old theme—sometimes an old Catholic and conservative theme— now put to radical new music.[86] This, indeed, was a recurrent feature of the patriotic motifs of 1938: they blended the old and the new in a powerful symphony, capable of arousing a very varied audience—which, as a rule, would not have considered dancing together. Denunciations of "imperialism," for example, did not necessarily imply a commitment to radicalism, and they easily led into conventional historical invocations of 1810: the alien exploitation of Anglo-American companies was assimilated to that of the Spanish colonial past: the companies treat Mexico as "their fief" as a "colonial fief," or a "colonial country" rather than a free nation. "The Mexican Republic is not a colony," declared an indignant official press. In this, of course, popular—actually, CTM— terminology followed that of elite nationalists like Beteta; and, in a sense, it mirrored the quasi-colonial assumptions of magnates like Deterding.[87] This the government encouraged. The official press de- nounced "the feudal conditions which the petroleum barons maintained in their oil fields" and the "condition of a colonial country" that Mexico suffered—until now. "For those who feel themselves to be colonial masters, no crime is so abominable as the attempt of subjects to behave like free men."[88] Historical allusions were to be seen on the marchers' placards: in Tampico, "the dates 1810 and 1938 appeared, the first referring to the independence of Mexico and the second to the indepen- dence of the workers."[89]

The official press harped on this, a staple theme. "Economic indepen- dence" was being fought for in 1938 just as political independence had been won in 1810; the economic tyranny of the oil companies was a throwback to the eighteenth century, when "feudal" (sic) exploiters ransacked colonies and made fortunes for European metropolises.[90] Cárdenas's broadcast of 18 March—Lombardo explained, also by radio— was "tantamount to a declaration of economic independence in the same way as the one issued in 1821 marked the political independence of

Mexico"; "after more than a century," Lombardo went on, "the political revolution had produced—dialectically—the economic revolution."[91] "Let us renew the thread of our history," *El Nacional* exhorted: "first, political independence, then internal emancipation, today the implacable rupture of the umbilical cord which ties us to imperialism."[92] Supreme Court judge Icaza came up with a different, and apter, analogy: with "a little good will," he declared, the conflict could have been avoided; but, now that it was unavoidably thrust upon the Mexican people, it was "perhaps as well . . . in order that the people of Mexico might have an opportunity to temper their steel and to repeat a struggle similar to that which ended with the death of Maximilian."[93] The concept of race, too, offered a means to link old images—reminiscent of the ancient *indígenismo* of Fray Servando—to the new radical *indigenismo* of the 1930s. Demonstrators were summoned onto the streets of Mexico City, "the cradle of the race," to display their support for the government, while the Department of the Federal District organized—as an "affirmation of the spirit of the race"—a historical reconstruction of the birth of the Fifth Sun at Teotihuacán.[94] Again, provincial opinion (the Bakers Unions of Ahualulco, Jalisco: a major center of anti-Spanish protest in the late colony) echoed such official imagery: it was time for the sons of Mexico's "brave and oppressed race, which in its own time displayed its patriotism" to assert themselves in the face of a new oppression.[95]

"Imperialism" thus easily entered the vocabulary of many who were neither Marxists nor Lombardistas nor even necessarily left-of-center radicals. It afforded a bridge between the minority left, strong for popular frontism, anti-fascism, and anti-imperialism (imperialism, that is, in the modern, Marxist sense), and the majority, for whom "imperialism" was essentially an additional epithet within the long litany of traditional patriotic invective: "these imperialist companies . . . [these] exploiters . . . tyrants (*berdugos* [*sic*]), assassins, Pariahs."[96] Here we encounter a much older, mainstream discourse. It is the discourse of traditional patriotism, especially liberal patriotism. Its emphases are political: that is, it stresses less economic subjection or exploitation than insults to Mexican honor, decorum, prestige, integrity, sovereignty. The key words are: *decoro nacional; integridad nacional; soberanía nacional.* Thus: "the Government of Mexico has done nothing more than maintain national decorum and the prestige of its institutions." The basic question was no longer the labor dispute but rather the companies' defiance of the Supreme Court: "to rebel thus against a definitive resolution means to deny the sovereignty of Mexico."[97] Blood, too, is a recurrent traditional image (as it was in Zapata's Plan de Ayala, for example): the foreign companies have drawn "a constant hemorrhage (*perpetua sangría*) from Mexico's subsoil"; "independence is won with blood"; "the Nation writes its history in its own blood." And the concluding demand is for national unity above all, irrespective of class or ideology: "divisions based on differences of opinion, or party or group allegiances, yield before the supreme imperative of national security."[98]

No less traditional was the cult of the caudillo. As never before, Cárdenas was elevated to mythic status. Here was a president disliked by many (notably, the urban middle class), and scarcely the embodiment of Mexican macho values. True, he was tall and athletic, but he was also somewhat simple in dress, wooden in manner, and weak-chinned in appearance; his oratory was poor, he eschewed violence, he rarely drank, and he abhorred bloodsports and gambling. Nevertheless, Cárdenas now won converts far beyond his old political constituencies—workers, peasants, and leftist activists—and became a heroic symbol of the nation in its struggle against foreign oppression. If contemporary rhetoric was— I shall suggest in a moment—positively Churchillian, the hero-worship recalls, even literally, Canning's famous toast to Pitt the Younger in 1802: "Here's to the Pilot that weathered the storm." Thus, "like an accomplished and serene pilot" ("serene" is a recurrent epithet) "placed in command of a drifting ship, who espies port far off in the midst of a storm, but who espies it and is resolved to reach it, the President steered with alacrity" and speedily accomplished the decisive act of expropriation.[99] Thus, "national sovereignty was asserted by the voice of a man who is the depository of unanimous popular confidence"; thus, Cárdenas, "for his ability to embody the genius of our nationality at the critical moment, deserves endless recognition in the annals of Latin American liberty."[100] Street placards similarly lauded Cárdenas and his bold resolution: "three years of Cárdenas in power are a thousand years of conquests and revolutionary emancipation, which no-one else had achieved"; "we workers salute the virile attitude of Cárdenas." "Virile attitude" cropped up in laudatory messages, too; freemasons applauded their fellow mason for his "strong-man spirit"; he was the "Michoacán [Seigneur de] Bayard."[101] It was as if many of Cárdenas's compatriots were surprised as the dour reformer, worthy but dull, was suddenly transformed into the bold patriot, who had tweaked the tail of the British lion and the beard of Uncle Sam and done both with apparent impunity. "The general feeling here," the British Minister reported in April 1938, "is that the President has 'got away with'" the expropriation to "a degree exceeding all expectation." "A clever steal," they considered it in Durango. Government circles thus evinced a new self-confidence. "The national pride is aroused," Foreign Minister Hay told Daniels, "and there is no doubt that the oil matter will work out well"; Cárdenas himself was said to be "in a mood of extreme self-congratulation and self-confidence."[102]

The president thus tasted the nectar of nationalist adulation; it did not, perhaps, go to his head, but it gave him a sensation—of unprecedented popularity, of patriotic exaltation—that was bound to affect his politics. It also represented, perhaps, the fulfillment of his adolescent dreams of glory.

Meanwhile, contemporary rhetoric not only deemphasized but even denied the economic dimension of the conflict. Thus, the struggle concerned higher, spiritual values: Cárdenas's broadcast was "an appeal to [his listeners'] most intimate spiritual realities." It was an appeal positively Churchillian in some of its emphases, in its call for sacrifice, for—in so many words—blood, toil, tears, and sweat. "If it becomes necessary we will sacrifice all the constructive activities in which the Nation has entered during my period of Government," the president proclaimed over the radio.[103] The newly acquired petroleum was a responsibility, not a bonanza (the contrast with the assumptions of the late 1970s is striking); it would take an uphill struggle to meet the challenge, but the Mexican people would be equal to it. "No matter the sacrifice which we have to assume," declared the official press, "our people is temperate, the Government is honest, and, in payment for the redemption of the national patrimony, they will both know how to withstand the privations which economic reprisal may produce."[104]

Of course, this was good, realistic politics, since reprisals were in the offing. But the theme of sacrifice, of belt-tightening, of stoicism, went beyond prudential tactics. It exemplified the mood of the time. The motif of blood recurs: "liberties are won with sacrifice and independence with blood." The oil workers promise "whatever sacrifice may be necessary rather than to allow the capitalist imperialists to trample on our laws and national honor." The CTM proposes a special tax, greeted by *Excelsior* with the headline "the people's sacrifice." The military commander of Yucatán makes an ostentatious family contribution to the petroleum indemnity fund and stresses, in an open letter to the president, the need for "personal sacrifices," a theme that Hay stresses in conversation with Daniels, and that Cárdenas himself takes up, warning a crowd of 200,000 in the Zocalo that "labor will have to bear its share . . . to guarantee the Nation's 'claim to independence.'"[105]

It is almost a case of *fiat justicia, ruat economia:* "Let the collapse come; let our money depreciate, let us be corralled in the economy of isolated peoples; let the Mexicans' belt be tightened ten holes. But let the country's independence take precedence over lusts, over ambitions, over the will of the public enemies of democracy."[106] Street placards pick up the theme: "The patriotic policy of President Cárdenas in the petroleum conflict must be supported at whatever sacrifice by every Mexican" (San Luis slogan). And Foreign Minister Hay tells the U.S. ambassador that "his countrymen were united in this resolve and ready to make any sacrifices to meet their objectives."[107] Those who call for sacrifice, of course, are often not the ones who practice it. There was, no doubt, much genuine patriotism and sense of self-abnegation upon which the government could count. But, behind the calls for unity and sacrifice there was something of a hidden or latent agenda. And here we broach the question of the deeper politics of the expropriation, and of the legacy it left the country. To understand this, we need first to say something about popular reactions to the expropriation, then, finally, to see how they were channeled—even manipulated—in the interests of this hidden agenda.

The conventional view, already mentioned, is that the expropriation rallied broad support in an unprecedented display of Mexican patriotism. It is probably true that the reaction was unprecedented. Nationalist rallies had been attemped during the armed revolution—in protest at the U.S. occupation of Veracruz, for example—but they were of scant impact or duration.[108] Those of 1938 were bigger, better organized, and often more genuine. Up to 200,000 took to the streets in Mexico City (a "monstrous demonstration," in the garbled words of the U.S. ambassador); 20,000 each in San Luis, Monterrey, Tampico, and Guadalajara; 6,000 in Juárez; 3,000 in Piedas Negras. In several communities, these were the biggest street demonstrations ever witnessed: "unprecedented popular demonstrations," for example, took place in southern Sonora (Guaymas, Ciudad Obregón, Navojoa).[109] These were not, of course, spontaneous eruptions (though the occasional *manifestación espontánea* was claimed, and the president, addressing his assembled state governors, had stipulated that, in respect to public support, "no quiero nada que no sea espontáneo").[110]

In fact, of course, these were carefully organized events. Even before the expropriation, as labor and agrarian groups, emulating the oil companies, lobbied and propagandized, the government declared an imminent national petroleum week, during which teachers and officials would go to the people "to explain the background of the present oil controversy and the policy which the government is following to free the country from foreign monopolies."[111] Thereafter, certain key groups distinguished themselves in the work of mobilization: government departments, the labor unions, the teachers, ejidal commissions, veterans' associations, and masonic lodges. The CTM probably played the biggest role, not only marshaling demonstrators but also organizing write-in campaigns (the Cárdenas papers are full of letters and telegrams, many of them from CTM affiliates, following common formulae). Organized labor, the American ambassador correctly observed, enjoyed an influence out of proportion to its numbers. Unions provided the backbone of support in cities like Mérida and Piedras Negras. In particular, major industrial unions like the miners and the oil workers themselves were well briefed as to the precise details of the conflict (each "knows to the Nth degree how many Americans work in these fields and their compensation").[112] Networks of solidarity spread widely, linking city to countryside, mobilizing diverse groups such as the Revolutionary Federation of Laguna Region Workers, who, a week before the expropriation, demonstrated in support of the oil workers' claim; or the Sindicato de Trabajadores de Transporte Fluvial de la Industria Platanera y Similares de Tabasco, who pledged their support for Cárdenas "ante el case petrolero y platanero de esta entidad."[113] These were both CTM affiliates; and the CTM had its own agenda in respect to the oil expropriation (it was not simply an agent of the government). This agenda concerned both policy—the CTM was for nationalization and popular frontism— and also personnel: the CTM wanted to dislodge enemies (state governors like Cedillo and Yocupicio) and promote its friends.

Teachers also played a key role. They spread news of the conflict in remote Yucatan. They passed the word on to ejidal commissions, who cabled their support to the president. And they were prominent in the big street demonstrations, their placards particularly numerous, as they paraded their pupils, tricolors flying, in front of U.S. consulates.[114] Thus, while some citizens, like those of Tinguindín (Michoacán), received the news of recent events from the press (a controlled, subsidized and self-censored press); or even from pamphlets scattered from the air by government planes (at Mérida and Guaymas); others, perhaps more, relied on the local *maestro*, or on union and ejidal committees.[115] For, in a good many communities, literacy and newspaper circulation were still limited and the radio had not yet made an impact: in the border town of Matamoros, for example, opinion and information lagged behind those of neighboring Brownsville; even in metropolitan Guadalajara, the press, hit by strikes and closures, played only a small role (even when newspapers came out, they remained editorially inscrutable), leaving the work of propaganda and mobilization to other groups, political and clerical.[116] If in Guadalajara the pulpit preached national solidarity, elsewhere Masonic lodges (which could be working- as well as middle-class in composition) played their part, backing up a president who was also a masonic Grand Master; while, especially in the capital, the agencies of the federal government counted on their massive patronage to get crowds on to the streets. Here, on 23 March, all public offices, banks, and shops were closed, and government employees had to check in and out as the demonstration proceeded; "Quienes faltarán se harán acreedores de las sanciones respectivas" read the official instructions.[117] So, too, at Agua Prieta customs officials had to parade, like it or not (and some allegedly did not). And, soon, municipal and federal officials, army officers and trade unionists began to make their contributions, spontaneous or prompted, to the ill-fated petroleum indemnity fund.[118]

The newly expanded ejidal sector also provided a host of recruits. Agraristas and ejidatarios were prominent in demonstrations at Torreón, hub of the recently reformed Laguna; at Durango, where they "were brought into the city by trucks at the expense of the state government"; at Ensenada, where "a very high percentage of the persons who took part in the demonstration were agrarians from the various ejidos in the neighborhood of the community," who allegedly attended "under threat of punishment for failure to do so"; and at Agua Prieta, where "agrarians ... and certain other leftist elements" took the lead, which the reluctant customs officials followed.[119] Official indigenista organizations also spread the word; the press claimed, lyrically and unconvincingly, that "even the most ignorant Indians intuitively know of the greatness and gravity of the step which our government has taken."[120] There is little hard evidence of this. However, communications to the president do suggest that awareness of this national issue had penetrated to self-confessed remote corners of outlying states like Tabasco; they also suggest, if only by their indifferent spelling, some genuinely popular, as opposed to official, support: condemnations of the "empreza imperializta El Aguila" from an agrarian committee near Agua Dulce, Veracruz; "Lásaro Cardenas, sinsera felisitación" from building workers in Cd. Anáhuac, Nuevo León.[121]

What this reveals, obviously enough, is the newfound capacity of the state to tap popular support and, further, to manipulate mass organizations. "Newfound" because the operation was much more successful than previous attempts (the 1914 mobilization—admittedly undertaken in difficult circumstances, yet spurred by outright invasion—was amateurish in comparison: the levers of power were, in those days, feeble or nonexistent). March 1938 thus offers an ideal example of the new *política de masas* which, it is often asserted, was the chief legacy of the Mexican Revolution. But, from this perspective, it is a revealingly ambivalent example. For the mobilization was far from unanimous, enthusiastic and compelling (as it is often depicted); it revealed the fractures as well as the solidarities of "revolutionary" political society. Its scope was certainly a tribute to the growing organizational powers of unions, ejidal committees, teachers, masonic lodges. But its content was less impressive. The mobilizers could count on genuine support—it would be quite wrong to see the whole episode as one of sheer manipulation—but they sometimes had to work hard upon apathetic populations, and their efforts were not always successful. Nor were their objectives as disinterested and transparent as sometimes suggested.

Here, of course, the evidence may be questioned. U.S. consuls were probably very ready to discern apathy and manipulation. On the other hand, some commented on the "enthusiastic support" given to the government, for example, by the labor unions at Piedras Negras.[122] Others made distinctions: in Mérida, the consul accosted "persons with whom he is acquainted (who were) on their way to form the parade and many of them said, in their inimical (*sic*) manner, 'mi sindicato me ha mandado que yo vaya, y qué voy a hacer?'"; yet, the consul went on, "there are many who are absolutely loyal to the labor syndicates and to the government."[123] Elsewhere, apathy was stressed: at Monterrey (not altogether surprisingly); at Durango (also a traditionally conservative city); at San Luis (likewise); and border towns like Ensenada, Nuevo Laredo, and Piedras Negras (bar the labor unions).[124]

Three points are worth making about these reports of alleged apathy. First, apathy—to the extent that it existed—did not prevent sizable demonstrations' being mounted. The greater the apathy, the greater must have been the pulling power of official clientelism. Second, the country was far from homogeneous. Even a cursory analysis reveals significant variations by regions and classes. As regards regions, it is not surprising that conservative towns like Monterrey, San Luis, or Durango should drag their feet. Here, demonstrations were chiefly the work of leftist syndical and agrarian minorities, then engaged in battles with conservative opponents. In some states, indeed, the politics of the oil expropriation hinged upon these old and deep divisions; far from indicating a unanimous patriotic sentiment, they simply provided another chapter in a long saga of local political conflict. In Sonora, for example where the CTM was at loggerheads with the conservative Govenor Yocupicio, the unions and agrarians (especially those of southern Sonora) used the oil issue to mobilize against the governor; but Yocupicio, an old political hand, smartly and apparently successfully jumped aboard the patriotic/petroleum bandwagon himself.[125] In San Luis, a similar confrontation was being enacted, although here the pressure of the *cardenista* forces, now possessed of a new patriotic issue, forced the less canny Cedillo into a fatal rebellion.[126] In Sinaloa, too, the petroleum issue was taken up by rival factions, contesting for power in a notoriously fractious state;[127] while in Jalisco, the *callista* old guard, politically bloodied but unbowed, used the issue to reassert their political legitimacy and to reach a modus vivendi with the powerful church hierarchy—who, of course, were also playing politics with their newfound sentiment of *ralliement*. We will return to that case in conclusion. Wherever one looks, it seems, the politics of national unity appear, on closer inspection, to resemble the politics of local faction.

These regional distinctions are also bound up with class. Monterrey's ostensible apathy had a lot to do with the political predominance of the powerful Nuevo León bourgeoisie who—no archetypal national bourgeoisie here—opposed the expropriation, though they preferred to do so silently and covertly, anticipating with relish the "disastrous defeat" that they thought Cárdenas would eventually suffer.[128] This pattern was common across the nation, and it must seriously qualify the picture of national unanimity that some accounts suggest. One insider got it right: according to Víctor Manuel Villaseñor,

> the version that the Mexican people, to a man, impelled by a
> patriotic impulse, gave Cárdenas the gift of their unconditional
> support in those decisive moments now forms part of the legend of
> our history. Nothing is more false. True, the real people, the
> humble workers and common employees, responded. . . . But this
> was not the case with the employers' sector, the ghosts mourning
> for the Porfiriato, the enriched "revolutionaries," nor for many
> men and women of . . . the middle class who, in their little circles,
> gleefully commented that "snouty is now heading for a fall." In
> hypocritical fashion, they feigned solidarity with the expropriation,
> but they did not relax their efforts to undermine the regime.[129]

More recently, Lorenzo Meyer concurred—in a sense—when he observed that "the nationalisation was popular because Cárdenas was popular."[130] True, for some sectors and regions; but then Cárdenas was also very *unpopular* in many sectors and regions. Of course, critics rarely dared openly oppose the president for fear of appearing unpatriotic or downright traitorous (and there were plenty of timely reminders: "to depart from the line of duty at this moment," warned the official press, "would be to betray the Nation").[131] But the lukewarm attitude of some was clear to observers.[132] For the moment, the critcs held their tongues. "There is strong feeling against the Cárdenas policies by Mexicans of wealth and the old Scientificos (*sic*)," the U.S. ambassador wrote, "they believe they [the policies] tend towards Communism and are hostile to such policies as expropriation. . . . But they are unorganised, have no political influence, and, when discussing any real organisation against the policies they do not like, they throw up their hands and ask 'what is the use?' Moreover, they are Mexicans and are unwilling to be regarded as lining up against their country when to do so will be to risk being called traitors and friends of foreign exploiters."[133]

So the disaffected bourgeoisie kept silent or joined the patriotic chorus *faute de mieux*. "My country right or wrong" (or "right or wrong, our country," as *Ultimas Notícias* put it, in English, misquoting Stephen Decatur) was a sentiment plugged by the press and clearly espoused by some anti-*cardenista* conservatives.[134] In Piedras Negras, "some who did not believe in the advisability of the expropriation . . . are now, for patriotic reasons, giving their support."[135] Meantime, the Monterrey bourgeoisie was not alone in opposing the expropriation and, further, in rejoicing at the prospect that—as Torreón businessmen believed—the execrated Cárdenas government had "undertaken more than it can succesfully handle."[136] At Agua Prieta, too, commercial interests were against the policy; at Durango "the sentiment and sympathy of the substantial class of citizens of this city was (*sic*) almost unanimously cemented in favor of the oil companies"; Cárdenas was "greatly and heatedly maligned" by businessmen in San Luis; while at Tampico "businessmen and professional men believe that the Government has made a very grave mistake in expropriating the oil companies."[137]

But the smartest conservatives discerned a positive advantage lurking in the politics of expropriation. They foresaw that it would further weaken an already shaky economy, and that, once the euphoria passed, Cárdenas's prestige would very likely wilt. A few *enragés* entertained the possibility of Cárdenas's overthrow (as did U.S. Secretary of State Sumner Welles, to a degree). But this was a vain hope. The army—if not unanimously enthusiastic—was fundamentally loyal, as were the vast majority of political officeholders.[138] Cedillo's revolt in May 1938 thus proved an instant failure; the threat of fascistic exiles like Nicolás Rodríguez excited the border press more than the Mexican public.[139] The more numerous cautious and canny conservatives, however, did not flirt with rebellion but looked instead to a more gradual political solution: a progressive erosion of *cardenismo*, a retreat from radicalism, the eventual peaceful establishment of a more congenial conservative regime.[140] Thus, even as the expropriation went through and Cárdenas's prestige—we are told, probably correctly—reached its peak, plans and predictions were already being made to ensure that a more conservative leader would succeed him. The name of Maximino Avila Camacho, Governor of Puebla, was touted; the touts got the right *apellido*, the wrong *nombre de pila*.[141] In general terms, however, they were not far wrong. Cárdenas's subsequent transition (1938–1940) from patriotic hero to presidential lame duck was surprisingly swift and debilitating.

The expropriation alone did not bring that about. The pendulum would have swung anyway; powerful forces—clericals, conservatives, *callistas*, fascists, and PNR/PRM "moderates"—were aligned against the president, awaiting the moment to strike. For some years, they had contested his reforms locally, subterraneanly, and often successfully. Now, after 1938, they began to organize more openly, nationally, and noisily. Within the PRM, they mobilized the center/right and blocked the left; outside, they formed the PAN and the host of right-wing parties and lobbies that pullulated in the years 1938–1940.[142] The expropriation was, however, important in accelerating this shift. It did so in two principal ways. First, on the socioeconomic front, it forced the government to retrench. The economic problems of 1937 were compounded: capital flight accelerated; the peso sank from 3.60 to 5.00 to the dollar in a matter of weeks; imports slumped instantly (sales of cars, refrigerators, radios virtually halted); tourism faltered; the government failed to meet its payroll and had to cut back on costly social reforms.[143] In respect to the oil industry itself, Cárdenas at once promised the companies a fair indemnity and guaranteed that further expropriations were out of the question. The oil expropriation had been "a totally exceptional measure which will not be extended to other activities in the country." The press blazoned this same guarantee.[144] The mining industry was safe, and radical hopes of further nationalizations were dashed.

What is more, the quest for economic stability led the government into confrontation with organized labor, its oldest, best ally. This was not entirely new—the government had always discriminated in its legalization of strikes—but now judgment erred on the side of caution, even conservatism. On the radio, Cárdenas appealed for "absolute tranquillity in centers of work, the encouragement of production, and effort that was unanimous and productive, without prejudicial distractions": in other words, hard work and fewer strikes.[145] In some regions the effect was immediate. In Jalisco, "several strikes which had been threatened have been called off or indefinitely postponed."[146] The miners were obliged to drop their demands for a collective contract and were urged by the president "to slow down the tempo of unrest in the mining industry in order not to embarrass the Mexican Government."[147] The railwaymen, too, as they entered upon their brief period of control of the railways, did so under stringent financial conditions. And the oil workers soon found themselves at loggerheads with Cárdenas over the rationalization of the newly nationalized industry. As early as the spring and summer of 1938, it was clear that labor militancy was fast diminishing. The mines and smelters were quiet; at Torreón, Guadalajara, Chihuahua, and elsewhere the unions were on the defensive. By 1940, as the presidential election loomed, many of the major industrial unions were in open dissent, even to the extent of supporting Almazán; the *cardenista* coalition, which had seemed so potent in 1934–1937, was in open disarray. The oil nationalization did not cause that decline, but it contributed to it in significant measure. For, like their Bolivian counterparts, the Mexican revolutionary leadership found that nationalization, far from consolidating radical forces, served instead to divide them, pitting previously allied unions and *políticos* against each other, to the advantage of the conservative opponents of both.

In addition, the nationalization and the patriotic jamboree that ensued had a decisive *political* effect. The rhetoric of unity, patriotism, sacrifice, and serenity was well suited to the policies of retrenchment that now came to predominate. Class struggle was deplored; Mexicans should pull together for the common good. In this ideological shift, the expropriation proved crucial because it afforded a common stage for radicals, moderates, and conservatives, all of whom—for their quite different reasons—could now join in the chorus. All social classes should recognize that patriotism was not a question of shouting in street demonstrations, but rather of accepting hardship with stoicism, warned *Excelsior*; "from this day forth," proclaimed *Ultimas Notícias*, in distinctly Vichyite mood, "deeds, not parades, not words"; "work and more work"; "no more talk of class struggle, do not seek to practice it; that struggle makes us forget that we are one big family, one sole Nation, one will and one chief: Cárdenas."[148]

The local manifestations of this new political climate were varied and cannot be pursued here. But the case of Jalisco was interesting—not necessarily typical. Traditionally Catholic and conservative, possessed of strong *callista* elements within official circles, Jalisco offered a classic example of how the expropriation afforded an opportunity for moderate and conservative interests to recover the political initiative. Here, the Chamber of Commerce and Industry at once offered to collaborate with the state governor in a "patriotic effort of all Mexicans without distinction of beliefs, opinions, or socioeconomic categories"; thus displaying that "the Mexican people is capable of unity, coordination and resolute effort." It was, however, indispensable that this be done "under the standard of national union," for if "so noble a task were defiled by becoming a class or party manoeuvre," it would necessarily fail; furthermore, it could not be accepted "that these ends are incompatible with the honest work and legitimate property of those who are not wage-earners" (i.e., capital, too, had its place in the *union sacrée*).[149] This entrepreneurial *démarche* was promptly followed by a pastoral letter from the archbishop, staking a similar claim for the Catholic constituency: "We Catholics, who profess patriotism as one of the teachings of our religion, must, as Catholics set an example"; collections for the petroleum indemnity fund would therefore be taken in Jalisco's churches. The letter was to be followed up by further exhortations "assailing Communism and other radicalism and urging moderation."[150] These overtures met with a favorable official reception since, in Jalisco, "practically all of the principal state and municipal officers and PNR leaders are former Callistas and, although they climbed on the Cárdenas bandwaggon as a matter of political expediency, several are believed not to be very enthusiastic Cardenistas."[151]

Accordingly, the state governor spoke out, tacitly accepting the proferred olive branches of church and private enterprise. It was time, he declared, to terminate "the period of material and spiritual agitation and of adjustments which necessarily followed the violent phase of the Revolution"—and which responded to "social necessity" rather than "legal precepts"—and to achieve a "strict interpretation of the accomplishments of the revolution, preventing excesses which are so harmful to the social order which it is our duty to develop and protect." Now, "national consciousness fully appreciates that the present situation . . . requires harmony and unlimited coordination of the activities of all elements . . . (and) strict compliance with the laws so that every one and every group may enjoy the broad guarantees which the laws provide"; specifically—and "without abandonment of my revolutionary principles," the governor assured his listeners—the state administration will "endeavour to bring about the greatest possible cooperation and harmony . . . in an era of tranquillity and of work, based upon respect of small rural properties and in . . . just understanding of [the] problems of labor, avoiding all excesses contrary to the spirit of our laws."[152] This statement—vague and "susceptible of widely different interpretations," as the U.S. consul put it—is nevertheless clear in its intent. "It may be taken," the same consul cautiously concluded," . . . as an intended favorable gesture to business and industry."[153] He was right. But it was also a warning to organized labor and *agrarismo* and an endorsement of *pequeña propiedad*. Thus, it neatly summarized the concerns and appeals of the newly resurgent center/right. It was also—we can see with hindsight—a perfect prototype of the bland, reassuring rhetoric that characterized Avila Camacho's presidential campaign—and presidential term—when the external threat against whom Mexicans had to unite, work, and mobilize was no longer U.S. imperialism but Axis aggression.

Here was the latent agenda of the politics of expropriation: a statement that things had gone far enough; that it was time for retrenchment; that order and legality must prevail; that strikes must cease; that class solidarity must give way to national solidarity; that church, commerce, industry, and property must be protected; that, in short, the *cardenista* experiment had run its course. That there would no doubt have been such a reaction, oil expropriation or no, is certain. Whether, without the expropriation, it would have been so swift and successful is debatable. Certainly the expropriation, by virtue of its rhetoric and results, dealt the anti-*cardenistas* a winning hand. Above all, it obliged the administration to connive at its own demise by demanding syndical restraint, curtailing agrarian reform, dropping socialist education, espousing a bland patriotism, and promoting safe middle-of-the-road machine politicians. Much better that *cardenismo* perish at the friendly hands of the unknown soldier, Manuel Avila Camacho, than the calloused mitts of the old caudillo, Saturnino Cedillo. That was the safe, decorous, bloodless way to proceed. Ironically, the oil expropriation, which was the high point of the Cárdenas presidency, thus contributed significantly to the collapse of the *cardenista* project. From that high point, it was downhill all the way; and the kinetic energy built up in the exciting days of spring 1938 powered, above all, the resurgence of the political center and right.

Notes

1. Lorenzo Meyer, *México y Estados Unidos en el conflicto petrolero (1917–1942)* (Mexico City, 1968), is the best study.

2. Ibid., pp. 19, 29, 31.

3. Alan Knight, *U.S.-Mexican Relations, 1910–1940: An Interpretation* (Center for U.S.-Mexican Studies, University of California, San Diego, 1987), offers a recent résumé.

4. Jonathan Brown, "Why Foreign Oil Companies Shifted Production from Mexico to Venezuela during the 1920s," *American Historical Review* 90 (1985), pp. 362–385.

5. Meyer, *México y Estados Unidos*, pp. 176–188.

6. Ibid., p. 19. Meyer's figures do not suggest a significant relative fall in exports during the mid-1930s; other sources do. A detailed report, "Industria de la refinación y recursos nacionales de abastecimiento de productos petroleros," 18 Jan. 1935, gives exports of all categories of petroleum products, by volume, at only 34.5 percent of total production for 1934 (first ten months): Archivo General de la Nación, Presidentes, Lázaro Cárdenas, 545.3/236 (henceforth, AGN-LC). A State Department memo., 812.6363/3267, 23 March 1938, puts exports at just over 50 percent.

7. Luis González, *Historia de la revolución mexicana, 1934–40: Los artífices del cardenismo* (Mexico City, 1979), p. 51; the report of Ortiz Rubio in AGN-LC 527/6 gives details of Petromex performance.

8. Virginia Prewett, *Reportage on Mexico* (New York, 1941), p.117; Daniels, Mexico City, to Hull, 19 March 1938, State Department Archives, Documents Relating to the Internal Affairs of Mexico, 812.6363/3107 (henceforth: SD).

9. Meyer, *México y Estados Unidos*, chap. 8; Joe C. Ashby, *Organized Labor and the Mexican Revolution under Lázaro Cárdenas* (Chapel Hill, N.C., 1963), chap. 9.

10. Frank L. Kluckhohn, *The Mexican Challenge* (New York, 1939), p.10; Daniels, Mexico City, 19 March 1938, SD 812.6363/3103.

11. Memo of G. FitzMaurice, 31 March 1938, in FO 371/21465, A2690.

12. *Times* (London), 11 April 1938. A subsequent Foreign Office memo, Balfour, 1 Dec. 1938, FO 371/22770, A393, stressed the "malevolent advice and machinations" of Lombardo.

13. Daniels, Mexico City, 21 March 1938, SD 812.6363/3111. Múgica certainly had no qualms about encouraging German trade and investment: Múgica to Cárdenas, 23 March 1937, enclosing a commercial initiative from the German

Embassy, in *Desdeldiez*, July 1986, pp. 121–130.

14. Eduardo J. Correa, *El balance del cardenismo* (Mexico City, 1941), p.151; Miguel S. Wionczek, *El nacionalismo mexicano y la inversión extranjera* (Mexico, 1967).

15. O'Malley, Mexico City, 6 Jan. 1938, FO 371/21462, A674.

16. Cárdenas to G.Vázquez, 26 Nov. 1936, AGN-LC 432.2/253 (my italics).

17. O'Malley, Mexico City, 22 Dec. 1937, FO 371/21462, A284. The Mexican government also contended that the Poza Rica agreement, by virtue of yielding "royalties," implied company acceptance of the old government claim to subsoil ownership rights; the British, preferring "profit-pooling" to "royalties," questioned this conclusion. The important point is that the government has reason to see the Poza Rica deal as a major advance. For the Huasteca offer, see memo of Daniels/Cárdenas conversation, 22 March 1938, S.D.812.6363/3141.

18. *Times* (London), 21 March 1938.

19. Marvin D. Bernstein, *The Mexican Mining Industry, 1890–1950* (Albany, N.Y., 1964), p. 184. General Motors began operations in Mexico in 1935, Chrysler in 1938.

20. O'Malley, Mexico City, 27 Dec. 1937, FO 371/21462, A524.

21. L. Duggan, Division of the American Republics, State Department to Secretary of State Sumner Welles, 5 April 1938, S.D.812.6363/3374. The original source of the information was probably Pierre Boal, Counselor at the U.S. Embassy in Mexico City (Boal and Duggan ran a hot line, bypassing Ambassador Daniels).

22. Cosme Panti and others, Local 30, STPRM, to Cárdenas, 20 Aug. 1937, AGN-LC 527.1/8.

23. Daniels, 24 Feb.1938, S.D.812.6363/3075; Luis González, *Historia de la Revolución Mexicana 1934–1940, Los días del presidente Cárdenas* (Mexico City, 1981), p. 178.

24. Daniels, Mexico City, 21, 28 Jan. 1938, S.D.812.6363/3069, 3070.

25. Ibid., 21 March 1938, S.D.812.6363/3119.

26. Boal, Mexico City, to Duggan, 8 Jan. 1938; Daniels, Mexico City, 31 Jan. 1938, S.D.812.6363/3067, 3072.

27. Daniels, Mexico City, 19, 21, 22 March 1938, S.D.812.6363/3103, 3119, 3139.

28. Ibid., 19 March 1938, S.D.812.6363/3103.

29. *Boletín Financiero y Minero de México*, 19 March 1938; Víctor Manuel Villaseñor, *Memorias de un hombre de izquierda, I, Del Porfiriato al Cardenismo* (Mexico City, 1976), p. 413. For the sake of brevity, consular reports will be cited simply by place, date, and source location, thus: Guaymas, 31 March 1938, S.D.812.6363/3381.

30. Both the original quotation and the Bourbon analogy are taken from George Philip, *Oil and Politics in Latin America. Nationalist Movements and State Companies* (Cambridge, 1982), p. 225.

31. O'Malley, Mexico City, 30 Dec. 1937, FO 371/21461, A19.

32. Daniels, Mexico City, 19 March 1938 (twice), S.D.812.6363/3103, 3107. E. David Cronon, *Josephus Daniels in Mexico* (Madison, 1960), p. 183, questions whether the companies' belated offer of $7.2 million really represented an attempt at compromise.

33. It is often asserted that, at this critical juncture, Cárdenas offered the company representatives his personal word that the pay award would not have to exceed $7.2 million, to which a representative replied, "that is hardly sufficient," thus incurring presidential ire and prompt expropriation. The original source (see Cronon, *Josephus Daniels*, p.184) is a private communication of Pierre Boal to E. David Cronon. However, Eduardo Suárez, who was present at the meeting in question, deems this "absolutely untrue": Suárez, *Comentarios y recuerdos* (1926–1946) (Mexico City, 1977), p. 193.

34. William Cameron Townsend, *Lázaro Cárdenas, Mexican Democrat* (Ann Arbor, 1952), p. 44.

35. Francisco Múgica, "Su paso por la Huasteca Veracruzana (1928)," *Desdeldiez*, Sept. 1984, pp. 34–86. The boom-and-bust character of the petroleum enclaves exercised many official minds: "the regions where the oil industry is established. . . .develop an artificial and unreliable existence, since their prosperity is transient; when the industry is paralysed . . . they experience a situation of general inactivity, bringing poverty to the . . .working classes, while the exploiters dispose as they please of their profits": Secretaría de Economía Nacional, Ley de Petróleo, 30 Dec.1935, Exposición de Motivos (the work of a committee including Ramón Beteta): AGN-LC, 545.2/67.

36. Murray, Mexico City, 15 July 1935, FO 371/18708, A6865.

37. O'Malley, Mexico City, 19 Jan. 1938, FO 371/21462, A481.

38. Romana Falcón, *Revolución y caciquismo. San Luis Potosí 1910–1938* (Mexico City, 1984), p. 264; Dudley Ankerson, *Agrarian Warlord Saturnino Cedillo and the Mexican Revolution in San Luis Potosí* (DeKalb, Ill., 1984), p. 179.

39. Ortiz Rubio to Cárdenas, 15 July 1937, AGN-LC 527.1/19.

40. Cf. L. Denny, *We Fight for Oil* (New York, 1925).

41. O'Malley, Mexico City, 4 Jan.1938, FO 371/21461, A98, stressed the "intense suspicion of [the] Mexican authorities of [the] companies' capacity to conceal their real profits." For an early example of the companies' propensity to cry "Wolf!": Meyer, *México y Estados Unidos*, pp. 48–49.

42. Murray, Mexico City, 17 Sept. 1935, FO 371/18708, A8586, quoting Assheton of the Aguila Co. On alleged conditions in the oil zone: Antonio Rodríguez, *El rescate del petróleo Epopeya de un pueblo* (Mexico City, 1958), pp. 39–66.

43. Philip, *Oil and Politics*, p. 206; Cowdray to Bowring, 16 Dec. 1913, S. Pearson Papers, box A3.

44. O'Malley, Mexico City, 21 Dec. 1937, FO 371/21462, A285.

45. T. R. Armstrong to Sumner Welles, 9 May 1938, S.D.812.6363/4003.

46. Prewett, *Reportage*, p. 108.

47. González, *Los artífices del cardenismo*, p. 119.

48. Enrique Krauze, *Lázaro Cárdenas, General misionero* (Mexico City, 1987), pp. 16–18.

49. Kluckhohn, *The Mexican Challenge*, p. 144.

50. The same analogy occurs to González, *Los días del presidente Cárdenas*, p. 180. Prewett, *Reportage*, p. 125, comments: "Cárdenas' method in the face of a serious threat was always to take the bold course."

51. Krauze, *Lázaro Cárdenas*, pp. 40–50, which in turn tends to follow

Victoriano Anguiano Equihua, *Lázaro Cárdenas, su feudo y la política nacional* (Mexico City, 1951).

52. Kluckhohn, *The Mexican Challenge*, pp. 96–97; Cronon, *Josephus Daniels*, pp. 17–25.

53. R. C. Tanis, State Department, memo of conversation with Bohanon of Standard Oil of New Jersey, 19 March 1938, S.D.812.6363/3208.

54. O'Malley, Mexico City, 11 April 1938, FO 371/21465, A2820.

55. L. P. to Godber (Aguila Co.), 18 March 1938, FO 371/21463, A2139.

56. Nora Hamilton, *The Limits of State Autonomy, Post-Revolutionary Mexico* (Princeton, N.J., 1982), pp. 190–191, 223–225; the quotation from Beteta in O'Malley, Mexico City, 6 Jan. 1938, FO 371/21461, A145.

57. González, *Los días del presidente Cárdenas*, p. 178; Suárez, in his memoirs, remains inscrutable.

58. Both Huerta and Carranza, from their very different standpoints, refused to make unpalatable political concessions in return for proffered U.S. financial aid. Such stances, of course, derived from a broader, politically bipartisan suspicion of any U.S. manipulation (Knight, *U.S.-Mexican Relations*, pp. 31–33).

59. Leopoldo Palazuelos and Jorge González Guevara to Cárdenas, 1, 2 June 1937, AGN-LC 432.2/253.

60. Communications to Cárdenas from: Prescott Allen, 29 May 1937; José Tamborrel, 2 June 1937; J. de la Torre, 20 Aug. 1937; R. Yocupicio, 7 June 1937; Cooperative de Plataneros de Ojitlán, 31 May 1937: in AGN-LC 432.2/253.

61. Report of Francisco Urrutia (Gobernación informer?) on meeting of Comité de Solidaridad Huelga de Trabajadores Petroleros, Mexico City, 2 June 1937, AGN-LC 432.2/253. As Ramón Beteta explained to the Dutch ambassador, "while...no distinction could be drawn between labor issues and politics....this [the labour] factor constituted a permanent unknown" (Philip, *Oil and Politics*, p. 215); even Kluckhohn, fond of stressing centralized, conspiratorial decision making, believed that "sometimes the unionists are mere government tools; at others, an independent force" (*Mexican Challenge*, p. 219).

62. Memo by Duggan, 5 Jan.1938, S.D.812.6363/3065; O'Malley, Mexico City, 21 Dec. 1937, FO 371/21462, A285, adding that Anderson is "rather inclined to violence" and "not at all amenable to moderating advice" from U.S. diplomats.

63. Ashby, *Organized Labor*, p. 100; Bernstein, *Mexican Mining Industry*, p. 181.

64. E. D. McLaughlin, U.S. Commercial Attaché, Mexico City, 19 March 1938, enclosed in S.D.812.6363/3108.

65. Daniels, Mexico City, 19 March 1938, S.D.812.6363/3092.

66. Ibid., S.D.812.6363/3104; *El Nacional*, 19 March 1938. Asarco—a critical historian states—did not in fact collude with the oil companies in 1937; but other lesser mining companies, he further suggests, "dream(ed) of the united front— the simultaneous closure of all properties—by which they hoped to paralyze the government and stir up local forces of reaction to rise in revolt": Harvey O'Connor, *The Guggenheims* (New York, 1937), p. 340. Cronon, *Josephus Daniels*, p. 181, agrees that Asarco rebuffed the oil companies' overtures.

67. Bernstein, *Mexican Mining Industry*, p. 184; Anatol Shulgovski, *México en la encrucijada de su historia* (Mexico City, 1985), p. 367.

68. Ashby, *Organized Labor*, pp. 99–101; Bernstein, *Mexican Mining Industry*, p. 196.

69. F. Feuille to State Department, 21 March 1938, FO 371/21465, A2690.

70. English text of speech in S.D.812.6363/3153; Daniels, Mexico City, 21 March 1938, S.D.812.6363/3109.

71. Daniels, Mexico City, 20 March 1938, SD 812.6363/3108.

72. Kluckhohn, *Mexican Challenge*, p. 129.

73. Memo of Balfour, 1 Dec. 1938, FO 371/22770, A393.

74. *Times* (London), 11 April 1938; the same correspondent later penned a fuller account: R. H. K. Marett, *An Eye-Witness of Mexico* (London, 1939), p. 227.

75. Daniels, Mexico City, 24 March 1938; Tampico, 2 March 1938, S.D.812.6363/3221, 3114; KG to Godber, 22 March 1938, FO 371/21164, A2217.

76. Cf., for example, Bernstein, *Mexican Mining Industry*, pp. 182, 184, with references to contemporary "xenophobia" and "antiforeign actions," culminating in the "hysterical xenophobia" and "riotous celebrations" of March 1938. Guaymas, 31 March, and Durango, 4 April 1938, S.D.812.6363/3381, 3420, come closest to reporting xenophobia; but in neither case is the evidence impressive (some slogans and discourtesy at Durango; a tourist scare at Guaymas, where the consul assured a prospective tourist party that "so far as could be foreseen, their brief trip to Guaymas involved no particular danger"). The *Douglas Daily Despatch*, 24 March 1938, in S.D.812.6363/3188, reported an enthusiastic demonstration across the border in Agua Prieta: "utterances were fiery in the extreme but not particularly anti- foreign . . . ; there were no disorders and no utterances indicating any possible anti-American activity."

77. Torreón, 1 April; Guadalajara, 23, 29 March; Matamoros, 31 March; Nuevo Laredo, 23 March; Piedras Negras, 5 April; Mexicali, 7 April; Tampico, 24 March, 4 April; Monterrey, 24 March 1938; S.D.812.6363/3363; 3365, 3409; 3376; 3185; 3385; 3396; 3143, 3357; 3171; *Excelsior*, 26 March 1938.

78. Knight, *U.S.-Mexican Relations*, pp. 59–69.

79. González, *Los días del presidente Cárdenas*, p. 172.

80. *El Nacional*, 27 March 1938; Jan Bazant, *A Concise History of Mexico from Hidalgo to Cárdenas* (Cambridge, 1979) p. 187; cf. Prewett, *Reportage*, p. 121 ("wildest enthusiasm"); Kluckhohn, *Mexican Challenge*, p. 121 ("tremendous burst of nationalist enthusiasm"); Correa, *Balance del cardenismo* ("orgy of flagwaving"), p. 151; Shulgovski, *Mexico en la encrucijada*, p. 353 ("ardent support amongst the widest sections of the population").

81. Guadalajara, 23 March; Monterrey, 24 March 1938; S.D.812.6363/3365, 3171.

82. Jesús José Zazueta, president, Comité Ejecutivo Agrario, Bacobampo, Sonora, 9 March 1938; Lorenzo Vázquez, Sindicato Unico de Trabajadores de la Enseñanza, Querétaro, 2 June 1937; Marta Toledo, Frente Unico Pro-Derecho de la Mujer, Tapachula, 4 June 1937; all to Cárdenas, AGN-LC 432.2/253. Tampico, 23 March 1938, S.D.812.5353/3140, enclosing local broadsheet. In compiling evidence of contemporary images, I have used 1937 as well as 1938 sources.

83. Daniels, Mexico City, 24 March 1938 (twice), S.D.812.6363/3194, 3220.

84. San Luis, 23 March 1938, S.D.812.6363/3186.

85. Monterrey, 24 March 1938, S.D.812.6363/3171.

86. *El Nacional*, 19 March 1938, proclaims revolutionary Mexico to be "el

guión del continente"; banners in Monterrey (see n. 85) hail Cárdenas as "the Liberator of all Latin America from imperialistic Yankee control." For conservative and Catholic versions of anti-Americanism, Knight, *U.S.-Mexican Relations*, pp. 43–46.

87. Communcations to Cárdenas from Prof. José Gamboa, Kimbila, Yuc., 15 March 1938; José Solís, tramworkers union, Mexico City, 16 Feb. 1938; Julio Almeyda Soria, teachers union, Veracruz, 23 Feb. 1938 (which replicates Gamboa's terminology), AGN-LC 432.2/253; *El Nacional* 17 March 1938; Philip, *Oil and Politics*, p. 217, quotes Beteta to O'Malley: "[the] presence of the big foreign companies was symptomatic of [the] semi-Colonial system of Mexico."

88. *El Nacional*, 21 March 1938.

89. Tampico, 23 March 1938, S.D.812.6363/3197.

90. *El Nacional*, 19 March 1938.

91. *El Universal*, 19 March 1938. The notion that 1938 represented an "affirmation of national economic independence," paralleling the political independence of 1810 (or 1821) was standard: e.g., Graciano Sánchez and Congreso Regional Indígena, Tamazunchale, to Cárdenas, 17 March 1938, AGN-LC 432.2/253.

92. *El Nacional*, 19 March 1938.

93. O'Malley, Mexico City, 16 March 1938, FO 371/21465, A2865.

94. Daniels, Mexico City, 30 March 1938, S.D.812.6363/3260.

95. Secundino Córdoba to Cárdenas, 5 June 1937, AGN-LC 432.2/253.

96. Marta Toledo, Frente Unico Pro-Derecho de la Mujer, Tapachula, to Cárdenas, 4 June 1937, AGN-LC 432.2/253.

97. *Excelsior*, 21 March, *El Nacional*, 17, 21 March 1938; communications to Cárdenas from Florentino Almaza, Local 3 STPRM, El Ebano; Vidal Ramírez, Local 28, Las Choapas, 16 March; Departamento Agrario workers, AGN-LC 432.2/253, 16 March 1938.

98. *El Nacional*, 19 March 1938; *Universal Gráfico*, 19 March 1938. Constantino Pérez, Tampico Strike Solidarity Committee, 1 June 1937, denounces the oil companies "who take away Mexico's gold, won with our blood," and Teodoro Tejeda, Local 10 STPRM, speech at Minatitlán 1 June 1937, citing the authority of Lincoln to the effect that liberty is bought with blood: AGN-LC 423.2/253.

99. *Ultimas Notícias*, 19 March 1938. *Universal Gráfico*, 19 March, calls for "respect for the law and serenity"; *Ultimas Notícias*, 16 March, "an energetic but serene atttiude."

100. *El Nacional*, 19 March 1938.

101. San Luis, 23 March 1938, S.D.812.6363/3186; Pascual Coss, Gto, 17 March; Carlos Zepeda, "Renaissance" Lodge of National Mexico Rite, 26 March, to Cárdenas; anniversary eulogy by Narciso Fernández, 30 March 1940, AGN-LC 432.2/253.

102. O'Malley, 3 April 1938, FO 371/21465, A2593; Durango, 6 April; Daniels, Mexico City, 25 March 1938, S.D.812.6363/3420, 3219; O'Malley, Mexico City, 5 April 1938, FO 371/21465, A2689.

103. *Ultimas Notícias*, 19 March 1938; S.D.812.6363/3153.

104. *El Nacional*, 19 March 1938.

105. Ibid.; Florentino Almaza, Local 3 STPRM, El Ebano, communicating the

resolution of 550 oil workers to Cárdenas, 16 March 1938, AGN-LC 432.2/253; *Excelsior*, 23 March 1938; Mérida, 31 March, Daniels, Mexico City, 27 March, S.D.812.6363/3354, 3164; *Excelsior*, 23 March.

106. *El Nacional*, 19 March 1938.

107. San Luis, 23 March 1938, S.D.812.6363/3186; Daniels, Mexico City, 27 March, S.D.812.6363/3164.

108. Alan Knight, *The Mexican Revolution* (2 vols., Cambridge, Eng., 1986), vol. 2, pp. 158–162.

109. Daniels, Mexico City, 24 March; San Luis, 23 March; Monterrey, 23 March; Tampico, 23 March; Guadalajara, 23 March; Juárez, 23 March; Piedras Negras, 30 March; Guaymas, 31 March 1938, S.D.812.6363/ 3194, 3186, 3126, 3124, 3365, 3123, 3278, 3381.

110. Luis Paz de Hoyos, Nueva Rosita, Coa., 13 March 1938, referring to the "spontaneous demonstration" of support mounted by Local 14 of the Miners' Union, AGN-LC 432.2/253; *El Nacional*, 25 March 1938.

111. Daniels, Mexico City, 17 March 1938, S.D.812.6363/3100.

112. Daniels, Mexico City, 19 March; Mérida, 31 March, Piedras Negras, 24 March 1938, S.D.812.6363/3354, 3385.

113. Victoriano Cuellar, Fed. Rev. de Trabajadores de la Región Lagunera, 13 March 1938; STTFIPST, n.d., March 1938, to Cárdenas, AGN-LC 432.2/253.

114. "Informados por el maestro de la Escuela Federal de este pueblo de los conflictos entre el Gobierno . . . y las empresas petroleras extranjeras," the *ejidatarios* of San Pedro del Tongo, Nazas, Dgo, send a "vote of adhesion" to the president, promising that, in whatever eventuality, "los campesinos sabremos estar con Ud," 2 Feb. 1938, AGN-LC 432.2/253. Agua Prieta, 24 March 1938, S.D.812.6363/3188.

115. "Por prensa diaria enterámonos problema petrolero país": José Mejía, comisario ejidal, Tacatzcuaro, Tingindín, Mich., to Cárdenas, 15 March 1938, AGN-LC 432.2/253. According to Ambassador Daniels (no enemy of the administration), 26 March, S.D.812.6363/3175, "the Mexican Department of Press and Publicity is exercising a close supervision of what is published in the newspapers here at the present time"; a reading of the press tends to corroborate this. Mérida and Guaymas, 31 March 1938, S.D.812.6363/3354, 3381, on aerial propaganda (which cost one aviator his life).

116. Matamoros, 21 May, Guadalajara, 24 March, 4 April 1938, S.D.812.6363/ 4000, 3383, 3409.

117. Daniels, Mexico City, 24 March 1938, S.D.812.6363/3192. Again, Daniels' sympathy for the administration strengthens the evidence.

118. Agua Prieta, 24 March, Piedras Negras, 5 April, Mérida, 31 March 1938, S.D.812.6363/3188, 3385, 3354. Donations to the indemnity fund—cash, pigs, wedding rings—made good publicity; but the final sum raised (which was never disclosed) did not reach initial ambitious objectives; Cárdenas eventually asked that the donations be returned: Suárez, *Comentarios*, p. 195. A string of consular reports comment on fund-raising attempts, generally minimizing their impact: S.D.812.6363/3372, 3416, 3420, 3972, 3984, 4044.

119. Torreón, 1 April, Durango, 24 March, Ensenada, 23 March, Agua Prieta, 24 March 1938, S.D.812.6363/3363, 3246, 3168, 3188.

120. *Ultimas Notícias,* 23 March 1938.

121. Ernesto López, Ejido Morelos, Cunduacán, Tab., 11 March; Santiago Lara, Comité Ejecutivo Agrario "El Burro," Agua Dulce, Ver., 29 May 1937; Máximo Contreras, Sind. Ind. de Obreros de Construcción, Cd. Anáhuac, N.L., 8 March 1938, to Cárdenas, AGN-LC 432.2/253.

122. Piedras Negras, 5 April 1938, S.D.812.6363/3385.

123. Mérida, 31 March 1938, S.D.812.6363/3354; though the consul qualifies his last statement: "They would be loyal to any movement and to anyone in power."

124. Monterrey, 24 March; Durango, 24 March; San Luis, 23 March; Ensenada, 23 March; Nuevo Laredo, 23 March; Piedras Negras, 30 March 1938; S.D.812.6363/ 3171, 3246, 3186, 3168, 3185, 3278.

125. Guaymas, 31 March 1938, S.D.812.6363/3381.

126. Ankerson, *Agrarian Warlord,* p. 158.

127. Mazatlán, 1 April, 14 May 1938, S.D.812.6363/3307, 4008.

128. Monterrey, 21 March 1938, S.D.812.6363/3134.

129. Villaseñor, *Memorias,* pp. 414–415.

130. As told to Philip, *Oil and Politics,* p. 531.

131. *El Nacional,* 17 March 1938.

132. For example: Nuevo Laredo, San Luis, 31 March 1938, S.D.812.6363/3279, 3305.

133. Daniels, Mexico City, 19 March 1938, S.D.812.6363/3107.

134. Ibid., 20 March 1938, S.D.812.6363/3097; *Ultimas Notícias,* 19 March 1938.

135. Piedras Negras, 30 March 1938, S.D.812.6363/3278.

136. Torreón, 2 April 1938, S.D.812.6363/3315.

137. Agua Prieta, 24 March; Durango, 24 March; San Luis, 26 March; Tampico, 4 April 1938; S.D.812.6363/3188, 3246, 3244, 3357.

138. Memo of Welles conversation with Castillo Nájera, 21 March 1938, S.D.812.6363/3153. On the army: Daniels, Mexico City, 19 March; Agua Prieta, 21 May; Chihuahua, 13 May 1938; S.D.812.6363/3107, 4001, 4004. The gist of these (and other) reports was that the army was basically loyal and hostile to sedition (this was amply confirmed with the Cedillazo); however, plenty of officers disagreed with the tenor of Cárdenas's policy. Villaseñor, *Memorias,* pp. 415–416, comments on the fascist leanings of the junior officers of the day.

139. Matamoros, 19 May 1938, S.D.812.6363/3997.

140. British officials, too, whose opinions had historically aligned with those of the Mexican well-to-do, hoped that U.S. policy might involve "encouraging moderate opposition groups . . . to feel that they enjoy American sympathy": Balfour memo, 1 Dec.1938, FO 371/22770, A393.

141. Tampico, 16 May 1938, S.D.812.6363/3982.

142. Ariel José Contreras, *México 1940: industrialización y crisis política* (Mexico City, 1985), offers a good analysis.

143. The border and oil regions were probably hardest hit: for example, Matamoros, 18 May; Nuevo Laredo,18 May; Tampico 21 May; Agua Prieta, 21 May; Chihuahua, 13 May 1938; S.D.812.6363/3988; 3995; 3996; 4001; 4004. Of course, those who did not buy imports and who grew their own subsistence crops

were cushioned against the impact of inflation.

144. Daniels, Mexico City, 22 March 1938, S.D.812.6363/3139; *El Nacional*, 2 March 1938.

145. *El Nacional*, 27 March 1938.

146. Guadalajara, 29 March 1938, S.D.812.6363/3409.

147. Balfour memo, 1 Dec.1938, FO 371/22770, A390; Alberto Bremauntz, *Material histórico de Obregón a Cárdenas* (Mexico City, 1973), pp. 182, 216: Cárdenas warns the miners against encouraging "useless upheavals," advocates harmony between labor and capital, and guarantees the rights of capital, the petroleum expropriation being a "unique case."

148. *Excelsior*, 21 March; *Ultimas Notícias*, 23 March 1938.

149. Manifesto of Cámara Nacional de Comercio e Industria, Guadalajara, 31 March 1938, in S.D.812.6363/3356.

150. Guadalajara, 4 April 1938, S.D.812.6363/3383.

151. Ibid., 29 March 1938, S.D.812.6363/3409.

152. Ibid., 7 April 1938, S.D.812.6363/3416.

153. Ibid.

5. Worker Participation in the Administration of the Petroleum Industry, 1938–1940

Ruth Adler

La Trobe University, Bundoora, Victoria, Australia

The years of the presidency of Lázaro Cárdenas were characterized by a radicalization of the Mexican labor movement and by government policies intended to advance the interests of the working class within the economic framework of promoting nationalist capitalist development. Labor's militancy was reflected in an increasing number of industrial conflicts caused by demands for higher wages and better working conditions, and, in some cases, for greater participation in the administration of production. The government, for its part, responded to these developments by supporting labor in so-called just conflicts with capital, and by promoting the formation of workers' cooperatives and, as in the case of the National Railways of Mexico, workers' administrations. In the oil industry, the Cárdenas years witnessed the labor conflict that culminated in the 1938 expropriation and subsequent reorganization of production in which the workers participated.

This chapter will analyze the experience of worker participation in the administration of the nationalized oil industry in Mexico between 1938 and 1940, and the debate that developed in relation to this question during this period. The text consists of four sections that examine, respectively, labor initiatives to gain control of the industry prior to the expropriation, the experience of the union administration of the oil fields and refineries in the months following March 1938, the debate over the issue of worker control that occurred during the Second Special Convention of the Mexican Oil Workers Union (Sindicato de Trabajadores Petroleros de la República Mexicana, STPRM) in 1939, and the origin of the 1940 Conflict of Economic Order, which resulted in a substantial reorganization of the industry. It will be shown that, although there was strong support for the concept of labor control of the industry among the oil workers, the union decided to reform its official policy on this question during the Second Special Convention of the STPRM in 1939. In this respect, it will be argued that the reasons for this change in attitude derived from the fact that the workers were not covered by a collective contract that defined and protected wages and conditions, and that from mid-1939 onward, the resolution of this question was of utmost importance for the STPRM. It will also be shown that the union was under considerable pressure from the government to accept a reorganization of the industry that would reduce the operational costs of production and that the workers perceived their interests to be under threat by the proposed changes.

Labor and Control of Production

The origins of the demand for worker control of the oil industry are to be found during the 1937 Conflict of Economic Order. As is well known, this conflict had its origins in a campaign by the STPRM to achieve the implementation of an industrywide collective contract that had been drafted during the union's First Special Convention in 1936. Although the final aim of thc STPRM in this dispute was the implementation of a collective contract and not the modification of the existing structural organization of the industry, nevertheless, as the conflict developed into an issue of national political importance, certain elements within the union began to conceive of the expropriation and transfer of the oil properties to the workers as a possible solution.

The first such initiative came from Local 30 of the STPRM in Poza Rica, Veracruz, in 1937 and arose in the context of a conflict that had developed between the local and the Compañía Mexicana de Petróleo El Aguila. The origins of this conflict were the following: In 1937, Delegation 2 of Local 1 of the STPRM (based in Ciudad Madero, Tamaulipas) became independent, forming Local 30. Until this time, the workers of Local 1 and its delegations had worked under the same collective contract; however, when the delegation gained its autonomy, the company refused to apply the existing collective contract to the new local. Local 30 presented the company with a petition of demands that included the creation of permanent positions for workers who were, for all intents and purposes, permanent employees of the company, but had hitherto been regarded as temporary employees, and the application of a salary scale similar to that which was in effect for Local 1.[1] Negotiations between the workers and the company produced limited results and on 12 July 1937, the local decided to call a wildcat strike for 21 July.[2] This action was supported by neither the National Executive Committee of the STPRM nor the government, both of which viewed the strike decision as evidence of lack of discipline and argued that the Poza Rica workers should have awaited the outcome of the Conflict of Economic Order, which was being litigated in thc Federal Commission of Conciliation and Arbitration.[3] In spite of this opposition, Local 30 managed to maintain the strike for fifty-seven days until an agreement was reached with the company on 15 September 1937. This agreement provided for the creation of 250 new permanent positions and for the implementation of a salary scale similar to that in force for the workers of Local 1.[4] The company complied with part of the agreement immediately, but then argued that it was not in a position to implement the remaining terms because they referred to questions that were being contested in the Conflict of Economic Order.[5] As a result of the company's failure to implement the agreement in its totality, the Poza Rica workers decided to organize a series of stoppages to force El Aguila's compliance.[6]

In August 1937, during the strike, a commission of workers from Poza Rica proposed a solution to the conflict to President Lázaro Cárdenas. According to the local's proposal, the Poza Rica oil properties should be expropriated and given to the workers to be administered as a cooperative.[7] Cárdenas gave careful consideration to the workers' suggestion but, several months later, rejected it. According to the president's reasoning, the STPRM had won a favorable decision from the Federal Commission for Conciliation and Arbitration, which invalidated the local's claim that its conflict with the El Aguila company could be resolved only through the expropriation of the Poza Rica properties. Furthermore, it was the president's view that no definitive action on this question should be taken until the result of the companies' appeal to the Supreme Court of the Nation against the ruling of the Federal Commission of Conciliation and Arbitration was known.[8] The government's attitude on this question was a reflection of its policy of exhaustion of all channels before resorting to coercive action against the companies.

Local 30's initiative represented the first attempt by workers to modify the existing structure and property relations of the industry. In relation to the Poza Rica workers' proposal, this initiative considered the creation of a cooperative and not a workers' administration. This distinction is important because, under cooperative management, the industry would have remained a private concern in which the workers would have become shareholders, whereas under a workers' administration, the property of the oil fields and refineries would have been transferred to the state, and the workers would have assumed a managerial role. That the workers requested specifically that the El Aguila company be run as a cooperative is of interest because in other sectors of the labor movement this issue was also being discussed, and, in some cases, this type of organization had been rejected as inappropriate for industries that had been expropriated. For example, at this time, the railway workers were discussing the form the union administration of the nationalized lines was to take and had rejected the idea of forming a cooperative. The Mexican Railway Workers' Union (Sindicato de Trabajadores Ferrocarrileros de la República Mexicana, STFRM) argued that, under a cooperative organization, the existing collective contract would have been rendered null and void. Also, the railway workers' terms of employment would have been subject to a process of negotiation with an administrative council, the results of which might not have been favorable to the railway workers because they might have lost the benefits that were protected in the existing agreements. Given that in the 1930s the railway workers' contracts were considered to be among the most advanced then in force in Mexico—in terms of benefits, work conditions, and wages provided—the STFRM's reluctance to support the formation of a cooperative is understandable. Furthermore, in the STFRM's view, the formation of a cooperative would have been an ideologically retrogressive step because the workers would have become shareholders in a private concern and thereby would have ceased to form part of Mexico's revolutionary trade union movernent.[9]

The decision of Local 30 to push for the formation of a cooperative is, nevertheless, understandable in the context of the political reality of the time and the special circumstances affecting the Poza Rica workers in 1937. First, the government had actively promoted the formation of cooperatives, and in many industries this type of organization had proven to be politically and economically viable.[10] Second, under a cooperative form of organization, the workers would have gained complete control of the management of production because they would have become shareholders responsible for electing an administrative council composed of their own constituents. This administrative council would have been free to formulate the terms of the collective contract applicable to the workers. Given that the Local 30 workers did not have a collective contract with the El Aguila company, they perceived that their interests would not be endangered in the least by the formation of a cooperative. Finally, it is also possible that the Local 30 workers demanded the formation of a cooperative in order to avoid becoming federal employees. In 1937, many workers in industries that had been nationalized, such as the railways, were concerned about this issue because there was no legislation in force that protected the rights to strike and of free association of government employees. Furthermore, there had been considerable public discussion about this question, and the Chamber of Deputies was in the process of debating legislation to define the rights and terms of employment of these public sector workers. By late 1937, this issue still had not been resolved, and workers in newly nationalized industries, regardless of whether they had previously been covered by collective contracts, were reluctant to subject themselves to the determinations of the state, regarding the terms of employment, salaries, and work conditions. The decision of Local 30 to favor the formation of a cooperative offered the Poza Rica workers the best possibility of guaranteeing the rights and conditions of labor, of preserving their independence, and, in the final analysis, of putting an end to the conflict with the El Aguila company .

During the 1937 Conflict of Economic Order, the petroleum workers demonstrated their willingness to cooperate with the government and to assume responsibility for the administration of production if necessary. In February 1938, the secretaries of all the locals met with Cárdenas to discuss the future of the industry should the government be forced to intervene in the petroleum workers' conflict and to order the expropriation of the oil properties. The president's representatives requested that each local draft organizational plans stating how production would be administered at a local level in such an event.[11] The locals responded enthusiastically and within weeks had drafted contingency plans.[12] Another aspect of the presidential petition was that locals ascertain whether administrative and technical staff would support the government in case of expropriation.[13]

The government's decision to incorporate the STPRM in the administration of production did not mean that it was contemplating the formation of a cooperative or a workers' administration. Cárdenas's strategy was to provide the STPRM with a limited and local role, and meant that, in the event of expropriation, the government would control the administration of production at a national level. From the government's point of view, it was necessary to permit the union administrative control at a local level because it depended on the cooperation of the workers to ensure that production continued. The STPRM accepted its designated role, and not even in Local 30 was it suggested that the workers be given complete control of the administration of production in the event of expropriation of the oil companies.

The Expropriation and the Local Administrative Councils

The expropriation was announced by presidential decree on 18 March 1938 at 10:00 p.m.[14] Immediately afterward, the workers occupied the oil fields and refineries in order to effect a stoppage (of all save essential activities) that had been called for midnight[15] and to guard the installations against possible sabotage attempts by agents of the expropriated companies.[16] (At midday, the Federal Board of Conciliation and Arbitration had declared that existing collective contracts had been suspended because of the companies' failure to comply with the *laudo* of 18 December 1937; hence, the National Executive Committee of the STPRM had ordered that members abandon work at midnight on 18

March 1938.) The occupation of the oil properties signified the beginning of the period of direct union administration of the industry.

On 19 March 1938, the National Executive Committee of the STPRM issued emergency instructions concerning the organization of production. According to the directive, *consejos locales de administración* were to be designated in each local. Each *consejo local* was to consist of the local secretary, the secretary of labor, and a member of the local vigilance committee, and was to ensure that production continued without serious interruption and without altering the existing organization of production. Each *consejo local* had the authority to designate the personnel for positions of responsibility and was to manage production in the various departments and dependencies of the expropriated companies. These instructions were to remain in force until the permanent administrative organization of production had been decided.[17] The National Executive Committee also ordered that work be resumed, and within a few days production had normalized.

At the same time, the government moved to establish a body to coordinate the administration of production at a national level. On 19 March 1938, representatives of the STPRM and the Secretariats of Treasury and Public Credit and National Economy formed a commission to discuss problems related to the production and distribution of petroleum and its derivatives. On 20 March 1938, the Consejo Directivo del Petróleo was established. This agency consisted of seven departments: Production, Transport and Storage, Refining, Sales and Distribution (external and internal), Finance, Accounting, and Administration. It had an administrative board of nine members, three of whom were designated by the STPRM.[18] A department was also established to coordinate petroleum exports.[19] This agency was a dependency of the Secretariat of National Economy and did not have union representation in its management. Following the announcement of the formation of these agencies, the National Executive Committee of the STPRM issued another directive, qualifying its instruction of 19 March 1938, to the effect that movement of administrative staff was to be done in consultation with the Consejo Directivo del Petróleo and that questions related to production were to be directed to the Secretariat of National Economy.[20]

The *consejos locales* administered the industry until the formation of Petróleos Mexicanos and the Distribuidora de Petróleos Mexicanos in July 1938. Since they had been formed to administer only temporarily, the *consejos locales* adopted the practices of the companies in relation to the administrative and technical organization of production, and— with the exception of exploration, which was suspended with the expropriation—productive activities continued as before. Furthermore, the *consejos locales* were not responsible for such matters as the distribution and sale of petroleum products, the purchase of equipment and spare parts, or the transport of production—these activities became the responsibility of the central administration of the industry.

Nevertheless, in local matters, the *consejos locales* had considerable freedom of action. They named departmental heads, and resolved problems related to the employment of staff and working conditions.[21] For example, following the expropriation, many workers were left without employment. Furthermore, there was an instruction from the Consejo Directivo del Petróleo to curtail the number of temporary employees. The *consejos locales* decided how to implement the reorganization and how to assist the affected workers.[22] Similarly, when the STPRM secured payment of salaries for the May 1937 strike (which provoked the 1937 Conflict of Economic Order) and the implementation of a number of clauses from the 1937 *laudo* (e.g., the forty-hour week), the *consejos locales* decided how these concessions would be applied.[23]

In general terms, the experience of union management of production was varied. In some locals, such as Local 30, production continued without serious interruption and there was a process of consultation between the *consejo local* and local members. At each local meeting, the *consejo local* presented a report on its activities, and members discussed and ratified its decisions. Complaints against decisions of the *consejos locales* were also dealt with by the local assembly.[24]

In other locals, however, serious problems developed during the period of the union's management at a local level. In a number of cases, available labor was used inefficiently or in unproductive activities, with the result that production slowed down or virtually halted.[25] Furthermore, certain elements of the petroleum workers' union were alleged to be corrupt and in league with interests that were opposed to the expropriation. In the latter part of 1938, a scandal erupted concerning the activities of Local 3 (El Ebano, San Luis Potosí) leader Juan Zamora and his associates in the period preceding and immediately following the nationalization. The controversy began in 1937 when Zamora expelled seventeen members of the local who had opposed certain actions and decisions of the local leadership and had attempted to oust the incumbent Local Executive Committee. Specifically, it was alleged that Zamora, in contravention of the existing collective contract and union regulations, had made a number of agreements with the Huasteca Petroleum Company that were deemed to be detrimental to the interests of Local 3 workers. It was further alleged that Zamora had misappropriated local funds amounting to $4,700, and, in a bid to avoid the application of legal sanctions against himself, had unsuccessfully attempted to file injunction (*amparo*) proceedings in the district courts of Tampico, Pachuca, Mexico City, Tuxpan, Toluca, and Puebla. Finally, it was claimed that he had attempted to foster division within the union by conducting a campaign in the northern zone locals against the national leadership of the union.[26]

In November 1937, San Luis Potosí authorities issued orders for the arrest of Zamora and two associates, Eduardo Toscano and Pablo F. Reyes, all of whom were subsequently apprehended. The three did not, however, remain in custody according to later testimony of the General Executive Committee of the STPRM, their release was procured as a result of instructions from the state governor, Saturnino Cedillo,[27] who in May 1938 rebelled against the Cárdenas government over long-standing disagreements with aspects of the regime's policy on education, labor relations, and agrarian reform.[28] Union funds amounting to $16,000 were, according to documentation held by the Local 3 Executive Committee, diverted for the legal defense of Zamora and his cohorts.[29] It was also alleged that Zamora had falsified the accounts of the local's cooperative, with the result that members did not receive their share of the profits and that, following the delivery of the Federal Commission for Conciliation and Arbitration's *laudo* in December 1937, Zamora and associates had initiated *amparo* proceedings on behalf of the sanction against the tribunal's decision.[30] Because matters of greater importance subsequently occupied the attention of the National Executive Committee, the question of Zamora's activities was temporarily forgotten, and, following the expropriation, Zamora was appointed Field Superintendent in the region. During this period, Zamora and his associates allegedly engaged in the theft of equipment and materials belonging to the local petroleum administration and in acts of "peaceful sabotage" on local installations. Such acts included the allowance, through negligence or by design, of excess pressure buildup in a number of the zone's oil wells, with the result that considerable damage, including the emulsification of certain wells, occurred.[31] In mid-1938, local members opposed to Zamora's control of local union affairs again began to take steps to have him removed. Zamora, who by this stage had acquired the status of a *cacique*, violently attempted to repress the opposition. Tarring and feathering, pesticide "baths," assault, and, in two cases, murder[32] were among the tactics employed by Zamora's group to suppress dissident elements.

In July 1938, Zamora and cohorts were removed from the leadership positions they occupied and were expelled from the local by the Local Vigilance Committee.[33] Following this, Petróleos Mexicanos dismissed Zamora from the position of field superintendent.[34] The National Executive Committee of the STPRM ruled the findings of Local 3 to be justified, and in October 1938 he was formally expelled from the union.[35] The local, in a special meeting held in the same month, decided to apply the exclusion clause to thirty other individuals associated with the Zamora clique.[36] The workers who were expelled by the Zamora group were, as a result of these developments, reinstated as members of the local and as employees of the local petroleum administration.[37]

The union's intervention in the Zamora matter did not, however, end with his expulsion. The General Vigilance Committee urged locals to petition judicial authorities in San Luis Potosí to arrest and charge Zamora and his associate, Eduardo Toscano, who had also been involved in criminal activities, including the murder of a worker who had been opposed to the Zamora clique.[38] Zamora was arrested on 15 October 1938, and criminal charges were brought against him.[39] The workers who were expelled for allegedly collaborating with him also refused to let the matter rest, and in 1939 sought the support of President Cárdenas and the General Vigilance Committee in a bid to be reinstated. Cárdenas and the members of the latter organization supported their petition, arguing that the interests of the industry would be best served if the expelled workers, in spite of any association with Zamora, were given an opportunity to demonstrate their willingness to cooperate with the government and the union in the future administration of production. The Local Executive Committee was adamantly opposed to this proposal on the grounds that the reinstatement of these workers would provoke serious divisions within the union.[40] The matter was, however, subsequently discussed in a special session of Local 3, and by a majority of votes the local decided to reject the request that the workers be reinstated as a group, although members agreed that individual cases be considered on their merits at a special meeting to be held at a later date.[41] Zamora was subsequently tried by judicial authorities in San Luis Potosí, but was acquitted in 1940 on the grounds that there was insufficient evidence to substantiate the charges against him.[42]

Duality of functions of union members who occupied positions of responsibility in the nationalized industry was another question that arose in the wake of the expropriation. In a number of locals, it was occasionally decided that Local Executive Committee members who also sat on the *consejos locales* be relieved of their union commissions.[43] The leadership of the STPRM also supported this policy. When Juan Gray, secretary general of the STPRM, was appointed to the position of Head of Administration and Personnel in the Consejo Directivo del Petróleo, the National Executive Committee issued a directive that STPRM officials occupying technical or administrative positions in the industry be given a fortnight to decide which of the two functions they would continue to perform.[44]

By mid-1938, there was considerable discontent in various locals concerning the conduct of the *consejos locales* and accusations that they did not consult with members about production decisions.[45] In some locals, relations between members and the *consejo local* were so strained that the latter was forced to resign. In Local 21 (Arbol Grande, Tamaulipas), for example, the *consejo local* was forced to resign after a dispute over a number of decisions he had made about the security of local oil installations. The origins of this conflict were the following: The president of the *consejo local*, Juan Aviña, alleged that in various departments, especially the refinery, there was frequent theft of materials. As a result, the *consejo local* decided that tight security of the installations would be necessary in order to discover the thieves. This security was to extend to all departments, and not even trucks would be permitted to leave the premises without a thorough inspection. This decision provoked the hostility of a number of members, who argued that it showed bad faith on the part of the *consejo local* toward the workers. After considerable discussion in a local meeting held in July 1938, the *consejo local*/Local Executive Committee was obliged to resign.[46] That members could force the resignation of the *consejo local* suggests that workers exercised considerable control in questions of local control.

The union management of the industry lasted until July 1938, when Cárdenas ordered that the *consejos locales* be disbanded, and Petróleos Mexicanos and the Distribuidora de Petróleos Mexicanos were established to administer the industry permanently. In spite of the opposition of certain locals,[47] the decision was accepted by the National Executive Committee of the STPRM.[48] Nevertheless, the committee fought to maintain union participation in the administration of the industry. Hence, in June 1938, following the promulgation of the decrees that created Petróleos Mexicanos and the Distribuidora de Petróleos Mexicanos, the STPRM dispatched a commission to discuss the question of worker participation in the administration of the two organizations. Under the legislation that created these two bodies, the STPRM had three of the nine positions in the administrative council of Petróleos Mexicanos and no representation in the Distribuidora. After negotiating the matter with Cárdenas, it was decided that the STPRM would have four representatives on the administrative council of Petróleos Mexicanos and two on the council of the Distribuidora.[49] Although these changes were hailed as victories by the STPRM, in reality they did not increase the degree of political control exercised by the workers in the management of the industry because the union was still in a minority in the administrative councils of both agencies.

After the formation of Petróleos Mexicanos and the Distribuidora de Petróleos Mexicanos, the workers' demands for increased participation in the administration of the industry grew more radical. For example, in a meeting of Local 30 members in August 1938, Eduardo Pérez stated that it was necessary for the oil workers to know whether they were employees of the government or shareholders in a cooperative, and proposed that the industry be organized as a cooperative. It was agreed that a commission would study the suggestion and submit a proposal for discussion at the next oil workers' convention.[50]

Furthermore, at a 1939 mass meeting held to celebrate the first anniversary of the expropriation, Rafael Gómez, Treasurer of the STPRM, spoke of the success of union participation in the management of the industry and called on the government to give workers complete control of the administration of production, that is to say, that a workers' administration, such as existed in the National Railways of Mexico, be established.[51] These sentiments were reiterated in May of the same year in an article published in the oil workers' journal *Guía*, which discussed the tasks of the upcoming STPRM convention.[52] Possibly the most developed expression of these ideas was to be found in an article written by Local 4 (Mexico City) activist B. M. Gutiérrez, who argued that trade unions should struggle for the creation of workers' administrations and that labor control of the management of production should be defended at all cost.[53]

The spirit of these demands indicates that the ideological position of the STPRM had changed on the question of worker control. Until 1939, the union had limited its demands to increased STPRM participation in the administrative council of Petróleos Mexicanos or, as in the case of proposals of Local 30 leader Eduardo Pérez, the formation of a cooperative in the industry. From early 1939 onward, however, the workers demanded the formation of a workers' administration. This change in political orientation can be attributed to two factors. First, the creation of a workers' administration was a solution compatible with existing conditions and more feasible than, for example, the formation of a cooperative. In order to understand this, it is necessary to recall that in 1939 the state was the owner of the expropriated properties and the creation of a workers' administration would have implied that the control—but not the property—of the oil industry would have been transferred to the workers. In contrast, the creation of a cooperative would have meant that both the property and the administration of the oil industry would have been transferred to the union—a proposition that the government would not have accepted. Second, the Workers' Administration of the National Railways of Mexico had existed for almost a year (it was set up on 1 May 1938), and, at that time in labor circles, it was regarded as a great success and a triumph for the working-class movement. Evidence of this is found in the fact that in 1939 *Guía* published various articles extolling the virtues of the railway administration.[54]

The Second Special Convention of the STPRM

The question of a workers' administration in the nationalized oil industry was debated extensively during the Second Special Convention of the STPRM. This convention was convened in June 1939 to discuss problems related to the structure and administration of the nationalized oil industry and to working conditions. The question of worker control was analyzed in the context of discussion concerning the second point of the convention's agenda—the legal and administrative organization of the industry.

The issue provoked strong debate and was the subject of a number of discussion papers submitted to the Commission on Legal Matters (Comisión de Asuntos Jurídicos), which had been designated to prepare a relevant policy document. In all the papers presented there were a number of common threads: the necessity of protecting workers' interests in the nationalized petroleum administration; recognition of the critical national and international political and economic problems precipitated by the expropriation, the desire that the union's participation in the management of production at a base level be recognized in its representation in the industry's administrative bodies at a national level; that the interests of cost and administrative efficiency would be best served by the fusion of the Distribuidora de Petróleos Mexicanos with Petróleos Mexicanos; and, finally, that under no circumstances should the oil properties be returned to the expropriated companies.[55] The discussion papers differed, however, on the form that worker participation in the nationalized industry should take. For example, Local 22 (Agua Dulce, Veracruz) proposed that the existing state of affairs should continue for the time being and that, in due course, a legislative bill be drafted providing for the eventual transfer of the industry to the workers. Local 5 (Mexico City) argued that the ultimate aim of the STPRM should be the creation of a workers' administration, and that, in the meantime, members should declare themselves in favor of a mixed government-union administration. Local 1's position was that the industry should be managed by a mixed administration of the government and the STPRM in which the latter had a majority in the administrative council. The National Executive Committee maintained that the immediate goal of the STPRM should be the creation of a workers' administration and that a special commission be appointed to report on its feasibility.[56] This possibility was also supported by the Confederation of Mexican Labor (Confederación de Trabajadores de México, CTM) delegate to the convention, Vidal Díaz Muñoz, who, in an inaugural address, called on the government to give the workers complete responsibility for the management of production.[57]

The commission decided that, although a workers' administration was the ideal form of management for the nationalized oil industry, it was not feasible at that point in time. In its statement to the convention on the issue, the commission alluded to the political and economic difficulties that had arisen in the wake of the expropriation. In this context, it pointed to the fact that the Mexican government still had not reached a settlement with the companies regarding compensation for the oil properties, to the boycott that had been imposed on the sale of Mexican petroleum in the international market, and to the campaign that was then being waged by the political Right against the policies of the Cárdenas government. It was the commission's view that these problems would only be aggravated by a government decision to give the administration of the industry to the workers.[58]

The commission also rejected a cooperative form of organization for the industry. According to its policy statement, the creation of a cooperative, in which individual workers became shareholders, would represent a major departure from the class and ideological interests of the oil workers because they would inevitably become "shamefaced" members of the bourgeoisie (*burgueses vergonzantes*). The commission hastened to warn that nothing could be more dangerous for the long-term interests of Mexico's labor movement.[59]

The commission concluded that the immediate interests of the industry would be best served by a continuation of the existing mixed government-union administration. It argued, however, that this structure be modified to the effect that the government and the STPRM be equally represented in the administrative council of Petróleos Mexicanos. It also recommended that the administrative councils of Petróleos Mexicanos and the Distribuidora de Petróleos Mexicanos be one and the same.[60]

The adoption of these findings as official STPRM policy represented the abandonment of the pro-workers' administration position that the union had advanced only a few months previously. There are several explanations for this change in attitude. First, since the nationalization, the oil workers had not been covered by a collective contract and many of the clauses in the 1937 *laudo* had not been implemented. Although the STPRM had been negotiating with the government for the gradual application of the *laudo*—and, by mid-1939, 125 clauses had been implemented[61]—it is evident that this was a fundamental concern for the workers because, immediately after the Second Special Convention, the union demanded that Petróleos Mexicanos sign a collective contract.

Furthermore, it is clear that this had been a cause of worker discontent for a considerable time. For example, in June 1938, when Cárdenas visited the Veracruz oil producing regions, workers in many zones expressed their dissatisfaction that the 1937 *laudo* had not been implemented. On one occasion, in a meeting with workers from Cerro Azul, Cárdenas explained that the *laudo* had not been applied in its totality because of the serious economic problems confronting the industry.[62] Such official explanations did not satisfy many workers, however. Shortly afterward, Local 1 and several other locals launched a campaign within the union for the creation of a special convention to clarify the legal position of STPRM members and to discuss questions related to the administrative organization of the industry.[63] Although the National Executive Committee opposed an attempt by various locals to convene a convention in December 1938—on the grounds that it was working for the resolution of the problems raised by the disgruntled locals, such as the government's failure to implement the contract contained in the 1937 *laudo*[64]—it was eventually forced to recognize the existence of considerable discontent among STPRM rank and file, and to convene the convention.

The discontent of certain elements of the petroleum workers' movement was demonstrated further in 1939 when a major conflict erupted in the Ciudad Madero refinery. For several months, the refinery workers had been demanding that the applicable salary scale be revised on the grounds that workers in the Central Zone, who performed similar labors, received higher wages.[65] In March 1939, Petróleos Mexicanos established a commission (Comisión Niveladora de Salarios) to investigate the alleged discrepancy. The negotiations did not advance to the satisfaction of the workers, and on 31 May 1939, the boiler department employees organized a work stoppage.[66] The administration of Petróleos Mexicanos characterized the workers' action as an act of sabotage, instigated by the expropriated companies,[67] and even Cárdenas intervened by sending a telegram warning that strict measures would be taken to avoid such acts of sabotage in the future.[68] In spite of this reaction from the industry's central authorities and the government, the boilermakers received support from other members of the local, and there were threats of a refinerywide strike.[69] The crisis was resolved in June 1939 when an agreement was reached providing for the establishment of a commission, composed of representatives of the union and the government, to investigate the reasons for the strike and the question of the salary scale applicable to the Northern Zone.[70] These developments indicate the workers' profound concern over the lack of a collective contract and over the discrepancies that existed throughout the industry—and had existed since the time of the companies—in relation to salaries and conditions of employment.

A second possible reason for the STPRM's decision to postpone its campaign for the creation of a workers' administration was that since

November 1938 the government and Petróleos Mexicanos had been calling on workers to make sacrifices in order to facilitate the economic recovery of the industry. By 1939, the industry was suffering from the effects of the boycott imposed by the expropriated companies and production and exports had fallen considerably. For example, the value of exports of crude petroleum and its derivatives fell from $42,254,963 in 1937 to $15,875,728 in 1938.[71] Furthermore, in 1938 the number of wells in production declined by 41 percent compared to 1937, and refinery production fell by 47.75 percent in the same period.[72] Initially, many locals reacted hostilely to Petróleos Mexicanos' demands that workers make economic sacrifices, arguing that such cooperation should first come from senior employees, who were alleged to have enriched themselves in the period following the nationalization.[73] Nevertheless, it is probable that the subtle and constant pressure that the STPRM modify its demands influenced its decision to abandon the pro-workers' administration policy.

A third possible reason for the change in STPRM policy is that the Left, the natural ally of the oil workers, was ideologically divided over the question of worker control of industry, and one of the socialist parties, the Mexican Communist party, had changed its position on this issue. In this context, it should be noted that when the Workers' Administration of the National Railways was established in May 1938, the Mexican Communist party had applauded the decision and had expressed its strong support for the concept of labor control of industry. However, in October 1938, the Central Committee of the Mexican Communist party approved a resolution to the effect that, in light of the financial problems that had beset the railway administration as a result of the government's failure to permit increases in cargo tariffs, worker control of industry was not feasible within the framework of capitalist economic relations. This resolution was adopted as official policy at the party's seventh congress in early 1939.[74]

In contrast, the adherents of Leon Trotsky supported the concept of worker control of industry, arguing that the labor administrations were vehicles through which the working class could advance its class interests. In 1939, Trotsky, writing under a pseudonym, expressed his views on the question of worker control in the nationalized oil industry in the journal *Clave*. He argued that the imperialist administration of the oil industry had been replaced by a local capitalist one, and in these circumstamces, workers should fight for the formation of committees in each local that participated in the administration of production, thereby setting the basis for an incipient labor control.[75] Although the political divisions between the Communists and the Trotskyists were not reflected within the oil workers' union, it is probable that the ideological disparity between the two also influenced the STPRM's change in policy.

The 1940 Conflict of Economic Order

In October 1939, following the Second Special Convention, the government, in response to the STPRM demand that Petróleos Mexicanos sign a collective contract, established a commission (Comisión de Contratación) to work on the issue. This commission consisted of labor and government representatives and offered the STPRM the possibility of defining, once and for all, the legal position and working conditions of members. The negotiations moved rapidly, and seventy clauses of a draft contract were approved.[76] The discussions, however, were suspended in December 1939, when Cárdenas called for a complete reorganization of the industry and asked the STPRM to formulate a plan to facilitate it. The government justified the proposed reorganization on the grounds that production costs, particularly in the area of wages, had risen substantially since the nationalization without a corresponding increase in productivity and that the industry was in a state of crisis because revenues from exports of petroleum products had fallen as a result of the boycott on Mexican oil imposed by the expropriated companies.[77]

The STPRM did not respond formally to the presidential petition. Consequently, the government decided to draft a plan to effect the proposed reorganization. The plan was issued on 28 February 1940, consisting of fourteen points that, in general terms, proposed: A reduction in the number of permanent employees to a ceiling defined as the number who were employed on 18 March 1938; the abolition of positions that were deemed unnecessary; the revision of administrative salaries; the reduction in the number of temporary employees to 10 per cent of the number of permanent employees; the suspension of housing allowance payments to employees whose salaries exceeded $1.85 per day; that positions left vacant be filled only if absolutely necessary; that the management of Petróleos Mexicanos and the Distribuidora de Petróleos Mexicanos be at complete liberty to transfer staff if necessary; that competence be the main factor in the determination of staff promotions; that the number of STPRM locals be reduced in order to complement the new administrative organization of the industry; and, finally, that field superintendents be nominated by the administration of Petróleos Mexicanos rather than by STPRM locals.[78]

Following the publication of this plan, the STPRM designated a commission to study how the proposed reorganization could be effected. Various possibilities were suggested within the STPRM, and in May

1940 the union presented its formal reply. In addition to submitting a proposal for the reorganization, the union called on the industry central management to implement fully the salary scale contained in the 1937 *laudo* and to discontinue the practice of discounting workers' salaries, as had been the case since 25 July 1938, when the government agreed partially to implement clauses of the said *laudo* referring to wages.[79] It also called for the fusion of the Distribuidora de Petróleos Mexicanos with Petróleos Mexicanos, and demanded that, on the administrative board of the new agency thereby formed, the STPRM have a majority.[80]

The STPRM response indicates that it had accepted the need for an administrative reorganization of the industry and that it was willing to cooperate with the government. It also demonstrates, however, that the general questions of work conditions and a collective contract were matters of utmost importance for the STPRM. Hence, while the union was prepared to compromise and accepted that Petróleos Mexicanos might not be in an economic position to implement fully the 1937 *laudo*, it is evident that the STPRM expected compliance with certain fundamental clauses, such as those relating to wages. The terms of the STPRM's answer to the government also suggest that the question of the administrative and legal structure of the industry was still a major preoccupation, although the demand for the creation of a workers' administration was not repeated.

The government agreed to study the STPRM's proposals for the reorganization of the industry and to examine the possibility of merging Petróleos Mexicanos with the Distribuidora de Petróleos Mexicanos. It did not, however, agree to discontinue the salary discounts on the grounds that to do so would have increased, rather than decreased, the industry's administration expenses. Nor did it agree to the STPRM suggestion that the union dominate the administrative board of Petróleos Mexicanos. The National Executive Committee argued that it could not give up the majority it had on the administrative councils of Petróleos Mexicanos and the Distribuidora de Petróleos Mexicanos, because this would imply a renunciation of the responsibility that the government had contracted before the nation for the administration of the oil industry.[81]

The terms of the official response to the STPRM proposal that the union have a majority on the administrative board of Petróleos Mexicanos indicate that the government had no faith in the capacity of the union to administer the industry and that it had definitely discounted the possibility of creating a workers' administration. The government's policy on this question was not merely a response to the difficult economic circumstances confronting the industry. It was indicative of a general change in the political orientation of the Cárdenas government. This change had been reflected in such developments as the decision to support the candidacy of Avila Camacho in the 1940 elections; in the undertaking, in the wake of the oil expropriation, not to nationalize other major industries; in the adoption of confrontationist tactics with labor;[82] and, finally, in the reduction in the rate of land redistribution in the program of agrarian reform.

The reasons for this change are complex. First, in the international arena, Mexico was confronting serious political and economic problems. These problems were caused by such factors as the attitudes adopted by the governments of the United Kingdom and the United States in the wake of the oil nationalization, the boycott imposed by the expropriated companies, and the difficulties created by the outbreak of World War II for the sale of petroleum and other export products on the international market. Second, on a national level, the political situation was tense: 1939 and 1940 saw the emergence of a strong political Right, in the form of the Almazán party, which was opposed to the spirit of the *cardenista* political and economic agenda. Furthermore, the possibility existed that dissident military elements would again take to arms as had happened in the case of the Cedillo revolt in 1938. Finally, on the other side of the political spectrum, the Left, and particularly the Mexican Communist party, had adopted a policy of "unity at all costs." This policy was a direct result of the Comintern's 1936 decision to support the notion of "popular frontism" as a way of combating the spread of fascism and meant that the Mexican Communist party accepted the gradual modification of the most radical aspects of the *cardenista* political and economic agenda. Although the Comintern abandoned the policy of popular frontism in 1939 when the Soviet-German pact was signed, this did not result in a major modification of the Mexican Communist party's attitude toward the Cárdenas government, as is demonstrated by the fact the it supported the administration's official candidate in the 1940 elections.[83] In mid-1940, the full extent of the Cárdenas government's change in political orientation was still to emerge, but there is little doubt that the regime's attitude toward oil workers was symptomatic of a more general process.

In spite of the government's decision to examine the union's proposal regarding the reorganization, the regime decided to introduce a series of emergency measures to reduce production costs. The measures included: the abolition of unnecessary positions; further discounting of salaries that exceeded $130 per month; the elimination of overtime payments; and a reduction in the number of temporary employees. The administrations of Petróleos Mexicanos and the Distribuidora de Petróleos Mexicanos were also instructed not to fill vacant positions unless absolutely necessary, and were given the power to transfer staff at will.[84] These measures provoked the hostility of certain elements of the oil workers' union, and there was general criticism of the actions of STPRM representatives on the administrative boards of Petróleos Mexicanos and the Distribuidora de Petróleos Mexicanos for having accepted the government decision to reorganize the industry.[85] Furthermore, there was a government campaign against oil workers who opposed the reorganization. For example, in one pamphlet that was circulated by the secretary of communications and public works, such workers were characterized as "bad revolutionaries," "bad Mexicans," and "traitors to the homeland"![86]

In these circumstances, the negotiations between the government and the union regarding the reorganization did not advance, and, in July 1940, oil industry authorities filed a Conflict of Economic Order suit against the STPRM in the Federal Commission of Conciliation and Arbitration. In the demand, the plaintiffs described the economic circumstances of the industry since the expropriation and sought permission to implement a number of administrative and structural reforms, including a reduction in the number of temporary and permanent personnel. The plaintiffs also filed an incidental claim requesting the commission's authorization to implement a series of emergency measures in order to reduce the immediate administrative costs of production.

The 1940 Conflict of Economic Order was litigated over a period of several months, and on 28 November 1940 the Federal Commission for Conciliation and Arbitration handed down a decision against the STPRM. The *laudo* declared that there existed economic disequilibrium in Petróleos Mexicanos[87] and that it would, therefore, be necessary to implement a number of temporary measures in order to facilitate the recovery of the industry. It then authorized the administration of Petróleos Mexicanos to dismiss permanent employees and 25 percent of the doctors, lawyers, pharmacists, and drillers who were employed after 1 April 1938; to retrench temporary staff once they had completed the tasks for which they were contracted; and to reduce, by 10 percent, the salaries of workers earning more than $130 per month. It also ruled that workers who were laid off as a result of the implementation of the plaintiff's incidental claim of 25 July 1940 would not be reemployed and that industry authorities were not obliged to implement a collective contract.[88]

The decision to file the Conflict of Economic Order suit against the STPRM marked a fundamental change in the relations between the government and the union, and signified the end of any real worker participation in the administration of the nationalized oil properties. Furthermore, the presentation of the demand and the findings of the Federal Commission for Conciliation and Arbitration against the STPRM represented a major defeat for the workers because, in the final analysis, they emerged from the conflict without a collective contract and without the possibility of modifying the existing administrative or legal structure of the industry That is to say, by the end of 1940, the workers had no further possibility of increasing the union's participation, or of creating a labor administration, in the petroleum industry.

Conclusion

Several points emerge from this review of the oil workers' participation in the administration of the nationalized petroleum industry between 1938 and 1940. First, a workers' administration per se did not exist at any time between 1938 and 1940. This chapter has attempted to document the experience of worker participation in the administration of the expropriated oil properties and has shown that, until the formation of Petróleos Mexicanos and the Distribuidora de Petróleos Mexicanos in July 1938, the workers exercised de facto control of the means of production at a *local* level. After July 1938, the workers' participation in the administration of production was limited to minority representation in the administrative councils of Petróleos Mexicanos and the Distribuidora de Petróleos Mexicanos. As a result of this and the fact that the *consejos locales de administración* were abolished, the degree of effective control exercised by the workers was considerably reduced. Second, the emergence of the demand for worker control of the industry has to be understood within the political context of the time. The period of the presidency of Lázaro Cárdenas witnessed the climax of an era of revolutionary nationalism in Mexico, and the experiments in labor administration and cooperative organization of production were the logical products of the political and economic philosophy of the regime. In the petroleum industry, the workers perceived the creation of a labor administration as a viable alternative to state management of the expropriated oil properties. In this context, the existence of an apparently successful workers' administration in the National Railways of Mexico influenced the STPRM's position on this question in 1938 and 1939.

Finally, the STPRM abandonment of the proworkers' administration policy in 1939 was the result of a combination of circumstances. The most significant of these were the fact that a majority of oil workers believed that certain conditions—such as the implementation of an industrywide collective contract and the economic recovery of the industry—were fundamental prerequisites to the successful establishment of a labor administration and, more important, the fact that the Cárdenas government had, as has been shown, changed its ideological position on the question of worker control of industry. The modification of the government's position on this and other questions signified the end of the era of revolutionary nationalism in Mexico and the transition to a period in which the philosophy of developmentalism dominated the political and economic programs of subsequent regimes.

Notes

1. Sinesio Capitanachi Luna, *Furbero, Palma Sola y Poza Rica: historia del petróleo y memorias de un trabajador jubilado en la industria*, 2 vols. (Xalapa, 1983), vol. 1, p. 448.

2. Minutes of the Local 30 meeting held on 12 July 1937, Archive of Local 30 of the STPRM, Pozo Rica, Veracruz (hereafter cited as Local 30), file no. 0033.

3. Joe Ashby, *Organized Labor and the Mexican Revolution under Lázaro Cárdenas* (Chapel Hill, 1967), p. 226.

4. Capitanachi Luna, *Furbero, Palma Sola y Poza Rica.*

5. Ibid.

6. Alberto J. Olvera, "Gestión del trabajo y acción obrera en la coyunturo de la nacionalización del petróleo: el caso de Poza Rica (1938–1939)," paper presented at the Primer Coloquio sobre Crisis, Proceso de Trabajo y Clase Obrera, Xalapa, Veracruz, 15–18 Oct. 1986, p. 11.

7. Capitanachi Luna, *Furbero, Palma Sola y Poza Rica*, vol. 1, p. 452.

8. Ibid., p. 453.

9. Marcelo Rodea, *Historia del movimiento obrero ferrocarri1ero en México (1890–1942)* (Mexico City, 1944), pp. 603–604.

10. During the presidency of Lázaro Cárdenas, cooperatives were established in the mining industry, in several of the lines that did not form part of the National Railways system, in a number of sugar refineries, and in the Mexico City abattoirs, to give a few examples.

11. Capitanachi Luna, *Furbero, Palma Sola y Poza Rica*, vol. 1, p. 453.

12. Typical of the administrative plans presented to the president were those of Local 30, which gave the Local Executive Committee extraordinary powers and permitted it to decide which workers would occupy positions of responsibility. The Local 30 plans also proposed that, in order to augment local finances, workers contribute 50 percent of their salaries for the establishment of a cooperative store. Minutes of the meeting of 24 Feb. 1938, Local 30, file no. 003-3.

13. Capitanachi Luna, *Furbero, Palma Sola y Poza Rica.*

14. Merrill Rippy, "El petróleo y la Revolución Mexicana," *Problemas Agrícolas e Industriales de México* 6:3 (1954), p. 117.

15. *El Mundo* (Tampico), 19 March 1938.

16. Francisco Colmenares, *Petróleo y lucha de clases en México, 1864–1982* (Mexico City, 1982), p. 95.

17. Juan García Hernández, *El cuchillito de palo* (Mexico City, 1967), pp. 21–22.

18. *La Prensa* (Mexico City), 21, 23, 24 March 1938.

19. This department was called the Department of External Sales and was directed by Gustavo Espinoza Mireles.

20. STPRM, National Executive Committee, circular no. 27, 21 March 1938, Local 30, file no. 0132.

21. Minutes of meeting of 24 March 1938, Local 30, file no. 003-3.

22. Ibid. In Poza Rica, for example, it was decided that the local would take appropriate action to ensure that temporary workers who were dismissed did not lose their acquired rights and that a list of affected personnel would be forwarded to the Consejo Directivo del Petróleo. The local also decided that workers who found themselves unemployed would be helped economically and would be employed by the union wherever possible.

23. Ibid.

24. See minutes of Local 30 meetings held between March and June 1938.

25. See "Report submitted to Francisco J. Múgica, Centro de Estudios de la Revolución Mexicana Lázaro Cárdenas, AC, Fondo Francisco J. Múgica (hereafter cited as CERMLC, Fondo Múgica), vol. 1 B2, document no. 29B.

26. Memo, Victor F. Sánchez, Secretary of Internal Affairs, and Manuel Gutiérrez B., Secretary of External Affairs, National Executive Committee of the STPRM, 8 Nov. 1937, Archivo General de la Nación, Mexico City, Ramo Presidentes, Fondo Lázaro Cárdenas del Río (hereafter cited as AGN Fondo Cárdenas), 432.2/29.

27. Memo, A. Martínez Rincón and A. Villaseñor, National Executive Committee of the STPRM, to President Cárdenas, 29 Sept. 1938, AGN Fondo Cárdenas, 432.2/29.

28. See Carlos Martínez Assad, "La rebelión cedillista o el ocaso del poder tradicional," *Revista Mexicana de Sociología* 16:3 (1979), pp. 709–729.

29. STPRM, Consejo General de Vigilancia, circular no. 31, 9 Sept. 1938, Local 30, file no. 0133.

30. Ibid.

31. Ibid.

32. Ibid., and Local 3, El Ebano, San Luis Potosí, Bulletín, 25 Oct. 1938, AGN, Fondo Cárdenas, 432.2/29. Zamora was accused of being the intellectual author of the murder of the president of the Local Vigilance Committee, Jesús de la Garza, on 10 Aug. 1938. According to internal documentation of the local, De la Garza had refused to cooperate with Zamora in the furthering of the latter's political ambitions and was therefore eliminated. At about the same time, another worker opposed to the Zamora group, Baltazar Gómez, was shot dead in broad daylight in the local electrical workshop. The assassin in this instance, Eduardo Toscano, was a close associate of Zamora. Toscano was subsequently expelled from the local.

33. Transcript of report of Bernardo G. Mortera, Federal Labor Inspector in San Luis Potosí, 8 Aug. 1938, AGN, Departamento Autónomo de Trabajo (hereafter cited as AGN DAT), Caja 241, Expediente 9.

34. Memo, Vicente Cortés Herrera, General Manager, Petróleos Mexicanos, to Godofredo F. Beltrán, Chief Executive to the Secretaría Particular de la Presidencia de la República, 24 Aug. 1938, AGN, Fondo Cárdenas, 432.2/29.

35. STPRM, Consejo General de Vigilancia, circular no. 39, 13 Oct. 1938, Local 30, file no. 0133.

36. Minutes of the special session of Local 3, Ebano, San Luis Potosí, of 17 Oct. 1938, AGN Fondo Cárdenas, 432.2/29.

37. Transcript of report of Bernardo G. Mortera, AGN DAT, C. 241, E. 9.

38. STPRM, Consejo General de Vigilancia, circular no. 38, 6 Oct. 1938, Local 30.

39. Ibid., no. 41, 17 Oct. 1938, Local 30.

40. Local Executive Committee of Local 3 to President Cárdenas, 17 Feb. 1939, AGN Cárdenas, 432.2/29.

41. Minutes of the special session of Local 3, 9 March 1939, AGN DAT, C. 217, E. 7.

42. Local Executive Committee of Local 3 to President Cárdenas, 19 Sept. 1940, AGN Cárdenas, 432.2/29.

43. For example, in Local 1 (Ciudad Madero) there was, shortly after the expropriation, a heated debate on the question of the duality of functions of the members of the *consejo local de administración*, and it was decided that they should be relieved of their positions as union officials. See *El Mundo*, 26 March 1938. Local 30 members also made a similar decision. See minutes of meeting of 18 April 1938, Local 30, file no. 003-3.

44. "Acuerdos tomados en asamblea del Comité Executivo General del día 16 de julio de 1938," in García Hernández, *El cuchillito de palo*, p. 47.

45. In Local 30, for example, there were various complaints of this nature and even allegations that the *consejo local* acted in an authoritarian fashion. Minutes of meeting of 7 July 1938, Local 30, file no. 003-3.

46. *El Mundo*, 15 July 1938.

47. The decision to dissolve the *consejos locales* was strongly opposed by Locals 1 and 30. Local 30 decided to comply with the presidential determination but to express its disagreement by requesting that the *consejos locales* continue to function, and, if this were not possible, that the 1937 *laudo* be implemented completely. It also demanded that the legal position of the STPRM in the new administration be defined. See *El Mundo*, 16 July 1938; minutes of meeting of 21 July 1938, Local 30, file no. 003-3.

48. STPRM, *Informes del Comité Ejecutivo General y Consejo General de Vigilancia o la Segunda Gran Convención General Extraordinaria del STPRM* (Mexico City, 1939), p. 22.

49. Ibid., p. 21.

50. Minutes of meeting of 25 Aug. 1938, Local 30, file no. 0033.

51. *Guía* (Mexico City), no. 5, April 1939, p. 29.

52. Ibid., no. 6, May 1939, p. 12.

53. B. M. Gutiérrez, *Las administraciones obreras de las industrias* (Mexico City, 1939), as quoted in: Colmenares, *Petróleo y lucha de clases*, pp. 108–109.

54. See "Los puestos administrativos," *Guía*, no. 4, March 1939, p. 23, and "Las administraciones obreras de las industrias," ibid., no. 8, July 1939, pp. 26–27, 35.

55. "Dictamen de la Comisión de Asuntos Jurídicos de Segunda Convención Extraordinorio del STPRM sobre el punto 2: organización jurídico-administrativa de la industria que convendría apoyar el sindicato por garantizar los intereses de los trabajadores," Mexico City (mimeo of the STPRM), 1939.

56. Ibid.

57. *Guía*, no. 8, July 1939, p. 2.

58. "Dictamen de la Comisión."

59. Ibid.
60. Ibid.
61. STPRM, Informes del Comité Ejecutivo General, p. 26.
62. Julio Valdivieso Castillo, *Historia del movimiento sindical petrolero en Minatitlán, Veracruz* (Mexico City, 1963), pp. 117–118.
63. Local 30, file no. 041.
64. Aurelio Martínez Rincón and Oscar Caraveo, memo, 31 Dec. 1938, Local 30, file no. 031-2.
65. Fabio Barbosa Cano, "El movimiento petrolero en 1938–1940," in Javier Aguilar García, coord., *Los sindicatos nacionales en el México contemporáneo*, vol. 1: *Petroleros* (Mexico City, 1986), p. 62.
66. *La Prensa* (Mexico City), 4 June 1939.
67. Ibid., 7 June 1939
68. Barbosa Cano, "El movimiento petrolero," p. 63.
69. *La Prensa*, 7 June 1939.
70. Ibid., 15 June 1939.
71. Rippy, "El petróleo y la Revolución Mexicana," p. 138.
72. Barbosa Cano, "El movimiento petrolero," p. 69.
73. Yaldivieso Castillo, *Historia del movimiento sindical petrolero*, p. 119.
74. Encarnación Pérez J., "En el sexenio de Cárdenas" in Arnaldo Martínez Verdugo, *Historia del comunismo en México* (Mexico City, 1985), p. 183.
75. Colmenares, *Petróleo y lucha de clase*, p. 116.
76. Valdivieso Castillo, *Historia del movimiento sindical petrolero*, p. 126.
77. Ibid.
78. *La Prensa*, 29 Feb. 1940.
79. STPRM, "Informes del Comité Ejecutivo General," p. 27.
80. Valdivieso Castillo, *Historia del movimiento sindical petrolero*, p. 127.
81. Ibid., p. 128.
82. In this context, it should be noted that in mid-1937 Cárdenas instructed the Federal Labor Department to discourage industrial action on the part of workers, and that the years 1937–1940 saw a substantial decrease in the number of strikes. This tendency is demonstrated in the following table.

Strikes and Strikers, 1937–1940

Year	Number of Strikes	Number of Strikers
1937	576	61,732
1938	319	13,455
1939	303	14,486
1940	357	19,784

Source: Jorge Basurto, *Cárdenas y el poder sindical* (Mexico City, 1983), p. 159.

By 1940, the government's tendency to oppose rather than support workers in their attempts to advance their class interests had been demonstrated in such developments as the reorganization of the oil industry, the decision to disband the Workers Administration of the National Railways of Mexico, and the fact that workers did not receive the support of either Cárdenas or the CTM in a major dispute that erupted with foreign-owned electrical companies.

83. For a discussion of the Mexican Communist party's attitude toward the Cárdenas government at this time, see Barry Carr, "Crisis in Mexican Communism: The Extraordinary Congress of the Mexican Communist Party," parts 1 & 2, *Science and Society* 50:4 (1986, 1987), pp. 391–414; 51:1 (1987), pp. 43–67.

84. Valdivieso Castillo, *Historia del movimiento sindical petrolero*, p. 129.

85. Ibid., p. 130.

86. Barbosa Cano, "El movimiento petrolero," p. 78.

87. The Distribuidora de Petróleos Mexicanos, as the result of an agreement signed between the government and the STPRM on 7 Aug. 1940, had been fused with Petróleos Mexicanos and was, therefore, no longer a party in the dispute.

88. Junta Federal de Concilación y Arbitraje, "Resolución de la Junta Federal de Conciliación y Arbitraje en el Conflicto de Orden Económico entre Petróleos Mexicanos y Socios (actor) y el Sindicato de Trabajadores Petroleros de la República Mexicana (demandado)" (Expediente A/940/5373/362), 28 Nov. 1940, AGN DAT,C. 209, E. 4

6. The Expropriation and Great Britain

Lorenzo Meyer
El Colegio de México, Mexico City
Translated by Lidia Lozano

When in March 1938 the government headed by General Lázaro Cárdenas decided to settle its dispute with foreign oil companies in radical fashion by resorting to expropriation, the Anglo-Dutch interests that owned the largest oil company then operating in Mexico, the Compañía Mexicana de Petróleo "El Aguila," were most affected. This enterprise had been founded under Mexican law in 1908, as a relatively minor part of an extensive economic empire controlled by the British firm S. Pearson & Son, headed by Weetman Pearson, later Lord Cowdray. However, within a short time, it had become the center of Pearson's interests in Mexico. In April 1919, Cowdray transferred control of El Aguila to the Anglo-Dutch consortium Royal Dutch–Shell, which ran the company until its expropriation nineteen years later.

After spectacular early success, which coincided with World War I, El Aguila's importance declined in the twenties, but recovered again in the early thirties with the discovery of the Poza Rica deposits. In 1938, the enterprise had a book value of $137 million, which made it one of the most important companies in Mexico.[1] Under the old regime, relations between El Aguila and Mexican authorities had been overtly friendly, but following the success of the *maderista* revolution in 1911, and especially after the proclamation of the 1917 Constitution, which nationalized oil deposits, the relationship was fraught with continual conflicts. It was not just a clash between the various oil companies and the Mexican authorities; it also involved the governments of the shareholders' countries of origin: the United States and Great Britain.

Following the Poza Rica discoveries, El Aguila decided that in order to recreate a favorable climate for a planned phase of expansion, the time had come to seek a definitive solution to its differences with the Mexican government. With this in mind, El Aguila executives and the Mexican authorities signed an agreement on 11 November 1937, which, in effect, granted the Mexican government a significant share of the value of future production of Poza Rica by way of royalties (35 percent)—an agreement to which the rest of the international oil community strongly objected.[2] The potential for collaboration between the big oil firm and the Mexican government that this agreement entailed never had a chance to be realized, because precisely at that point the conflict between labor and management, which had long troubled the oil industry, now intensified. El Aguila, along with the other foreign oil companies—which were essentially American in ownership—refused to accept the finding of the Mexican courts that favored the recently organized oil workers' national union, and openly challenged the authority of the Mexican president and government. The expropriation followed.

Return for Nothing

Since the very beginning of the Mexican Revolution, American and British policies had differed and even clashed in respect to their views of the Mexican situation and the best way to deal with it.[3] These differences surfaced once again after the oil expropriation. According to the British minister in Mexico, Owen St. Clair O'Malley, Mexico under the leadership of General Cárdenas had become a country under "advanced evolutionary socialism," whose central objective was to give ownership of land and industry to the masses, and, if this was not feasible, then simply to extract from capital the highest possible bonuses and wages for labor. Unfortunately, His Majesty's minister thought, this type of socialism would bankrupt the Mexican economy and confound its very objective: the betterment of the working classes. In O'Malley's view, given the dishonesty and incompetence of the officials surrounding President Cárdenas, such an outcome was very likely.[4] In his analysis of the Mexican situation, written on the eve of the oil expropriation, O'Malley voiced his fears that the strong nationalist drives of *cardenismo* would lead to decisions concerning the question of control of natural resources that would be contrary to British—and, in the long run, Mexican—interests. Nevertheless, he was confident that before any such thing happened, pressure from the United States would curb the pursuit of senseless social reformism that the Mexican government had embarked upon.[5] Clearly, the minister's optimism was proven wrong by the expropriation of 18 March 1938.

From an American perspective, the more important element in the relation between Mexico and the United States in 1938 was not the defense of its petroleum interests—which had already lost the strategic character they had enjoyed twenty years earlier—but rather the consolidation of an inter-American alliance in the face of the impending collapse of the international system that had emerged from the Treaty of Versailles. In order to achieve such an alliance, the United States had accepted the principle of nonintervention, and it was therefore inconceivable that it would resort to force against Mexico; besides, it feared that the fall of General Cárdenas's government might bring about a government with pro-fascist sympathies.[6] This accounted for the failure of three Foreign Office missions to Washington, which, in May, July, and August 1938, tried to persuade the State Department and President Franklin D. Roosevelt of the advantages of working toward a joint Anglo-American policy against the oil expropriation. The American refusal to work with the British arose from their different views on the legitimacy of the action taken by Mexico. As far as the United States was concerned, only the method of compensation, not the actual decision to expropriate the oil industry—which was within Mexico's rights as a sovereign nation—was open to discussion. On this question, Mexico proposed payment within ten years, while the United States demanded immediate compensation. His Majesty's government, on the other hand, questioned the very legitimacy of the expropriation and demanded from the Mexican government the immediate return of the seized companies to their legitimate owners.[7]

Three diplomatic notes dated 8 April, 20 April, and 11 May 1938 reveal the official position of His Majesty's government on the oil expropriation.[8] According to these notes, the Foreign Office accepted the sovereign right of any government to expropriate private property as long as the general interest required it and proper compensation was offered. However, the opinion in London was that, in the particular case of the Mexican oil expropriation, no substantive reason existed, and therefore it was arbitrary and unacceptable. Faced with the Mexican refusal to accept their protest against the expropriation of El Aguila, the British government insisted on its right to defend the interests of shareholders even though the company itself was not registered in Great Britain but in Mexico. In the third note of May 11, the Foreign Office, at Minister O'Malley's insistence, questioned the assurance given by the Mexican government, to the effect that oil company owners would receive adequate compensation. The source of doubt was Mexico's default on its old foreign debt and also on the 1937 annuity for compensation awarded to British claimants for damage to persons and property during the Revolution.

The Mexican response to the imputation of default on their international obligations was quick: O'Malley received the outstanding annuity payment, but, it was pointed out, "even states more powerful and with ample resources have no reason to feel proud of their record to pay every pecuniary obligation promptly." This paragraph contained a clear reference to the unpaid debt of Great Britain to the United States. But Mexico also took the opportunity to announce the withdrawal of its diplomatic

personnel from London; the Foreign Office had to do ... e with
O'Malley and his four assistants; and, not for ... ico and
Great Britain broke off diplomatic relati...

The British declared they were surpri... ion but
did not express regret. They immediatel... nent to
take charge of its affairs in Mexico, but... clined,
alleging that it was inadvisable that M... osition
of the two powers on the oil question t... result,
the Finnish minister became the political representative of British
interests, although in 1940 this role was more appropriately taken over
by the Dutch legation—Holland had never broken off relations with
Mexico. In London, the Cuban legation represented Mexican interests.
However, as on previous occasions, the consular corps was not affected
by the diplomatic rupture, and the British and Mexican consuls remained in their respective places. Thus, the consul general—first F. A.
Clough, then Thomas Ifor Rees—became the eyes and ears of the Foreign
Office in Mexico.

Great Britain welcomed the "hard" line of the Foreign Office. It was
clear that from the British point of view the most important factor in the
Mexican case was to establish a firm precedent of opposition to actions
such as Mexico's being taken elsewhere.[9] Besides, it was felt in Great
Britain that formal rejection of the expropriation, combined with adequate pressure, would soon force Mexico to reverse its decision. "There
can be no doubt," announced *The Economist*, "that Mexico will regret
the action it has taken."[10]

Pressures

At first, the British believed that, although the oil expropriation had
wide support in Mexico and it would not be easy to force Cárdenas to
back down, economic pressures against the recently nationalized industry would lead to bankruptcy within three months. After all, Great
Britain, the United States, and Holland controlled 83 percent of the
petroleum fleet, to which Mexico would have no access; on the other
hand, countries such as Germany, Italy, Norway, or Japan, which might
be tempted to buy Mexican fuel at discount rates, would not be able to
resist American pressure not to do so. And if that were not enough, with
the U.S. Treasury's suspension of purchases of Mexican silver—the
country's leading export—the popularity of the expropriation would
dwindle and Mexican public opinion would cry out for a return to the
status quo ante.[11] We know that British expectations were wrong.
Mexico found an independent oil entrepreneur in the United States,
William Davis, who was prepared to risk the wrath of the big companies

and their governments in return for windfall gains. Davis shipped Mexican crude oil to his refineries in Europe; meanwhile, Germany and Italy, followed later by Japan, ignored threats by Standard Oil (N.J.) and Royal Dutch–Shell, and proceeded to trade manufactured goods and grain for Mexican oil. Davis sent the first shipment of 12 million barrels of Mexican crude to Europe in a chartered tanker sailing under the British flag in July 1939—barely three months after the expropriation and about the time when the collapse of Mexico predicted in Great Britain should have occurred; to make matters worse, the press at the time reported purchases of Mexican oil by British companies.[12] El Aguila then tried to impound one of Davis's shipments as it entered a European port, but the company eventually lost the legal battle and was later faced with a counterclaim from Davis for damages, which dragged on for years.[13]

The loss of the American silver market—which was worth some $30 million a year—was a very harsh blow for the Mexican economy in 1938. Fortunately, however, the American boycott in this area was not absolute, although it did manage to reduce substantially Mexican silver sales overseas over a period of two years. In fact, the two great losers in the silver affair turned out to be the Mexican treasury and American miners, since the bulk of silver production at the time came from mines managed by Americans. Thus, while the treasury did not purchase the metal directly from the Bank of Mexico as it had done prior to March 1938, within a few months after the expropriation it was buying it again, this time in the free market, where Mexico placed its silver.[14] Economic pressure affected the behavior of some sectors of the Mexican economy, but not enough to force a reversal of the expropriation. Between 1937 and 1940, the Gross National Product rose by some 10 percent.[15] Thus, by the end of Cárdenas's administration there was little hope for those who had counted on economic problems to reverse the process of oil nationalization.

In May 1938, Sir Robert Vansittart—a British official and an old adversary of the Mexican Revolution—counseled that although Great Britain was not in a position to solve the problem created by the expropriation through direct military intervention, nothing could stop it from embarking on a psychological war against Cárdenas, creating the impression that British measures were responsible for whatever internal or external difficulties Mexico experienced.[16]

As a result of the expropriation, those in the Foreign Office responsible for Mexican policy looked back to the times when they had nurtured hopes that intervention by reactionaries like Félix Díaz, Victoriano Huerta, and Manuel Peláez would put an end to the governments of the Revolution and somehow restore the comfortable and predictable atmosphere of the old regime. It was precisely because of suspicions that El

Aguila was prepared to support the rebellion of General Saturnino Cedillo—the strongman of San Luis Potosí—that in April 1938 Sumner Welles, the undersecretary of state, warned the British ambassador in Washington against any attempt by the Anglo-Dutch company to encourage the rebellion, since further civil strife in Mexico might offer a great opportunity for "foreign intrigue," that is, for Falangist, national-socialist, or fascist influences.[17] When the *cedillista* uprising finally took place in May 1938, the federal government was able to isolate it with little difficulty and to finish it off by January 1939. There is no strong evidence to suggest that the oil lobby gave support to Cedillo, even though his political statements condemned Cárdenas's oil expropriation as an "antipolitical, antieconomic and antipatriotic" act.[18] In 1939, hopes that a military coup would bring about a political change in Mexico were revived, at least within the Petroleum Office in London, which tipped off the Foreign Office about an uprising to be led by Joaquín Amaro that would establish a military dictatorship in Mexico, this being "the only way to restore a proper sense of business, discipline and respect for property in this country."[19] Later, others hoped that General Cárdenas's loss of popularity and the 1939–1940 electoral campaign might achieve what neither Cedillo nor Amaro had achieved.[20] Hence the failure of the opposition candidate, Gen. Juan Andrew Almazán, must have been a further disappointment to those who hoped to reverse the expropriation through a change in government in Mexico.

It gradually dawned on those responsible for Mexican policy in London that, in fact, the fate of Anglo-Dutch oil interests in Mexico would depend less on Great Britain's actions than on the eventual settlement between the Americans and the Mexican government; unfortunately, relations between President Roosevelt and his own oil companies were not very good.[21]

By the end of 1938, there was an impasse. General Cárdenas asserted that his government would not oppose the resumption of relations with Great Britain as long as His Majesty's government took the initiative and did so unconditionally. It seemed pointless to the Foreign Office to seek normalization of relations with Mexico as long as the latter did not reconsider its attitude, for otherwise "leaders of other countries in Latin America where the British hold important petroleum concessions—i.e., Venezuela, Colombia and Peru—would be encouraged to think that it might be in their national interest to carry out a policy of theft like Mexico's." From the point of view of the Foreign Office, since the United States would not adopt a hard line and since a settlement with Mexico that involved government participation in the running of the oil industry was out of the question, the only remaining alternative was a policy of containment, designed to isolate Mexico, and to make its attempt to consolidate the nationalized oil industry as costly as possible, by adopting measures to cut off its markets and prevent it from importing vital equipment.[22] The question of a possible settlement involving the direct participation of the Mexican government in the management of the industry related to the fact that, by that time, the expropriated companies were negotiating with the Mexican authorities through an American attorney, Donald R. Richberg, to explore the possibility of settling their differences and setting up new companies in which both the expropriated firms and the Mexican government would be represented. However, the attempt eventually failed when no agreement could be reached on the question of who would have control over daily operations and how such control would be exercised.[23]

It is not possible to assess clearly how successful the British boycott of Petróleos Mexicanos (Pemex) was, simply because the American government and the oil companies adopted a similar policy. But it is clear that Pemex's hardships during the years following the expropriation were due to an inextricable combination of the efforts of both powers. In any case, the Foreign Office succeeded in dissuading those countries over which it had some influence from purchasing Mexican oil and from selling oil equipment.[24] When World War II broke out in September 1939, Mexico lost its European markets; but, with the United States and, later, Mexico joining the Allied forces, the American boycott of Mexican oil was relaxed.[25] However, what was really responsible for Pemex's survival was the fact that it was virtually able to dispense with foreign markets, concentrating instead on the domestic market. While in 1938 local hydrocarbon consumption accounted for 57 percent of production, four years later internal demand absorbed 81 percent of production;[26] within a short time, the link between Pemex and the world market was marginal, and British hopes to drown Mexico in its own petroleum became somewhat unreal.[27]

A Forced Reconciliation

As has already been pointed out, in early 1939 the British position was one of waiting; the intention was not to resume relations with Mexico and to continue the boycott until that country changed its position on the oil nationalization question—as a result either of economic bankruptcy or of a direct settlement between the Mexican government and the expropriated companies, which were then negotiating with Cárdenas. In the long run, it was felt the domestic market could not sustain Pemex.[28] The Mexican attitude, too, was one of waiting: waiting for the boycott's failure and for the time when the need to protect and support its other investments in Mexico would force His Majesty's government to take the initiative and unconditionally to resume diplomatic relations between the two countries. The outbreak of World War II broke the deadlock. At first, Great Britain had a good opportunity to tighten its pressure on Mexico, with the Royal Navy stopping oil shipments to Germany and also refusing to provide safe conduct for materials and machinery—already paid for—that Mexico had stored in German docks.[29] Mexico lost that equipment altogether when the Allies subsequently bombed the warehouses.

The beginning of the Second World War also saw a change of government in Mexico. British observers figured that under Manuel Avila Camacho's presidency, the left wing of the ruling party—in particular the loathed CTM (Confederación de Trabajadores de México, Confederation of Mexican Workers)—would lose power, and the right—not the extreme right, Falangist and fascist in tendency, which still constituted a threat, but rather a moderate right—would gain strength. The new president—who came to power on 1 December 1940, when the beleaguered British Isles had just won the Battle of Britain—was seen as an honest person, perhaps somewhat lacking in the toughness needed to put an end once and for all to the follies of the left, but definitely more friendly than Cárdenas.[30]

Mexico's open participation on the Allies' side was not very important from a British standpoint, because at the time the main sources of petroleum for the British war effort were Persia (now Iran) and Venezuela. Hence, despite the pressures of the war, the Foreign Office in 1941 turned down requests several times from the Ministry of War Economy to resume relations with Mexico in order to secure from it oil, minerals, and a few enemy ships trapped in Mexican ports. Furthermore, according to the Foreign Office, the resumption of relations with Mexico at such a time would work against British strategic interests because it would displease Venezuela and Persia, who might fear Mexican fuel would take away some of the British market. Thus, as far as the Foreign Office was concerned, Mexico's political and economic marginalization had to continue in order to force it to negotiate an agreement that would open the way for the return of El Aguila to Mexico.[31]

Those outside the Foreign Office who wished to normalize Anglo-Mexican relations because they felt it would benefit Great Britain's military interests soon found support abroad, in the person of Sumner Welles, who wanted to see Mexico better integrated into the antifascist struggle.[32] However, what truly changed the Foreign Office's analysis of Anglo-American relations was their realization in August 1941 that, given the lack of success of direct negotiations between the oil companies and the Mexican government (only the Sinclair company had agreed to a settlement that involved compensation, rather than the return of seized property), the American government had decided that the way forward lay in setting up a binational governmental commission that would determine the amount and method of payment of compensation to the American oil companies. The Foreign Office immediately asked its embassy in Washington to oppose such a settlement since it would put an end to the possibility of foreign oil companies' ever returning to Mexico.[33] Once again, the British plea was ignored by Washington, and in April 1942 a direct agreement with Mexico was reached on the amount and method of payment owed to American oil companies. Standard Oil and the other American companies that had supported its hard line—to negotiate for a return and to refuse compensation—felt abandoned by Roosevelt's government. While at first they rejected the terms of the settlement, eventually, in October 1943, they agreed to end their dispute with Mexico for a compensation of $30 million to be paid within four years ($14 million previously agreed on with the Sinclair group should be added to this payment).[34]

The 1941–1943 settlements constituted a victory for Mexico, for, just as the Foreign Office had feared, it then became virtually impossible to reverse the process of oil expropriation and nationalization. Only the wartime situation, which required close political, military, and economic collaboration between Mexico and the United States—throughout 1941 and 1942, a Japanese attack on the American West Coast via Mexico was feared, and a joint U.S.-Mexico defense commission was set up in January 1942—can account for American acceptance of the Mexican position over the interests of the powerful Standard Oil (N.J.). It then became clear to Great Britain that El Aguila had been abandoned to its fate by the only power capable of protecting Aguila interests.[35]

Toward the end of his administration, General Cárdenas asserted Mexico's solidarity with Great Britain in its fight against the Nazi and Fascist powers.[36] After Avila Camacho's rise to power, his foreign minister, Ezequiel Padilla—one of the strongest supporters of a pro-Allied policy within the cabinet—was more outspoken about Mexican solidarity with the British cause. Padilla even informed the British consul general that perhaps the time had come to resume relations between the two countries; a similar statement—backed by the press— was made by the chargé d'affaires of the Diplomatic Office in the Mexican Chancery, but London responded to neither gesture.[37] Nevertheless, when the British War Cabinet was told in August 1941 of the impending signing of an oil agreement between Mexico and the United States, it authorized the Foreign Office—against the latter's own view— to look into the possibilities of resuming diplomatic relations with Mexico, and it advised El Aguila on the expediency of reaching a settlement similar to that accepted by the American companies. The

Foreign Office acceded to the cabinet's request with one qualification: it would not force El Aguila to follow in the steps of the American companies since there was still a chance of something better in the indefinite future.[38]

Although until January 1941 the Foreign Office had deemed it unacceptable to resume relations with Mexico before the oil properties had been recovered, it soon set in motion the machinery to enforce a different policy.[39] The decision was justified within the Foreign Office in terms of the "friendly" behavior shown by Mexico immediately following the world conflagration and, above all, because of the "consultations" held on the matter with Great Britain's principal support in its fight against Germany: the American government.[40]

Beginning in September 1941, both the Mexican and the British press informed their readers that an early resumption of Anglo-Mexican relations was likely. Ezequiel Padilla reiterated the significant role the British nation was playing then as defender of world freedom.[41] On 2 August, Buckingham Palace informed the Foreign Office that the king had given his consent to the reestablishment of relations with Mexico, and eleven days later, London instructed the consul general in Mexico City to inform the Mexican government that His Majesty's Government felt the time had come to resume diplomatic relations, while retaining, nevertheless, its full rights on the oil question; the Mexican Foreign Ministry accepted the British condition and on 22 October 1941, the British and Mexican governments declared that they had formally resumed political relations. Although after a break of three and a half years these relations were back at the starting point, the British press did not criticize the resumption of relations and in fact it did not consider it disastrous that El Aguila should reach a direct agreement with Mexico along the lines proposed by the State Department.[42]

From Alliance to Final Settlement

The new British minister to Mexico, Charles Harold Bateman, arrived in February 1942, just before Mexico joined the Allied cause. Indeed, as Bateman was beginning to familiarize himself with his new post, Mexico declared war on the Axis countries, precisely because of a series of incidents brought about by the end of the American oil boycott: the sinking in May 1942 by German U-boats of two Mexican tankers that were carrying fuel to American ports. Thus, unintentionally, in mid-1942 Mexico and Great Britain found themselves to be allies fighting against the same enemy.

Before the resumption of Anglo-Mexican diplomatic relations, El Aguila's representative in Mexico, I. D. Davidson, had already contacted

Avila Camacho and his colleagues to raise the possibility of a settlement that would involve not compensation, but rather an association with the government that would enable El Aguila to retain control of its operations for an indeterminate but substantial period of time. At the end of this period, the company would be handed over to the Mexican government. Avila Camacho considered the offer, but in the end rejected it; according to Davidson, the maneuvers of Eduardo Suárez, finance secretary, who represented Cárdenas's influence inside the cabinet, were to blame for the rejection.[43]

The oil settlement between Mexico and the United States led El Aguila to fear that other countries, in particular Venezuela, would follow the Mexican example. On the other hand, the settlement signaled the end of the Anglo-Dutch giant's "united front" with Standard Oil (N.J.). Through the Foreign Office, El Aguila informed the United States that it was going to try to reach a direct settlement with Mexico, but it wanted Washington not to give Mexico any loans that might enable Pemex to exploit fields in El Aguila's former property. The State Department acknowledged the request but never responded to it.[44]

In 1943, President Avila Camacho put his foreign minister at the head of the negotiations with El Aguila. Ezequiel Padilla proposed that negotiations should be based on the following premises: (1) the oil question was essentially political; (2) El Aguila could not expect a settlement different from that reached by American interests; and (3) no settlement could seek to remove control of the oil industry from the Mexican government. After a series of talks with El Aguila, the Foreign Office decided to accept a Mexican proposal to appoint a committee of evaluators to determine the amount of compensation that should be paid to the Anglo-Dutch company.[45] When it looked as if negotiations were about to start, Mexico hardened its position and the talks collapsed. Legally, El Aguila was a Mexican company; therefore, only compensation to the company's British shareholders was open to negotiation. Furthermore, negotiations should also take into account pending demands by El Aguila's Mexican workers against their former employer. Bateman rejected these changes to the basis for negotiations, the British press backed him, and once again the Foreign Office blamed *cardenista* influence for sabotaging the settlement proposed by Padilla.[46] Yet, in his 1944 presidential address, Avila Camacho pronounced himself optimistic on the question of an early oil settlement with British interests, although, on the face of it, such optimism seemed unfounded. For the situation had become more complicated, since El Aguila now demanded payment for fuel delivered to the National Railways before 18 March 1938, as well as compensation for some property not included in the expropriation decree but that had nonetheless been seized by Mexico.

The Mexican government's response was to demand the payment of pensions for workers retired by El Aguila, as well as some taxes that remained unpaid at the time of the expropriation.[47]

Despite new demands and counterdemands, and despite Ezequiel Padilla's departure from the Foreign Ministry, oil talks between the British and the Mexicans continued, this time with the president directly involved. Finally, on 7 February 1946, it was announced that an agreement had been signed to appoint an Anglo-Mexican and Anglo-Dutch commission to evaluate the seized property. The Mexican commissioner was Ingeniero Enrique Ortiz; the British one, I. D. Davidson; it was understood that their joint report would be ready before the end of the presidential term in late November.[48] It was at this point that the Americans warned both the British and the Mexicans that it would not be advisable either to seek, or to grant, better terms for El Aguila than those reached in the 1942–1943 settlements. Should Mexico allow the return of foreign companies, every expropriated company without exception should be readmitted. The State Department warned that if this was not possible then it would be preferable that things remained the same—and Mexican petroleum deposits remained unexploited, as "reserves."[49]

When it looked as if a final settlement was near, the Mexican government raised further objections. It objected to the fact that the secret terms of the agreement—whereby only British and Dutch shareholders, not those of other nationalities, would be compensated—had been leaked; it was known that 75 percent of shares were in the hands of British and Dutch subjects, the rest belonging to French (20 percent), Swiss, and Danish shareholders.[50] There was a further complication: the Mexican evaluator argued that the taxes and pensions that El Aguila owed its workers—and that had been taken on by Mexico—amounted to $6,185,567, not the mere $100,000 claimed by the company. On 21 May 1946, the public was informed that the agreement of February 7 had been annulled, and the group of experts whom El Aguila was about to send to Mexico never left England. The British ambassador—for by now Anglo-Mexican relations had changed from legation to ambassadorial status—again blamed Suárez for sabotaging the agreement.[51] Avila Camacho left the presidency without having resolved the oil question.

It is clear that by the end of 1946 the British felt a greater need to reach a solution on the El Aguila case than the Mexicans. For Mexico, Great Britain no longer represented a power that might counteract, albeit in part, an American presence. The war effort had weakened it considerably, whereas the Americans had emerged at the undisputed center of the capitalist world economy; thus, the postponement of a final settlement with the Anglo-Dutch petroleum interests did not matter to

Mexico. For the British, on the other hand, the situation was totally different. It was known that the dollar reserves accumulated by Mexico during the war were dwindling fast; it was plain to the British that unless an agreement was reached while Mexico had dollars, the oil question would remain unresolved for a long time.[52] Hence, even before Miguel Alemán, successor to Avila Camacho, had formally assumed power, the British ambassador began talks with him on this question. Alemán was cautious, but he did not shun discussing the subject with the ambassador.[53] The latter, who thought very highly of Alemán, did not hide his optimism: at last, the end seemed near.[54]

With a view to creating an even more favorable climate for the coming talks, El Aguila informed authorities in London that it would no longer object to the purchase of Mexican oil products; in other words, the boycott of Mexican oil by the British, who had sustained it the longest, came to an end.[55] The government of Miguel Alemán asked the British that the impending negotiations be kept secret, but someone in London could not resist the temptation of informing the press of what was happening, to see whether El Aguila shares went up, which indeed they did. This upset the Mexican government, though not sufficiently for it to postpone the talks.[56]

Ambassador Bateman thought that the new negotiations should be conducted, at least formally, between the oil company—which after all was Mexican—and the government of Miguel Alemán, without conferring on them the status of official bilateral talks. Neither El Aguila nor the Mexican government liked the suggestion, but eventually it was agreed to proceed on these terms, and the Mexican government ended up thinking that a situation that diminished the political consequence of the whole question worked to its advantage.[57]

The British came prepared for the negotiations with an estimate of their 1938 losses: according to their figures, the value of El Aguila's plants was $76,312,585, but that of its oil and gas deposits was $310,260,000, which included some 2,100 million barrels in proven reserves and some 690 million in probable reserves.[58] The commissioners who would debate the final destiny of this prodigious wealth were, on behalf of Mexico, the director of Pemex himself, Antonio J. Bermúdez, and on behalf of El Aguila, Prof. Vincent Charles Illing, an expert on the oil economy, who kept in constant touch with El Aguila's man in Mexico, Davidson. A request by the Dutch government to send a representative to the talks was turned down. Sessions between them began secretly on 15 July 1947 in Bermúdez's residence; it was agreed that only the final outcome would be made public, and then only if an agreement was reached.[59]

Two sums formed the basis for the talks. Illing demanded a payment of $257 million on behalf of his clients, while Bermúdez offered only $43.9 million. Following the precedent set by the negotiations with the Americans, both parties soon settled on a sum of $87 million, which was later rounded up to $90 million, though Mexico then proceeded to lower its offer to $75 million. The latter sum Illing accepted on condition that the possibility of a return to the Mexican fields was left open—a request that Bermúdez neither rejected outright nor conceded, leaving it up to his counterpart to nurse hopes for the future. This being the state of affairs, on 24 July, Bermúdez delivered his final offer: $81.25 million to be paid within fifteen years at 3 percent interest that would become effective retrospectively to the time of the expropriation, the first payment to be made in 1948 and all secondary claims by one party against the other to be dropped. By the time Mexico finally settled its debt to El Aguila, it would have paid $130,339,000 for property—hydrocarbon deposits included—with a market value of $387 million. By 2 August, the documents were drawn; the agreement was to involve simply El Aguila and the Mexican government. The company executives in Europe were not altogether happy with the settlement; given the size of the proven reserves of Poza Rica, they had expected a higher amount, as well as the participation in the deal of HMG, but faced with the alternative of turning down a partial compensation for damages and waiting for an indeterminate future that might never come, they accepted the offer. The agreement was signed on 29 August 1947, the date when the negotiations that had taken place in Bermúdez's residence were made public.[60]

By way of an epilogue, it should be pointed out that Professor Illing left Mexico convinced—at any rate, so he told his clients—that the agreement of August 1947 had not closed the book on the history of British and Anglo-Dutch petroleum interests in Mexico, but merely a chapter. Pemex, Illing said, lacked the resources and competence to achieve the necessary level of production, and in the long run the Mexican company would have to reopen its doors to foreign capital. At that time, Royal Dutch-Shell would be able to come back to Mexico. Ambassador Bateman never entertained any illusions on the subject but the company executives did, and they asked the Foreign Office to watch out so that they might be able to take advantage of any opportunity arising in the future.[61]

When the time came in 1948 to make the first compensation payment, Mexican finances were in trouble, and Royal Dutch–Shell took advantage of the conjuncture to communicate to Mexico that the 1947 agreement could be canceled: the company would renounce compensation in exchange for renewed talks with a view to its return to Mexico. The government of Miguel Alemán rejected the offer and instead made the first payment punctually on 18 September.[62] Thus, time proved Bateman right: Mexico would not reopen its doors to the big oil companies.

Conclusions

It is not necessary to dwell long on these. The winding-up of large British investments in Latin America became inevitable as Great Britain lost its central position in the world economy and spent a significant part of assets accumulated overseas in its efforts to survive a German offensive in two world wars. Nevertheless, the manner in which this took place was not predetermined, at least not in the case of Mexico.

If El Aguila had not supported the position taken by American companies against General Cárdenas's government and had instead taken advantage of the opportunities offered by the 1937 agreement on cooperation between itself and Petromex, it is highly likely that its presence in Mexico would have lasted a good many years longer, and that the nature of the Mexican oil industry would not be what it is today. Yet things did not turn out that way. El Aguila and the Foreign Office reacted to the creation of the STPRM (Sindicato de Trabajadores Petroleros de la República Mexicana, Union of Oil Workers of the Mexican Republic) and to the revival of Mexican nationalism as represented by *cardenismo*, by adopting traditional policies, hoping for a repetition of the process that had culminated ten years earlier in the agreements between Calles and Morrow.

The history of the relationship between the Mexican revolutionary regime and British interests is one of systematic opposition by the latter to any attempts by the former to reduce the burden of external dependence. There is no doubt that the oil industry was one of the areas where the conflict manifested itself with greater intensity. In 1937 and 1938, British interests attempted to reenact the process of resistance to Mexican nationalism that had worked so well before, without taking into account the fact that the Mexican government—indeed, the regime—had changed; it was now stronger as a result of the mass politics of *cardenismo*; American pressure, too, was greatly reduced as a result of the Good Neighbor Policy set in motion by Franklin D. Roosevelt's government.

Without American support for its rejection of the decree of expropriation of 18 March, there was very little His Majesty's government could do to force Mexico to back down, short of an economic boycott. Here, again, British conjecture was wrong, for Mexican oil found a market in Europe, which enabled the consolidation of the expropriation throughout those critical years, 1938 and 1939. Wrong, too, were Great Britain and Holland's speculations that it would be impossible for Pemex to survive purely on the strength of the domestic market. Last, the prediction that the Mexican government would not be able to take charge of such an obviously complex business as the oil industry also turned out to be inaccurate.

The way in which El Aguila was compensated meant, among other things, that Mexico did not pay the full value of the oil deposits claimed as its own by the company. In fact, by compensating only a third of total property value—an amount that approximated very closely the book value declared by the company during its final year of operations in Mexico—the last vestiges of the Calles-Morrow agreement were destroyed, and the original spirit of Paragraph 4 of Article 27 of the 1917 Constitution at last came into effect.

Notes

1. Lorenzo Meyer, "Los petroleros británicos, el nacionalismo mexicano y el gobierno de su majestad británica (1901–1947)," in Miguel S. Wionczek (ed.), *Energía en México. Ensayos sobre el pasado y el presente,* (Mexico City: El Colegio de México, 1982), p. 18.

2. The terms of the agreement can be found in: the Public Record Office (hereafter PRO), the Foreign Office (hereafter FO) 371, Volume (hereafter V) 20634, A1451, 1822, 2003 and 2178/132/26; *Times* (London), (20 Nov. 1937), and *The Economist* (20 Nov. 1937).

3. On this, see the classic study by Peter Calvert on the differences between the United States and Great Britain on Mexico: *The Mexican Revolution, 1910–1914. The Diplomacy of Anglo-American Conflict* (Cambridge, Eng.: Cambridge University Press, 1968).

4. PRO, FO 371, V.21482, A 1975/1975/26, O'Malley's annual report to the Foreign Office, 9 Jan. 1938.

5. Ibid.

6. For a study of the American position, with particular reference to the implications of the so-called Good Neighbor Policy, see Bryce Wood, *The Making of the Good Neighbor Policy* (New York: Columbia University Press, 1961).

7. PRO, FO 371, Foreign Office to its embassy in Washington, 4 May 1938, V. 21469, A 3403/10/26; memo from Balfour from the Foreign Office on 1 Dec. of that same year, V. 21477, A 8808/10/26; Foreign Office minutes signed by Thomas Hohler, 29 April 1943, V. 34005, A 3981/3981/26.

8. The British notes and the Mexican replies can be found in: British Government, Foreign Office, *White Paper, "Mexico No. 1"* (London: His Majesty's Stationery Office, 1938).

9. *The Economist* (16 and 30 April 1938).

10. Ibid., 2 April 1938.

11. Ibid.

12. Lorenzo Meyer, *México y Estados Unidos (en el conflicto petrolero (1917–*

1942). Mexico City: 1968), pp. 411–415; *Times* (London) (27 and 28 July 1938); *The Economist*, (2 July 1938).

13. PRO, FO 371, J. T. V. Miller from El Aguila to the Foreign Office, 25 July 1947 V.60936, AN 2709/72/26.

14. Meyer, *México y Estados Unidos*, p. 416.

15. Nacional Financiera, *La Economía Mexicana en Cifras* (Mexico City: Nacional Financiera, 1965), p. 29.

16. PRO, FO 371, Petroleum Office to Imperial Committee for Defense, 12 May 1938, V. 21469, A 3663/10/26.

17. PRO, FO 371, British embassy in Washington to Foreign Office, 30 April 1938, V. 21469, A 3404/10/26.

18. Meyer, *México y Estados Unidos*, p. 350.

19. PRO, FO 371, Starling, from the Petroleum Office to Balfour, 22 Feb. 1939, V. 22778, A 1453/84/26.

20. *The Economist* (10 July 1939).

21. Ibid., 21 May 1938.

22. *Times* (London) (19 and 21 July and 3 Nov. 1938); PRO, FO 371, "Memorandum on the Oil Question," signed by J. Balfour from the Foreign Office, 1 Dec. 1938, V. 21477, A 8808/10/26.

23. For an analysis of these negotiations, see Meyer, *México y Estados Unidos*, pp. 395–403; *Times* (London) (28 Feb., 15 April and 21 June 1939); *The Economist* (24 June and 19 Aug. 1939).

24. An example of the above is the British request to the Australian government to stop a barter of copper for oil with Mexico, *Times* (London) (25 Sept. 1940).

25. Meyer, *México y Estados Unidos*, pp. 415–428.

26. J. Richard Powell, *The Mexican Petroleum Industry, 1938–1956*, (Berkeley: University of California Press, 1956), p. 79.

27. In a report to his superiors, the British General Consul in Mexico in 1938 pointed out that it was impossible for Pemex to survive while depending solely on the domestic market, PRO, FO 371, V. 22780, A 1678/1685/26.

28. *Times* (London) (9 May 1939).

29. Ibid., 23 Dec. 1939.

30. PRO, FO 371, secret report from the Ministry of Information to the Foreign Office, 23 May 1941, V. 26067, A 3886/281/26.

31. PRO, FO 371, Foreign Office minutes dated 16 Jan. and 30 March 1941; Foreign Office to its embassy in Washington, 1 March 1941; and Foreign Office to the General Consul in Mexico, 30 March 1941; British Embassy in Washington to the Foreign Office, 30 Sept. 1941, Vs. 26061 26062, A 364, 1928, 1009, 7882/47/26.

32. PRO, FO 371, Ministries of War Economy and Information to the Foreign Office, 18 March and 23 May 1941, V. 26067, A 1921/47/26 and A 3886/281/26.

33. PRO, FO 371, Foreign Office minutes and telegram to its embassy in Washington dated 26 and 28 Aug. 1941, V. 26064, A 6580/47/26.

34. An account of the negotiations and final settlement can be found in Meyer, *México y Estados Unidos*, pp. 452–457.

35. PRO, FO 371, Foreign Office minutes dated 4 Sept. 1941, V. 26064, A 6580/47/26.

36. *Times* (London) (20 Sept. 1940).

37. PRO, FO 371, Bateman to the Foreign Office, 31 March 1942, V. 30571, A 3742/133/26; *Times* (London) (4 Aug. 1941); *La Prensa* (8 and 13 Aug. 1941).

38. PRO, FO 371, minutes from the War Cabinet dated 8 Sept. and from the British embassy in Washington to the Foreign Office, 9 Oct. 1941, V. 26064, A 7331 and 8178/46/26.

39. PRO, FO 371, Foreign Office minutes dated 16 Jan. 1941, V. 26061, A 364/47/26.

40. PRO, FO 371, Bateman to the Foreign Office, 31 March 1942, V. 30571, A 3742/133/26.

41. *Times* (London) (29 Aug. and 3 and 4 Sept. 1941); *La Prensa* (6 Sept. 1941).

42. PRO, FO 371, Bateman to the Foreign Office, 31 March 1942, V. 30571, A 3742/133/26; *The Economist* (25 Oct. and 1 and 22 Nov. 1941).

43. PRO, FO 371, British General Consul in Mexico to the Foreign Office, 1 Feb. 1941, and Davidson to El Aguila, 3 March 1941, V. 26062 A 606 and 3149/47/26.

44. PRO, FO 371, Bateman to the Foreign Office, 20 Feb. 1942, and Foreign Office minutes signed by T. Hohler, 29 April 1943, V. 33994 and 34005, A 2328/901/26 and A 3981/3981/26.

45. PRO, FO 371, Bateman to the Foreign Office, 10 Jan. 1944, and Foreign Office minutes signed by T. Hohler, 29 April 1943, V. 38312 and 34005, AN 293/138/26 and A 3981/3981/26.

46. PRO, FO 371, Bateman to the Foreign Office, 10 Jan. and 14 Feb. 1944, V. 38312, AN 293 and 798/138/26; *The Economist* (16 Oct. 1943); *Times* (London) (27 April, 5 and 22 Oct. 1943, and 17 March and 26 Oct. 1944).

47. PRO, FO 371, Bateman to the Foreign Office, 15 Jan. 1946, V. 51592 AN 338/338/26.

48. *Times* (London) (8 and 9 Feb. 1946); *The Economist* (16 Feb. 1946).

49. National Archives of Washington, State Department documents (hereafter NAW), Record Group (hereafter RG) 59, Ambassador Messersmith to the State Department, 21 April and 31 Aug. 1945, 16 Feb. and 28 Oct. 1946, 812.6363/4-2145, 8-2645, 1-2346, 2-2346 and 10-2846, and Broden to Briggs in the State Department, 24 Oct. 1946, 812.6363/ 10-2146.

50. PRO, FO 371, Foreign Office minutes dated 7 Aug. 1947, V. 60936, AN 2833/72/26.

51. PRO, FO 371, Ministry for Fuel and Energy to the Foreign Office, 14 March 1946, Bateman to the Foreign Office, 25 March 1946 and 16 Jan. 1947, Godber to Davidson, 6 May 1946, V. 51579 and 60940, AN 764/ 13/26, A 967/13/26, A 397/395/26, AN 1366/13/26; *Times* (London)(21 May 1946).

52. PRO, FO 371, Davidson from El Aguila to G. Leigh-Jones, 27 Feb. 1947, V 60934, AN 1004/72/26.

53. PRO, FO 371, Foreign Office minutes, 24 Dec. 1946, V. 51581, A 3790/13/26.

54. PRO, FO 371, Bateman to the Foreign Office, 24 Feb. 1947, V 60940, AN 958/395/26.

55. PRO, FO 371, Foreign Office minutes, 29 March 1947, V. 60934, AN 1223/72/26.

56. PRO, FO 371, Davidson from El Aguila to G. Leigh-Jones, 27 Feb. 1947, V.

60934, AN 1004/72/26; *Financial Times* (1 March 1947).

57. PRO, FO 371, Bateman to the Foreign Office, 12 Dec. 1946 and 23 Jan. 1947; Foreign Office to Bateman, 24 Dec. 1946; and Foreign Office minutes dated 6 Jan. 1947, V.

58. PRO, FO 371, G. Leigh-Jones to E. A. Berthoud, from the Ministry for Fuel and Energy, 17 April 1947, V. 60934, AN 1429/72/26.

59. PRO, FO 371, Bateman to the Foreign Office, 7 July 1947, V. 60936, AN 2348/72/26.

60. PRO, FO 371, Illing's reports to the Foreign Office dated 24 July and 2 Aug. 1947; Foreign Office minutes of 14 Aug. 1947, V. 60936, AN 2761, 2762, and 2821/72/26.

61. PRO, FO 371, two undated memoranda from Illing to the Foreign Office; Bateman to the Foreign Office, 9 July 1947, V. 60936, AN 2764, 2765/ 72/26, and AN 2521/604/26.

62. *Financial Times* (12 Aug. 1948).

7. The Expropriation in Comparative Perspective

George Philip
London School of Economics and Political Science

Too much has been written by historians about the "lessons of history." Whether the various participants in and observers of the Mexican expropriation learned anything valuable from history is debatable; however, they do not seem to have been doomed to repeat it. No significant properties owned by oil companies in Latin America were expropriated between 1938 and 1960. Subsequently, the pace of expropriation quickened. There was a wave of nationalizations, of mineral as well as oil properties, between 1968 and 1976 (in Peru, Bolivia, Chile, Venezuela, and Ecuador), at the end of which period "old style" blocks of foreign capital dominating large areas of Latin American extractive economies had largely disappeared. In the Middle East, the story was fairly similar. After a major battle over expropriation (Persia 1950–1953), Middle Eastern governments lowered their aspirations for control and instead bargained with foreign companies within fairly strict limits until the old order broke down after 1970.

For many interests, the Mexican nationalization was a calamity that should not be allowed to happen again. Obviously, the oil companies and the U.S. government thought so (though for different reasons and with different results), but much of Mexico's postwar political (and, even more obviously, business) elite made it clear that they had serious reservations about certain aspects of the expropriation. Thus, when in 1960 President López Mateos was preparing to nationalize the electric power industry, an article in *Excelsior* summed up the official view about worker's control:

> The federal government has not forgotten past experiences, particularly in regard to the two activities which were the headaches of their time, the railroads and the petroleum industry. The government did not purchase the electric companies at a cost of 600 million pesos in order to turn them over to the workers. From the experience gathered over the years the government has recognized

fundamental errors in this system or practice which was followed in the Ferrocarriles Nacionales and presently in Petróleos Mexicanos.[1]

If the Mexican elite later came to think this way, it can scarcely be supposed that other Latin American elites saw the nationalization in more favorable light. Certainly, they did not immediately seek to follow the Mexican example; there was some limited symbolic action in Peru and Ecuador,[2] but in Venezuela the Foreign Office was told that:

> There are occasionally references in the press to eventual nationalisation of the oil industry as a desirable aim but I can find no indication that these references are in any way connected with events in Mexico and oil companies are not uneasy for the present. Position of companies is normal and there are no indications of endeavours from outside the industry to gain a foot-hold. From discreet enquiries I have been able to make, I learn that Venezuelan officials are inclined to regard Mexican expropriation as an unwise move.[3]

In any case, the international environment changed sharply soon after March 1938 with the outbreak of war. Within the decade, three external conditions that had shaped events in Mexico changed completely. There was no longer a significant British presence in the Latin American oil industry. It was no longer true that the Roosevelt administration and big oil cordially detested each other. The U.S. government had become converted to the idea of playing a global role and, from around 1947, found its main enemy in the Soviet Union and international Communism. *Cardenismo* was a creature of the New Deal, not the Cold War.

The Latin American Oil Industry in 1938

Mexico was not the only case of its kind, but it was one of the most important. The first significant oil nationalist campaign in Latin American history was led by Hipólito Yrigoyen in 1928. The first legislation permitting the setting up of a state oil monopoly passed in Chile in 1932 (although this remained largely a dead letter). The first outright expropriation of a foreign oil interest was that of Standard Oil in Bolivia, taken over in March 1937. The Mexican nationalization was, however, far more significant than all of these events taken together.

For one thing, an actual expropriation was a far more serious matter than a mere market closure. There has never been anything in international law to prevent governments' protecting or sealing off their domestic markets from imports or foreign investors. Moreover, even before 1938, oil technology was sufficiently internationally available and standardized for Latin American governments (and probably even Latin American entrepreneurs) to have had the option of developing locally owned oil industries. This is particularly true of the downstream sectors, notably refining. Thus, Bethlehem Steel was in 1925 given a turnkey contract to build an oil refinery for YPF (Yacimientos Petrolíferos Fiscales) in Argentina, and the British subsidiary of Foster Wheeler built the La Teja refinery in Uruguay in the early 1930s. Once a local refinery had been set up, the state company could very easily move into marketing (which, perhaps surprisingly, was the most profitable sector of all during the 1920s, though no longer so by 1938). Where there was a problem with the supply of oil, the Soviet Union was, from about 1930, willing to move into the gap.

Apart from the public policymaking limitations inherent in many Latin American countries prior to 1945, the most difficult sectors to enter were exploration and development and, even more so (at any rate after 1928), international exporting. The Argentine government had the interesting experience of discovering a large oil field (the largest ever discovered in Argentina) apparently by mistake, but, with this exception, no Latin American company (state or private) proved able to handle a significant exploration effort until after the Mexican expropriation.

This structure suggested the appropriateness of a kind of ISI model for, at any rate, some Latin American oil industries. This is in fact what happened in the relatively more developed but also oil-importing Southern Cone countries. The Chilean and Uruguayan governments used their bargaining power to force down marketing profits and also introduced local capital (private in the Chilean case, public in Uruguay) into that sector. Subsequently, both had oil refineries built that formed the backbone of their state companies; both ventured into exploration after 1945, but with only limited success in the case of Chile and none at all in the case of Uruguay.

YPF in Argentina really came of age during the 1920s when, under Mosconi, it proved able to organize construction of a national refinery and to challenge the marketing position of the multinationals. This development paralleled, though it did not precisely connect with, the oil nationalist campaign mounted (but not seen through) by Yrigoyen.

Oil nationalization in the Southern Cone, then, involved importer governments; oil nationalism involved seeking control over their home markets. Exporter governments elsewhere in Latin America, however, rarely challenged the foreign oil companies (in the 1930s, Ecuador, Peru, and Colombia, as well as Mexico and Venezuela, were exporters). Barriers to entering the international oil market were indeed extensive.

Following the Achnacarry agreement of 1928, the major oil companies were able to establish an effective oligopoly that squeezed unintegrated independent producers as well as national operators. International oil was subjected to a dual-pricing system; the open market price was rock-bottom, while crude oil carried by the major companies through integrated channels to a quota-determined market commanded a significant premium. (It was, indeed, a major grievance of the Mexican government that Mexican oil was treated as "free market" oil due to the formal differentiation of the Mexican and Canadian Eagle companies.)

However, the Mexican industry was not typical of the oil-exporting Latin American countries, either. Certainly, oil was an important source of foreign exchange in 1938, but already most production was being consumed domestically and local consumption was on a rapidly rising trend. Even if all export markets were blocked, the Mexican industry could keep going at a reduced level of activity. The loss of exports was more serious, but even that was less immediately critical than it would have been in Venezuela (and later would be in Iran). Moreover, thanks to the Poza Rica find, the Mexican reserve position was healthy indeed. Pemex could, and indeed did, neglect oil exploration for a decade while continuing to increase production from existing reserves (from the 1938 low point); if this had not been an option, it is hard to see how the Mexican government could have avoided reversing policy during the 1940s. In fact, it was not until the late 1960s that Pemex was faced with an urgent need to increase its oil reserves; not until the early 1970s did it actually do so. No other Latin American government could have followed such a strategy. Elsewhere even relative neglect of new exploration activity would lead (in Peru, *did* lead) to a rapid decline in the productive potential of the oil industry.

The politics of expropriation in Mexico, however, were still serious enough. Expropriation was regarded in 1938 as having serious legal and international implications. These impinged particularly on the British government, since the British Empire was an importer of oil and needed to feel able to control its sources of supply, particularly in the event of a European conflict for which the Petroleum Department (unusual for Whitehall at that time) was actively preparing.[4]

As might therefore have been expected, the strongest reaction to the expropriation came from Eagle (Shell) and the British government. What was of concern to them was not so much the loss of properties in Mexico as the fear that, unless Mexico was made such an example of as to discourage emulation, it would mark the beginning of a trend. (The Bolivian case was seen, rightly, as too unusual and insufficiently important to create any danger of emulation; British government papers barely refer to it.) As we now know, the fears of a "domino effect" proved to be exaggerated. Meanwhile, Washington, with a range of concerns to consider, took a far less legalistic view of the takeover.

Oil and Bargaining

The first impression, that there is no event in Latin American oil history that closely resembles the Mexican expropriation, is borne out further when one considers some of the specific factors that lay behind the nationalization. It may be useful to look at some rational maximization considerations before going on to consider internal political factors.

Oil nationalization is far more likely to occur when the companies concerned are perceived to have lost interest in their properties, or, in some cases, never to have had any in the first place; it is less likely when they are in the full flow of expansion. A similar judgment can be made about mining companies; the generalization would fit Cerro de Pasco in Peru (nationalized at the end of 1973) and the Gran Minería in Chile (nationalized by Allende).[5]

There are several reasons why this might be the case; two-person non-zero-sum bargaining theory would suggest that the optimum time to expropriate is when the host government has little prospect of attracting fresh investment but before existing investment has depreciated excessively. A more psychological theory would suggest that resentments gradually accumulate against any large foreign-owned resource enterprise and that expropriation occurs after a criticial threshold is reached; the quality of local diplomacy as conducted by the companies can lengthen or shorten this process but not reverse it. Finally, the companies themselves may respond to political trouble either by trying to conciliate (which is likely to include an offer of expansion) or by running down their holdings in anticipation of worsening conditions. If they adopt the second strategy, their incentive to make concessions to avoid political problems gradually diminishes, and expropriation becomes increasingly probable.

When we look at specific examples, the International Petroleum Corporation (IPC) in Peru and the oil companies in Venezuela had run down their assets for years before their expropriation. IPC had been particularly intransigent in Peru for a long time. The Venezuelan companies were not so much intransigent (though they were often uncooperative) as positively eager to be nationalized provided that they were satisfied with the compensation offered. Conversely, Gulf Oil was still investing in Bolivia at the time of its expropriation in 1969, but there is no evidence of its taking a hard line with the Bolivians; its problem was more in choosing the "wrong" set of friends. Similarly, the oil refineries in Cuba were virtually new when Castro expropriated them in 1960.

Here, however, the expropriation followed the oil companies' decision to follow the advice of the U.S. government (rather than their own better judgment) in refusing to refine Soviet oil.

The Mexican case would in some respects seem to fit the general pattern of expropriation following a loss of corporate interest. Production had peaked in 1921, exploration during the later 1920s had been unsuccessful, and the U.S. companies had long ceased to take their Mexican holdings particularly seriously. If Mexican oil production (and oil revenue) had been rapidly increasingly during the 1930s, then Cárdenas would have been faced with a different set of options and his choices might have been different; an expanding industry might in any case have managed to find the 26 million pesos ($7.2 million) that were required to settle the 1938 dispute.[6]

After the Mexican case, foreign companies ceased to expect a policy of nationalization to fail because of pure unfeasibility. It would, of course, be an exaggeration to say that after 1938 oil company statesmanship was everywhere of the highest quality; in 1942, the State Department felt bound to intervene to head off an apparent deadlock in negotiations with the Venezuelan government, and Anglo-Iranian badly mishandled negotiations with Iran in the late 1940s. Nevertheless, the Mexican nationalization was an event that shook expectations, and corporate strategies thereafter for the most part did become more sophisticated. In Latin America, at any rate, their subsequent mistakes were in general different ones.

Again, because the Mexican case was new and unexpected, there was generally a high degree of uncertainty as to how the various interests involved would react. There can be no doubt that the British government (at any rate, in the shape of those quite junior figures who had been covering Mexican events) and the oil companies overestimated the amount of support they could expect from Washington. Washington was itself taken by surprise (partly because Ambassador Daniels, himself surprised by the expropriation, took little trouble to keep the State Department informed about what was going on). In the event, Washington offered only very limited support to the companies (a fact that the shrewder Mexicans, such as Portes Gil, soon picked up);[7] New Deal politics, both national and international, and the United States's own security in respect to oil supplies turned out to be the crucial factors.

On the other hand, the Poza Rica discovery does not fit this pattern at all. Mexican Eagle was expecting to be able to launch a major expansion in Mexican production; it had in 1937 persuaded Cárdenas to ratify an agreement on development and royalties of the Poza Rica field. Since Cárdenas had made it clear toward the end of his negotiation with the companies that he was looking for some kind of compromise, it would surely have paid Eagle (if not necessarily the U.S. companies) to have avoided confrontation.

The reason, surely, why Eagle in particular did not pursue a late compromise with more energy was that it miscalculated what would happen if Cárdenas did expropriate. It was clearly expected that the Mexican government, if it did not fall, would be unable to operate the industry and would be forced to return the properties.

This calculation was not wholly bizarre. Even Cárdenas is known to have expressed some private doubts about whether he could make the expropriation stick. A failed attempt to expropriate would have put the companies in a very strong position in subsequent negotiations. However, this point was also not lost on the Mexican government, which was willing to accept considerable costs rather than admit defeat. It has in fact been a common mistake of "First World" actors (by no means exclusively oil companies) to underestimate the lengths to which Third World leaders have been willing to go to control their own territories when their authority was threatened. This lesson would be relearned in Persia in 1950, Egypt in 1956, Cuba in 1959–1961, and in Vietnam over a full generation. If the stakes were high enough, an expropriating government could see to it that expropriation "worked" simply by refusing to back down—almost irrespective of the costs involved.

During and after the Second World War, however, Washington and the oil companies became much more closely associated.[8] At first, Washington exerted strong leverage on the companies; later, the pattern of influence tended to flow more in the other direction. Subsequent U.S. oil companies that found themselves embattled in South America (or the Middle East) did not lack support from Washington. On some occasions, indeed, this association proved a liability; Gulf Oil's position in Bolivia in the late 1960s was threatened as much by anti-Americanism as by opposition to Gulf Oil per se.

Over time, however, the fact that the Mexican nationalization did not turn out to be a complete failure was one of several factors gradually moving the balance of bargaining advantage away from foreign companies and toward host governments. A good indicator of this trend is what was expected by companies in the way of compensation following expropriation.

Originally, the meaning of "prompt, adequate and effective compensation" was that the expropriating government would be expected to hand the cash to the companies at the moment of the nationalization. Cárdenas immediately offered to indemnify the companies and had (in the shape of Mexican crude oil) the means of doing so. The companies refused even to discuss compensation, demanding instead the restitution of their holdings. When this line proved unviable, they demanded that compensation be paid for subsoil rights (i.e., the commercial value of lost oil reserves); eventually Washington refused to accept even this demand. Obviously, if from the beginning the oil companies had demanded no more than cash compensation from Cárdenas, the dispute would have been settled quickly and, almost certainly, the companies would have been paid more. (They might also have been able to negotiate management contracts, sales contracts, and so forth.)

What is being put forward here is not, of course, a serious counterfactual. What most concerned the companies (and the British government) about Mexico was not so much the loss of income as of control and the threat that other countries might seem to follow the Mexican example. The point is, rather, that dispute over the 1960s nationalizations was not over expropriation in principle but rather over compensation (i.e., money—a relatively bargainable commodity); if General Velasco in Peru had offered what Cárdenas offered in 1938, there would never have been an issue. Nor was there much of an issue in 1975 when the Venezuelan oil industry was expropriated.

In sum, if one takes a "bargaining theory" approach, then the Mexican expropriation resulted from some serious miscalculations, most of which were on the company side. The Mexican outcome both changed perceptions of what could occur and established some kind of precedent.

Mexican Politics and the Nationalization

In general terms, oil nationalization has in most Latin American contexts been directly related to domestic political considerations. While the popularity of oil nationalism can be exaggerated, it is unlikely to prove positively unpopular unless there are serious economic costs arising. There is a strong element in technocratic elite thinking that stresses the importance of national control over strategic (military or developmental) resources; mass emotion can also be aroused, from time to time, on issues relating to national sovereignty. (This, of course, is not true only of Latin America.) Nevertheless, even here Mexico's experience was highly distinctive in Latin American terms.

One major political difference between Mexico in the 1930s and the various South American republics both then and later was the absence, in Mexico, of a united "corporate" military with strong ideas and interests of its own. One of the main activities of South American military institutions has been to place a check on popular mobilization (which threatens the military command structure and therefore the position of senior officers).[9] There have been only a few cases (Bolivia during the 1950s, Argentina just at the end of World War II, Chile from 1971 to 1973) where the degree of mobilization in South American politics during the twentieth century has rivaled that of Mexico under Cárdenas. These few cases in South America also involved seizures of property.

It is not being s   oil was particularly the focal point of *cardenista* mobili   gh the militancy of the oil workers was real enough. The   Cárdenas had stirred up political forces that he was not   itrol; these political forces had begun to stimulate an increasingly ... _itening right-wing opposition. Whatever the full range of Cárdenas's motives may have been, it is likely that the "national unity" implications of a dramatic oil nationalization formed a serious argument in its favor.

In this sense, the Mexican nationalization ties in with the old Machiavellian maxim: "If in trouble at home, make trouble abroad"— abroad in this case including foreign-owned oil companies. I am not suggesting that this provides a full explanation for the expropriation; only that it helps to explain why Cárdenas took a step that the companies and foreign governments—who thought in terms of bargaining advantage—considered highly unlikely. What is of particular interest here is the suggestion that Cárdenas sought to use the spirit of national unity generated by the expropriation to end rather than extend his mobilizing program; it was a means of escape from impending conflict between the irresistible force of his radical support and the increasingly immovable object of bourgeois and middle-class alarm. (In this respect, the analogy that comes to mind is of Prime Minister Macmillan in and after 1957— in Harold Wilson's words, "waving the banner of Suez while leading his party away from it.")

There are few South American parallels to this kind of action. On the contrary, South American nationalists have sought to use their chosen issue to stimulate rather than check or channel popular mobilization; Galtieri's invasion of the Falkland Islands would be an example. The same process can also be seen when the issue has been oil nationalism; again, many of the mobilizing leaders have been military. General Velasco in 1968 was looking to create a personal popular base when he nationalized IPC in Peru and refused to pay compensation. In 1973, according to the CIA, General Fernández Maldonado (the Mining and Energy Minister in Peru) was seeking to confront the Cerro de Pasco mining company "with a view to nationalizing it . . . [his] . . . motive for proposing the measure is to seize on an issue of sufficient drama to make him the front runner to succeed President Juan Velasco Alvarado who is ailing."[10] In Bolivia, General Ovando was looking to win support from the Left when he nationalized Gulf Oil in 1969; he was attempting (unsuccessfully) to persuade the Left to forget his own part in the massacre of tin miners in 1965 and in the defeat of Che Guevara in 1967.

The Petrobrás campaign in Brazil offered the military in that country, somewhat lacking a role following the end of the Second World War and the Estado Novo and the experimentation with democracy that followed, "an extra political resource to strengthen its position in the center of the system."[11] It was precisely because military conservatives in Brazil were concerned with the use of "O petróleo é nosso" as a mobilizing slogan that they formed the ESG in 1949 and used the outbreak of the Korean War to initiate a strident anti-Communism (which also proved successful as a demobilizing slogan).

In South America, mainstream civilian politicians have not led oil nationalist movements as frequently as military figures. In important cases, democratic governments that have nationalized oil tried hard to avoid the issue's being treated in too popular a way Venezuela under Carlos Andrés Pérez is a case in point. As president, Pérez made the surprising choice of Valentín Hernández as oil minister as opposed to Hernández Grisanti; Hernández Grisanti, unlike Valentín Hernández, "was an important leader of Acción Democrática (AD) and had been for many years the party spokesman on oil matters. But President Pérez did not choose him because he thought that Hernández Grisanti could make use of the nationalization in order to convert himself into the next AD candidate for the presidency."[12] When the nationalization was negotiated, Hernández Grisanti publicly opposed the terms that provided for technical service contracts with the oil companies and boycotted Congress when the law was debated. Valentín Hernández, meanwhile, stated that "I consider that it is much better for the country not to have [nationalized] 'heroically' because that would not have allowed the oil industry, when nationalized, to bring in the income which the country requires for its development plans."[13]

A rare example of a civilian politician's using oil nationalism as a mobilizing instrument was Yrigoyen in 1928. It is doubtful that the oil issue contributed much to his popularity, but the factionalism of his second administration led to his early overthrow by the military. There are, it is true, other examples of oil nationalism being used for factional/tactical purposes (Peru between 1963 and 1968 would be an example),[14] but not during periods of intense popular mobilization. On the whole, civilian governments have tended to rely on clientele mechanisms for support; these are obviously vulnerable to economic setback and tend to discourage overt confrontation with powerful economic interests.

It is, however, instructive to consider those very few cases in South American history when there has been intensive political mobilization. Mineral nationalizations did occur in both Bolivia in the 1950s and Chile in and after 1971. There are some real parallels between the Mexican oil nationalization and the Bolivian tin expropriation. In Bolivia, there is some evidence that Paz and the Movimiento Nacional Revolucionario (MNR) leadership were seeking to damp down the process of mobilization by conceding to certain radical demands (tin nationalization and land reform); as in Mexico, the nationalization did nothing to demobilize a militant and troublesome labor force. (A difference here, however, would be that Mexican oil generated sufficient income to permit the "purchase" of a loyal, if corrupt, union structure; Bolivian tin did not.) Although the international implications of the Mexican act were far greater than those of the Bolivian, Washington in both cases responded in an essentially conciliatory way; it considered (rightly) that this was the best way of helping moderate or conservative members of the MNR or PRI overcome their more radical opponents.

The Chilean case, however, does seem quite different. Allende did not seek to use the copper nationalization as a kind of substitute for more domestically controversial reforms. He was instead a mobilizer who misjudged the balance of forces within Chile, above all underestimating the power of Chilean conservatism. Moreover, neither Washington nor local conservatives saw very much point in seeking to influence Unidad Popular in the direction of moderation (as they did with the PRI and the MNR); they wanted, instead, to remove it.

A further point of comparison in relation to domestic politics is the role of organized labor. As will be discussed in more detail elsewhere in the book, organized Marxist-led labor was a major factor in Mexico in 1938. It is generally true that official labor leaders have had more power in Mexican politics than organized labor has ever had (except during short periods of mobilized politics) in South America. There are no South American equivalents of Lombardo Toledano, Fidel Velázquez, or even La Quina. Nor was any other oil nationalization provoked by a labor dispute or followed by an experiment in workers' control such as occurred in Mexico after 1938 (although, as we have just seen, there is some kind of parallel with the Bolivian tin mines).

The Confederación de Trabajadores de México (CTM) was for many years (and perhaps still is today) one of the key pillars of the Mexican state. The precise nature of the relationship between Lombardo and Cárdenas is still to some extent a matter of conjecture, but there can be little doubt that, even if Lombardo did not actually urge the expropriation, he made it very clear that the CTM would support it and would show discipline during the difficult times ahead. (Both Cárdenas and members of the orthodox left, such as Silva Herzog,[15] were at times highly frustrated at the unruly nature of the oil workers—both before and after the expropriation.)

Whatever the nuances of this relationship, the point is that there are no South American equivalents. Movements such as Peronism were organized in a much more "top down" way than the CTM in 1938 (though not so obviously the CTM today); Venezuelan party politicians were, even at the beginning, careful to control the trade union and peasant leagues that, after the death of Gómez, they were beginning to create.[16]

A further factor is that the oil industry changed its industrial relations practices after 1945. The Mexican expropriation made the companies acutely aware of the potential dangers posed by militant labor movements elsewhere. In Venezuela, for example, the oil companies worked closely in the late 1940s with the AD government to co-opt labor moderates and undermine the more militant Communist-led tendencies; the result was costly in financial terms but of long-term political benefit. In the mid-1970s, the Venezuelan oil workers union, which had since 1958 opposed any precipitate oil nationalization, insisted on certain "technocratic" safeguards for the new state oil company if they were not to oppose the nationalization outright. In Peru also, the oil workers employed by IPC were poor and militant in the 1930s, well-paid and moderate by the 1960s. In Colombia, moreover, the U.S. Embassy was concerned in 1948 that "the labor unions in the petroleum industry are Communist-controlled and strikes brought about by the Communist leadership are aimed less at obtaining economic benefits for labor than at obtaining for the Communist labor leaders control of management of the oil companies."[17] By 1951, however, the same source was reassured that "labor conditions in the oil industry have been relatively stable due in large measure to increased salaries and other financial benefits obtained by labor under negotiated contracts."[18]

The companies also made greater efforts to train local managers and engineers (who were very few and far between in the Mexican industry in 1938), partly to reduce their operating costs but mainly to open promotion opportunities among the work force. So was born the corporate "good citizen." It was not only the companies, moreover, who did not wish for a repetition of the Mexican experience. Moderately reformist governments in South America (such as AD in Venezuela) did not want to be bounced into an economically damaging conflict with the oil companies against their better judgment as a result of the activities of militant oil workers.

The Politics of Aftermath

One important characteristic of the Mexican expropriation was its irreversibility. Not only were company properties not restored, but all efforts by the U.S. State Department to persuade the Avila Camacho and Alemán governments to issue new concession contracts failed. Against this, many of the South American nationalizations were partially reversed, or at any rate left incomplete.

Soon after the IPC expropriation, the Velasco government started negotiating with other oil companies anxious to invest in the Peruvian Amazonia. The Occidental contract was signed in 1971; a major deal with foreign operators, in copper rather than oil, was made over Cuajone at the end of 1969. After the expropriation of Gulf Oil in Bolivia, a compensation settlement was agreed upon within months; fresh foreign investment was attracted into oil exploitation by 1973. The expropriation of Gulf Oil in Ecuador at the end of 1976 was a signal for oil policy to move more, not less, in the direction desired by the remaining oil companies (notably Texaco).

In the cases of Bolivia and Ecuador, the reasons for this rapid change lay mainly in the ephemeral nature of domestic politics and, particularly, with the weaknesses of the forms of military radicalism attempted therein. The Peruvian case is rather more complex in that the authorities both intended the confrontation with IPC to be real and proved able to sustain it at least until the end of 1973. As we have seen, some of the military radicals positively enjoyed provoking Washington, hoping thereby to produce a response that would justify further radicalization. Yet, in Peru, the IPC confrontation did not really deepen. Jersey Standard could not effectively pressure the Peruvian authorities because, by that time, it did not export significantly from Peru and its operation was managed almost wholly by Peruvians; it did not have the options that the united front of companies had (and exercised) in the post-1938 period in Mexico. Washington did not want to escalate the conflict because it perceived the threat of generalizing confrontation (particularly, after June 1970, when it wanted to isolate Chile); its strategy was therefore to impose a limited set of sanctions and, when the climate seemed right, to intervene directly to break the deadlock. Washington's at any rate semiconciliatory stance over IPC was not very different from its position over Mexico.

What was different was the attitude of conservatives in these various countries. When politics in Peru, Bolivia, and Ecuador moved to the right, efforts were made to attract fresh foreign investment into oil exploration. This has also been the pattern in Argentina. However, in Mexico, President Alemán almost certainly had enough political strength to have allowed a partial reversal of policy with respect to Pemex. Why did he not do so?

A part of the reason was that Mexican conservatives, at any rate in late 1936, were not especially pro–United States or economically liberal; they preferred instead a kind of right-wing corporatism under a nationalist symbolism. They put little or no value on foreign oil investment in principle. However, it also appears that Mexican governments in the 1940s used Pemex (as later Mexican governments would use their nonaligned foreign policy) as a manipulative symbol, by this means holding left-wing support while at the same time pursuing anti-left policies in other areas. This "symbolic" outcome of the Mexican oil expropriation had much to do with the specific character of the Mexican political system. A further factor, however, may have been the different kinds of relationships set up between the oil companies and local interests.

The oil companies in Mexico had, during their years of expansion, established important relations with local and regional interests. Their connections with Peláez have been the subject of much conjecture, and the companies were also spending a good deal on royalty payments to local landlords. After the early 1920s, however, the decline of the industry and the radicalization of the Mexican Revolution took their toll. Central government (and the CTM) had become too strong, and the resources that the companies were willing to put into winning friends and influence were too limited; to the extent that Assheton and the other El Aguila managers were interested in a more flexible policy, they were firmly discouraged by Deterding. It seems, in fact, that the decision-making process with regard to Mexico was highly centralized in London and New York; it may be that the corporate head offices were hoping for (and helping to finance?) an attempt at rebellion by the exiled Calles in 1936.[19] There are complexities here, but the essential fact that by 1938 the companies had few if any local allies is scarcely in dispute. Mexican conservatives (the church hierarchy, Governor Alemán, etc.) supported the nationalization with genuine enthusiasm.[20]

In most South American countries, however, the foreign oil companies were concerned about acquiring domestic allies. In Colombia, for example, the companies (aided by the pattern of legislation) took active steps to co-opt local plutocrats—steps that the British government strongly approved. In Peru, after 1945, the International Petroleum Company used local oil managers as intermediaries so as to develop and strengthen relations with APRA (Alianza Popular Revolucionaria Americana); the problem for them was that they chose the wrong horse.[21] In Bolivia, Gulf Oil specifically offered to supply natural gas free within the province of Santa Cruz; the nationalization provoked so strong a reaction from *cruceños* that I earlier described Gulf's policy of local alliances as "posthumously successful."[22] In Argentina, the alliance struck between Jersey Standard (in particular) and local northern elites played a major part in the oil politics of the 1930s.[23] In Venezuela, Jersey Standard sought to build relationships with Acción Democrática during 1945–

1948. Although some smaller operations were more sympathetic to the reactionary right. Pérez Jiménez was later strongly—in retrospect, embarrassingly strongly—supported by the companies that helped persuade President Eisenhower to give him a military decoration. When Pérez Jiménez fell, the companies became unpopular. Jersey Standard responded by recalling Arthur Proudfitt—their man in Caracas during 1945–1948 and a man openly sympathetic to AD—to head the local company.[24] Shell and Jersey Standard also negotiated the entry of the companies into *Fedecameras*, which up until then had been mainly representative of domestically owned businesses; by all accounts, the oil companies used their *Fedecameras* membership to considerable effect.[25] They ran out of friends decisively only after 1970, when international commitments made it impossible for them to keep faith with the Caldera government.

These various alliances sometimes did give the companies a degree of political protection; at other times, by alarming potential oil nationalists, they may have hastened the end. What they do seem to have done was have an impact on the postnationalization politics; for foreign oil companies in general, if not always for the ones expropriated, there was often some form of life after nationalization. In Mexico, there was not. The Mexican expropriation was unusual in that it had a finality that makes an anniversary record appropriate.

Notes

1. Quoted in L. Wionczek, "Electric Power: the Uneasy Partnership,"in *Public Policy and Private Enterprise in Mexico*, edited by Raymond Vernon (Cambridge, Mass., 1964)

2. G. Philip, *Oil and Politics in Latin America: Nationalist Movements and State Companies* (London, 1982), chap. 2.

3. Document dated 18 March 1938, Public Record Office, London, British Foreign Office Papers (hereafter cited as FO), 371 A2389/1732/47.

4. J. Thynne, "British Policy on Oil Resources 1936–51, with Particular Reference to the Defence of British Controlled Oil in Mexico, Venezuela and Persia," PhD diss., London School of Economics, 1987.

5. On Cerro de Pasco, see D. Becker, *The New Bourgeoisie and the Limits of Dependency: Mining, Class and Power in "Revolutionary" Peru* (Princeton, N.J., 1979).

6. See E. Suárez, *Comentarios y recuerdos 1926–46* (Mexico City, 1977).

7. The Portes Gil archive at the Archivo General de la Nación in Mexico City casts some new light on official Mexican thinking during 1939 and 1940.

8. See, for example, D. S. Painter, *Private Power and Public Policy: Multinational Oil Corporations and U.S. Foreign Policy, 1941–54* (London, 1987).

9. G. Philip, *The Military in South American Politics* (London? 1985).

10. CIA Directorate of Operations, "Plans of Peruvian Government to Bring Pressure on Cerro de Pasco Mining Company with a View to Nationalizing It," (mid-April 1973).

11. L. Martins, *Pouvoir et développement économique: formation et évolution des structures politiques au Brésil* (Paris, 1977), p. 338.

12. Personal communication from Fernando Baez Duarte, 27 July 1983.

13. Quoted in Philip, *Oil and Politics*, p. 307.

14. G. Philip, "Policymaking in the Peruvian Oil Industry, with Special Reference to the Period October 1968 to September 1973," PhD diss., Oxford University, 1975.

15. See J. Silva Herzog, *Petróleo mexicano* (Mexico City, 1942).

16. D. Villaslobos, "The Incorporation of the Lower Classes into Venezuelan Politics," PhD diss., London School of Economics, 1986.

17. U.S. Department of State, *Foreign Relations of the United States, 1948* (Washington, D.C., 1952), p. 451.

18. FRUS, 1951, p. 1303.

19. Thynne, "British Policy on Oil Resources" (see note 4).

20. A. Michaels, "The Crisis of Cardenismo," *Journal of Latin American Studies* 2: 1 (May 1970), pp. 51–79.

21. Interview with former Shell manager in Peru.

22. Philip, *Oil and Politics*, p. 273.

23. Carl Solberg "YPF: The Formative Years of Latin America's Pioneer State Oil Company." In *Latin American Oil Companies and the Politics of Energy*, edited by John Wirth (Lincoln, Nebr., 1985).

24. *Fortune* (February 1949) published a long profile of Arthur Proudfitt.

25. L. Vallenilla Auge, *Declinación y porvenir del petróleo venezolano* (Caracas, 1973).

8. Technical and Economic Problems of the Newly Nationalized Industry

Fabio Barbosa Cano
Universidad Nacional Autónoma de México, Mexico City

Once the Mexican government had decided to nationalize the oil industry and once the nation had decided to bear the costs of making it work, the Mexican oil industry now under domestic management had found itself overwhelmed by multiple problems in nearly every facet of its activity. Beginning in March 1938, the new administrators had to unify the operations of an industry that previously had functioned separately among the various foreign companies. Such centralization necessitated the definition of a new management rationale (unity of direction, merging of management departments, combined functioning of separate installations taken from various companies, inventory transfer, industrial relocation) within the new organization of Petróleos Mexicanos, or Pemex, formed in July 1938. Yet, this necessary centralizing process could not be formally undertaken as long as an agreement with foreign interests affected by the expropriation was not yet defined, even if only on a tentative basis. Inputs such as financing, technology, and some manufacturing materials still came from abroad and would not be so easily substituted by domestic inputs. Therefore, delays in settlement with the American and British companies also forestalled resolution of a number of internal constraints on Mexican petroleum production in the 1940s.

Many of these problems had a definitive profile, for example, the technological vacuum left by the withdrawing foreign technicians, the dearth of imported inputs such as lead tetratile, the antidetonant ingredient in gasoline, and the inability to obtain repair parts, new equipment, and qualified personnel. Perhaps the most pressing problem was the immediate loss of foreign trade. Along with the collapse of oil exports came overproduction and overloaded storage facilities. Moreover, just days before 18 March 1938, the foreign companies had moved most of their tank trucks to the other side of the border. With scarce distribution equipment, the nationalized industry faced a bitter paradox—overproduction on the one hand, and the impossibility of meeting the needs of large areas within Mexico's own domestic market, on the other. More than anything, many Mexicans wanted to prove that the executives of the dispossessed oil companies were wrong. Those foreign managers had warned repeatedly that Mexico could not run its own oil industry.

The massive cooperation of the workers and the experienced union bureaucracy turned into a factor of utmost importance during the expropriation and the continuation of oil operations. Nevertheless, the enthusiasm and the national euphoria over the oil nationalization soon wore off. Several tensions arose from the new state of paralysis within the industry, and labor relations, as has been demonstrated, had become an acute problem unto itself.

This chapter proposes two hypotheses about Mexico's first efforts to manage its own oil industry. First, among the various problems mentioned above, one can separate those that could be considered conjunctural (i.e., those that pertained to the emergency situation created by the abrupt and unexpected expropriation) from structural problems that remained to plague the industry even into the succeeding decades. Second, the structural problems, defined by the technological horizon in which the Mexican oil industry found itself at the time of the expropriation, related to oil exploration, to the extraction of crude oil, and, finally, to the refining of light derivatives. Exacerbated by changes in the domestic market, these were chronic problems that could be attacked only through a renegotiation with the international oil industry, which in the late 1940s defined terms for renewing the flow of foreign equipment, technology, and financing into Mexico. Between 1938 and 1949, the Mexican managers of the nationalizaed oil industry grappled with both the conjunctural and the structural problems in order to make the oil expropriation work, which had been Mexico's goal in the first place.

Difficulties in the International Market

President Cárdenas, the new captains of industry, and some of the major union leaders insisted that, among the various problems created by nationalization, none had a more widespread impact and a more critical consequence than the loss of foreign markets. It turned out to be one of the results of the boycott that those foreign governments and companies affected by the expropriation had placed on Mexican oil in the international marketplace.[1] Even though it no longer was basically an exporting industry at the time of expropriation, the Mexican industry did depend on foreign trade. By 1937, the last year in which foreign companies operated fully, the production of crude oil had risen nearly to 47 million barrels. The exports of crude oil and its derivatives consisted of almost 25 million barrels, or 53.2 percent of total Mexican production. According to government reports, the boycott closed approximately 90 percent of those international sales outlets in the first weeks after the expropriation.[2] This meant that half of Mexico's potential production could not be placed in any market.

Although detailed statistical data on the effects of the boycott are not available, it is clear that the boycott was a devastating blow to the Mexican administrators. By the end of May 1938, the superintendent of the major oil field of Poza Rica informed the workers of a decision by the management in Mexico City that was to be observed at every oil field. All primary production activities were to be suspended immediately. At this same time, he also informed the workers of problems created by the boycott: the danger of a seizure if the oil was shipped abroad and the scarcity of domestic storage facilities. He also mentioned that alternatives to exporting "were under study," consisting of "either injecting the production into old oil wells, restricting production or, as a last resort, burning it."[3]

As the major production zone, Poza Rica presented a special situation, and production there not only was soon resumed but even increased. Other oil fields, however, suffered a different fate entirely. Based on reconstruction of the industry's situation by the end of 1937, it is possible that there were at least 45 oil fields distributed among 4 large zones: the Northeast Border Zone, the Pánuco River Basin, Poza Rica, and the Southern Zone. From these 1937 fields, 15 (1 of every 3 fields then in production) disappeared in the years following the expropriation. That is, they were totally closed, a situation that continued for more than five years.[4] In 1937, there were 1,039 oil wells working, distributed among the 45 fields. When production was decreased after 1938, many wells also had to be closed down. By 1938, the number of oil wells in operation had declined to 756, that is, 1 out of every 4 had been capped. By the beginning of 1940, there were 807 oil wells in full production.[5]

The process of eliminating oil fields was not homogeneous. As was pointed out, production at Poza Rica soon recovered; the same happened in the Pánuco River Basin. However, two zones underwent especially devastating effects. The Northeast Zone, the most recently discovered production, collapsed completely and was erased from the Mexican oil map for nearly a decade. The situation in the Southern Zone was also very difficult, as the number of oil wells in production decreased there from 306 in 1936 to approximately 200 during the eight-year period following the expropriation. Productivity in the Southern Zone dropped to half during that period.[6] Workers and employees were immediately affected by the consequences of this reduction in the production; transitory workers were fired everywhere. Some locals of the Sindicato de Trabajadores Petroleros de la República Mexicana (STPRM) lost significant number of members. Local 3 at El Ebano lost its delegation once belonging to the Compañía "Cosmos," and Local 10 of Minatitlán lost a delegation at the oil field of San Carlos in Tabasco. The two zones most seriously affected by the restriction in production, the Northeast and the Southern Zones, lost whole locals, such as Local 25 in Nuevo León and Local 19 in Tabasco. These territories were completely deserted during the new period that started in 1938.[7]

However, there seems to be an ambiguity in that the oil wells and fields were closed for almost a decade even though the foreign markets were not closed that long. Indeed, Mexico's external markets revived quite soon. In 1940, it was officially reported that "foreign trade had begun to improve." The Mexican government was forced, against its will, to increase its sales substantially to Germany and Italy from 1938.[8] Also, deliveries of Mexican oil to Japan started as early as March of the same year. These new customers grew in importance until, in 1939, they were purchasing 65 percent of all Mexican oil exports. On the other hand, and even though the boycott of Shell and Standard Oil was far from over, sales to the United States also were resumed in 1938. The former general manager of the Sales Distribution Office of Pemex, Prof. Jesús Silva Herzog, reported that in August 1938 a sales contract for 10,000 barrels of oil from Poza Rica had been negotiated with the Eastern States Petroleum Company of Houston. As Silva Herzog explained:

> The contract was not advantageous from a commercial point of view, yet it had been advisable to sign it because it was wise to introduce nationalized oil into the United States for the first time after the expropriation and start winning the battle against the boycott of the big companies, little by little.[9]

By 1939, trade with the American market had almost been reestablished. Mexico was exporting 75 percent of what could be considered the normal quota prior to the nationalization. By 1940, concurrent with its agreement of indemnification, the Mexican government began to sell oil to the Sinclair Group and the First National Oil Corporation, and Mexico also was making other so-called spot-market sales. At the beginning of August 1939, the Distribution Office of Pemex was "turning down orders because all its production had been committed already."[10] Silva Herzog himself arrived at a somewhat surprising conclusion when he stated that, by 1940, more oil was being sold to the United States than before the nationalization of the oil industry.[11] It may not be an exaggeration to state that the foreign trade problem of the Mexican oil industry was virtually over within a year of the March 1938 expropriation.

Nevertheless, during the second half of 1939, Mexico's external sales suffered a hard, though contradictory, blow. The outbreak of war in Europe shattered its links to its fascist customers. Sales dropped again but only for a short while, because war in Europe also motivated the American interests to reach agreement with Mexico. The necessary collaboration among democracies (including the eminent signing of military defense and economic cooperation pacts) was not consistent with the existence of an oil boycott by the big American and British oil interests. Soon after the Germans and Russians marched into Poland in October 1939, the former secretary of defense of the Hoover administration, Patrick Hurley, approached the Mexican Embassy in Washington as a "mediator." According to Miguel Alemán, Hurley had the support of the State Department to begin negotiations on behalf of the Sinclair Group over the question of indemnities for the expropriation.[12] The final document was signed by Mexico and Sinclair on 1 May 1940. Apart from its particular terms and the relatively minority character of the companies involved (40 percent of all American investment in Mexican oil and 15 percent of its production before expropriation), the agreement was of great significance as a breakthrough in the impasse between the international oil interests and Mexico. The larger companies, especially Standard Oil of New Jersey, maintained their initial intransigence. In fact, an agreement was concluded with Jersey Standard and the other American companies in 1943, even though it was virtually imposed on them by the U.S. government.[13] Regarding the general tendency to reach an agreement, Silva Herzog says:

On May 10, 1939, Germany began its advance over Holland. This Second European War from that moment on turned into one of dreadful and enormous proportions. The problem over the nationalization of the oil companies in Mexico, partially solved through an agreement with Sinclair, became of secondary importance.[14]

Considering this chapter's concern for the resumption of oil production, it is important to emphasize that the Sinclair agreement comprised payment in crude oil from Poza Rica, and twenty million barrels were delivered between 1940 and 1948. Mexico's foreign markets were back.

We can conclude, therefore, that the continuing fall in Mexican production and the closing of oil wells and fields cannot be explained only by disturbances in the international market. The ruptures in foreign markets were very serious, but they were transitory and conjunctural in nature. Even so, Pemex and the Mexican government (and several historians as well) often insisted that the international oil boycott was the principal determinant for all the early difficulties in the Mexicanized oil industry, omitting many other problems. In actuality, beginning in 1940, the foreign market started to lose its importance. The Mexican economy, stimulated by war, entered into a phase of great activity, devouring virtually all domestic production.

Difficulties in Primary Activities

Yet the decreased production and its bitter consequences, like the closing of oil wells and fields, not only continued during the years from 1941 to 1946 but even became more serious, making the structural problems more evident to Mexican managers than the circumstantial. The fall in Mexican oil production continued for ten years; not until 1946 were the 1937 levels of production reestablished. From 1942 to 1944, production had declined so much that it became necessary to ration consumption. The phenomenon of decline carried itself over into other aspects of the oil industry, comprising an authentic Mexican petroleum crisis in itself.

The oil industry of Mexico consisted of primary activities, industrial transformation, and distribution. The primary activities, those related to oil extraction, depended upon exploration, the results of which may be expressed in two distinct aspects: the discovery of new oil fields and the confirmation of oil reserves. Due to technological limitations, that is, lack of equipment and qualified personnel, exploration was totally suspended during the first five years after the nationalization. It was not until 1942 that the Strategic Explorations Department was included in the organizational chart of Pemex. That year, Pemex general manager Efraín Buenrostro reported that the United States "has been conceding us priorities which now permit us to import U.S. equipment and raw materials."[15] Buenrostro also explained that the prolonged suspension of exploratory activities had been the result of "the denial of some companies to supply us with materials" and of "the boycott from international oil interests." Even though in 1940 and 1941, "the possibility of buying those elements was present," he concluded, "we only took limited advantage because of financial problems and the lack of a sufficient number of experts."[16] Nevertheless, even when the new exploration department had gathered more than a hundred geologists and geophysicists in 1943, its work proceeded without any success. Results in exploration may be expressed through discoveries, but there were none in the first five years following expropriation, prompting criticism from the nation's newspapers.[17] In 1948, Pemex technical subdirector, Antonio M. Amor, had to admit that:

[t]he daily press has referred to [Pemex's] poor success in relation to the exploration job and indeed there is reason for its criticism, regardless of the cause, because we have not had any real success in the detection of new deposits nor in the enlargement of current production wherever it may be possible to do so.[18]

The situation was desperate. Manuel Rodríguez, Pemex's first exploration manager and engineer, sought help even from Divine Providence: "I ask the heavens for just a bit of luck," he said in his speech during the Third Convention of Technicians of the Department of Exploration.[19]

As pointed out, the discovery of new oil fields constitutes one of the most spectacular results of exploratory work. The other aspect, although more discreet, is just as important. Exploratory drilling and geophysical research contribute information on geological aspects of the subsoil and of deposits already being exploited. This information provides the basis on which oil reserves are determined and their size and value are assessed. Of course, these evaluations are mere hypotheses that, in turn, production drilling proves true or false. Yet, knowledge of reserves enables the oil enterprise to plan efficiently for future work, since all decisions concerning exploitation rely upon knowledge of oil reserves.

Due to the poor performance in exploration, the production of crude oil was carried out without consideration of any technical knowledge of the size and distribution of Mexico's oil reserves. In 1948, Pemex's exploration submanager, Jorge León Cumming Castañeda, made a public statement about "an extremely alarming circumstance, the relation between oil reserves and production would reach its safety limits by 1948.... A crisis may be upon us in 1950."[20] The official figures divulged by Pemex do not contradict the drop that we have mentioned; the decline in the relationship between reserves and production is even more alarming. The reserve-production relationship dropped from an index of 29 in 1938 to 21 in 1948. The large reserves claimed to be confirmed for 1943 through 1945 (1,515 million barrels in this last year) may seem like simple statistical manipulations, not only because of the ineffective exploratory activity then being undertaken but because Mexican oil reserves were determined for the first time since the expropriation by the engineer Manuel Rodríguez Aguilar. According to his research, the reserves consisted of 821 million barrels.[21] Pemex's estimate of oil reserves simply had no relation to its capacity to explore, a capacity that, for the moment, was nearly nonexistent.

During this period, the production policy of Pemex assumed different forms: the increased extraction of Mexican crude oil without the discovery of new oil fields rested on a gradual exhaustion of those wells remaining in service. Under these circumstances, a healthy production policy aimed at the preservation of the oil mantles in the zones of operation was impossible. These difficult conditions prevailed until the beginning of the 1950s, when a change finally took place. Our conclusions are not intended by any means to undermine the historical success of the expropriation, but only to gain a better knowledge of the reality of nationalization. On the other hand, this is not a novel criticism. Actually, it was the secretary of national patrimony who, in 1963, brought this matter to the public's attention, explaining oil field exhaustion as an unavoidable necessity:

> The production policy followed until 1950 was not essentially different from that followed by the foreign companies just before 1938. In fact, extracting operations continued at full capacity. Nevertheless, the difference lies in the fact that the nationalized industry was forced to do so as a result of the world boycott it underwent in the acquisition of equipment and materials, the lack of Mexican technicians and the impossibility of getting them from other countries, and finally the supplying difficulties imposed by war along with the accelerated growth of the internal demand. This policy [of maximum extraction] had been applied consciously and deliberately by foreign companies in order to obtain maximum economic growth of the country.[22]

As early as 1940, a commission of experts, including the engineer José López Portillo y Weber and the economists Enrique Sarro and Miguel Materola, cooperated in the writing of a document—considered by Silva Herzog as a "moderate and truthful report of the state of affairs in the Mexican oil industry." The report concluded: "Production in the oil fields of Pánuco, the Golden Lane, and the Isthmus, with the exception of Acalapa, are in a great decline, and no more wells should be drilled in them because they would diminish the possibility of recovering all the oil within the strata."[23] As we have insistently demonstrated, however, this sound advice could not be followed.

In summary, crude oil production during this period tended toward decline, stressed the "safe" zones of easy oil extraction, and emphasized the production of light crudes. The Northeast had been abandoned entirely by Pemex; actually, foreign interests whose four small fields in the Northeast were not expropriated remained in production.[24] The Southern Zone was partially dismantled (especially in the swampy region of Tabasco where El Aguila company had started operations), and Poza Rica held the dubious honor of becoming the oil zone of major production. In 1937, Poza Rica contributed 39.8 percent of the total Mexican production, and, by 1940, it had increased to 64.5 percent. In general, during the whole period, Poza Rica accounted for more than half of total Mexican production.[25] It became the very core of the oil industry, pumping its production into every refinery in Mexico. For this reason, a pipeline was built to link Poza Rica to other refineries in Tampico as well as to the refinery in Azcapotzalco, which it had been supplying since 1932. Even the plant at Minatitlán refined Poza Rican crude. "The fall in production in the Southern Zone has forced Pemex to carry crude oil from Poza Rica to Minatitlán, just to maintain that refinery in operation," Silva Herzog reported.[26]

The Resumption of Operations in the Northeast

How could this exaggerated reliance on production from one field have been overcome? How could efficiency in production have been obtained? How could reserves have been increased? How could the production policy have been reversed? Only with capital and access to new technology. To illustrate, the nationalized industry inherited sixteen drilling rigs from the expropriated companies, only eight of which were capable of reaching depths of 2,952 feet. When difficulties later were overcome in the problematic Southern Zone, the average well had to be drilled to depths of 6,562–8,202 feet.[27] Drilling rigs, as any other machinery, required a supply of energy to be transmitted to a rotating table, which in turn acted as a gear to spin the drill; the drill had a bit at its bottom that accomplished the perforation. At that time, steam was still used to produce the energy of the drilling rigs, though some gasoline or diesel engines were also used.[28]

The renewed flow of capital and technology, so necessary for modernizing exploration and exploitation, implied a redefinition of relations between Mexico and the foreign companies that possessed capital and technology. It implied also a new participation of private foreign interests in the oil industry. The rapprochement between Mexico and the foreign interests heralded a new stage in the history of the Mexican oil industry. At the beginning of 1947, many pacts were being negotiated that allowed the reinitiation of activities in the Northeastern Border Zone. Perhaps the most important agreement was signed in New York with Cities Service Oil Co. and its group of companies: Mexico Texas Petrolene and Asphalt Company, Sabino Gordo Petroleum Corporation, Compañía de Terrenos Petrolíferos Imperio, S. A., and Mexico Eastern Oil Company. The pact was divided into two parts, the first consisting of a final agreement over the indemnities between the Mexican government and this trust.[29] The companies received $1,000,000 as payment for their investments, concessions, and properties. With this pact, nearly two square miles of the Northeastern Border Zone that had not been included in the 1938 expropriation now became part of the national patrimony.[30] The second part of the agreement was called the "Contrato de financiamiento y comisión." Among its clauses: (1) Mexico Cities Service was to finance and supply materials, equipment, and manpower for the exploration and extraction of crude oil and gas and the construction of storage facilities and transportation; (2) Mexico Cities Service could sell half of its total production in foreign markets; (3) and the remaining 50 percent of production would be applied to Mexico's commission, government taxes, and Pemex's debt to Cities Service.[31] The Mexican public did not find out about these agreements until the machinery, technicians from Cities Service, and hundreds of workers began arriving at Reynosa.[32] Soon Mexico negotiated similar pacts with other foreign oil companies. The extent of participation over crude oil and the territory each company was granted varied, but all were negotiated for the Northeastern Zone only. The companies included The Texas Company, Cía. Mexicana de Gas, Inversiones, S.A., Petróleo y sus Derivados, S.A., Perforadora Southeastern, S.A, of the Southeastern Oil Co. (owned by Texans Carlos and Federico Wiegand, Ambassador Oil Co., Thomas Williams, Rhodes and Sullivan, Astra Co., Edward S. Burt, and Latina Drilling Company, among others).[33] It is noteworthy that none of the big pre-1938 oil concerns, like Shell and Standard Oil New Jersey, were included in these agreements.

The Resumption of Operations in the Southeast

In 1949, other deals known as "risk contracts" were also signed. Their basic features delineated all the exploratory activities that were to be performed by the contracting company, and if they turned out to be unproductive, the companies would assume the loss. For risk contracts, the Southern Zone was favored, where exploration was thereby resumed. Pemex even granted these companies portions of submerged land in lakes and on the oceanic shelf, and some land also was granted in the Northeastern and Poza Rica oil fields. Perhaps the most important contract was that signed with the Independent Oil Company of Mexico, whose participants included Sunray Oil of Tulsa, Signal Oil and Gas of Los Angeles, Phillips Petroleum of Bartlesville, Hancock Oil of Long Beach, Globe Oil and Lario Oil and Gas companies of Wichita, Keep Rock Oil of Chicago, Ashland Oil of Ashland, Ralph K. Davis of San Francisco, and J. S. Abercrombe of Houston. Similar contracts were also signed with Edwin Pauley, Isthmus Development, Cía. Perforadora del Golfo, S. de R. L., and Sharmex, S.A.[34] Once again, Mexico and Pemex chose to sign these contracts with the independent oil firms rather than the multinational companies.

Institute of Latin American Studies

31 Tavistock Square

London WC1H 9HA

The drilling technology that was used in Mexico now underwent an important change, similar to the technological revolution of the twenties when rotary drilling was substituted for the percussion method. In 1949, for the first time, the so-called directional well system and the turbodrill were introduced. With these methods, drilling was not performed vertically but at an incline, introducing a "fixed tubing," which contained the drilling apparatus at its point. Its advantage was that now the entire length of the valve stem did not rotate, as in rotary drilling, but only the bit at the point. When working in the swampy region of Tabasco and Campeche, this new drilling technology avoided constantly rubbing the walls of the well and diminished the danger of their collapse, which up to then had occurred frequently. Now crews could drill to the great depths required to bring in the coastal fields along the Gulf of Campeche.[35]

Exploration and production were radically modified, and a spectacular reassessment of Mexican oil reserves took place. In the Northeastern Zone, the discovery of the Camargo oil field was announced. Other discoveries included Reynosa (gas and oil), Valadeces, and the productive structure called the 18 de Marzo. In 1949, the Brasil and Francisco Cano oil fields came in, and during the following years, the Caimán, Maguey, Monterrey, Mexicano, and Treviño oil fields, all in the Northeast, also came on-line. Soon, the zone would be defined as the main producer of natural gas in the country, producing 272 million cubic feet in 1958, even more than Poza Rica.[36] The Reynosa refinery was built and became the most important facility for processing gas.

The rediscovery of the Southern Zone began in 1949. The first new oil field in Tabasco, named Fortuna Nacional, was located near Macuspana. In the succeeding months, the Mexican press was happily reporting in its headlines: "New and wealthy oil zone has arisen in the Southeast. Great enthusiasm for success in explorations in States of Campeche and Tabasco. Data reveal oil in Chiapas too. Dawn of prosperity for Tabasco and Campeche."[37] The participation of foreign contractors was not concealed; one of the news reports mentioned that Bermúdez had toured the zone accompanied by a large group of people in three airplanes, one of which belonged to Edwin Pauley and Poncet Davis, head drilling contractors of the Xicalango and Tortuguero wells.[38] In 1951, the José Colomo, largest oil strata in the zone, was discovered. A year later, close to Poza Rica, the so-called prolongation of the Golden Lane was also discovered. In a slightly exaggerated tone, *El Universal* commented: "Facts are evident and speak for themselves. From 1932 to 1938, that is, six long years, no field was discovered; from 1938 to 1945, eight more years, just one. But it so happens that from 1947 to 1952 . . . thirty-one fields are found!"[39] The available information does not permit us to distinguish whether all the exploratory achievements of this new stage were products of the new technology.[40] Yet, the data suggest a strong correlation between Mexico's conclusion of drilling contracts with foreign companies and the discovery of new production in the Northeastern and Southern Zones.

Bottlenecks in Refining

Not only did Pemex technicians confront structural problems in exploration and exploitation during the first decade of Mexican management of the oil industry, but they also faced severe limitations in maintaining refining throughputs. At times, Mexico experienced shortages of gasoline because it possessed few of the additives. The dynamism of economic expansion of the 1940s consequently was somewhat constrained until the structural problems could be resolved. At the time of nationalization, Petróleos Mexicanos came into possession of five big refineries: the Ciudad Madero refinery near Tampico (which produced 42 percent of primary distillation), the Minatitlán refinery (26 percent), the Arbol Grande refinery near Tampico (11 percent), the Azcapotzalco refinery in Mexico City (10.7 percent), and the Mata Redonda refinery near Tampico (7.8 percent). Five smaller refineries and six topping plants also were in operation.

While conditioned, or, to be more precise, constrained by technological limitations, the Mexican oil industry in 1938 was producing four different types of gasoline. Refined gasoline had an octane index of 57, having gone through redistillation and purification processes.[41] The octane index of refined gasoline was increased by the addition of lead tetratilene and by mixing direct gasolines with "cracked" gasolines. Disintegrated or cracked gasoline, whose octane level varied from 67 to 93, was produced in modern thermal disintegration plants. Only three of Mexico's ten refineries at the time had such cracking plants.[42] The third kind of gasoline, natural gasoline, was recovered from gas by absorption or compression. Lighter than the lightest gasoline obtained by direct distillation and disintegration methods, natural gasoline was not a final product but one that was mixed with others. Finally, crude gasoline was the name for a refined product obtained from the ebullition towers that were unable to get well fractioned cuts. It was not a final product either, and had to undergo additional distillation. The statistical information available for the 1940s does not reflect the production of these four types of gasoline.[43] Between 1938 and 1940, these refineries experienced a drastic drop in the production of gasoline. Only half of 1937's gasoline production was being matched in 1940. And Mexico's refineries would not reach their former levels of production until ten years later.

Serious problems also emerged in reaching minimum octane levels in the gasolines. As mentioned before, octane content was achieved by mixing various grades of gasoline or by adding what was called a TEL additive. The latter had an antidetonant characteristic: a few drops in the engine's carburetor air inlet sufficed to diminish the explosive sounds, thus resulting in a smoother and quieter ride. TEL additive was imported. However, after the nationalization, sales to Mexico were totally suspended by the company having the monopoly on its production, Ethyl Gasoline Company, an affiliate of Du Pont Chemical. As the government explained in 1940, "the boycott and limitations imposed by the big oil trusts on the acquisition of anti-detonant products to be mixed with gasolines, explain the reason for the poor quality of the nationalized plants' production of gasoline during the first months of 1938."[44]

The Mexican government, therefore, resolved to produce its own TEL additive and built a plant three miles from Mexico City known as Confidential One, or C-1. The factory maintained industrial secrecy "because TEL production had become a war industry." In February 1940, just as production was being achieved on an industrial scale, serious cases of toxication developed, affecting half the workers in the C-1 plant; several died.[45] Then, in August 1940, a fire destroyed the plant, and the official report to President Cárdenas suggested that the factory had been "sabotaged." (An investigation of who was responsible for this sabotage was initiated, but this writer, as yet, has found no summary of its results.)[46] The C-1 plant was reconstructed at the same location in 1942, when the flow of capital and technology from the United States was partially resumed despite limitations imposed by the wartime economy. Even then, however, the plant worked with numerous interruptions. From January 1943 to March 1944, TEL additive could not be produced, for lack of raw materials, and the same thing occurred in November and December 1945 and in January and February 1946.

Such refining difficulties compounded certain problems in supplying the growing domestic market for petroleum products. Immediately after the nationalization, the state enterprise had a relatively favorable refining situation: the existing industrial facilities permitted the refining of 79.5 percent of the total production of crude.[47] At the same time, Pemex faced a demand for its refined products dominated by fuel oil, known as Combustóleo (72 percent of all refined products), and of light distilled products or gasolines (15 percent of all refined petroleum) and diesel oil (5 percent). At first, Pemex's existing refining capacity had no problems in meeting this small demand for light derivatives, but not for long.

The intense economic activity during the Second World War, the reorientation of the oil industry toward the internal market, and, above all, the changes in its structure toward producing for the burgeoning demand for gasoline as opposed to fuel oil, soon taxed the refining capacity of Pemex. The complaints and protests, particularly from Northern Mexico, over the scarcity of petroleum products grew as the decade of the 1940s advanced. There were even times when the supply was rationed—there is no way of knowing whether the complaints resulted from production problems or from simple distribution difficulties. But it is true that a black market in oil products emerged along with a phenomenon called *coyotaje* or the marketing of Mexican petroleum by those with political influence.[48] While the lack of data complicates our estimation concerning the magnitude of the problem, it is possible to conclude that a gap existed between supply and demand (especially of light derivatives) within an increment of 12 percent from 1938 to 1940.

The construction of three new refineries—a second at Azcapotzalco in Mexico City, another at Salamanca, and a third at Reynosa—somewhat reduced these supply difficulties. The refineries were inaugurated between 1946 and 1950. Foreign companies directed the equipment design, the inspection of machinery and materials, and the operations.[49] Mexico also secured foreign financial support in the form of a bank loan for the new Mexico City plant. Yet, at the same time, Mexican technicians, domestic materials, and internal savings contributed to the construction of these refineries. As César Baptista, a Pemex technician, affirmed:

> When Petróleos Mexicanos was born, the fact that all major changes to its units had been decided and planned abroad became evident. Its plants were planned and designed outside the country, mainly in the United States. Our institution [Pemex] found itself lacking specialists for these constructions of a high technical level and was forced to hire the services of foreign companies. Yet, at the same time, it began educating and training Mexican technicians who would be able to start taking charge of this work.[50]

Clearly, the Mexicans were beginning to solve some of the bottlenecks in refining, and by 1947 they had returned gasoline production to its 1937 levels. Indeed, refined petroleum products also surpassed their earlier limits, so that they could be distributed in sufficient quantity to meet the brisk internal demand. Mexico was learning the oil business.

This analysis has not attempted to deal with the policies of the various early administrations of Petróleos Mexicanos. Rather, our attention has been focused on the technical and economic problems that arose during the first three administrations, those of Cortés Herrera, Buenrostro, and Bermúdez, and the solutions that Bermúdez, especially, attempted during his first years in Pemex's management. In fact, the text explains what Bermúdez considered to be the principal accomplishments of his administration. Due to new oil-field discoveries, the increase of reserves, and the construction of new refineries and gas-treatment plants, Bermúdez hailed 1950 as the beginning of "Pemex's golden age."

This reexamination perhaps permits some reflection on the structural problems that afflicted the nationalized petroleum industry during the first decade of its existence. These structural problems were defined by the scarcity of technology and capital, which explains Mexico's subsequent renegotiations with foreign capital and the reentry of foreign companies into the Mexican petroleum industry. Maybe this experience demonstrates that by not applying themselves to the creation of technological capabilities within Pemex, the Mexican managers found that the pledges they had made at the time of nationalization and their genuine desire to secure the nation's economic independence were limited somewhat by the need to negotiate again with those important actors of the international economic scene, the foreign oilmen.

Notes

1. President Cárdenas, Cortés Herrera, and Buenrostro insisted that the most urgent problem concerned the loss of the external market. See especially "Conflicto de orden económico en la industria petrolera," Archivo General de la Nación [hereafter cited as AGN], Trabajo, Caja 209, exp. 4. The head of the CTM, Vicente Lombardo Toledano, agreed in his final speech before the Third Special Convention of the Sindicato de Trabajadores Petroleros de la República Mexicana in *Guía, órgano del STPRM*, no. 26, Jan. 1941.

2. Jesús Silva Herzog, *Petróleo mexicano: historia de un problema* (Mexico City: Fondo de Cultura Económica, 1941), p. 209; México, Secretaría de la Economía Nacional, *Seis años de gobierno al servicio de México, 1934-1940* (Mexico City: La Nacional Impresora, 1940), chap. on "Petróleo"; Fabio Barbosa, "Situación de la industria petrolera en 1938," mimeo, paper presented at Xalapa, Veracruz, 10-11 Sept. 1987.

3. The orders specified that exploring and exploiting activities be suspended. See "Actas de las asambleas de la Sección 30," Poza Rica, 27 May 1938, Archivo de la Sección 30 del STPRM, Poza Rica, Veracruz.

4. See Barbosa, "Situación de la industria petrolera." In 1945, there were only thirty oil fields in operation. Pemex, *Anuario estadístico 1983* (Mexico City: Pemex, 1985), p. 36.

5. Silva Herzog, *Petróleo mexicano*, p. 189; Enrique González Casanova y Agustín Acosta, "Nota preliminar a la reedición," in *El petróleo de México* (Mexico City: Secretaría de Patrimonio Nacional, 1963), p. 30; Lorenzo Meyer, *México y Estados Unidos en el conflicto petrolero (1917-1942)* (Mexico City: El Colegio de México, 3d ed., 1981), p. 409; Pemex, *Anuario estadístico 1983*, p. 39.

6. Pemex, "Informe de la gerencia de explotación," internal document, (Mexico City: Pemex, 1947). Among the zones that survived, the Southern

showed the steepest decline. In 1937, it produced 9,993,517 barrels of crude and, in 1943, just 45 percent of that amount.

7. Local 19 underwent a somewhat a similar process in the Tajín field, although some of its personnel were reassigned to Local 30 of Poza Rica. Local 14 also closed down when its workers were left with nothing to do. This field had belonged to the Imperial, which had been a pipeline company. See the documents in Archivo General de la Nación, Mexico City [hereafter cited as AGN], Ramo Presidentes, exps. 432/847, 432.1/14.

8. México, Secretaría de la Economía Nacional, *Seis años de gobierno*, p. 204; Silva Herzog, *Petróleo mexicano*, p. 203. The latter relates that these transactions did not consist merely of exchange but also included deals for boat building and, within a few months, hard currency.

9. Ibid., pp. 199–200.

10. In 1937, 7,847,771 barrels of crude oil and derivatives were exported to the United States; in 1938, 3,326,614 barrels (42 percent of the amount of the previous year); and in 1939, 5,860,150 barrels (75 percent of the 1937 figure) (ibid., p. 210). On the rejection of new orders, see Meyer, *México y Estados Unidos*, p. 409.

11. Silva Herzog (*Petróleo mexicano*, p. 210) bases his statement on the preliminary statistics of the first half-year of 1940.

12. Ibid., p. 173; Alemán, *La verdad del petróleo*, p. 448.

13. See especially Meyer, *México y Estados Unidos*, pp. 443–460.

14. Silva Herzog, *Petróleo mexicano*, p. 186.

15. Efraín Buenrostro, "Informe del director general de Pemex, 18 de marzo de 1943," *Los veinte años de la industria petrolera nacional* (Mexico City: Pemex, 1958), p. 95.

16. Ibid., pp. 95–96.

17. On the exploration personnel, see Pemex, *Anuario estadístico*, p. 35. In 1945, a field called "Misión" was "discovered" in the Northeastern Zone. Because it was located in an oil field abandoned in 1938, the announcement of its discovery suggests not a "discovery" at all but a timid return of Pemex to an old oil zone it had abandoned earlier (Antonio J. Bermúdez, *The Mexican National Petroleum Industry: A Case Study in Nationalization* [Stanford, Calif.: Stanford University Press, 1963], pp. 220–221).

18. *Novedades*, 6 Jan. 1948.

19. Manuel Rodríguez Aguilar, "Discurso en la clausura de la III Convención de Técnicos de la Gerencia de Exploración," Mexico City, Jan. 1948, Archivo de Petroleos Mexicanos, Mexico City [hereafter cited as Archivo de Pemex].

20. At the time, the Mexican press was publishing headlines such as "Mexico urgently needs new oil fields" and "Serious danger that the production will not meet demand." At a convention on the subject, experts were saying that the "safe limits" had been reached (*Novedades*, 6 Jan. 1948).

21. Manuel Rodríguez Aguilar, "Reservas petroleras: una exposición de las posibilidades petrolíferas de la República Mexicana," mimeo (Mexico City: Pemex, 1941). Even more absurd are the figures published in other sources. The Consejo Nacional de Ciencia y Tecnología has stated that in 1944 "reserves increased to 786,850,000 barrels" (*El petróleo en México y en el mundo* [Mexico City: CONACYT, 2d ed., 1980], p. 248).

22. González Casanova and Acosta, *El petróleo de México*, p. 33.

23. The complete text of this report may be found in AGN, Trabajo, caja 209, Exp. 4. Also see Silva Herzog, *Petróleo mexicano*, p. 285.

24. Operated by the Compañías Mexicana de Gas, these four fields provided fuel for Monterrey's modern industry through a gas line constructed from Texas to Monterrey. See José S. Noriega, *Influencia de los hidrocarburos en la industrialización de México* (Mexico City: Banco de México, 1944); Antonio García Rojas, "La exploración petrolera en México de 1938 a 1963," mimeo (Mexico City: Pemex, 1963), p. 6.

25. See Pemex, "Informe de la Genercia de Explotación," mimeo (Mexico City: Pemex, 1947), pp. 32–37.

26. Silva Herzog, *Petróleo mexicano*, p. 188.

27. Jorge de la Vega Domínguez, "La industria del petróleo en México: Algunos aspectos de su desarrollo y de su problema financiero," Licenciatura thesis, UNAM, 1957, p. 86. De la Vega collaborated with Pemex general manager Jesús Reyes Heroles from 1964 to 1970. Also see Agustín Cué Cánovas, "La industria petrolera después de la expropiación," *El Popular*, 23 March 1948. Tabasco's average production is 13,836 barrels per well (Fortuna Nacional, La Venta, Ogarrio, and Chilapilla fields). In 1957 in the Colomo field, the most important in that zone, there were thirty-five wells with an average depth of 8,858 feet (Pemex, "Informe de la Gerencia de Explotación," mimeo [Mexico City: Pemex, 1963], p. 17).

28. Cómite Ejecutivo General del STPRM, *Petróleo* (Mexico City: STPRM, 1939), p. 26.

29. This group consisted of eleven companies (of which only two were specifically mentioned in the decree of 18 March: Imperial Gas and Fuel Company and AGWI Oil Company). On 17 April 1942, a pact was signed that allowed payment to seven of them; when the agreement was settled, this dispute was solved with the other four (see *Diario Oficial*, 18 May 1948). Some authors, such as Lorenzo Meyer, erroneously affirm that Cities Service had been closed since 1940.

30. This land was located at San José de las Rusias Hacienda, in Aldama and Soto La Marina municipalities; Sabino Gordo in Aldama municipality; and Buenavista de las Papayas, in the municipalities of Soto la Marina and of San Fernando, all in the state of Tamaulipas.

31. Pemex, "Actas del Consejo de Administración, acta número 331, 8 April 1948, vol. 6, pp. 156–158 and acta número 312, 28 March 1947, vol. 6, p. 52, Archivo de Pemex.

32. *Excelsior*, 3, 4, 11, 24 April 1948.

33. Pemex, "Actas," no. 315, 6 June 1947, vol. 6, p. 72; no. 345, 20 Dec. 1949, book 6, 246–2477; no. 349, 25 Feb. 1949, book 6, p. 265, Archivo de Pemex. Inversiones and Petróleo y sus Derivados were Mexican companies, which were to drill fifty-seven oil wells and be compensated at the rate of U.S. 50¢ per barrel for ten years.

34. Amid the scarce official and authorized information that addresses this theme, see the press bulletin of Pemex informing the Mexican public of these first *convenios*, especially *El Nacional*, 6 March 1949; also Pemex, "Rescisión de Contratos CIMA," mimeo (México City: Pemex, 1969, pp. 6–21); additional

information may be found in Miguel Alemán, *La verdad del petróleo*, pp. 675–698. Information relative to some of the contracts may be found in Pemex, "Actas," no. 410, 28 Feb. 1952, book 7, pp. 266–267; no. 379, 30 June 1950, book 7, p. 107, Archivo de Pemex. These agreements have raised numerous controversies focused mainly on their juridical aspects: the form of payment (crude oil) to the companies or the excessive valuation of that oil. In 1951, Antonio Bermúdez told oil entrepreneurs from Dallas that "49 percent of the drilling of new wells was performed by contracts" (*El Nacional*, 4 March 1952). In some later years, the contractors even surpassed Pemex in the number of wells drilled in Mexico. In 1961, for example, Pemex drilled 288 wells, and the contractors, 440 (Pemex, *Anuario estadístico*, p. 34).

35. On drilling technology, see José Colomo, "Actas del Consejo de Administración de PEMEX," no. 367, 2 Dec. 1949, vol. 6; interview with Antonio J. Bermúdez, *Novedades*, 27 Oct. 1949.

36. Pemex, Gerencia de Explotación, "Informe de producción, 1958," mimeo (Mexico City: Pemex, 1959), p. 87.

37. *El Nacional*, 10 Feb. 1950; *El Popular*, 17 Feb. 1950.

38. *El Nacional*, 10 Feb. 1950.

39. *El Universal*, 6 Sept. 1952. According to the official reports of Pemex, by 1949, 9 new fields had been opened up; by 1952, the new fields had added up to 21. The total number of wells in operation had risen from 1,267 in 1949 to 1,511 in 1952 (Pemex, *Anuario estadístico*, p. 39).

40. The following information seems to establish a relation between the activities of the contractors and the discovery of the "New Faja de Oro" or the "Prolongación de la Faja de Oro" and "la Faja de Oro Marina." From 1951 to 1953, the sea prospects located in the Gulf of Mexico, which formed a wide arch with its center off the coast of Tuxpan, were evaluated. During this period, 16 wells were drilled: 2 wells in Isla del Toro and the other 14 in Cabo Rojo. Oil was found in 3 of them, belonging to the Abra formation from the Middle Cretacic, which produces soil petroleum. Data obtained in these wells, together with a later geophysical evaluation, permitted the discovery of the northern portion of the submerged arch that afterward would become the New Faja de Oro (see *El petróleo en México y en el Mundo* [Mexico City: CONACYT, 1980], p. 253). Concerning the oil wealth of the Southern Zone, the workers' representative on the Administration Board, Manuel Fernández Rustrian, said in 1949: "The expropriated oil companies . . . knew of the existence of a rich oil zone whose secret they had closely maintained. This region is located in the southern part of Las Choapas, on the coast of Tabasco and has been studied and classified by Japanese, Norwegian, English and American geologists. . . . These mantles were kept . . . as the richest of the reserves." Mexican technicians could not begin its exploitation, he said, "because they did not have the materials and equipment" (*Excelsior*, 14 March 1949).

41. The Secretaría de la Economía Nacional issued the first regulations regarding the octane content of gasolines in 1936 (see *Diario Oficial*, 22 Feb. 1936). The information on gasolines is found in Gustavo Ortega, "La industria petrolera mexicana: sus antecedentes y su estado actual," *Boletín del Petróleo*, 35:1–3 (1933); Carlos E. Bermúdez, "La elaboración de gasolinas para Pemex,"

Primera Convención Técnica Petrolera Mexicana (Mexico City: Pemex, 1950), pp. 425–434.

42. The thermal cracking plants were found at the former El Aguila refinery at Ciudad Madero, the El Aguila refinery at Minatitlán, and the Huasteca refinery at Mata Redonda.

43. Nevertheless, Silva Herzog offers some statistics that are disaggregated relative to refined and crude gasolines. See Silva Herzog, *Petróleo mexicano*, p. 190.

44. México, Secretaría de la Economía Nacional, *Seis años de gobierno*, pp. 206–207.

45. Between May and Aug. of 1940, 32 of 68 workers at C-1 developed symptoms of toxication; eleven of these were gravely affected, and two were fatalities (Pedro Alegría Garza, "Aspecto médico-industrial del Tetraetilo de Plomo en México," *Primera convención técnica petrolera mexicana*, vol. 2, pp. 92–104).

46. "Extracto del memorandum del Doctor Teófilo García Sancho," AGN, Papeles Presidenciales, Fondo Lázaro Cárdenas, exp. 432.2/253-28.

47. Silva Herzog, *Petróleo mexicano*, p. 189. Other authors have elevated the percentage. "In 1937, 95.1 percent of total crude production was refined. It was an expression of the policy of "differential taxation" that was favoring the export of refined products and added to the cost of crude and semi-elaborated products" (González Casanova and Acosta, *El petróleo de México*, p. 19).

48. *Tiempo*, 20 Oct., 17 Nov. 1944: *Excelsior*, 1, 6, 13, and 23 Feb., 15 March 1945.

49. Carlos L. Corcuera Riva, "Modernización de la refinería de Azcapotzalco," in Pemex, *Servicio de información*, no. 40 (Dec. 1946), pp. 40–48; Pemex, *Actas del consejo de administración*, no. 326, book 6 (26 June 1947), pp. 73–74.

50. César O. Baptista, "Fabricación y diseño nacional de equipo y plantas para las refinerías de Petróleos Mexicanos," *Primera convención técnica petrolera*, vol. 1, p. 453.

9. The Consolidation and Expansion of Pemex, 1947–1958

Isidro Morales
El Colegio de México, Mexico City
Translated by Lidia Lozano

During the administration of Antonio J. Bermúdez, between 1946 and 1958, Pemex faced a major challenge: to integrate the oil industry vertically under state control. The Mexican public company had to take control simultaneously of the production, processing, and marketing of oil. Until then, only the big international companies had had the degree of integration that the new state company now sought.

From the very beginning, this vertical integration proved hard to establish. On the one hand, production of crude oil had to be maintained and increased; on the other, it was necessary to develop a refining industry that would be virtually wholly geared toward a constantly expanding domestic market. Furthermore, the new company had begun as a nonprofit-making institution, to provide public services according to criteria of social utility. The 1938 expropriation decree inevitably made it a focus of nationalist symbols and rhetoric. Hence, the activities of Pemex were governed by criteria other than those followed by private companies. Even within the context of Mexican public companies Pemex was unique, because of the symbolic weight conferred on it by the act of expropriation.

In this chapter, I will look at the expansion achieved by the industry in the areas of production, refining, and distribution, during a period that could be categorized as one of company consolidation. I will also review the policy of subsidies and price freezes that Pemex pursued as an essential element in its strategy to promote the industrialization of the country. I will consider the costs and sacrifices incurred by the company in pursuit of the goals assigned to it by the state, and, finally, I will look at the benefits granted to labor in order to curb the mobilization that had taken place since the expropriation.

The Framework of Pemex

In 1950, Bermúdez summed up the objectives of Pemex in the following way: to conserve and to develop petroleum resources fruitfully; to supply the home market with abundant petroleum products; to export only secondarily, once internal demand had been satisfied; to contribute to public expenditure through the payment of taxes; to improve the cultural and social standards of oil workers; and to benefit communities in the oil producing zones.[1] Bermúdez also conceived of Pemex as a service company rather than a profit-seeking one, whose general aim was to support the industrialization project set by the state in the early forties. As a member of the generation that had experienced *cardenismo*, Bermúdez considered the oil expropriation and the subsequent creation of Pemex as a decisive step in the country's search for "economic freedom." The "decalogue" of Mexican oil policy was formulated during the Bermúdez administration. Its fundamental premise was that hydrocarbon reserves were a national resource; the mission of Pemex was to preserve and to enlarge such resources—symbols of Mexico's "freedom" and economic sovereignty—and to exploit them for the benefit of national projects.

Some general principles on oil policy followed from this basic premise. First, the future development of the industry would be directed inward rather than outward as had been the case when oil was in the hands of private companies. The industry's expansion and growth efforts would be directed toward the satisfaction of a home market for oil products. Exports would be realized only in a situation of oversupply or insofar as they were necessary to finance imports. These were the assumptions that made up the conservationist thesis passed on by the Bermúdez administration to its successors and that prevailed until the beginning of the 1960s. According to this thesis, increases in production had to respond to growth in internal demand and should never be guided by the needs of the international market. Oil in Mexico was a source of energy, not of foreign exchange.

During this period, according to Bermúdez, an "oil mystique" was developed that embodied the defense of "economic sovereignty"—of which Pemex was a symbol. This mystique involved the joint efforts of both managers and workers to turn Pemex into a viable company, despite the serious limitations faced by the industry following the expropriation. It was this "mystique" that, in Bermúdez's view, made possible the consolidation of the nationalized industry during his administration.[2]

In spite of these nationalist principles, the industry in fact had to adapt its norms to the actual conditions within which it operated. The Petroleum Law of 1941 had left untouched both the properties that had survived the expropriation decree and the confirmatory concessions approved by the Law of 1925 and its 1928 reform (which had recognized them in perpetuity). The Law of 1941 also contemplated the creation of "mixed societies" between the state and Mexican private capital to carry out exploitation. The participation of foreign capital was not included in this category.[3] However, the Law of 1941 did not ban the participation of foreign capital in the drilling, exploration, and development of wells, a fact that later paved the way for the signing of "risk contracts" with American companies.

It was not until the proclamation of the Statutory Law of Article 27 of the Constitution in November 1958 that these concessions were finally revoked and became state property. Thereafter, too, the participation of private capital was confined to service contracts with Pemex, the terms of which excluded the transfer of a percentage of production as a method of remuneration. With the proclamation of the Statutory Law, the basic petrochemical industry also came under the control of Pemex, since the legislation of 1941 had sanctioned the participation of Mexican private capital in this strategic sector of the industry.[4]

Exploration and Production

As Bermúdez said, exploration and production are the backbone of the industry. At the beginning of his administration, both had fallen well behind, and it was necessary to boost them in order to achieve the new targets set up by the public company. For the first few years following the expropriation, Mexican technicians had difficulty estimating the country's reserves. Lack of knowledge and resources, together with the fact that companies had removed relevant geological reports from their archives, hindered exploration work. Even so, the companies had passed on to Pemex four producing provinces, among which Poza Rica, apart from being very prolific, had been discovered only recently. The remaining fields were in the region of El Ebano–Pánuco (San Luis Potosí and Veracruz), the Faja de Oro (the Gold Lane—Tamaulipas and Veracruz), and the region of the Isthmus of Tehuantepec. In 1947, 88 percent of proven crude oil reserves were in Poza Rica.[5] In fact, Veracruz, together with the subsequent discoveries in the Reynosa and in the Nueva Faja de Oro (the New Gold Lane) fields, made up the mainstay of Pemex production until the early seventies.

Right from the very first months, Bermúdez greatly encouraged exploration and development drilling. The goal was a parallel increase in production and reserves. At that time, it was thought that total extraction should not exceed 4 percent of available reserves per annum; such balance would maintain and maximize the exploitation of hydrocarbon resources in the long run. Tables 1a and 1b show the growth in drilling from 1941 onward; they reflect the participation by private, even foreign, contractors, which, as I mentioned above, was allowed under the 1941 law. In an effort to gain support from the union of oil workers, the latter

Table 1a. Exploration Drilling (1941–1958)

		Exploration Wells		
	Pemex	*Contractors*	*Total*	*Success Rate(%)*[a]
1941–1946	31	—	31	16.0
1947–1952	127	110	237	35.0
1953–1958	457	70	527	30.0

[a] This index is calculated by dividing the number of producing wells into the total number of drilled and explored wells. The column was taken from Ana María Sordo and Roberto López, *Exploración, reservas y producción de petróleo en México, 1970–1985* (Mexico City: El Colegio de México, 1988).
Source: Pemex, *Anuario estadístico, 1985* (Mexico City, 1986), pp. 32–33.

Table 1b. Development Drilling (1941–1958)

		Development Wells	
	Pemex	*Contractors*	*Total*
1941–1946	159	—	159
1947–1952	560	291	851
1953–1958	1,187	434	1,621

Source: Pemex, *Anuario estadístico, 1985* (México City, 1986), pp. 32-33.

was granted the power to negotiate contracts with private Mexican individuals. At that time, however, what was needed were equipment, experience, and financing, which foreign companies were in a position to offer; so Bermúdez signed "risk contracts" with a few American companies.

Sixteen of these contracts were signed between 1949 and 1951. However, only five remained in force: two with the Compañía Independiente Mexicano-Americana (CIMA), and one each with Edwin W. Pauley, Sharmex, and Isthmus Development. The contracts granted companies ten to fifteen years to carry out the exploration and development of wells. If drilling was successful, Pemex undertook the reimbursement of their investment, guaranteeing a return of between 15 and 18.25 percent of the production value of wells discovered over a twenty-five-year period.[6] However, "risk contracts" did not produce the desired results. As from 1953, contractors favored development drilling over exploration drilling. Between 1953 and 1958, Pemex drilled 520 exploratory wells, contractors only 70. Besides, most exploration during this period was carried out in oil fields that had been producing since the 1930s.[7] Drilling did not bring about a substantial increase in total production either; in 1958, Pemex obtained only 2 percent of its production from wells managed by contractors.[8]

Since some sectors of the Mexican political class criticized the negotiation of such contracts, Bermúdez defended their legality by describing them as simple work contracts. The Law of 1941 had banned foreign participation in exploitation contracts with Pemex. Article 47 of the same law, however, authorized the negotiation of work contracts without distinguishing between Mexican and foreign capital. A "variant" to this kind of contract, in the form of a windfall payment based on the value of oil extracted, was stipulated. In 1952, the Office of the Attorney General sanctioned the constitutionality of such contracts.

Nevertheless, Pemex made significant advances in exploration throughout those years. Five new producing provinces were discovered during this period. However, exploration was not without its problems. For example, greater importance was attached to gravimetric and seismological studies than to geological ones. According to experts, the neglect of geological and geophysical work was counterproductive because it delayed and hindered the diagnosis of diverse areas.[9] During Bermúdez's second administration, exploratory studies dropped appreciably due to the financial restraints that began to have an effect on company activities. Finally, the estimates upon which exploratory drilling work was based turned out to be too optimistic. For example, it was reckoned that each new well would add 18.8 million barrels of proven reserves, but from 1947 to 1952, each well added an average of only 5.7 million barrels.[10] Even so, the discovery of new fields had an effect on the level of reserves, which declined until 1948, increased in 1949, only to drop again the following year. From 1951 onward, reserves grew at a faster rate than annual production.

During the period covered in this chapter, production of crude oil was erratic. From 1947 to 1951, the average annual increase in production was about 9.6 percent, and from 1952 to 1958, it was 4.2 percent. While some specialists believe that the drop in production was brought about by the lack of adequate production plans,[11] the decline in exports of crude oil from 1952 onward also was significant. It had been agreed since its creation that the bulk of Pemex's production would be directed toward the home market. Nevertheless, exports continued to play an important role during the Bermúdez administration. On the one hand, they helped achieve a balance in Pemex's terms of trade; on the other, they secured additional financial resources to support the plans for the expansion of the industry. In fact, during the first Bermúdez administration, exports showed a significant rise. A portion of this income went to pay off part of the compensation owed to expropriated companies.[12]

According to Bermúdez, the policy of Pemex from the early fifties was to boost exports of oil products, since their value was higher than that of sales of crude oil and they generated more sources of employment. After 1953, manufactured products began to displace sales of crude oil until they virtually supplanted them. However, the fall in crude oil exports also resulted from the fact that production in the oil fields barely managed to meet domestic demand; in 1957 and 1958, Pemex had to import significant amounts of crude. While in Pemex's balance of trade the volume of exports always exceeded the volume of imports, their composition was quite unequal. The main export product was fuel oil, but Pemex had to purchase gasoline, kerosene, diesel and lubricants, products whose value was much higher than that of fuel oil. For that reason, and despite the fact that the volume of exports was greater than that of imports, Pemex's balance of trade between 1953 and 1957 showed a deficit of 1,536.1 million pesos.[13] This worsened the company's financial position and called into question the success of its marketing policy.

Despite his concern to increase exports and their value, Bermúdez never regarded reintegration into the world market as a major exporter as a viable alternative. The possibility of sustaining an export market was difficult for Mexico. By the 1950s, the marketing of crude oil was a virtual monopoly of the big companies, which, of course, had boycotted the purchase of Mexican crude. In the years following the expropriation, Mexico had had to sell its exports at 12 to 15 percent below world prices. Later, in 1952, an oversupply in the international market depressed prices by 20 percent. In order to maintain the competitiveness of its exports, Mexico had to cut its prices by 30 percent.[14] Having finished his second term of administration, Bermúdez announced that "Mexico is not and never shall be a large exporter of oil. It is illusory—and it would be very damaging—to expect oil, exported in large quantities, to become the workhorse of our economy or the panacea of our economic ills."[15] Bermúdez reaffirmed his position in the mid-seventies, when domestic and international conditions favored the country's becoming once again a major exporter of crude oil.

Refining and Domestic Consumption

During Bermúdez's term, the refining industry received a decisive boost, turning Pemex into a fully integrated enterprise. In this sector, Pemex faced the following challenges: to relocate refineries in order to supply areas with the highest consumption; to increase refining capacity and improve the yield of crude oils; and to ensure domestic supply through a network of pipelines and the improvement of land transport.

The relocation of plants was necessary to ensure Pemex's supply to the domestic market. All but one of the six refineries in operation since the expropriation (Azcapotzalco) were on the Gulf Coast. Refineries were near the oil fields because up to that time the oil industry had been geared toward exports. Of refining capacity, 89 percent was situated in the coast, whereas 75 percent of demand came from the Center and the North of the country. The old refinery at Azcapotzalco was dismantled, and a new one, built on the same site, began operations in 1946, with a capacity of 50,000 b/d. The target of this refinery was to meet demand from the country's capital and its outskirts, and in 1955, because of the rise in consumption, its capacity was increased to 100,000 b/d. By 1958, Azcapotzalco was the largest plant, and could meet the country's demand for aviation fuel.

The old Minatitlán refinery was dismantled in 1954, and a new one began operations in 1956. The new refinery's great innovation was its catalytic cracking plant, the first in Mexico. At the beginning of 1947, there were only two thermic cracking plants, built at the refineries of Ciudad Madero and Mata Redonda. By 1956, similar plants had already been set up in Azcapotzalco, Salamanca, and Reynosa. By 1958, there were catalytic cracking plants operating in Azcapotzalco and Ciudad Madero.[16] In 1950, two new refineries, Reynosa and Salamanca, began operations. Although its refining capacity was limited (4,000 b/d), the Reynosa refinery was a success for Pemex since the company carried through the design and construction in five months. In 1955, its capacity was increased to 10,000 b/d. The Salamanca refinery began processing 30,000 b/d. Its target was to supply the Bajío area and to ease pressure on Azcapotzalco. In 1955, a lubricants plant was built there, with a view to curtailing imports of lubricants, which weighed heavily on Pemex's balance of trade.

The laying of pipelines also received a boost alongside the enlargement and building of refineries. Since the priority at this time was to integrate productive oil fields and centers of consumption, pipeline construction was concentrated in the Center region and the Bajío. In 1947, the pipeline network barely extended to 998 miles; in 1957 it covered 4,154 miles.[17] The most important pipelines built during this period were: Poza Rica–Azcapotzalco (1946); Poza Rica–Salamanca (279 miles), completed in 1950; Lagos-Guadalajara (116 miles), Lagos-Aguascalientes (45 miles) and Salamanca-Morelia (66 miles), completed in 1953; Minatitlán–Salina Cruz (155 miles), completed in 1951; and Tampico-Monterrey (306 miles), completed in 1956.

By the end of Bermúdez's term, Pemex had secured the supply of oil products to the center of the country, the most important consumer region. At the same time, a branch line had been built to facilitate access to the northern region and the Pacific. Even so, in the late 1950s there were supply problems in the states of Zacatecas and Durango, the border regions of the Northwest, the West Coast, and the states of Oaxaca and Chiapas.

The infrastructure built to process and distribute crude oil was the mainstay of the company's internal supply policy. This was essential to meet the growing domestic consumption encouraged by a policy of low prices and subsidies. Consumption of oil products grew at an annual rate of 7.1 percent between 1945 and 1954, and 6.7 percent between 1955 and 1960. Such growth rates surpassed even the increase in GNP recorded during those years.[18] The growth in consumption of oil products also underwent a qualitative change. Global demand shifted toward light products (gasoline, kerosene, and diesel) at the expense of heavy products. Whereas, in 1938 73 percent of demand had been for heavy products, by 1958 the latter accounted for only 40 percent of consumption, refined products accounting for the remaining 60 percent.[19]

This change in the patterns of consumption of oil products was linked, no doubt, to the industrial transformation experienced by the country under the governments of Miguel Alemán and Adolfo Ruíz Cortínes. During these years, hydrocarbon production made possible the development of the motor industry: it paved roads, generated electricity, and displaced other sources of primary energy.[20] The supply of refined products accelerated the mechanization of transport and at the same time encouraged the motor industry. Between 1945 and 1955, freight trucks increased from 60,000 to 200,000; cars, from 98,000 to 267,000; and tractors, from 12,800 to 59,500. Diesel now began to displace coal engines.

On the other hand, the supply of fuel oil and natural gas encouraged the installation of thermoelectric plants. Thus, while in 1945 thermal plants accounted for 40.6 percent of electricity-generating capacity, by 1955 the percentage had risen to 52.5 percent.[21] By the end of the fifties, 75 percent of electricity produced in the country came from hydrocarbons. These, in turn, satisfied 92 percent of the country's energy requirements, while coal accounted for 5.5 percent and hydraulic energy for only 2.5 percent.[22]

Pemex's support of industrialization policies was not confined to the supply and distribution of crude oil and refined products. The company's marketing strategy played a key role in stimulating both industrial and private consumption. The growth in consumption, even above and beyond the domestic supply of refined products, was due, in great measure, to the low prices that prevailed throughout this period. According to Bermúdez, domestic prices for oil products rose on average by 185 percent, whereas prices in the country in general rose by 459 percent.[23] As table 2 shows, only at the end of the fifties did real prices for Pemex products recover. This was the result of Bermúdez's decision to raise the price of some refined products shortly before reaching the end of his administration. Although keeping the price of oil products below the rate of inflation was a deliberate state policy, the company's director did not support it. During his second administration, Bermúdez publicly sought a review of prices that would take into account the rise in company costs and the national level of prices. The director was of the opinion that Pemex prices should remain at a moderate level, but they should not undermine the "financial health" of the company.

The government's policy, however, was to subsidize consumption at the expense of Pemex's own finances. Bermúdez estimated the loss in company earnings caused by the deterioration in domestic sales prices between 1954 and 1958 at $10 billion. This is equivalent to more than half of total company earnings between 1953 and 1958, which attests to the kind of sacrifice made by the company.[24] Therefore, the rapid growth in hydrocarbon consumption and the displacement of other energy sources by oil and gas can be accounted for only in terms of the low-price policy sustained by Pemex throughout this period. Under this policy, between 1947 and 1957 Pemex granted direct subsidies to important sectors of the economy, such as railways, public transport, and energy, to the tune of 2,080 million pesos, which equaled 9.1 percent of the accumulated earnings of Pemex during this period.[25]

Securing Company Earnings

One of the most significant changes experienced by the oil industry when it came under state control was in its financial structure. While the old companies had obtained resources primarily from exports, Pemex would have to secure its earnings from domestic sales. During the period that concerns us, domestic sales represented 85 percent of total sales earnings. A further difference between Pemex and the private companies was the administration of its own financial resources and the distribution of what might be called the oil surplus. Pemex expenditure was geared to satisfy the growth of subsidized consumption. Thus, outlays were intended to create and encourage consumption rather than to adjust to demand. A significant amount of the company's financial

Table 2. Change in Real Price[a] of Various Oil Products in Mexico (pesos per liter)

	1950	1955	1960
Gasoline (supermexolina)			
Sale price	0.90	0.81	0.88
Index	100.00	90.90	98.00
Kerosene			
Sale price	0.31	0.22	0.35
Index	100.00	71.00	113.00
Diesel			
Sale price	0.29	0.24	0.35
Index	100.00	83.00	121.00
Liquified Gas			
Sale price	1.19	0.78	1.03
Index	100.00	66.00	87.00

[a] 1965 prices (12.5 pesos = $1). The deflator used was the consumer price index.
Source: ECLA, *La industria del petróleo en América Latina: Notas sobre su evolución reciente y perspectivas* (New York: United Nations, 1973), p. 63.

surplus (additional earnings after operation costs have been covered) was transferred to the state in the form of taxes or to other industrial sectors through subsidies. Because of this, the internal savings of Pemex were insufficient to finance necessary investments and to expand the industry to suit the country's new needs. In fact, the gap between company earnings and investment became its Achilles' heel.

Growth in Company Spending

Internal resources for investment progressively declined throughout the period because spending also progressively increased. It is not surprising that expenditure should have been greater than investment. Under expenditure, Pemex's accounts included disbursements for the purchase of operational products and materials, taxes and tranfers to the federal government, personnel wages and benefits, subsidies and losses, interest, and financial obligations. During the period studied, expenditure accounted for between 87 and 95.3 percent of income from sales. During the first Bermúdez administration, income from sales grew faster than disbursements, but during his second term the situation was reversed, which explains the substantial drop in company savings.[26]

The distribution of expenditure throughout this period was as follows: 29.2 percent for purchase of operational products and materials; 25.5 percent for taxes and transfers to the government, including payments to compensate expropriated companies; 24.7 percent for wages; 13 percent for subsidies; and 7.6 percent for interest on its debt.[27] The fact that the acquisition of products and materials was the most important category of total disbursements simply reflects Pemex's growing activity. Such disbursements increased because of the rise in the price of materials, especially following the 1948–1949 and 1954 devaluations, which increased the deficit in the company balance of trade for these years.[28] Taxes and transfers to the government also represented a significant percentage of company expenditure, and Pemex thus became the country's leading taxpayer. Between 1947 and 1957, it payed 5.2 billion pesos in taxes and other payments, which amounts to roughly a fourth of total government income for that period. The transfer of "petropesos" to the state became a strategic item in the financing of public expenditure. While the bulk of transfers were based on product sales, in particular of gasoline, Pemex also made payments for royalties and interest on property acquired from expropriated companies. The royalties had been payments made by the expropriated companies for the use of private land. Throughout this period, Pemex compensated most of the landowners through the purchase of their rights.[29] In 1947, it was agreed that from that date Pemex would make the compensation payments to El Aguila for the next fifteen years.[30] In the final years of the second Bermúdez administration, the loss of income and increase in operational costs meant that the company fell behind with its tax payments. In 1958, Pemex owed 190 million pesos ($15.2 million) in tax arrears, which revealed its difficult financial situation. According to José Rentería, if during the last three years of the Bermúdez administration prices had been raised by an annual rate of 18 percent, Pemex would have met its obligations by 1958 and would have had no extra burdens on subsequent years.[31]

Wages and salaries also represented a significant part of company expenditure. Although wages lagged behind the inflationary spiral, Pemex was, from the start, a company that generated more employment than any other productive sector of the Mexican economy. Given the aggressiveness of the Sindicato de Trabajadores Petroleros de la República

Mexicana (STPRM), the state was forced to grant workers exceptional labor conditions. As already mentioned, Pemex also incurred sacrifices as it subsidized railway transport and energy, to which should be added losses incurred through the import of oil products, which it bought at current international market prices but sold at controlled prices in the domestic market.

Given the structure of its expenditure, Pemex was vulnerable to charges of inefficiency in its operations. In 1944 its losses were estimated to be in the neighborhood of $10.3 million a year.[32] A study carried out in the fifties for the World Bank reached similar conclusions when it emphasized that the company had been unable to recoup its capital.[33] For his part, Oscar Guzmán has estimated that during this period the combined costs of exploration and extraction increased continuously (from 53¢ a barrel in 1946 to 75¢ in 1958.) In fact, it was the primary production stage that raised Pemex's operational costs, since overall refining costs actually went down.[34] Bermúdez publicly denounced the "dearth" of financial resources experienced by the company in the late fifties, but he attributed it to price controls imposed by the government, and never mentioned that it might have been caused by the company's inefficient operations.

To measure Pemex's efficiency using criteria applicable to private companies might be confusing. Since its inception, we have seen, Pemex was endowed with a "set of symbols" and a rationality that differentiated it from private enterprises. Some authors have suggested that the company's efficiency should not be measured by the volume of its net profit. In their view, the yield on its investments must be offset by their effect on the entire social and economic structure of the country.[35]

From this perspective, the company's expenditures and sacrifices bore fruit. However, to evaluate company activities on the basis of general social and economic consequences may lead to an underestimation of the mistakes and shortcomings of its internal management. Given the very nature of its business, Pemex could not escape the exigencies peculiar to the petroleum industry: investment cycles, the uncertain character of exploration, technological innovations, and so on. The plurality of Pemex's functions (as both a producing enterprise and promoter of a "social-symbolic-economic" state policy) has on occasions generated conflicts within its internal management and in its relation with the state. During the second Bermúdez administration, there were disagreements between the director and the chief executive on the pricing policy that squeezed the company's real earnings. Throughout his administration and in subsequent years, Bermúdez reasserted that financial strengthening of the company was compatible with its developmental function as long as an adequate pricing policy was pursued and subsidies and expenses "foreign" to the company were canceled. Bermúdez also demanded greater independence for the company vis-à-vis the state and that strictly political activities should not interfere with his administration.[36] At the same time, given the complexity of the company's functions and its subordination to the policies of the chief executive, its production and financial activities could not escape the vicissitudes of power.

In Search of Credit for Investment

Since government control of pricing policy coupled with the rise in expenditures meant that Pemex's savings were insufficient to finance expansion, it became clear to the government of Miguel Alemán that expansion would have to involve the participation of foreign capital. But the terms of such participation were a delicate issue, given existing legislation, the symbolic burden carried by the company, and the refusal by the expropriated companies to participate on the basis proposed by the Mexican government.

In 1944, when the Mexican government sought a loan from the United States, Washington replied that it did not grant official loans to sectors where private capital was available for use.[37] The reference was clear: Mexico had to reach an agreement with the expropriated companies to ensure the future expansion of the industry.[38] The refusal reflected disagreement within the U.S. government on how to ensure oil production in Mexico. From that date until the summer of 1950, when credit was granted indirectly, the State Department, with support from high officials in the Departments of Defense and Navy, opposed the granting of credit to Pemex. Its position reflected the attitude of the big oil consortiums that the Mexican government had to change its legislation and accept their participation in the direct exploitation of Mexican oil. For their part, the U.S. President and Congress adopted a more flexible attitude. While they did not oppose the participation of the companies in the Mexican oil industry, they thought Pemex should receive financial support without having to renounce its monopoly on ownership and exploitation. The crucial goal for both the White House and Congress was to support the expansion of Mexican production (a question that at that time was taboo), thus making possible an increase in the export of crude and refined products, and strengthening the "security" of hemispheric supplies.

Bermúdez became aware in good time of the split among U.S. officials, and he set out to win the support of both the executive branch and Congress. Under these circumstances, in early 1948, the Mexican government presented to the U.S. ambassador—in secret—the bases for reaching agreements with private companies. The proposal stipulated that 80 percent of costs would be repaid should productive wells be discovered, and that profits of between 10 and 20 percent would be allowed.[39] Although the big companies rejected the Mexican proposal, the position of Pemex and of the government had now become clear. The participation of companies would be restricted to "risk contracts" that did not confer on them any rights to the subsoil or to the exploitation and distribution of crude. By mid-1948, Bermúdez's strategy became clearer. On the one hand, he began negotiations with independent investors—like Gordon Duke and Edwin Pauley—in order to interest them in drilling contracts, thus breaking the big companies' bloc. On the other hand, he had extended an invitation to the Committee on Interstate and Foreign Trade of the American Congress (which favored granting credit to Pemex) to visit installations and to appraise their needs.

The committee, headed by Senator Wolverton, visited Mexico in August and September of that year. During their stay, Bermúdez showed them the company's five-year plan, which gave priority to exploration and production aiming to increase the latter from 167,000 b/d in 1948 to 365,000 b/d in 1953. If this figure was reached, the country would be in a position to export 280,000 b/d by 1953.[40] This level of exports contrasted with the 36,000 b/d that Mexico was exporting in 1948 and even with the 70,775 b/d that it would export in 1955, when total exports reached their peak. To underline the scale of the effort Pemex was willing to undertake, the plan assumed a pessimistic scenario in which high deficits in the production of crude were forecast if the necessary investment was not made. On this basis—and in order to reach the above targets—Pemex estimated an investment in the five-year period 1949–1953 of $470 million, 80 percent of which would be invested in exploration and drilling.[41] An investment of this size could not be made with Pemex resources alone.[42]

The plan was intended to excite the interest of the U.S. Congress and to obtain additional resources for expansion. Bermúdez let the Wolverton Committee know that if the United States were to grant financial aid for this program "there would be no problems with regards to its share in the oil extracted."[43] Bermúdez was not opposed to the participation of direct American investment, but it was his view, which he shared with Miguel Alemán, that it should be confined to the signing of "risk contracts" comparable to those negotiated with small companies.

In early 1949, the Wolverton Committe published its report: it asked the U.S. government to extend credit to Pemex, though not to the extent suggested by Bermúdez. Rather, the committee deemed that part of the investment should be covered by private oil companies, insofar as "reasonable" conditions existed in the country for the development of their activities. However, the report mentioned that any U.S. aid program had to take into account the impact of the oil nationalization on the nationalist and political experience of the Mexican people. The report also stressed the significance that the development and expansion of the Mexican oil industry had for both Mexico and the United States. It mentioned such targets as an oil pipeline through the Isthmus, the construction of gas conduits to centers of consumption in both Mexico and the United States, and the building of a refinery on the Mexican Pacific Coast. The report pointed out that the significance of American aid had to be judged in the light of the strategic, diplomatic, and economic consequences for both countries.

However, the committee's recommendation encountered stubborn opposition in the State Department and among high-level U.S. officials. Their position had not changed: no credit would be given where private capital could collaborate, a position that protected the interests of the big companies. To extend credit would set a bad precedent in countries where the oil consortiums were active. It might even encourage them to nationalize their industries as Mexico had. The State Department was taking into account criticisms raised by the big companies on the proposal of "risk contracts," which, according to the Texas Company, were unacceptable. Standard Oil of New Jersey asked for a change in the 1941 law, to sanction the participation of foreign capital in the composition of "mixed societies." Gulf made its return to Mexico conditional on taking charge of production and sharing profits with the Mexican government. The companies were pressing also for a change in the tax structure to which they would be subjected.[44]

In March 1949, Bermúdez went to Washington to make a loan application to Eximbank. His proposal was for $203.4 million, less than half the investment required by his five-year plan. During his stay, Bermúdez made known the agreement reached with the company CIMA, citing this agreement as proof of his "good disposition" toward private capital. In the summer, the American government responded to the application, in a way that reflected once again existing divisions in Washington. The State Department reiterated its position of not extending direct loans to the oil industry; nevertheless, having considered the precarious financial situation of Pemex, Washington was prepared to offer an aid program for the development of refining, sales, and transport. In return, the Mexican government was asked to carry out legal reforms that would pave the way for the participation of private companies in exploration through "mutually acceptable" contracts.[45] Faced with this demand, the Mexican government withdrew its application, stressing its dismay that the U.S. government had let political factors interfere in the case of a financial request.[46] A year later, at Truman's instigation, Eximbank gave a loan for $150 million—to the Mexican government, not to Pemex—which Nacional Financiera managed as a loan for development investments. Thus, the U.S. president got around obstacles interposed by the State Department and indirectly supported financing of the Mexican oil industry, at a time when the Korean War necessitated the safeguarding of hemispheric supplies of hydrocarbons.[47]

The politicization of access to financial resources shows the difficulties encountered by Pemex and the Mexican government in financing the expansion and integration of the oil industry. The big American companies had constituted themselves as a powerful pressure group to lobby against all aid to Pemex. However, after 1951–1952, when new oil fields were opened in Venezuela as well as the Middle East, the big oil companies gradually lost interest in maintaining a foothold in Mexico. This meant that the administrative agencies of the U.S. government could adopt a more flexible attitude in regard to Pemex's activities.[48] Given the lack of official loans, Pemex began to secure loans from commercial banks that, though given under strict conditions, narrowed the gap between the company's savings and its investment needs, particularly during Bermúdez's latter years. Securing domestic resources was also important. Of the financing for the Salamanca refinery, 56 percent came from national savings, through the issue of bonds by the Patronato del Ahorro Nacional (the National Savings Board). Nacional Financiera also issued bonds to finance company investment. In 1958, domestic savings accounted for 28.4 percent of Pemex's investment. Thus, despite the company's shortage of resources, the limitations to the country's domestic savings, and the political and financial difficulties in securing external savings, Pemex increased its investments in real terms in 1958 from 107 million pesos ($8.6 million) to 913 million pesos ($73.1 million) (see table 3). During this period, Pemex's investments held a very important place among total public investment. Investment in the oil and energy industry gradually displaced investment in railroads. The latter sector, which in 1939 accounted for 30.9 percent of total public investment, had dropped to 11.9 percent in 1959, while Pemex accounted for 26.0 percent.

The Company's Managerial and Labor Control

The vertical integration of the oil industry had to face challenges not only of a technical and financial nature but also of a political and managerial nature. The reorganization of the industry into a single enterprise involved the concentration of technical, financial, and administrative decision making under a General Management and a Council

**Table 3. The Structure of Financing of Pemex Investments
(1939–1958)** (in millions of 1950 pesos)[a]

	1939	1947	1949	1951	1953	1955	1958
Total	77	107	271	354	415	687	913
Own resources	77	107	256	329	363	574	80
Domestic financing	—	—	—	—	—	—	260
External financing	—	—	15	25	52	113	573

[a] 8.65 pesos = $1.

Source: President's Office, *México, inversión pública federal 1925–1963* (Mexico City: Dirección de Inversiones Públicas, 1964), pp. 73–86.

of Administration, and it required that the STPRM mediate the demands of a heterogeneous labor force, dispersed in different regions of the country. The concentration of decisions and demands into these bodies turned both company and union directorates into extremely powerful institutions.

Under the 1938 decree of expropriation, Pemex was to be a decentralized public company responsible for specific tasks relating to the development of the oil industry. Its legal constitution and the very requirements of the industry gave the institution its own space independent of political commitments undertaken by successive governments. Nevertheless, from Pemex's inception, its activities had been subordinated to the policies of the Mexican state, and such subordination was assured through the government's power to appoint most of the company's top management.

According to the 1938 decree, the management of Pemex would be in the hands of a nine-member Council of Administration, from which the director general would be chosen. Six of its members, who would represent the company, would be appointed by the government, which would have the power to remove them, including the director general, should it deem it appropriate. The three remaining members would be selected by the union.[49] A 1940 decree changed the proportion to five members selected by the company and four by the union.

The vertical control of the company followed from the power of the director general to appoint the managerial cadre in his administration. Among them were the three subdirectors: for production, for administrative and legal affairs, and for business, who in 1951 were joined by a subdirector for finance. With the aid of the subdirectors, the director general also appointed four managers (for production and exploration, for refineries, for domestic sales, and for exports), and the remaining middle managerial cadre.[50] The managerial structure of Pemex could not escape the presidentialist structure of the Mexican political system, which the Cárdenas government had consolidated. Control of Pemex was exercised not only through such vertical appointments but also through the government's control of its earnings and expenditure, through the tax policy to which it was liable and through the price control imposed on its products, the changing of which depended ultimately on the government. Given the close link between company management and the government in power, Pemex's autonomy vis-à-vis the state depended to a large extent on the political strength of the director, a strength that did not emanate from his formal powers but from the skills of each individual director, from his contacts and support within and outside the company. This was the case with Bermúdez and later with Díaz Serrano. In any case, the leadership capability of the director general has always been subject to the kind of ties he could establish with the president of the republic.[51]

The managerial capability of the company director has depended, too, on the kind of compromises and balances reached with the STPRM, since from the very beginning the oil union enjoyed unusual political strength. One of the reasons is that the STPRM has been a national industrial union; that is, it has gathered the entire labor force upon which rest the company's multiple activities, basing its power on the number of members as well as on the geographical areas it represents.[52] The biannual revision of the collective labor contract became a barometer of the relative strength of company and union, a question that was more clearly defined at the beginning of the administration of Miguel Alemán. In view of the tough negotiations—which were postponed because of the presidential changeover—over the collective contract in the summer of 1946, the union called a strike in December, to put pressure on the newly established government. The response of the new president was blunt: military intervention in oil installations, and the dismissal and replacement of union leaders.[53] The blow to the union was indicative of labor policy throughout the administration of President Alemán. For the oil workers, these drastic measures were the culmination of a policy that had begun in the final years of Cárdenas's government, and that aimed at counteracting the power and militancy of the union. The state thus sought both to consolidate the controlling capacity of the director and the top managerial cadre (conferring on them, for example, the power to hire, dismiss, or suspend part of the labor force), and to reduce the burden of wages and benefits on company expenditure.[54]

Following this blow to the union leadership, a mixed commission was created to discuss the terms of the new contract, a process that would also entail the demarcation of the union's area of action. Thus, the new General Executive Council would be made up of leaders who were "collaborationist" (vis-à-vis company and state). In this way, the government sought to extend its control over the company's labor agencies and to neutralize one of the objectives of union struggle: to obtain control of the company. In fact, the creation of vertical political clienteles was a distinctive feature of the institutionalization of the Revolution, and Pemex was not immune to this process. Government encouragement of a "collaborationist" union bureaucracy could be pursued only through concession, not coercion. Hence, company management and government were ready to negotiate with the union a whole range of privileges and benefits, which, managed by the union bureaucracy, became the means to maintain control over its rank and file.

One of the most important concessions was the union's power to hire personnel and to admit members, a power based on a "gentleman's agreement" reached in the summer of 1947, which also granted the union power to participate in work contracts agreed between the company and private enterprises. The intervention of the union took place at several levels: contractors working on drilling had to employ the company's union members; the union could act as intermediary when engaging private companies, and it could also form "cooperatives" to carry out work contracts that would receive preferential treatment from management subject to "prior tender and under equal conditions."[55] With greater participation in the productive activities of the company and the power to hire personnel, the STPRM was given powerful weapons that in the hands of its leaders would help them control the rank and file. While opening the way for corruption within Pemex, the powers conferred on the union proved to be functional to the objectives set by the state: to control and discipline the labor force, to contain their wage claims, and to turn the union into a vehicle for advancing, rather than obstructing, the integration and development of the industry.

During this period, strikes and union mobilizations were curtailed, and the real income of oil workers dropped considerably. Thus, while in 1946 the index of the average real income was almost 65 percent relative to 1938, in 1958 it was 44.4 percent.[56] Nevertheless, it is important to note that the drop in wages was more than compensated by an increase in benefits. Whereas in 1946 almost 80 percent of labor payments consisted of salaries and wages, in 1958 the latter accounted for 48.1

Table 4. Pemex Increase in Workers Hired, 1938–1958 (selected years)

Year	Permanent	Temporary	Total
1938	14,786	2,814	17,600
1947	20,025	8,797	28,822
1952	24,255	11,533	35,788
1958	28,668	16,864	45,532

Source: Pemex, *Anuario estadístico 1985* (Mexico City, 1986), p. 139.

percent; that is, the remaining 51.9 percent were supplementary payments.[57] Benefits were of different kinds: provision of a savings fund to provide financial aid to workers buying or renting accommodation; establishing schools in oil towns and complementing teachers' salaries; building hospitals, clinics, and union quarters; and setting up consumer cooperatives and establishing scholarships for the technical training of workers.[58]

Pemex also became an important source of employment in a country where a high unemployment rate was a constant feature of the economy. As can be seen from table 4, the number of Pemex workers grew by 157 percent between 1947 and 1958. In relation to 1938, the increase was 258 percent. The increase took place in spite of the fact that company management fought for a reduction in temporary personnel. The power of the union to hire was further strengthened by the fact that Pemex became a labor exchange that offered attractive benefits for its workers. The hiring of a worker entailed his participation in a series of labor privileges that few companies could offer. Furthermore, workers could "bequeath" their jobs to close relatives. At the same time, the union managed the hiring for two types of payroll: temporary and permanent. Unlike temporary workers, plant workers had job security and enjoyed full benefits. Being hired, joining the union, finding a position in one or other class of employment, or changing from one to the other, were matters dealt with at the discretion of the union leadership.[59] Accordingly, union leaders could develop a clientele among the rank and file, which in turn facilitated greater control over the labor force. Thus came into being veritable union *caciques*, whose power sprang from corrupt practices. The most notorious case during this period was that of Superintendent Jaime J. Merino and Pedro Vivanco of Poza Rica, who turned the sale of jobs and temporary contracts, as well as the imposition of leaders and the violation of wage-scale rights, into everyday practice.[60] In December 1957, the Chamber of Deputies declared job selling fraudulent, but the practice was not eliminated from union activity.

The difficulties in eradicating corruption lay to a considerable extent in the fact that it represented the "perverse effects" of practices promoted and sponsored by company management and the state itself. Such practices were the price for running a vertical organization, held together by the creation of groups and clientele around leaders capable of negotiating sinecures and power-sharing. This structure has proved functional in disciplining the labor force, and transforming it, in turn, into an ally in the development of the productive and commercial activities of the company.

While these powerful faculties have strengthened the union bureaucracy, they have also become a potential source of weakness. Access to such enticing powers promotes divisions among leaders and the denunciation of these practices, opportunities, and privileges from which some are excluded. During the time of Bermúdez, internal dissidence within the union was common,[61] but it did not succeed in challenging the "collaborationist" alliance between union bureaucracy, company management, and the state as a constituent element of the organization of Pemex. This alliance proved to be fundamental for the consolidation of the vertical integration of the company and the expansion of its activities undertaken by Bermúdez and his successors.

Conclusions

During the twelve years of the Bermúdez administration, Pemex became a totally integrated company, from well to pump. One of the company's main objectives—the supply of a constantly expanding domestic market—was successfully attained. To achieve this, Pemex encouraged exploration and increased its reserves. Production grew along with consumption, and a transport and distribution network linking production areas with major centers of consumption was consolidated. Pemex boosted consumption, through a policy of subsidies and price freezes, and it generated "social gains" by granting juicy benefits to union personnel.

However, the first phase of expansion of the company exposed the costs and sacrifices implied in its goals of social and industrial development. Antonio Bermúdez himself reckoned, years later, that the golden age of the public company came to an end in the latter years of his second term. In his view, it was the dearth of Pemex's financial resources, which had been sacrificed on the altar of an indiscriminate policy of subsidies and benefits, that thwarted the achievement of another Pemex objective: the "economic independence" of the country. With this comment, Bermúdez denounced the increasing dependence on foreign financing for company investment and expenditure. He denounced, too, the fact that dependence had been accentuated in order to achieve political goals—subsidies, prize freezes, benefits—while rational technical and economic criteria had been cast aside.

The conflict between the goals of Pemex and the cost and means to achieve them continued into the decade following the Bermúdez administration. It did not, however, prevent Pemex from continuing to expand its activities, particularly in the areas of natural gas, petrochemicals, and scientific research. Yet, the "dearth" of financial resources that had begun to manifest itself under Bermúdez reached greater proportions in the late 1960s and early 1970s. This brought about significant changes in oil policy and laid the foundations for the reintegration of Mexico into the world market as a major exporter of crude.

Notes

1. *Informe del director general, 1947–1952* (Mexico City: Pemex, 1952), pp. 94–102.
2. Antonio J. Bermúdez, *La política petrolera mexicana* (Mexico City: Joaquín Mortiz), 1976, pp. 38–43.
3. The only contract for exploitation based on the 1941 Petroleum Law negotiated by the government was with Hilario Millán in October 1945 for a period of thirty years, which bound him to pay the federal government 12.5 percent of total production. The contract was canceled in 1955. See Antonio J. Bermúdez, *Doce años al servicio de la industria petrolera mexicana, 1947–1958* (Mexico City: Conaval, 1960), pp. 30–31.
4. See the "Ley Reglamentaria del Artículo 27 Constitucional en el Ramo del Petróleo" (November 1958) in Pemex, *Marco jurídico básico* (Mexico City: Pemex,1983), pp. 18–21.
5. "Informe del Comité Wolverton a la Cámara de Diputados de los Estados Unidos," in *Problemas Agrícolas e Industriales de México*, 1954, no. 4, p. 144.
6. Miguel Alemán Valdez, *La verdad del petróleo en México*. 3d ed. (Mexico City: Grijalbo, 1977), pp. 675–680.
7. George Philip, *Oil and Politics in Latin America* (Cambridge, Eng.: Cambridge University Press, 1982), p. 335.
8. Bermúdez, *Doce años*, pp. 31–34.
9. Ana María Sordo and Roberto López, *Exploración, reservas y producción de petróleo en México, 1970–1985* (Mexico City: El Colegio de México, 1988).
10. Ibid.
11. José Rentería G., *La descripción del plan sexenal para la industria petrolera mexicana, 1959–1964* (Mexico City: Pemex, n.d.), pp. 8–22.
12. Sordo y López, *Exploración. reservas y producción*.
13. Bermúdez, *Doce años*, pp. 154–159.
14. *Informe del director general*, Pemex, March 1953, p. 13.
15. Bermúdez, *Doce años*, p. 164.

16. Ibid., pp. 91–92.

17. Informe del Comité Wolverton, p. 142; Pemex, *Informe del Director General, 1958*, pp. 16–17.

18. Between 1946 and 1956, the average annual rate of growth in GNP was 6.1 percent; see Leopoldo Solís, *La realidad económica mexicana: retrovisión y perspectivas*. 6th ed. (Mexico: Siglo XXI, 1980), p. 111.

19. See Ernesto Lobato López, "Las finanzas de la industria petrolera de México," in *La industria petrolera mexicana* (Mexico City: UNAM, 1958), p. 77.

20. In 1960, however, the oil industry accounted for only 3.4 percent of the GNP and 11.7 percent of industrial production. See *La industria petrolera en México* (Mexico City: Secretaría de Programación y Presupuesto, 1980), p. 23.

21. See Enrique Padilla Aragón, "La industria petrolera y su influencia en el desarrollo industrial," in *La industria petrolera mexicana*, pp. 59–61.

22. Bermúdez, *Doce años*, pp. 284–287; E. Lobato López, "Las finanzas," p. 74.

23. Bermúdez, *Doce años*, pp. 222–240.

24. Bermúdez, *La política petrolera*, p. 54.

25. Lobato López, "Las finanzas," pp. 76 and 79.

26. Ibid.,p. 80; Oscar Guzmán, "Las finanzas de Pemex, 1938–1958" (Mexico City: El Colegio de México, 1985), pp. 39–49 (mimeo).

27. Lobato López, "Las finanzas," p. 80.

28. Between 1952 and 1954, Pemex accounted for 15 percent of the country's imports of capital goods and services. To this, one should add imports of oil products, which it then sold at lower prices in the home market. See George K. Lewis, "An Analysis of the Institutional Status and Role of Political Economy," PhD diss., University of Texas, 1959, p. 378.

29. Pemex bought the bulk of royalties at below their value. They had been valued at 3,796.7 million pesos, but the company paid 183.4 million (Bermúdez, *Doce años*, pp. 26–29).

30. Pemex paid $8.72 million a year until 1962. But in 1960 these payments became part of its tax payments.

31. José Rentería, "Análisis financiero de la industria petrolera nacionalizada" (Mexico City: Pemex), 1964, p. 12.

32. See José Noriega, *Influencia de los hidrocarburos en la industrialización de México* (Mexico City: Banco de México, 1944), p. 277.

33. See Michael Tanzer, *The Political Economy of the International Oil and the Underdeveloped Countries* (Boston: Beacon Press, 1970), p. 288.

34. In real terms, refining costs went down from $140.23 per barrel in 1952 to $92.08 in 1958; see Guzmán, "Las finanzas," pp. 43–44.

35. In the study mentioned above, Michael Tanzer assesses the achievement of Pemex on the basis of what he calls the "social rate of return" of its investment. See particularly chap. 22, which deals with the Mexican company.

36. Bermúdez, *La política petrolera*, p. 52.

37. Nevertheless, that same year Eximbank had granted $10 million to modernize the Azcapotzalco refinery, which would produce aviation fuel for sale to the United States.

38. See N. Stephen Kane, "The United States and the Development of the Mexican Petroleum Industry, 1945–1950: A Lost Opportunity," *Inter-American Economic Affairs* 35 (1) (summer 1981), pp. 45–72; Thomas Wood Clash, *Unitec*

States Efforts to Re-enter the Mexican Petroleum Industry, 1942–1946 (Buffalo: State University of New York, 1973).

39. Blanca Torres, *Hacia la utopia industrial* (Mexico City: El Colegio de México), 1984, p. 198.

40. "Informe del Comité Wolverton," p. 146.

41. Ibid., pp. 143–146.

42. At an exchange rate of 8.65 a dollar, $470 million equaled 5,937.5 million pesos. The accummulated investment of Pemex in current pesos, between 1949 and 1953, was 1,949 million of which only 213 million came from external resources. See Secretaría de la Presidencia, *Inversión Pública Federal 1925–1963* (Mexico City: Dirección de Inversiones Públicas, 1964), pp. 25–28.

43. "Informe del Comité Wolverton,"p. 146.

44. Alemán Valdez, *La verdad del petróleo*, pp. 627–629; Torres, *Hacia la utopia*, p. 196.

45. Torres, *Hacia la utopia*, p. 208; Kane, *The United States.*

46. See the text of the Mexican reply in Alemán Valdez, *La verdad del petróleo*, pp. 666–667.

47. Torres, *Hacia la utopia*, p. 212.

48. Ibid., p. 213.

49. The 1938 decree under which Pemex was formed established that the six government appointees would be made up as follows: two put forward by the Finance and Public Credit Office, three by the National Economy Office, and one by the National Petroleum Board. Later, under the Organic Law of 1971, the election of members to the Board of Directors was to be done directly by the government. See "Decreto que crea la constitución petróleos mexicanos," published in *Marco jurídico*, pp. 13–15.

50. Under the 1938 decree, the Council of Administration would appoint the company's officials, but it could delegate its powers to the director general, which is what did in fact happen.

51. On this question, see George Philip's appraisal in *Oil and Politics*, p. 366.

52. In 1935, the union had 32 sections, cut down to 22 with the trade-union reform of 1946. The division into geographical areas was as follows: the North, with headquarters in Tampico, Tamaulipas; the Center, with headquarters in Poza Rica, Veracruz; the South, with headquarters in Coatzacoalcos, Veracruz. The General Secretariat moved around every three years to one or other area (see Angelina Alonso and Roberto López, *El Sindicato de Trabajadores Petroleros y su relación con Pemex y el estado, 1970–1985* [Mexico City: El Colegio de México, 1986], pp. 32–35, 65).

53. Ibid., pp. 78–79.

54. The demand made by Bermúdez before the Conciliation and Arbitration Board on 21 Dec. 1946 pointed out that the financial problems faced by the company were mainly due to the "excessive" burdens of the collective labor contract (Alemán Valdez, *La verdad del petróleo*, p. 610; also, Alonso and López, *El sindicato*, pp. 68–78).

55. Cf. the text of clause 36 of the collective contract in Alonso and López, *El sindicato*, pp. 80–81.

56. Ibid., p. 77.

57. Ibid., p. 84.

58. Bermúdez, *Doce años*, pp. 200–204, and the director's reports during that period.

59. Alonso and López, *El sindicato*, pp. 55–61 and 83.

60. Ibid., pp. 55–61. See also Ella Fanny Quintal, "La Sección 30 del STPRM," in *Los Sindicatos Nacionales Petroleros* (Mexico City: Ed. G.V., 1986), pp. 289–328.

61. See Philip, *Oil and Politics*, p. 332; Alonso and López, *El sindicato*, p. 90; O. Pellicer de Brody and J. L. Reyna, *Historia de la Revolución Mexicana 1952–1960. El afianzamiento de la estabilidad política* (Mexico City: El Colegio de México, 1978), p. 74.

10. Pemex during the 1960s and the Crisis in Self-Sufficiency

Isidro Morales
El Colegio de México, Mexico City
Translated by Lidia Lozano

The chief priority of Pemex in the 1960s continued to be the supply of the domestic market at subsidized prices. This conformed to an economic policy geared to industrialization and to the nationalist principles that underlay the activities of the company, even if practice did not always coincide with principle, and the latter did not serve to promote more efficient policies. Exports continued to be entirely secondary, and union *cacicazgo* became an established labor practice.

Nevertheless, there were significant qualitative changes compared to the period of consolidation. Between 1960 and 1977, the industrialization of natural gas and the manufacture of petrochemical products were the dynamic sectors, but at the same time reserves dropped and production lagged behind consumption. The years 1966–1973 were a critical period for the industry, since during this time imports of oil products increased, and from 1971 onward Mexico became a net importer of crude oil. The imbalance in the company's terms of trade was not merely circumstantial, but rather the product of uneven structural development. That is, there was a lack of coordination and planning between the different company activities, which prevented key sectors in the industry, such as exploration, transport, and financing, from enjoying continuity and support.

In this chapter, I analyze the political, technical, and financial reasons that brought about the serious crisis, which Pemex faced in the first three years of the 1970s. This crisis ended in 1974, and Pemex entered a new phase of development that opened up unprecedented opportunities.

Oil Autonomy through Monopoly

Despite the expansion of the 1960s, the guiding principles of the company did not differ substantially from those that had prevailed in the preceding decade. On the contrary, the doctrine that identified state control over oil resources with the strengthening of nationalism and the exercise of sovereignty gained in intensity.

In part because of the heritage of the expropriation, this second phase of Pemex's expansion was uneven, entailing sacrifices that made its position difficult in the early seventies. Exploration did not get steady backing in these years; drilling for crude did not always take into account the technical requirements to ensure optimum recovery; the impetus given to petrochemicals diverted resources from priority sectors; and the sales price freeze from 1959 to 1973 restricted the financial prospects of the company. All these imbalances revealed a lack of planning and coordination on the part of the directorate. At the end of the 1960s, Jesús Reyes Heroles—the then company director—conceded that the development of Pemex involved the coexistence of several sectors that operated at different levels, causing bottlenecks, miscalculations, and delays in engineering works.[1] However, he further pointed out, there was no model to demarcate the role of a company like Pemex in a mixed economy; only the "grand guidelines and objectives of the Revolution" were available.[2]

While pragmatism characterized company policy, nationalist principles continued to guide Mexican oil policy. Under Reyes Heroles, the principle that the industry's autonomy was safeguarded by the control of resources gained new momentum. A nationalist emphasis became evident in two areas: first, with the cancellation of risk contracts signed during the first Bermúdez administration and of service contracts that proliferated during the administration of Gutiérrez Roldán; and, second, in the development of the petrochemical industry.

Between 1969 and 1970, five risk contracts signed with American companies were canceled. While the time limit for the drilling and development of wells had expired in 1964, payments for reimbursements and compensations continued through 1974–1975. Some companies (e.g., Pauley) had taken this opportunity to ask for a renewal of their contracts. While legally the renewal of such contracts was banned, under the administration of Gutiérrez Roldán, Pauley had succeeded in renewing the contract that covered the Tabascan continental shelf. Pauley even requested that it be granted more territory for drilling. The director of Pemex, with the support of the National Resources Secretary, considered the presidential changeover a favorable conjuncture to renew the contract. But the renewal did not go through, partly because of the intervention of Antonio Bermúdez, who sent Gustavo Díaz Ordaz, shortly before the latter became president, a memorandum in which he expressed his total opposition.[3]

During the Reyes Heroles administration, the companies demanded repayment of investments made after their contracts expired; that is why the government opted for "voluntary cancellation," paying companies in advance for compensations to which they were still entitled.[4] Reyes Heroles announced the cancellation in terms of a "reclamation" of the lands granted to contractors, so that a "clear fulfillment" of the petroleum legislation might be carried out.[5] The termination of many contracts signed between Pemex and private individuals during the Gutiérrez Roldán administration was also justified in this way. The contracts had been granted to boost exploratory drilling, but contractors had confined themselves to developing wells, thus increasing costs and employing Pemex personnel and equipment at subsidized rates.[6]

While it is true that with the cancellation of private contracts the government was laying down the boundaries for competition between private and public investment, the Directorate of Pemex was also pointing out that the control of the oil industry remained in its hands in order to ensure the economic autonomy of the country. The demarcation of such boundaries in the petrochemical industry provides a further example of this.

The Statutory Law of 1958 had granted Pemex control over those oil by-products "potentially useful as basic industrial raw materials," by which it was understood that the basic petrochemical sector remained in the company's hands. Soon after, it was established that private capital could develop secondary petrochemicals, with the participation of foreign capital being limited to 40 percent. To remove any doubts regarding the definition of basic petrochemicals, the government released a list of sixteen products in 1960.[7] During the administration of Gutiérrez Roldán, however, serious attempts were made to enable foreign companies to manufacture basic petrochemical products,[8] attempts that were opposed by ex-director Bermúdez and, probably, by those sectors identified with company doctrine. Thus, the state monopoly over this sector of the industry was defined more precisely during the administration of Reyes Heroles. In 1967, the number of basic petrochemicals was increased to forty-five, the industry received a decisive boost, and a law was passed to regulate it. Thus, in early 1971 the regulations of Article 27 of the Constitution were extended to petrochemicals. They defined basic petrochemicals, excluded private individuals, and created a Mexican Petrochemical Commission that, together with the National Resources Office, was to decide which products of "fundamental economic or social concern to the country" were to be developed by the state with the participation of Mexican private capital. The remaining chemical products could be manufactured by private individuals, but with the permission, and under the supervision, of the state. Once again, the participation of foreign capital was limited to 40 percent.[9]

With these provisions, the state reasserted the nationalist principles that had underpinned Pemex since the time of the expropriation. One such nationalist principle was the total and direct control over the industry that the company alone exercised. From this perspective, the concession of opportunities for private interests, national or foreign, was considered a sign of weakening of the country's oil autonomy. Hence, Reyes Heroles declared that during his term in Pemex he had "rescued" the basic petrochemical industry,[10] thereby denouncing Gutiérrez Roldán's attempts to open up the sector to private capital interests.

On occasion, however, the guiding principles of Pemex proved too rigid, obstructing necessary changes. Such was the case with marketing policy during the administration of Reyes Heroles. During these years, Mexico stopped exporting crude, exports of gas and oil products lost momentum, and, at the same time, imports of distillates and liquefied gas increased, giving rise between 1970 and 1974 to a deficit in Pemex's trading account. Up to 1971, Pemex opposed imports of crude, despite the fact that refineries had underutilized capacity that could have absorbed imported crude, contributed toward a reduction in the imports of oil products, and reduced the financial pressures on the company balance of trade. While Jesús Reyes Heroles based his refusal to import crude oil on economic arguments, the weighty reason was that he feared a deterioration in company autonomy and in the country's independence.[11] But this policy was changed in the early years of the administration of Antonio Dovalí Jaime, when Pemex opted to import crude oil in order to reduce its trade deficit costs.

Finally, it is worth mentioning that the foundation in 1965 of the Mexican Petroleum Institute (Instituto Mexicano del Petróleo, IMP) also aimed to encourage the development of an "autonomous" and "sovereign" oil industry; the function of the IMP was to train technicians and scientists to further the expansion of the industry. This institution's research into seismology, gravimetry, and magnetometry played an extremely important role in the discoveries of Sonda de Campeche.

Phase 2 of Expansion: Oil Self-Sufficiency

As in the earlier period, hydrocarbon production in the 1960s and early 1970s grew at a constant rate. In this period, the production of natural gas—which became a key resource in the Mexican energy balance—was decisive in the growth of total production. Nevertheless, hydrocarbon production for these years increased by almost 90 percent. Proven reserves, however, rose by barely 25 percent, bringing about a drop in available reserves, which stood at twenty-six production years in 1959, but only seventeen production years in 1973. By then, Pemex estimated that the minimum coefficient between reserves and production had to be twenty years. The imbalance between the growth in production and reserves summed up the magnitude of the crisis that developed in the industry through the sixties. Two crucial reasons account for the imbalance: first, the lack of continuity in the exploration policy launched during the Bermúdez administration; second, an endemic company problem: its financial bottleneck.

Under the administration of Pascual Gutiérrez Roldán (1959–1964), exploratory drilling did not continue with the momentum of past years. Research barely expanded, and exploratory wells increased by only 8 percent compared to the previous administration. The bulk of activity in this field was concentrated in developing productive wells. In fact, during the Gutiérrez Roldán administration, development drilling experienced a rare boom, since it increased by 96 percent compared to the previous term. The boom was generated by private contractors, who carried out over half the drilling.[12] The neglect of exploration delayed the discovery and development of new oil fields. It should be kept in mind that exploration has uncertain results and its development requires long cycles; as many as twelve years may lapse between the beginning of exploration and the discovery of a new oil field.

An attempt was made to change the situation during the administration of Jesús Reyes Heroles. Exploratory drilling gained momentum but development drilling fell behind: the majority of drilling contracts with private individuals were canceled and Pemex regained control over these activities. At the same time, geological research took priority over geophysical research, and together with the support of a new center for interpreting data—attached to the IMP—the pace of discovery of new oil fields quickened.[13] Thus, Sitio Grande and Cactus, areas that later were found to be part of the Samaria and Pueblo Nuevo structures, were discovered in 1969. By 1973, these structures were adequately developed, opening up new prospects for the national production of crude oil. Toward the end of the Reyes Heroles administration, the exploration of the continental shelf of the Gulf of Mexico and of the Mesozoic region of Chiapas was also pushed forward.[14]

Nevertheless, no new petroliferous region was discovered during the 1960s; the revaluation of reserves relied on the development of previously discovered fields, which explains their falling behind growing production. But there were also financial reasons that accounted for the lag in exploration. During this period, "surface" oil fields came to an end and deep drilling started; from then onward, Pemex began drilling beyond 9,800 feet, raising exploration costs. Drilling also became more burdensome with the proliferation of third-party contracts, for this encouraged corruption and the performance of services at the expense of Pemex installations and equipment. The cancellation of risk contracts in turn dealt a blow to investment in exploration, because of reimbursements made to compensate companies.

The inadequate savings capacity of Pemex at this time was also responsible for the lag in exploration. While the company did finance these activities throughout the period, in the view of ex-director Bermúdez it might have done so in greater measure had the aim been to avoid a deterioration in reserves. According to Bermúdez, the discoveries made in the early 1970s (Samaria and Sitio Grande) might have been made earlier had the company taken steps to increase reserves in proportion to production.[15] But this would have required establishing such a priority (which Gutiérrez Roldán declined to do), and achieving a steady increase in investment in exploration. But the latter was virtually impossible, given the progressive decline in surplus company earnings, due, above all, to the freeze in sales prices effective until 1973.

Consequently, throughout the period studied, the extraction of crude relied on previously known oil fields. The bulk of production came from the Poza Rica region and the districts of El Ebano–Pánuco and Cerro Azul in the North. In some instances, extraction was carried out in aging fields, whose low rates of production prevented any increased exploitation. Only at the end of the 1960s did the southern oil fields begin to increase their share in total supply: in 1965, they provided 37 percent; in 1973, 50.8 percent of total flow. The rise was brought about by the new discoveries made in the region during those years. Beside the low productivity of fields, Pemex also engaged in overexploitation, especially during Pascual Gutiérrez Roldán's management. The drilling boom of those years did not increase production significantly because it centered on productive oil fields, and involved an excessive subdivision of the strata, which affected the pressure of wells and appreciably reduced the return on resources.[16] This overexploitation was curbed under Reyes Heroles, when drilling areas were enlarged and contracting to private companies was restrained. Reyes Heroles also encouraged the development of offshore oil fields in Tampico and the Faja de Oro (the Golden Lane), even though production costs were high. At the same time, efforts were made to maximize the recovery of crude through the injection of gas or water into the wells. A further reason for the lag in production was deficiency in the infrastructure for collection and storage; until 1968 there were no adequate plans for pipelines surrounding productive fields, which led to failures in the maintenance of installations, including leaks and accidents.[17]

Growth in Consumption and Imports

Between 1960 and 1972, the average rate of annual growth of hydrocarbon production was 4.1 percent, and that of consumption was 9.9 percent.[18] These figures neatly sum up the balance between hydrocarbon supply and demand in this period. Unable to close the gap in the early 1970s, Pemex had to resort to increased imports of crude. In economic and symbolic terms, the situation had serious consequences for the industry, since Pemex had a trade deficit that put further pressure on its delicate financial situation, and it was unable to meet one of the basic objectives set since its creation: self-sufficiency in hydrocarbons.

Several factors accounted for the increase in consumption; one of them was, undoubtedly, the capacity of Pemex to extract and market natural gas. The 1960s mark the takeoff of the gas industry in Mexico: whereas in 1959 consumption of gas had been a bare 91.2 billion cubic feet, by 1970 it was 394.5 billion cubic feet.[19] Gas is important in the energy supply of Mexico because it can replace fuels with lower calorific content (such as fuel oils), whose use creates more pollution. In 1960, gas accounted for 17.4 percent of the demand for energy products (gas, distillates, and fuels); in 1970, its share had risen to 30.4 percent.[20]

While a domestic market for natural gas was created, a surplus supply—which increased in the latter part of the decade—was generated. Part of the surplus was exported to the United States, part was reinjected, but a fair amount had to be burned, not because of saturation of the domestic or export markets, but rather because of the lack of adequate collection and treatment facilities (in 1970, 6.6 percent of gross production was exported, 26 percent was burned). Nevertheless, in the early 1970s gas production stagnated due to the drop in reserves in Reynosa and Ciudad Pemex; exports to the United States fell and by 1974 had stopped altogether.

Rapid industrialization during those years also accounted for the notable increase in gas consumption. For some twenty years after 1957, Mexico experienced what economists have called a phase of *desarrollo estabilizador* (stabilizing development), based on a model of economic policy embodying the following premises: the freezing of exchange rates (the peso stayed at 12.5¢ till 1976); a curb on inflation (between 1957 and 1967 prices rose at an annual rate of 3.9 percent, whereas in earlier years they had grown at 10 percent); and the securing of foreign income through debt to finance imports needed for industrialization. The outcome is well known: the Mexican economy grew at an average annual rate of 6.2 percent, with the manufacturing sector—which grew by 8 percent—as its pivot; the process of import substitution of intermediate and durable goods, and the enlargement of a domestic market constituted by the growth of the middle sectors, were consolidated.[21] Some economists have labeled this period of sustained growth with low inflation rates the "Mexican miracle."[22] While extraeconomic factors also intervened in this "miracle"—such as the control over workers and *campesinos* exercised by the official party—it cannot be denied that the uninterrupted flow of goods manufactured by Pemex formed the basis for these changes in the Mexican economy. By 1958, Pemex had set up a completely integrated industry designed to pump out the energy resources necessitated by industry. In the 1960s, this supply of basic resources expanded in both quantitative and qualitative terms, involving both gas and petrochemicals.

The structure of demand for oil products responded to this process. During these years, the concentration of consumption in light distillates grew at the expense of heavy fuels, a trend that had already emerged by the end of the 1950s. As a result, fuel oil lost its dominant place vis-à-vis gasoline, gas oil, and diesel. The rise in income of the Mexican middle and upper sectors and the price freeze on energy products (cf. table 1), which constituted a further subsidy to consumption, combined to boost energy consumption. While all this continued to be justified in terms of the role assigned to Pemex in the social and industrial development of the country, waste was encouraged, the gap between demand and production widened, and company income was further reduced.

During this period, no new refineries came into operation, although under the management of Pascual Gutiérrez Roldán steps were taken to build another refining center in Mazatlán in order to solve problems of supply to the Pacific coast. Initial purchases for the project were made, but construction was interrupted in the early days of Jesús Reyes Heroles's administration. The interruption was justified in financial terms, on the grounds that it was preferable to expand existing refining centers, but the reasons were political, since officials of the previous administration were among the contractors building the new refinery.[23]

In the early 1970s, a new refining center was built at Tula, but it did not start operations until after the industry had begun its process of outward expansion. Until 1973, Mexico still relied on refineries modernized or built in the 1940s and 1950s, which supplied their different areas of "influence" unevenly. At the beginning of the seventies, there were six supply poles in the country. Each of them, with the exception of the Pacific coast, had one or more refineries. The eastern and southeastern regions were self-sufficient; the first was served by the Madero refinery, the second by the Minatitlán refinery. The northeastern region had the Reynosa refinery, but it also absorbed surplus from Madero and Salamanca. In the border areas of this region, far removed from marketing agencies,

Table 1. Variation in the Real Price of Various Mexican Oil Products
(pesos per liter)[a]

	1960	1963	1966	1968
		Gasoline		
Sale price	0.88	0.86	0.76	0.73
Index (%)	100.00	97.70	86.30	82.90
		Kerosene		
Sale price	0.35	0.34	0.31	0.29
Index (%)	100.00	97.10	88.50	82.80
		Diesel		
Sale price	0.35	0.34	0.31	0.29
Index (%)	100.00	97.10	88.50	82.80
		Fuel Oil		
Sale price	0.129	0.125	0.112	0.106
Index (%)	100.00	96.900	86.800	82.100
		Liquefied Gas		
Index (%)	100.00	97.0	86.4	82.5
		Natural Gas		
Sale price	0.12	0.13	0.114	0.11
Index (%)	100.00	108.30	95.000	91.60

[a] 12.5 pesos = $1; 1 liter = .264 gallons.
Source: ECLA, *La industria del petróleo en América Latina* (Mexico City: United Nations, 17–25 April 1986), p. 63.

demand was met with imports. The Poza Rica and Azcapotzalco supplies were not enough for the Center region, which needed transfers from Minatitlán. Salamanca, in turn, supplied refined products to the Center-North region. The Pacific coast was starved of Pemex products, since the cancellation of the Mazatlán refinery had left it without a supply center. The storage plant in Salina Cruz (Oaxaca), fed by pipelines from Minatitlán, was largely responsible for supplying this region. Deficits were met with imports from Curaçao, Aruba, and, occasionally, the United States.[24]

Refining capacity expanded constantly, but processing increased unevenly. Between 1971 and 1973, as new processing plants were given priority, stripping capacity increased by 19 percent (more than it had between 1959 and 1965). In 1973, for example, a combined unit of atmospheric and vacuum stripping with a capacity of 110,000 b/d, which made it one of the biggest in the world, came into operation in Salamanca, and doubled the refinery's installed capacity. In contrast, the capacity for cracking and viscosity reduction increased rapidly up to 1967 but thereafter stagnated. Rapid growth occurred at first because Pemex had given a high priority to the conversion of heavy fuel in order to increase the supply of distillates. Shortfalls were met with imports which, as mentioned above, grew by the end of this period. As new oil fields of light crude were discovered from 1972 onward, cracking took a second place.

At the end of 1973, most refining centers, with the exception of Reynosa and Poza Rica, had a refining system of comparable complexity: plants for atmospheric and vacuum stripping, catalytic cracking for heavy gas oils, hydrodesulfurizers for naphtha and intermediate distillates, converters of primary naphtha into high-octane gasolines, and so on. However, between 1966 and 1973, Pemex encountered difficulties supplying the domestic market. The problem was not merely circumstantial, but rather the product of the imbalance experienced by the industry in the 1960s as a result of its policy of exploration, production, refining, and financing, and of the pattern of domestic demand.

The crisis in self-sufficiency was reflected in the company's balance of trade. From 1966 until 1973, Pemex stopped exporting crude for the first time in its history. Other exports, basically fuel oil, natural gas, and surplus petrochemical products, fell gradually, whereas the volume of imports increased. After 1970, the company's balance of trade was unfavorable, and the deficit, which in 1973 was over $3 billion and accounted for 21.4 percent of the country's balance of payments current account deficit, continue to worsen.[25] The deficit reflected not only the inequality in the terms of exchange but, above all, the substantial increase in Pemex's imports.

Pemex's trade deficit, in both physical and monetary terms, summed up the critical point reached by the Mexican petroleum industry. A significant cause was the lag in the extraction and production of crude oil, so that refining capacity was not fully utilized (in 1970 and 1973, 81.9 percent and 73.8 percent, respectively, of nominal refining capacity was utilized).[26] But refineries did not just lack crude for processing; deficiencies in the systems of distribution and collection also contributed to an increase in imports. Such was the case of imports of fuel oil and liquefied gas, and, to a lesser extent, of natural gas. Gasoline and diesel purchases, too, rose even though from late 1971 Pemex would have preferred to import crude rather than refined products. This revealed the inadequacy of refineries to manufacture these distillates in sufficient quantity.[27] The effect of demand was also decisive in these imbalances, because the price freeze until 1973 subsidized consumption and encouraged waste.

Financial Deficit

With the rise in prices of Pemex products at the end of 1958 and through 1959, earnings from company sales increased by just over 25 percent as compared to 1958. At the same time, negotiations with the Treasury transformed tax obligations that burdened Pemex into a debt to be repaid over ninety-nine years. Payments would be made through the issue of negotiable bonds with an annual interest of 8 percent, to be known as "stock-bonds B." That is, the tax obligations of the company were not canceled, but instead were transformed into a debt whose balance would be paid off on a long-term basis. This, at any rate, meant that Pemex did not have to make very significant transfers.

At the same time, the administration of Pascual Gutiérrez Roldán undertook some new initiatives: it promised to remove all unnecessary financial burdens and to put an end to unwarranted expenses, and it committed itself to raising the productivity of capital and labor.[28] The negotiation of the company's new tax obligations was an example of the first intention. Until 1958, Pemex had paid some 21 percent of its gross earnings in taxes; after 1960, it paid only 12 percent.

Pemex also looked to a more balanced financial structure. The company's six-year plan for 1959–1964 stipulated the need to maintain a bottom price to cover three areas regarded as fundamental: operation costs, financial obligations and investment for expansion, and the creation of a fund for contingencies.[29] This indicated that new prices might not remain steady and that at least they would correspond to the level of inflation. This was not such a far-fetched possibility given that, as could be deduced from the plan, Pemex had at least a group of technicians and officials committed to the rescue of the company's financial balance. Its former director, Antonio Bermúdez, was the main spokesperson for this group. A few years later, he suggested that the price at which Pemex sold its products had to take into account the following requirements: replacing the value of raw materials, covering operational costs, and "providing a foundation" to support further investments.[30]

It is apparent that neither Bermúdez nor the 1959 six-year plan envisaged complete financial self-sufficiency for Pemex. But implicitly they were suggesting that the securing of financial resources outside the company should be kept to a minimum. This would mean not only a reduction in its level of indebtedness but also the elimination of transfers and costs that substantially depleted its own earnings. For Bermúdez, the priority at that time was to ensure company growth, in order to enable it later to transfer resources to other less efficient productive activities.

Plans and statements notwithstanding, the financial structure of Pemex deteriorated from the time of Pascual Gutiérrez Roldán. Prices remained frozen until 1973. While it is true that the period under study here was characterized by a much lower inflation rate than in the 1940s and 1950s, by the end of Gutiérrez Roldán's administration Pemex prices had already fallen relatively by some 80 percent.[31] Nor was efficiency in productivity achieved, for while the cost of extraction of one barrel of crude oil had been $1.03 in 1958, in 1964, in real terms, it was $1.48. The proliferation of *contratismo* and the overexploitation of oil fields undoubtedly contributed to the rise in extraction costs. However, costs also rose in the refining industry, from 61¢ per barrel to 88¢ over the same period.[32]

The freeze in sales prices and the failure to develop a more efficient productive structure narrowed the options available to secure additional resources. Throughout those years, exports of crude and other oil products were no longer an important factor in company earnings; on the contrary, they lost momentum and were overtaken by the imports that the company was forced to make. Besides, during the 1960s—in contrast—prices for crude in the international market experienced a downward trend. OPEC was created in 1960 precisely to stop, albeit unsuccessfully, this fall.[33] Therefore, the chances that Mexico would reenter the export market with a measure of success were virtually nonexistent, both because of the lack of a significant surplus for export and because of adverse conditions in the world oil market. If it sought to finance the bulk of new investment with its own resources, the only alternative open to Pemex was to increase domestic prices and to reduce costs; otherwise, as long as it did not curb its expansion, it would have to resort to indebtedness. As is known, it pursued the latter option.

It is not clear why prices were kept frozen for so long. The official line was justified in terms of industrial and social development policies that had been entrusted to the company since its inception. While Pemex may have been compelled by these goals to maintain low prices for its products, it did not have to freeze them. It is likely that government authorities thought that to maintain the price of oil products in real terms would have inflationary effects, and would threaten one of the objectives of the economic policy then championed: the stability of consumer prices. There is no evidence, however, to suggest that projections and discussions were carried out to analyze the consequences that a rise in Pemex prices might have had on the country's economy. It is probable that a further reason for the price freeze was of a political nature. A rise would have had repercussions on the government's relations with industrial groups and with working-class sectors. It cannot be denied, however, that company inertia helped to encourage such a policy of subsidies. Just as imports of crude oil, notwithstanding their economic justification, had been taboo during certain periods, so the freeze of Pemex prices became a shibboleth of the benefits of a nationalized company. It would take time to change tendencies and images of this nature.

Pemex's earnings were depleted not only by the price freeze but also by the growth in expenditure, transfers and investments necessitated by expansion. For example, while payments to labor did not account for a larger share of company expenditure, they did grow in absolute terms, which at times made possible a rise in workers' real wages;[34] in addition, the disbursements of benefits that formed part of the modus vivendi between the company and the union were even higher than wages throughout that time.

At times, operational costs rose faster than earnings; during the years that concern us in this study, these costs absorbed the largest share of Pemex's resources. In 1965, they accounted for 69.1 percent of total company outgoings; in 1972, 52.3 percent; and in 1973, 59.3 percent [35] While Pemex's tax burden stood, on average, at 12 percent of its gross earnings, transfers to public funds exceeded this percentage, because of contributions to states, social works, and the redemption of stock bonds. Nevertheless, between 1971 and 1973—critical years for the finances of the company—the federal government transferred funds to Pemex by way of subsidy refunds. This extraordinary income came to represent in 1972 and 1973, respectively, 6 percent and 4.74 percent of total earnings. Although Pemex continued to contribute significantly to public finance, during this period its share in the government's total tax revenues dropped. In 1958, it contributed 6.1 percent of state tax revenues; in 1973, it accounted for 3.3 percent.[36] Throughout those years, Pemex paid most of the taxes derived from oil activities (only a small percentage was paid by private individuals), but the tax burden on the extraction of crude was reduced and the sales tax on gasolines and light products was raised.

Company investment underwent a great boost in the latter half of the 1960s; in 1965, it absorbed 16.2 percent of total income (including financing), and in 1967 and 1968 it absorbed 41.6 percent and 38.0 percent, respectively. However, between 1970 and 1973, investment lost momentum: in the former year, it had taken 21.4 percent of total income, in the latter, 17 percent (see table 2). This trend was also evident in the oil industry's share of total public investment. Whereas in 1968 its share was 21.9 percent, in 1973 it had dropped to 15.5 percent.[37] Paradoxically, investment lost momentum as the company increased its income from both domestic and foreign sources. That the higher income from external resources did not bring about higher investment was due to the fact that part of this credit was needed to cover operational costs and the repayment of a growing debt.

Facing a decrease in its resources and plagued by an inability to reduce inefficiency, Pemex resorted to credit: in 1965, credit accounted for 11.2 percent of total company income; by 1967, it had already risen to 21.2 percent; in 1970, it was 36.3 percent; and, by 1973, it was 34.3 percent.[38] Company indebtedness was consistent with the economic policy pursued by the governments of the period, since one of the key tenets of a *desarrollo estabilizador* was that the lack of domestic savings should be covered by foreign savings. Between 1959 and 1964, despite endeavors to the contrary, Pemex continued to depend on short-term loans, which accounted for 92.3 percent of net indebtedness for that period.[39] However, from the later 1960s, Pemex succeeded in negotiating long-term credits (new loans averaged six to ten years), and foreign financing gained in significance among company debts. In 1970, the external debt of Pemex stood at $439 million; in 1973, it was $727 million. Nevertheless, the company's external debt as a proportion of total public sector debt remained constant, holding at approximately 10 percent throughout these years.[40] In 1973, the most critical year in the second phase of expansion of Pemex, company indebtedness stopped being an instrument for investment and became a threat to its very financial structure. In that year, Pemex diverted 20.2 percent of total outgoings to debt payments; it also financed 17 percent of operational costs, 46.8 percent of debt settlement, and 68.4 percent of investment with borrowed resources (see table 3).

Consolidation of Union Power

Despite the vertical nature of its management, the disorganization and size of Pemex contributed to increased inefficiency in some of its operations. At times, warehouses were overstocked with perishable

Table 2. The Balance of Trade of Pemex, 1959–1973

| | *Volume (thousands of barrels)* | | | | *Value*[b] | |
	Exports[a]	Imports[a]	Balance	Exports	Imports	Balance
1959	13,270	6,016	7,254	365.9	117.5	248.4
1961	15,159	3,713	11,446	434.6	240.8	193.0
1963	18,718	2,287	16,431	495.7	115.5	380.2
1965	19,845	1,255	18,590	528.1	95.5	432.6
1967	17,984	3,624	14,360	595.4	250.2	345.2
1969	16,263	8,652	7,611	537.1	515.2	21.9
1971	17,079	17,760	-681	433.7	1,041.6	-608.3
1973	8,699	47,769	-39,070	442.8	3,594.7	-3,151.2

[a] Includes crude and oil products.
[b] Includes exports of natural gas and exports and imports of petrochemicals.
Source: Up to 1969, Michele Snoek, *El comercio exterior de hidrocarburos y derivados en México, 1970–1985* (Mexico City: El Colegio de México, 1987), p. 176; for 1971 and 1973, unpublished thesis for MA in economics, El Colegio de México, p. 131.

products, while other sectors suffered from a shortage of spare parts.[41] During the Reyes Heroles administration, attempts were made to solve some of these problems through administrative reforms. However, these reforms did not involve a substantial change in the vertical structure of the administrative pyramid.

In 1971, the Mexican Petroleum Organic Law was passed, which expanded the Council of Administration to eleven members: six representing the Directorate, five the union. The government would appoint both the six members and the director general. The union representatives could not check presidential control of company management because by then the sphere of action between company and union had been well defined. Since 1947, the leaders of the oil workers had given up trying to control decision-making posts within the company. In exchange, the government had granted them the "management" of the rank and file and substantial opportunities for power within what some authors have labeled "the Mexican oil system."[42] Indeed, during these years, the most significant fact from a labor perspective was the consolidation of the oil union as a power parallel to the company. The foundations of this power were laid during the Bermúdez administration and were consolidated in subsequent years.

One of the bases of union power was its capacity to recruit company personnel. To do so, the union grouped together the majority of workers

Table 3. Allocation and Origin of Pemex Resources in 1973

	millions of pesos[a]	%
Operational Costs		
Own resources	13,093.3	74.5
Financing	3,001.0	17.0
Extraordinary resources	1,460.6	8.3
Total	17,555.0	100.0
Debt Settlement		
Own resources	3,180.4	53.1
Financing	2,880.0	46.8
Total	5,980.4	100.0
Investment		
Own resources	1,658.9	31.5
Financing	3,596.8	68.4
Total	5,255.7	100.0
Work by Third Parties		
Own resources	795.0	100.0
Final Stock		
Financing	1,185.4	100.0
Payments to Treasury of the Federation		
Final stock	1,280.3	100.0

[a] 12.5 pesos = $1.
Source: Pemex, *Memoria de labores de 1973* (Mexico City, 1974), p. 145.

in the oil industry, both temporary and permanent. Company and union agreed that no more than 10 percent of permanent workers and no more than 5 percent of temporary ones would be *empleados de confianza* ("trusted workers," i.e., management appointees). This severely limited the Directorate's powers of recruitment, and forced it to focus on creating a technical and bureaucratic elite responsible for carrying out the industry's "vital" decisions. The rest of the labor force was in the hands of the union leadership. In fact, company workers did not have a choice. Working for the company meant automatic enrollment in the union, and union fees were deducted from pay packets. There were repeated attempts to form independent associations, but they never enjoyed the support of either management or incumbent presidents. In 1970, an attempt was made to create a union of technicians, professionals, and others who, besides not wanting to be attached to the STPRM, were trying to regulate promotion procedures within Pemex, since changes in salary often responded to relations of *compadrazgo*, rather than professional qualifications. However, the Labor Office banned the formation of the new union and forced workers to join the official union. Furthermore, during the early years of Luis Echeverría's government, 3,600 professionals who were *empleados de confianza* were subject to union rules,[43] further indicating the concern of government authorities not to weaken the hegemony of the STPRM.

The alliance between the top union leadership and top management throughout this time was fruitful, because potential or real labor conflicts, likely to make trouble for Pemex and the government, were adroitly "managed" by the union bureaucracy. The policies of hiring and of compulsory membership were key elements guaranteeing the management of the labor force. Hiring was characterized by a system of "self-recruitment," which depended on permanent workers' jobs being distributed to family members or according to the recommendation of union members. In 1961, the union also received the right to provide the labor force for "works" carried out by third parties. These "works" laborers, also known as *pelones*, were not union members but they depended on the union for jobs in works involving Pemex. Thus, the union controlled a large number of unskilled laborers, engaged in a diversity of tasks, who in turn had to pay the union for each contract to which they were assigned.[44] The union control of the labor force ranged over different levels of specialization and competence from works laborers to engineers and professionals. As a result of the recruitment system of the STPRM, the hiring of new personnel did not always meet company requirements and needs (in 1965, Jesús Reyes Heroles admitted that there was overmanning).[45] Indeed, the rate of hiring was higher in the 1960s than in the previous decade,[46] and for that reason production of crude oil per worker dropped in the early 1970s, in contrast to the rise in per capita production.[47]

It is important to point out that the ratio of temporary workers to total hired personnel increased; in 1961, they accounted for 32.5 percent of the labor force, and in 1973, 40.4 percent (see table 4). The hiring of temporary workers was functional both to the union and to the company, which in this way had at its disposal a malleable labor force that could be increased or reduced depending on company needs. Temporary workers also made payments to the union, but they did not have a right

Table 4. Composition of Pemex Personnel (1959–1973)

	Permanent (1)	Temporary (2)	% (2)/Total	Total	59=100 Index
1959	29,324	16,371	35.8	45,695	100.0
1961	31,134	15,024	32.5	46,158	101.0
1963	32,858	16,747	33.7	49,605	108.5
1965	34,315	19,658	36.4	53,973	118.1
1967	38,448	24,224	38.6	62,672	137.1
1969	41,789	26,610	38.9	68,399	149.6
1971	44,153	31,345	41.5	75,498	165.2
1973	45,633	31,023	40.4	76,656	167.7

Source: Pemex, *Anuario estadístico 1985*, p. 139.

to all benefits enjoyed by permanent workers. The possibility of offering them a permanent job was a very effective manipulative tool in the hands of union leaders. A necessary requisite for such an offer was "union militancy," which not only served to reinforce clientelist practices but also produced significant economic gains for the union; on occasion "militancy" had to be proved by working without pay on a union farm or in a union shop.[48]

As a result of the manipulation to which many temporary workers were subjected, significant movements were organized in 1962 and 1967, with a view to either standardization or independent organization. The union's response in 1967 was to start a register of "supernumerary members"—a position to which temporary workers with six years of work could aspire—who qualified as candidates for permanent jobs and could be considered "active members."[49] The union's response was effective, because it curtailed discontent among temporary workers and further perfected the clientelist practices of its recruitment policy. The union's capacity to control was also enhanced by its link with the official party, a link that grew stronger through the period. At the end of the sixties, three union members were selected to liaise between the PRI and locals of the oil workers. Their integration into the CTM enabled leaders to continue their political careers within the ranks of official organizations.

Unquestionably, a crucial element in union power was its ability to control internal conflict and rivalries through the rotation of leaders in key posts and the maintenance of a balance among the three regions that made up the oil map: the North (centered on Ciudad Madero, an industrial suburb of Tampico), the Center (Poza Rica), and the South

(Minatitlán). Nevertheless, it was impossible to prevent the formation of regional powers within each zone. The most important bastion of oil power since the nationalization was Minatitlán, a traditional oil region that had gained more momentum with the development of petrochemicals, an industry where leaders became extremely powerful through a network of "influence."[50]

In the 1960s, however, the northern region, under the leadership of Joaquín Hernández Galicia (La Quina), who had led Local 1 in Ciudad Madero and was general secretary between 1961 and 1964, began to displace Minatitlán as the center of union power. Hernández Galicia's tactics were to maintain an aggressive union stance vis-à-vis the government, without actually confronting it; instead, he devoted himself to negotiating and "managing" benefits for union members. Indeed, throughout this period benefits rose faster than wages, a trend that had emerged at the time of Bermúdez. At the end of the 1960s, wage disbursements accounted for only 40 percent of company labor costs, the rest being benefits.[51]

Hernández Galicia's success lay in vying with Pemex for "social development" works. Thus, union locals began to participate in the social and political life of oil towns, which necessitated an increase in their funds. During his time as general secretary, contractors working with Pemex gave 2 percent of their investment to the union's social fund. Hernández Galicia ensured that all locals benefited from these transfers, and he pressed, albeit unsuccessfully, for an increase in his members' share of company profits.[52] In this way, the union leader projected a generous and paternalistic image to the rank and file.

When he left the leadership of the union, Hernández Galicia became director of the STPRM's Program for Revolutionary and Social Works, a post from which he controlled union finances. Farms, consumer shops, and recreation centers were set up. The financing of the program was secured not only through transfers managed by La Quina, but also through the "contributions" of *pelones* and temporary workers as payment for the assignment or renewal of contracts.[53] Through the administration of "social development," Hernández Galicia became the most powerful union leader of his time, and he turned the STPRM into one of the most powerful unions affiliated with the CTM. The strength of Hernández Galicia and of the northern region was consolidated in the early 1970s when Barragán Camacho became general secretary. The latter was Hernández Galicia's right-hand man; they joined forces to eliminate or co-opt opposition groups.[54]

In 1973, the system of secret and individual ballot was ended and a mechanism for collective balloting was set up. Until then, union representatives had been chosen on an individual basis, but thereafter they were to be chosen by a system of tickets, which reduced the opportunities for the representation of dissident groups. At that time, the power of the union equaled that of Pemex: hence, the alliance between the top union leadership and the directorate became crucial as Pemex had to confront the changes that the oil industry underwent after 1974.

Conclusion

The neglect of exploration activities and the proliferation of *contratismo* during the administration of Pascual Gutiérrez Roldán had serious repercussions for the development in the late 1960s and early 1970s of Pemex's reserves and its extractive activities. The high level of consumption throughout this period, encouraged by an indiscriminate policy of subsidies and price freezes, deepened the crisis of self-sufficiency. If one takes into account transfers to the Treasury and the growth of its labor force—a highly militant labor force in terms of its claims for privileges and benefits—it is easy to understand why external indebtedness became the solution to the further financing of Pemex.

Halfway through Echeverría's presidency, the industry faced a challenge: it had to revitalize its own resources in order to encourage the exploration and extraction of crude and thus overcome the crisis of self-sufficiency. One way to get ahead, as Bermúdez had observed, was to rationalize company expenditure and investment and to ensure that sales prices covered costs. However, an international event altered the terms in which the problem had been posed. In October 1973, international crude prices rose dramatically and OPEC emerged as the one organization capable of capitalizing on the new conditions prevailing in the world market. Given that the potential of reserves in the Mexican Southeast was known by then, exports of crude became a new option to increase the financial resources of Pemex. The debate in 1974 and 1975 concerned the volume of exports needed to increase company finances and thus to boost investment. Exports were conceived of as a financial resource of the company, not of the government. But as the country entered a financial crisis, which peaked in 1976 with the devaluation of the peso (thereby putting an end to the *desarrollo estabilizador*), the Mexican government found in Pemex and in exports the easiest solution to the country's liquidity crisis.

Notes

1. Pemex, *Política petrolera. Informes del director general (1968–1969–1970)* (Mexico City: Pemex, 1970), p. 74.

2. Ibid., pp. 43–44.

3. See "Memorandum urgente de Antonio J. Bermúdez para el Sr. Lic. Gustavo Díaz Ordaz, Presidente electo de México," in Angel Hermida Ruiz, *Bermúdez y la batalla por el petróleo* (Mexico City: Costa-Amic, 1970), pp. 195–198.

4. The contract with CIMA was canceled on 5 June 1969 after a payment of $18 million. The one with Sharmex was canceled on 25 Nov.; they were paid $950,000. On 8 Dec. the Isthmus Development Company was compensated for similar reasons, with $359,000, and on 27 Feb. 1970 Edwin Pauley was paid $4.4 million (making a total of $23.745 million). All compensation was below the value asked for by the companies; see Miguel Alemán Valdez, *La verdad del petróleo en México*. 3d ed. (Mexico City: Ed. Grijalbo, 1977), p. 695.

5. Pemex, *Política petrolera (1968–1970)*, p. 55.

6. Bermúdez opposed the proliferation of these contracts; his reasons can be found in "Memorandum de Antonio J. Bermúdez para el señor ingeniero Pascual Gutiérrez Roldán en relación con las perforaciones de pozos por administración y por contrato," in Hermida Ruiz, *Bermúdez y la batalla.*, pp. 190–193; see also A. J. Bermúdez, *La política petrolera mexicana* (Mexico City: Ed. Comaval, 1960; Ed. Joaquín Mortiz, 1976), pp. 69–70.

7. Among them were sulphur, ammonia, dodecylbenzene, and carbonic anhydrid (Michele Snoeck, *La industria petroquímica básica en México, 1970–1982* [México City: Colegio de México, 1986], p. 21).

8. Indeed, they tried to develop these products in association with Dow Chemical and to build a polythene plant with another private company. Bermúdez opposed these projects; see the memoradum he sent to Pascual Gutiérrez Roldán in Hermida Ruíz's study cited above, pp. 187–189, and also Bermúdez, *La política petrolera*, p. 71.

9. See the text of the law in Pemex, *Marco jurídico básico* (Mexico City: Pemex, 1983), pp. 40–49.

10. See Pemex, *Política petrolera (1968–1970)*, p.55.

11. Jesús Reyes Heroles thought it inadvisable to substitute imports of oil products for crude on the grounds that the cheapest crude oil available was 20 percent more expensive than the one produced at home. According to the director, it would also entail the "loss of jobs" by many Mexicans and the future dependence of the country on foreign supplies. Nevertheless, in 1972, when it was decided to favor imports of crude rather than oil products, Pemex estimated savings of 35 million pesos ($2.6 million). See Pemex, *Política petrolera (1968–1970)*, p. 7, and Michele Snoeck, *El comercio exterior de hidrocarburos y derivados en México, 1970–1985* (Mexico City: Colegio de México, 1987), pp. 36–37.

12. See Pemex, *Anuario estadístico, 1985*, pp. 32–33.

13. The development of reserves is secured not only by having access to advanced techniques of exploration, but also by the correct interpretation and integration of data gathered. In Mexico, the analogical processing of data began effectively with the creation of IMP. The first center for digital processing of geophysical data was set up there in 1970. It was an extremely important step, since until then all information gathered by Pemex was processed in the United States. See Rogelio Ruíz, "Estrategias y políticas para el fortalecimiento de la

capacidad tecnológica interna," pp. 9–10 (mimeo).

14. See Ana M. Sordo and Roberto López, *Exploración, reservas y producción de petróleo en México, 1970–1985* (Mexico City: Colegio de México, 1988).

15. Bermúdez, *La política*, p. 72.

16. See the section on production in Sordo and López, *Exploración, reservas,* cited above.

17. Ibid.

18. Eduardo Turrent Díaz, "La industria petrolera mexicana, 1965–1973," thesis, Colegio de México, p. 60.

19. For the same period, gas consumption in the petroleum industry rose from 5,364.6 to 21,922.1 million barrels. However, in 1970 Pemex produced 30,870.3 million barrels and exported only 7,925.1 million barrels. See ECLA, *La industria del petróleo en América Latina: notas sobre una evaluación reciente* (New York: United Nations, 1972), p. 129.

20. Ibid., p. 118.

21. Leopoldo Solís, *La realidad económica mexicana: retrovisión y perspectivas* (Mexico City: Siglo XXI, 1976), pp. 108–122.

22. See Roger Hansen, *La política del desarrollo mexicano.* 9th ed. (Mexico City: Siglo XXI, 1979), pp. 57–96, 225–270.

23. Pemex, *Política petrolera. Informes del director general, 1965–1966–1967* (Mexico City: Pemex, n.d.), p. 6; see also Michele Snoeck, *La industria de refinación en México, 1970–1985* (Mexico City: Colegio de México, 1989).

24. Snoeck, ibid.

25. Snoeck, *El comercio exterior*, p. 39.

26. Snoeck, *La industria de refinación.*

27. Detailed analysis of the imbalance in Pemex's terms of trade in Snoeck, *El comercio exterior*, pp. 36–42, and E. Turrent Díaz, *La industria petrolera*, pp. 126–138.

28. Pemex, *Informe del director general*, 1971, pp. 13–14.

29. See G. José Rentería, "Análisis financiero de la industria petrolera nacionalizada," Mexico City, Pemex, 1964, pp. 1–2.

30. Bermúdez, *La política petrolera.*, p. 85.

31. Oscar Guzmán, "El saneamiento financiero del desarrollo estabilizador, 1959–1964," Colegio de México, n.d., pp. 3–5 (mimeo).

32. Ibid., p. 9.

33. The price of crude oil in the international market went up in the latter half of the 1950s as a result of the Suez crisis, but by 1960 it had already fallen. Saudi Arabia crude, which in 1958 had been quoted at $2.08 per barrel, was down to $1.86 in 1960. Between 1961 and 1970, the price remained frozen at $1.80 per barrel. Crude exported by the major producing countries experienced a similar trend. In 1960, three Arab countries (Iraq, Kuwait, and Saudi Arabia) and two non-Arab countries (Iran and Venezuela) formed OPEC in order to stop the fall in prices. See the synthesis of the prevailing structures in the international oil market during those years in ECLA, *La industria del petróleo en América Latina: notas sobre su evolución reciente y perspectiva* (Mexico City: United Nations, 17–25 April 1986), pp. 42–66.

34. Between 1958 and 1964, Pemex's average daily payment per worker in real terms increased by 34 percent. See Guzmán, "El saneamiento," p. 10.

35. Pemex, *Memoria del labores*, 1965, 1972, 1973.

36. Secretaría de Programación y Presupuesto, *La industria petrolera en México*, 1980, p. 51.

37. Ibid., p. 49.

38. See Pemex, *Memoria de labores*, 1965, 1972, 1973.

39. Guzmán, "El saneamiento," p. 17.

40. Francisco Colmenares, "Problemas de rentabilidad y productividad en la industria petrolera mexicana (1970–1984)," Mexico City: 1985, p. 147 (mimeo).

41. Pemex, *Política petrolera*, pp. 63–67.

42. Marie France Prévot-Schapira considers the "oil system" as the economic, social, and geographic space in Mexico within which oil activity has taken place. See her article "Trabajadores del petróleo y poder sindical en México," in *Energía en México. Ensayos sobre el pasado y el presente* (Mexico City: Colegio de México, 1982), pp. 143–169. Also "Les travailleurs du pétrole au Mexique," in *Cahier de Sciences Humaines* 23(2), 1987, pp. 277–286.

43. Angelina Alonso and Carlos Roberto López, *El sindicato de trabajadores petroleros y sus relaciones con Pemex y el estado, 1970–1982* (Mexico City: Colegio de México, 1986), p. 99. See also Antonio Salazar Segual, "El movimiento sindical petrolero, 1960–1980" in Javier Aguilera (ed.), *Los sindicatos nacionales petroleros* (Mexico City: G.V. Editores, 1986), p. 276.

44. Prévot-Schapira, "Trabajadores del petróleo," pp. 154–155.

45. Pemex, *Política petrolera*, pp. 43–44.

46. Between 1950 and 1980, recruitment to Pemex's labor force grew at an annual rate of 3.2 percent, but between 1960–1970 it rose by 4.3 percent (Alonso and López, *El sindicato*, p. 97).

47. See Turrent Díaz, "La industria petrolera," p. 62 (art. 51); Alonso and López, *El sindicato*, p. 85.

48. Rosalía Pérez Linares, "Vigencia y formas del charrismo en el STPRM," in *Los sindicatos nacionales petroleros* (Mexico City: G.V. Editores, 1986), p. 119.

49. In turn, there was a stipulation that supernumerary members could not, in case of death, pass on the "candidature" for a permanent job to one of their children (Alonso and López, *El sindicato*, pp. 201–202).

50. Prévot-Schapira, "Trabajadores del petróleo," pp. 163–167. See also, by the same author, "Pétrole et nouvel espace industriel au Mexique, Coatzacoalcos-Minatitlán," 1981, thesis for Third Cycle PhD, Université de Sorbonne Nouvelle, Paris.

51. Alonso and López, *El sindicato*, p. 85.

52. Ibid., pp. 93–94.

53. Prévot-Schapira, "Les travailleurs," p. 281.

54. In fact, several union locals were unhappy and complained about the nomination of Barragán Camacho, but it had the support of the incoming president, Luis Echeverría. The opposition to Hernández Galicia led to the creation in 1971 of the National Petroleum Movement. The Independent Movement of Lázaro Cárdenas was founded soon after; however, neither thrived (Alonso and López, *El sindicato*, p. 98).

11. The Oil Industry and Mexico's Relations with the Industrial Powers

Gabriel Székely
University of California, San Diego

Mexico's oil industry generated the impressive sum of $110 billion dollars in export revenues from 1975 to 1987. Most studies of this period have focused on the economic and political constraints that kept Mexico from translating these resources into modest but sustained economic and social development.[1] Few have been concerned, however, with a systematic analysis of the oil industry's export strategy in these years and its relationship with the government's pursuit of other national objectives. In particular, this chapter looks at the Mexican government's 1980 initiative to seek greater economic security and political independence through foreign trade diversification. This search proved very costly because the strategy to diversify foreign trade focused solely on reducing exports of crude oil to the United States from 80 percent (1975 to 1980) to 50 percent of the total in subsequent years.[2]

The 1980 initiative marked the first time that explicit linkages between foreign trade and security policies were established. The benefits from import substitution industrialization (ISI) and the dominant economic and political position of the United States had caused Mexico to be only marginally concerned in the past with identifying options for diversifying foreign economic relations. The high demand and dependence on imported oil of the industrialized countries represented a genuine opportunity for trade diversification. However, some of the government's assumptions to support this objective either failed to materialize, or the associated policies were not carried through to their ultimate consequences. For example, while the government's projection in 1980 of a 50 percent increase of crude oil exports to 1.5 million barrels per day (mbd) in 1982 proved accurate, estimates that real crude oil prices would continue rising by a yearly average of 6 percent through the 1980s proved disastrous.[3] Moreover, it was assumed that through the expansion of crude oil sales industrial powers could be attracted to play a larger role in the Mexican economy, and that Mexico could thus gain access to carefully selected foreign markets. Paradoxically, government policies did not support the diversification of the scope of international operations of the oil industry itself, and they showed only a limited concern for encouraging changes in the volume and the structure of nonoil exports—at least until late 1985. As a result, the oil industry's export potential was not fully developed, a series of related economic objectives were not achieved, and political independence was not strengthened. A plausible explanation of these outcomes lies in the failure of policymakers to draw a clear distinction between the long-term goal of diversifying exports across a broad range of products and foreign markets, and the short-term oil export policy aimed at reducing once and for all political dependence on the United States.

Crucially, it will be argued that the decision to diversify crude oil export sales away from the U.S. market obscured the real issues. The critical change for a successful and sustained diversification program does not involve the geographical destination of oil exports per se, but rather the ability to allocate revenues efficiently to make progress in the following areas: (1) to reduce the vulnerability of the oil industry that is associated with a high degree of dependence on exports of a commodity subject to wild price fluctuations, such as crude oil; and (2) to allocate resources toward expanding the volume and diversifying the structure of nonoil products exported by private and public firms. Strengthening Mexico's position in the world economy as well as its negotiating leverage with the United States was and continues to be contingent upon accomplishing these two goals. Alternatively, the decision to stress the diversification of crude oil export markets has led to a mixed record of accomplishments and failures.

I have argued elsewhere that President López Portillo's administration, under which Mexico's oil industry burgeoned, postponed economic reforms because it could count on oil revenues and huge foreign loans.[4] The lack of planning, the waste of resources, as well as several unfavorable international economic conditions, resulted in López Portillo's leaving his successor, in 1982, one of the most intractable and persistent economic crises in the nation's history. President Miguel de la Madrid focused his attention on bringing down inflation and the public sector deficit, with only limited success. It was not until 1985 that he decided to begin implementing economic reforms that could bring about the much expected diversification of Mexico's foreign economic relations. This trend accelerated at the end of 1987, when the economic crisis deepened and the government concluded that it could no longer sustain most of the old economic policies.

Because the oil industry does not exist in a vacuum, this chapter also looks at the outcomes resulting from changes in foreign trade policy and at evolving relations with the main countries targeted by Mexico's diversification program (Japan, Spain, France, Great Britain, and Canada).

Assessment of Mexico's Diversification Program

There is a vibrant debate in the development literature on the merits and drawbacks of ISI compared to export-led growth. While development policy is usually based on a combination of these two strategies, the one that stresses the growth of exports appears critical for small nations that are willing to attain a greater command of the skills and resources needed to interact on their own with the world economy.

Governments play a crucial role in encouraging the growth of exports. First, they must implement the appropriate policies in a consistent fashion. This includes, for example, maintaining a competitive foreign exchange rate for the local currency and cutting down bureaucratic red tape to facilitate foreign trade transactions. In addition, public agencies provide subsidies and incentives; they help to develop information and commercial networks, to train managers and supporting staff to deal successfully with the complexities characteristic of world markets, and to encourage new attitudes to cope with changing conditions in those markets.[5] Further, the tasks of selecting industries that offer the best prospects of becoming internationally competitive, and of allocating government resources in support of these industries, are technically and politically complex and require the skillful leadership that governments provide.

Diversification involves structural changes in the economy that are likely to be resisted by domestic groups whose interests are hurt by the new government policies. Governments must be able to build sufficient political support and new social coalitions favoring export-oriented programs. Because foreign events, trends, and actors often play an important role triggering policy changes, governments usually find themselves in a delicate position. This is all the more significant when countries have experienced painful domestic economic adjustments and have mastered the resources, the political will, and the flexibility needed to adapt to changes in the international economic environment, just to find that these are not sufficient conditions to gain access to the markets they seek to penetrate. *Market access* constitutes a security priority for developing countries because their economic performance depends, to an increasing degree, on their ability to sell their goods in foreign markets.[6] This is an issue of comparable importance to the security interests of industrial powers as regards their access to critical raw materials in the developing world.[7] Successful governmental negotiations to open new opportunities in foreign markets are thus critical.

Governments therefore provide a variety of functions to support the growth of exports. That politics play as important a role as economic considerations do in establishing a nation's foreign trade strategy, is shown in decisions such as that taken by the Mexican government affecting the oil industry.

The Oil Industry

In 1980, oil had become the leading source of foreign currency with which to finance Mexico's record-high imports and ambitious development plans. The government announced that it expected crude oil exports to peak in 1982 at around 1.5 to 1.7 mbd, and to stabilize thereafter. In addition, Mexico's first National Energy Plan was published. Significantly, the plan included provisions to the effect that no more than one-half of crude petroleum sales were to be exported to a single national market; neither were such sales to account for more than 20 percent of the total oil import needs of any individual nation.[8]

The United States was the obvious target of this government program. The argument was twofold. First, if the United States became highly dependent on oil from its southern neighbor, Mexico's oil production, export, and pricing policies were more likely to be subject to U.S. pressures. This fear was founded on repeated expressions of concern and outrage by U.S. officials, in the tight market conditions that characterized the late 1970s, over the production and pricing policies of the leading oil producing nations within the Organization of Petroleum Exporting Countries (OPEC). From the perspective of Mexican leaders at that time, a strong argument favoring a policy of diversifying crude oil export markets was to expand their options and to protect the nation's political independence from foreign pressures. In addition, using oil exports as a means for diversifying economic relations with the rest of the world, rather than to deepen those relations with the United States, served Mexico's goal of making the traditional vulnerability of its own economy to abrupt changes in that of the United States more manageable. In particular, Mexican leaders did not want to see their oil exports and revenues reduced as a result of a sluggish performance of the U.S. economy. Their concern for Mexico's economic security was, therefore, another argument behind the decision to diversify.

It is noteworthy that the Mexican program, by deeds rather than by design, promised to bring about substantial benefits for the United States. For example, if the government achieved the objectives it proclaimed, such as strengthening the international position of the economy, it was fair to expect an increase in the trust of domestic and foreign investors regarding the government's economic managerial abilities. Such confidence had been shattered during the administration of President Luis Echeverría, when the public foreign debt increased fivefold and the peso was devalued for the first time in twenty-two years. More important, a share of Mexico's oil exports was directed to some of the closest U.S. political and military allies, including Japan and Israel. The United States had proved unable, due to national security directives that emanated from Congress, to respond favorably to demands for oil articulated by those two nations in the aftermath of the second oil price shock and the outbreak of hostilities between Iraq and the Iran of the ayatollahs. In the case of Israel, Mexico supplied over two-thirds of its oil needs in the 1980s. Additionally, the Mexican program was well-received by the U.S. Department of Energy, which was not thrilled by the prospect of seeing the United States become dangerously dependent on oil imports from a single major source, including Mexico. Finally, from the Department of Treasury's viewpoint, were Mexico to succeed in establishing sound financial relations with other industrial nations, its future demands on U.S. financial resources were likely to be kept within manageable limits. Raymond Vernon perhaps put it in the strongest and most explicit terms, arguing that the United States would benefit more from measures geared to deemphasize rather than to strengthen further its bilateral relationship with Mexico.[9]

From the Mexican government's perspective, it seems that the oil sector was chosen because export diversification would be achieved more rapidly and the outcomes would be more visible. This decision was facilitated by the eagerness of industrial countries to gain access to secure oil supplies, following the outbreak of hostilities in the Iran-Iraq War. Although their demand for imported oil had fallen from a peak 25 mbd in 1979 to 19 mbd in 1981, industrial countries continued substituting imports from OPEC—and particularly from Middle East suppliers—with oil from more secure sources like Mexico. The European market economies, for example, cut their crude oil imports from the Middle East from 8 mbd in 1979 to 2.5 mbd in 1985. Japan's 1985 crude oil imports from the Middle East (2 mbd) were 50 percent lower than in 1979. The United States reduced imports from this source as well, from 3 mbd in 1979 to a record-low 0.5 mbd in 1985![10]

In these circumstances, even after we discount the drastic fall in oil consumption and imports resulting from the new energy policies pursued by industrial countries, there was plenty of room for increasing Mexican exports in world oil markets. Table 1 shows a substantial expansion of Mexico's crude oil exports to industrial nations other than the United States, from an average 174,000 barrels per day (bd) in 1980 to 549,000 bd in 1985 and 634,000 bd in 1987. Japan, Spain, France, and,

Table 1. Mexico: OECD Oil Trade, 1975–1987 (thousands of barrels per day)

	Total Mexican Oil Exports	OECD, Total	United States	Canada	Japan	OECD, Europe	France	Great Britain	Spain
1975	94.2	94.2	94.2	—	—	—	—	—	—
1976	94.4	94.4	73.3	—	—	21.1	—	—	—
1977	202.0	178.0	176.8	—	—	1.2	—	—	1.2
1978	365.0	343.0	324.9	2.4	0.9	14.8	—	—	13.6
1979	532.8	492.0	448.8	—	—	43.2	—	—	42.9
1980	827.7	736.5	562.5	4.2	35.2	134.6	42.1	—	92.5
1981	1,098.0	915.7	546.7	46.1	76.5	246.4	71.7	18.3	151.5
1982	1,492.1	1,276.3	729.3	47.9	112.7	386.4	84.8	83.7	169.9
1983	1,534.8	1,347.4	823.2	39.7	120.1	364.4	82.6	85.4	161.8
1984	1,525.6	1,363.1	750.9	43.2	159.1	409.9	91.5	100.8	168.5
1985	1,438.2	1,299.8	750.7	34.6	158.2	356.3	85.5	66.2	181.2
1986	1,289.6	1,234.3	652.5	30.0	181.8	350.0	81.2	50.0	196.0
1987	1,345.4	1,304.0	631.0	25.0	191.0	452.0	85.0	80.0	208.5

Sources: Pemex, *Memoria de labores* (Mexico City, various years); *Pemex Bulletin* (Washington, D.C., various years); and monthly statistics supplied by Pemex and published in Mexico's national press.
Note: The Organization for Economic Cooperation and Development (OECD) comprises all the industrialized countries with a market economy. It is based in Paris.

to a lesser extent, Canada and Great Britain, figured prominently as Mexico's customers during this period.

It is important to note as well that while in 1980 32 percent of Mexican output was accounted for by Maya (heavy crude oil), production from new oil fields led to an increase of that share to 60 percent of total output in 1984 and in subsequent years.[11] The proportion of Maya in total exports of crude oil rose accordingly. Such changes in production and export patterns facilitated Mexico's successful penetration of new markets, even though world demand for oil was in decline. The reason is that demand for heavy crudes rose in the 1980s as a result of widespread plant conversions by refiners, who faced stiff competition and sought to improve their margin of profitability. Because the prices of heavier crudes were not set by OPEC, there was more room for negotiations over prices with crude oil suppliers eager to capture a larger share within industrial country markets.

Mexico was less fortunate in regard to the overall evolution of oil export prices, as real oil prices collapsed rather than increased in the 1980s (table 2). Moreover, because authorities have been slow in changing export prices to reflect market realities, Mexico recently has seen its oil sales and revenues reduced below expected levels. The continued decline of real oil prices and Pemex's inability to maintain its share of the world market in the competitive conditions of the present decade have hurt Mexico's economy. Domestic politics have also played a disturbing role in this regard. In 1981, for example, oil export prices were reduced and then increased in a matter of days, resulting in lower sales. These inconsistencies in setting export prices can be traced to the politics of the presidential succession in Mexico.[12] A governmental body (Comité para el Comercio Exterior de Petróleo, COCEP) was established in 1982 with the objectives of reaching consensus within the federal bureaucracy on commercial and export pricing policies, and preventing a repetition of the costly events of 1981. In 1985, the opinion of the secretary of energy prevailed over that government committee, however, and a new disaster could not be averted. Oil exports were temporarily cut in half because Mexico, in a näive show of solidarity with OPEC, maintained official export prices even though members of that organization were offering discounts to their customers behind the scenes.[13]

In 1986, the continued glut in world markets took its toll on Mexico with exports falling to their lowest level in the 1980s, 1.29 mbd. This was partly due to the fall of world oil demand, and partly to Pemex's pricing strategy for its exports. Pemex has not followed the "netback oil export pricing scheme," implemented by Saudi Arabia, where prices are based on the expected profits of refiners rather than on the old formula of official OPEC prices. Instead, prices are set according to the quality of

Table 2. Volume and Average Price of Mexican Crude Oil Exports, 1975, 1979–1987

	Volume (thousands of b/d)	*Export Price (annual average $/b)*
1975	94.4	11.60
1979	532.8	19.60
1980	827.7	31.25
1981	1,098.0	33.18
1982	1,492.1	28.64
1983	1,534.8	26.42
1984	1,525.6	26.82
1985	1,438.2	25.42
1986	1,289.6	11.84
1987	1,345.4	16.00

Sources: Petróleos Mexicanos, *Memoria de labores* (Mexico City, various issues); Petróleos Mexicanos, Coordinación de Comercio Internacional, *El sector petrolero mexicano, 1978–1983; Estadísticas seleccionadas* (Mexico City, April 1984), tables 15, 16.

each type of crude and the region of the world to which it is exported. For the Far East, for example, prices are set retroactively each quarter to reflect market changes; the prices of exports to Europe and the Western Hemisphere are adjusted on the basis of spot-traded crude oil and products.

A central problem has been that Pemex has lacked experienced traders operating and making decisions in the field—rather than in faraway Mexico City—to maintain its share of the world market as well as its privileged position within certain national markets. Within the United States, for example, the Saudis relegated Mexico to second place among the leading suppliers of crude both in 1986 and in 1987, despite rising imports in that country. Lower prices have benefited consumers in the United States, but they have also precipitated a reduction of domestic output. U.S. crude oil imports during 1987 averaged 5.2 mbd, or 40 percent above the record-low import level of 3.8 mbd for the year 1985.[14] In that two-year period, Saudi Arabia's crude oil exports to the United States rose from 130,000 bd to 690,000 bd, while Venezuela's position was also enhanced through a net increase in exports averaging 200,000 bd. In contrast, Mexico's position deteriorated as exports fell from 725,000 to 610,000 bd during the same period. Pemex also has been unable to take advantage of rising imports in the Canadian market, of which it was the leading foreign supplier of crude from 1980 to 1984. Pemex's exports to Canada have been reduced since 1985 (table 1), due to disagreements over prices; Great Britain and Venezuela have become the main beneficiaries, increasing their oil exports to Canada. There are other related aspects of crude oil commercialization policies that have not helped to enhance Pemex's position. Initially, the expansion of oil sales to industrial countries was contingent upon successful negotiations of long-term contracts. Further, Mexican authorities discouraged intermediaries by refusing to participate in crude oil processing agreements with oil multinationals, which purchase crude for use in their refineries around the world and then sell oil products to other parties. Because authorities contend that Mexico has no alternative but to be a price-taker in the world oil market, neither has Pemex developed an interest and the expertise to participate with oil sellers in spot market trading centers.[15] These policy directives were applied rather rigidly. They could not be sustained when conditions in the world market became highly competitive, and Pemex found itself unable to compensate the loss of income resulting from falling crude prices and shrinking sales with revenue from other sources.

Even more regrettable has been the scant attention paid to diversifying the scope of international operations of the oil industry. Pemex has failed to become a modern and aggressive trading agent in world markets commensurate with the size of its oil reserves, its assets, and its relative weight both in terms of production and exports of hydrocarbons. In particular, Pemex has specialized in exporting crude oil but has hesitated to seriously venture into downstream operations such as refining and petrochemicals. Alirio Parra, a leading oil expert and executive with Petróleos de Venezuela, has argued:

> state-owned majors cannot isolate themselves from market realities, because they may be more exposed to the uncertainties of a changing environment than many of the traditional integrated companies. To protect their long-term position, it is necessary that they develop strategies for becoming increasingly involved in the chain of processes that integrate the international market.[16]

That the strategy followed by Venezuela contrasts sharply with Pemex's is shown, for example, in the emphasis placed by Venezuela on downstream operations and exports. In the 1980s, Venezuela became the third largest supplier of refined products to the whole industrialized world. Only the Netherlands and the Soviet Union achieved higher export levels. Venezuela has sought joint ventures aggressively, with leading European companies such as Italy's ENI and West Germany's Veba Oel, in order to penetrate foreign markets and to protect its financial position from reductions in crude export prices.[17] Like Saudi Arabia, which purchased Texaco in 1988, Venezuela has also purchased Citgo and other refineries in the United States with a view to securing access for its own crude within this most important and strategic market. Because Mexico has not followed a similarly aggressive strategy, it has seen its role reduced in spite of rising imports of crude oil by the United States.

To be fair, the domestic political environment within which Pemex operates is highly restrictive and may have obstructed efforts at diversification. Pemex is subject to a myriad of budgetary controls and regulations. In addition, managers have to deal with the most corrupt and powerful of the nation's union bureaucracies. The leaders of the oil union, which belongs to the officially sanctioned national labor movement, have successfully resisted the assault and criticism that have originated periodically within the Office of the President of Mexico himself. Moreover, nationalistic feelings, rooted in the unhappy experience with U.S. and European oil majors before and after the expropriation of the industry, have discouraged executives from dealing with foreign companies. Because many such deals are needed in order to operate the industry, managers have disguised them in the past to avert politically embarrassing and economically costly domestic reactions.[18] It could be argued that there are structural factors built into the Mexican system that account for the underutilization of Pemex's potential within world markets. Be that as it may, of the total $95 billion export revenues earned by Pemex from 1980 to 1986, refined products accounted for only 5.4 percent and petrochemicals for 0.8 percent (table 3). Although Pemex has made massive investments to increase nominal production capacity in these two areas, 25 to 30 percent of such capacity remains idle. Thus, for example, in 1986 Mexico's refineries could process 1.8 mbd of crude oil (compared to 0.8 mbd in 1975), but actual production averaged 1.3 mbd. Further, actual production of petrochemicals in 1986 (12 million tons) contrasted with a 17.6 million tons nominal output capacity.[19] The ratio of exports over total output has been considerably low, averaging 10 percent for both the refining and petrochemical industries. To be sure, the data also show that some progress has been achieved in recent years with Pemex selling in foreign markets a growing share of output of refined products that are in excess of domestic needs. Moving further along this path is more urgent now that the long-term outlook for crude oil markets looks grim for produc-

Table 3. Mexico: OECD Trade, 1976, 1980–1986 (millions of U.S. $)

	Trade with World	OECD, Total	United States	Canada	Japan	OECD, Europe	France	United Kingdom	Spain
1976									
Balance	-2,645	-3,051	-1,897	-93	-205	-834	-152	-164	-27
Exports	3,655	2,383	1,873	48	101	355	29	26	23
Nonoil	3,092	1,820	1,431	48	101	234	29	26	23
Oil	563	563	442	—	—	121	—	—	—
Imports	6,300	5,434	3,770	141	306	1,189	181	190	50
1980									
Balance	-2,963	-1,885	-818	-204	-228	-594	94	-325	922
Exports	15,570	13,296	10,072	117	671	2,426	567	43	1,238
Nonoil	5,168	3,942	2,886	66	262	718	77	43	88
Oil	10,042	9,354	7,186	51	409	1,708	490	—	1,150
Imports	18,533	15,181	10,890	321	899	3,020	473	368	316
1981									
Balance	-3,342	-3,020	-3,282	256	62	-7	366	-148	1,492
Exports	19,646	16,224	10,716	661	1,157	3,674	900	242	1,921
Nonoil	5,072	3,968	3,149	104	234	465	16	33	14
Oil	14,574	12,256	7,567	557	923	3,209	884	209	1,907
Imports	22,988	19,244	13,998	405	1,095	3,681	534	390	429
1982									
Balance	6,710	5,740	2,941	293	673	1,871	613	660	1,479
Exports	21,214	17,804	11,129	584	1,450	4,626	931	913	1,815
Nonoil	4,736	4,482	3,269	83	300	566	33	37	26
Oil	16,478	13,322	7,860	501	1,150	4,060	898	876	1,789

Imports	14,504	12,062	8,188	291	777	2,755	318	253	336
1983									
Balance	14,200	12,284	8,076	261	1,192	2,767	505	761	1,465
Exports	21,819	19,182	13,034	467	1,512	4,160	832	916	1,617
Nonoil	5,654	5,031	4,079	83	247	713	37	113	12
Oil	16,165	14,151	8,955	384	1,265	3,447	795	803	1,605
Imports	7,619	6,898	4,958	206	320	1,393	327	155	152
1984									
Balance	13,150	12,208	7,690	288	1,411	2,877	698	829	1,524
Exports	24,407	21,084	14,130	495	1,868	4,577	928	1,020	1,703
Nonoil	7,941	6,371	5,533	67	219	540	27	39	37
Oil	16,466	14,713	8,597	428	1,649	4,037	901	981	1,666
Imports	11,257	8,876	6,440	207	457	1,700	230	191	179
1985									
Balance	8,665	7,472	4,387	158	986	2,033	541	394	1,486
Exports	22,108	19,577	13,341	393	1,709	4,113	816	678	1,700
Nonoil	7,341	6,405	5,569	106	248	763	13	66	30
Oil	14,767	13,172	7,772	287	1,461	3,350	803	612	1,670
Imports	13,443	12,105	8,954	235	723	2,080	275	284	214
1986									
Balance	3,917	3,282	2,891	75	294	45	142	-43	601
Exports	16,237	14,741	11,163	302	1,065	2,184	382	174	791
Nonoil	10,104	9,077	7,593	54	272	812	125	74	30
Oil	6,133	5,664	3,570	248	793	1,372	257	100	761
Imports	12,320	11,459	8,272	227	771	2,139	240	217	190

Sources: Author's estimates based on the sources identified in table 3.

ing nations. In addition to a greatly reduced demand, producers face stiff competition from a variety of sources, with the result that world markets continue to experience a glut.

There are indications that Pemex is beginning to develop a more international outlook. The strong links developed with Spain's refining industry hold particularly bright prospects for Pemex, especially since that country joined the European Economic Community in 1986. Spanish authorities invited the Mexican oil company to purchase up to 34 percent of the stocks in Petronor, a refinery in northern Spain. The funds and the steady supply of crude provided by Pemex over the last few years have been instrumental in ending Petronor's financial difficulties. It has become an efficient firm with expanded exports of refined products in the European market. In this light, the Pemex decision to purchase 10 percent of Repsol, another Spanish refinery, must be welcomed.[20] This type of investment has the advantage of isolating Pemex managers from several intractable problems at home, such as government controls and union corruption. For this reason, Pemex's investment ventures in Spain represent a model worth replicating in other markets.

The Pacific Petroleum Project with Japan constitutes another attempt to redress the pattern of missed opportunities in the 1970s and early 1980s. This $770 million project has been made possible through a special $500 million Japanese loan and the prospect of increased exports to markets in the Far East. It includes the building of pipes with greater capacity to send oil from provinces in southeast Mexico to the Pacific; increased storage capacity for preventing delays in filling up oil tankers at Oaxaca's Salina Cruz port; the expansion of available refining capacity; and a plant to export liquefied gas. The expectation was that Pemex would be in the position to penetrate markets in the Pacific Basin in the 1990s.[21]

The success of these projects, and indeed of the prospects for greater diversification, will depend on one crucial factor. Pemex managers must convince economic authorities to allow them more leeway in using financial resources that Pemex generates to fund its long-term development. According to oil executives, over 60 percent of revenues are provided to the government in royalties and taxes each year. Once operating expenses are deducted, little is left for the type of investments discussed here. Their expectations run high, however, because the Mexican government is now following a new approach toward control and allocation of the resources of various state-owned firms, such as telephones and the steel industry. Thus, in announcing in late 1987 a $15 billion investment plan for the next five years, Pemex's director general let it be known that negotiations are under way with the nation's treasury in order to fully finance these investments with Pemex's own resources.[22]

A related financial decision that affects petrochemicals has implications for the internationalization of the oil industry in the future. Until recently, Pemex had exclusive rights to import petrochemicals that it cannot supply in the domestic market. These are classified as "basic," or raw material products. Given prevailing controls over domestic prices implemented by other government agencies, Pemex in effect provided huge subsidies to consumers in the business sector. In 1986, the government decided to end such subsidies by reclassifying thirty-six "basic" products into a category known as "secondary," or manufactured petrochemical products, one of the few sectors within the oil industry where private business is allowed to participate. Consumers are thus free to engage in foreign trade operations and to reflect real costs in the price of their final products.[23] Private investments to expand output of these products have been slow to materialize, however, because business insists that it be allowed to participate in the production of basic petrochemicals as well. A decision on this critical policy issue is expected from the next administration after 1988. At the same time, Pemex plans to invest a share of its newly liberated resources in joint ventures in order to supply in the future some of these products. These joint ventures will take place both within Mexico and in foreign markets, and they will involve domestic and foreign business partners. This is therefore another way Pemex hopes to improve upon the quite limited achievements of recent years in diversifying both its sources of income and its international operations.

Mexico's Relations with Industrial Powers

Mexico's private industry has missed several opportunities brought about by the expansion of economic relations with industrial countries during the present decade. If we look beyond the United States, Mexico's trade with several industrial nations has surged during the 1980s. For example, Mexican exports to Canada, as well as to Japan, from 1970 to 1979, totaled $1 billion each. Table 3 shows a dramatic increase of exports, $3 billion to Canada, and $9.5 billion to Japan, during the years 1980 to 1986. Exports to the European market economies rose sixfold—to $26 billion—during the same period. Thus, while in 1975 only 10 percent of all Mexican exports were sold in Europe, that proportion rose to 19 percent during the 1980s. The problem, however, is that oil accounts for most of these export increases. The contribution of nonoil products to the total value of Mexican exports to each of these industrial countries averaged 20 percent from 1980 to 1986. To have a better idea of what this poor performance represents, consider that it takes Mexico a full year to export nonoil products to Canada worth $100 million. In contrast, it takes more distant developing nations like Korea only one month, and Brazil three months, to reach the same level of exports. Similarly, Mexico's nonoil exports to Europe in one year ($812 million in 1986), equaled the value of four months of Korean exports to Europe, and of two months of Brazil's exports.[24]

Not surprisingly, Mexico's foreign trade remains heavily concentrated within the U.S. market. Regrettably, however, opportunities have been missed even in this market. For example, while Mexico is the developing country whose products qualify for the greatest proportion of reduced duties under the U.S. General System of Preferences (GSP), it takes the least advantage of this scheme.

In 1986, the U.S. accounted for 75 percent of the total value of Mexico's nonoil exports, $10 billion according to table 3. Such a proportion would be even higher if we used U.S. rather than Mexican trade statistics. In the United States, import figures from Mexico's assembly plants include not only value added but the value of the whole product. This discrepancy in reporting methods may strengthen the case of producers and labor unions in the United States that oppose the maquiladora program. For example, according to the U.S. International Trade Commission, manufacturing imports from Mexico ($9.9 billion in 1985, of which over $4 billion originated in the maquiladoras) trailed only Korea's and Taiwan's when manufacturing imports from all developing nations are considered. Relatedly, although the U.S. General Accounting Office has reported that 68 percent of assembly plants in Mexico are U.S.-owned, congressional legislators are concerned about the growing role of Japanese firms. These firms have expanded their operations at the border and in central Mexico very rapidly, raising fears in Washington that Mexico is becoming a "back door" for the Japanese to circumvent protectionism within the U.S. market.[25] Mexico will face not only increasing competition from other industrializing countries but rising protectionism within the U.S. market as well.

I have discussed elsewhere the full range of issues that have arisen in connection with the emerging trilateral relation that involves Mexico, Japan, and the United States.[26] Japan's interest in Mexico's economy can be only partly explained by the evolving bilateral relationship in the oil arena, for Japan's long-term strategy toward Mexico responds to changes in the organization and patterns of world production. Japanese investments benefit from Mexico's geographical proximity to the U.S. market, from lower labor, transportation, energy, and other costs. Their central objective is to supply parts and components to Japanese firms, especially automobile and electronic industries, operating within the U.S. market. Yet the establishment along the U.S.-Mexico border of new types of small Japanese firms that supply parts to the giant electronics producers, such as Matsushita, Sanyo, and Sony, adds a new dimension to this phenomenon. These firms have come to Mexico to respond to the needs of their largest customers in Japan, who complain of the poor quality of U.S. and Mexico-made inputs. This competition is not being welcomed in either the United States or Mexico. Furthermore, Japan's position has become even more vulnerable after the United States ran a record-high $173 billion trade deficit in 1987; Japan alone registered a trade surplus of over $70 billion with the United States. Japanese firms within the United States are thus expanding their presence in order to respond to growing protectionism in that country. For example, it should not come as a surprise that while no Japanese automobiles were assembled in the United States in 1982, production of close to 1 million vehicles was projected for 1988. Japanese plants based in Mexico are expected to supply parts to the larger plants located on the U.S. side of the border.

It is worth stressing that, from Mexico's perspective, Japan represents the most promising option for diversifying its foreign economic relations. Mexico is receiving help to expand exports from the oil industry as well as from private business. In addition to the Pacific Petroleum Project, Japan has lent Mexico $500 million to complete a steel mill plant oriented toward foreign markets, and to promote nonoil exports with assistance provided by Japan's prestigious trading houses. Moreover, Japan has become Mexico's second largest trading partner, foreign lender ($15 billion), and foreign investor ($1.5 billion through 1987). These astute Japanese gestures have encouraged Mexican leaders to believe that Japan has not abandoned their country in times of crisis. This has contrasted sharply with Mexican perceptions that, in the 1980s, virulent attacks had been orchestrated, in U.S. official circles and in the media, out of desperation for the failure of Mexican leaders to tackle domestic economic and political difficulties. It could be argued that Mexico's diplomatic overture toward the United States' chief economic competitor has not been a casual decision.

With Japanese investments growing considerably within its principal market, the United States, Mexico's strategic importance to Japan will grow accordingly. These investments rose from $16 billion in 1984, to $30 billion in 1987; Japan trails only Great Britain and the Netherlands in the list of most prominent foreign investors within the U.S. market.[27] The long-term success of Japan's two-track investment strategy (investing both within the United States, and in countries like Mexico, to reduce direct exports to the United States) will depend on the continuing struggle in the U.S. Congress to resist the forces of protectionism. Relatedly, the domestic coalitions that are emerging in favor of and in opposition to maintaining a relatively free trading system will shape U.S. foreign trade policy for many years to come.[28] Experience suggests, however, that greater Mexican efforts are needed to collect and disseminate information to discourage measures that may limit access to the U.S. market; bilateral negotiations over specific export sectors constitute a step in the right direction.[29] It will also be necessary to stress that Japanese producers and exporters have the same right to participate in and operate from the Mexican market as U.S. businesses.

Compared to the unique circumstances that have fostered strong economic links with Japan, other projects to expand Mexico's economic relations with industrial powers have not been as important and they have not prospered. Canada has represented the other end of the continuum, while the growth of economic relations with Western European countries has fallen somewhere in between.

Energy provided the focus of Mexican-Canadian efforts to strengthen their bilateral relationship. Although Canada is a major oil producer and exporter, it is cheaper to import oil to supply eastern provinces than it is to pipe the oil across the continent from the country's western oil producing provinces. Mexico agreed in 1975 to supply crude oil to the Canadian market for ten years. While actual oil shipments were initiated until the end of that decade, Mexico alone supplied 20 percent of Canadian oil import needs in the early 1980s. Effective cooperation in other economic areas never materialized, however. The most important issue for Mexico involved policy coordination on natural gas export prices to the U.S. market, while Canada's main interest lay in the prospect of selling Mexico reactors for generating nuclear energy.[30]

Canadians pointed out that the size of their gas reserves and the volume of their exports to the United States are much larger than Mexico's, that the nature of their customers in the northern region of the United States is very different, and that they are prepared to reduce prices to maintain their share of the U.S. market, while Mexico is not. Such perceptions proved well founded because Mexico eventually suspended gas sales rather than meet U.S. demands for reduced prices in response to falling prices of crude oil. The perceptions and goals of the Mexican and Canadian governments on this issue were quite different.

As far as nuclear energy goes, Canada hoped to sell Mexico some of its homemade reactors. Under López Portillo, developing a nuclear energy program became one of the government's more ambitious plans. An investment of $50 billion was projected through the end of the century, bringing installed capacity to generate nuclear energy up to 20,000 megawatts. Because hydrocarbons supply over 90 percent of Mexico's energy needs, such a program was devised to reduce pressures to increase production of oil and gas that threatened an early depletion of Mexican fields. Before such plans were shelved by financially pressed President de la Madrid, important disagreements kept these two countries apart.

Mexico urged the Canadians to share their technology and knowledge so that the operation and maintenance of the reactors would fall under national control. This demand was denied due to the unhappy Canadian experience with India, which developed a nuclear weapon capability based on information supplied by Canada for peaceful purposes. Ottawa's insistence that Canadian personnel participate in overviewing the construction and operation of the reactors, along with the International Atomic Energy Agency, was rejected by Mexico City.

Mexico and Canada have shared economic and political concerns in relating to their common neighbor; they have disagreed with the United States on foreign policy issues, such as Central America and discussions on development-related matters in international forums. Despite much rhetoric, however, bilateral relations have been generally cool. This was particularly true once Prime Minister Brian Mulroney succeeded the more buoyant Pierre Trudeau, with whom Mexico's president cochaired the North-South Conference in Cancún in 1981. More important, little has been accomplished in establishing solid economic relations. The Mulroney administration ended the oil import agreement with Mexico while, in the 1980s, Mexico's nonoil exports to Canada and imports from that country did not expand significantly (table 3). The accumulated value of Canadian direct investments in Mexico through 1987 was a nominal $289 million.

As far as Europe is concerned, direct investments in Mexico before the oil boom amounted to $1.1 billion, climbing to over $4 billion by the mid-1980s; European loans to Mexico's institutions during the same period ranged in the billions of dollars. Spain, France, and Great Britain have been Mexico's most prominent oil customers in the European market. The governments of the first two countries have played an active role encouraging business deals with Mexico. Because Spain and France lack oil, their leaders have been more concerned with secure oil supplies. It has been argued as well that while industrial countries experienced a recession, growth in Mexico averaged over 8 percent from 1978 to 1981. Mexico was viewed as a particularly attractive market for allocating a share of surplus production and European investments.

A major foreign policy objective of the post-Franco regime has been to expand Spain's relations with the rest of the world, especially Europe and Latin America. Relations with Mexico had been severed during the Civil War and were not reestablished before 1977. In that year, oil began to flow from Mexico to Spain, though oil shipments increased significantly beginning in 1980. Spain became Mexico's second largest oil customer, as Pemex has supplied over 20 percent of that country's total oil import needs.

In the early 1980s, the government's Hispanoil negotiated purchases of up to 300,000 bd with governments from oil producing nations with half of the total coming from Mexico. This level of imports was subsequently reduced as private refineries began to purchase oil in the spot market at lower prices and thus enhanced their profitability. While Spain has shied away from signing long-term contracts preferred by Pemex, because the latter involve rigid commitments over prices, Spain has maintained nonetheless a solid oil relationship with Mexico. Reference has been made to the invitation extended to Pemex to buy stocks in Petronor, a refinery located in Bilbao, a deal that enhanced the prospects of an increased Mexican role within the European market in the 1990s.[31]

These accomplishments within the oil arena have not been matched elsewhere; it appears that Mexican business leaders have been unable or unwilling to develop opportunities in the Spanish market. Nonoil exports to Spain have averaged a negligible $30 million per year, with yearly imports of Spanish products valued at $200 million (table 3). At the same time, Spanish direct investments in Mexico reached $603 million at the end of 1987, while loans to Mexico's private and public institutions were worth about $1 billion.

There were great expectations as well in regard to the growth of Mexico's economic relations with France, but, as with Spain, much remains to be accomplished. While oil and gas resources are scarce in France, proved uranium reserves are the largest in Europe.[32] France enjoys a leading position in terms of production of nuclear energy and associated technology. French oil companies participate in commercial distribution in the domestic market, and are otherwise involved in several operations overseas. The state holds 40 percent of stocks in CFP-Total, and 66 percent in Elf-Aquitaine's. Their exports of technology and service contracts, as well as those of the Institute Francaise de Petrole, contribute significantly to enhance France's balance of payments. Elf specializes in oil and chemical production, while CFP's business is mainly in oil refining. Executives from both these companies are quite interested in selling their services to Mexico.

Mexican oil exports to France, 42,000 bd in 1980, averaged over 85,000 bd in the five subsequent years. Pemex's relations with CFP, which is its largest customer at the individual company level within Europe, have not always been smooth. In the summer of 1981, for example, CFP was one of the companies that put pressure on Pemex to reduce excessive prices. Because Mexico was late in responding, purchases were temporarily suspended. The Mexican Minister of Natural Resources threatened to terminate all public sector contracts with French companies unless CFP honored its commitments to Pemex. Oil relations between these two countries had become highly politicized. While cordiality was eventually reestablished, plans to implement in the European market an ambitious bilateral cooperation scheme involving Pemex and CFP fell through.[33] French direct investments in Mexico have been rather small, or about $596 million through 1987; financial institutions have a greater stake, however, as Mexico's public and private sectors owe France close to $10 billion. Few Mexican entrepreneurs export to France, as shown in table 3.

In regard to Mexico's relations with Great Britain, it is significant that, while that country is a major oil producer, it imports a large amount of petroleum that is handled by domestic and overseas refineries. The reason for these imports is that indigenous production of light crude oil must be supplemented with imports of heavier crudes that yield other products consumed by industry. Thus, for example, while domestic output in 1986 totaled 2.6 mbd, Britain exported 1.9 mbd and it imported 1.4 mbd of crude oil.[34] Britain's net oil exporter position and the limited participation of Middle East suppliers within its domestic market render that nation invulnerable to oil supply disruptions. Moreover, in the 1980s Britain helped to enhance the security of fellow industrial countries like France, Germany, and even the United States and Canada, all of whom import petroleum from the North Sea.

In striking contrast to Mexico's relations with Spain and France, the British government has not played an active role in the decision of Shell and British Petroleum (BP) to cultivate Pemex. In fact, Mexico ranks very low on the list of foreign policy priorities of Great Britain and its leaders. According to Pemex, oil exports rose from 18,300 bd in 1981 to 101,000 bd in 1984, and then fell to negligible amounts (table 1); Shell is its principal customer. That Mexico has oil and gas reserves likely to last for a decade or two longer than Britain's explains the latter's interest in Mexico. Additionally, British oil companies hold the expectation, shared by French oil executives, that Pemex will eventually be fully modernized and turn outward, thus finding their knowledge, expertise, and commercial networks valuable.[35] Other than these hopes and expectations in the oil arena, economic relations have also grown in limited fashion. There has been little trading of nonoil products, British investments have amounted to $987 million, and loans to Mexico about $8 billion.

Prospects for the Future

Although Mexico has achieved some progress expanding contacts with and attracting resources from several industrial countries, a lesson of this experience in the 1980s has been that there are limits to how far Mexico can go to diversify foreign economic relations beyond the U.S.

market. The United States remains an actor of overwhelming importance for Mexico's economy. The appropriate combination of policies, as well as the allocation of resources, that are needed to diversify exports across a broad range of nonoil products and foreign markets has been slow to materialize.

In this chapter, several explanations have been offered to account for the mixed record of Mexico's diversification program. First, Mexican decisionmakers are too easily swayed by emotional issues originating in the historic pattern of relations with the United States. As a result, their decisions sometimes reflect an aversion to dependence on the United States, with only limited consideration given to the associated short-term costs and longer-term consequences. For example, Pemex has been constrained by the policy to keep crude oil sales to the United States down to a certain level. Oil export revenues could have been higher had Pemex increased these sales at a time when world oil demand is falling but U.S. crude oil imports are rising. Moreover, Pemex could have followed a more rational policy of market diversification. Alternatively, exporting crude oil to more than forty customers in more than twenty countries has not been a carefully planned strategy. As a result, important economic agreements such as with Japan were delayed for several years because Pemex could not deliver all the oil that the Japanese expected. Japan and Spain offer the best prospects to penetrate the Far Eastern and European markets in the 1990s. Pemex must therefore be more responsive to the oil import requirements articulated by these two important customers.

Second, Mexico, like many other developing nations, misread international economic signals and fell into similar errors. For example, several assumptions regarding the evolution of world oil prices and of other international economic trends were not accurate, affecting both the formulation and the outcomes of government policies. The pace and the scope of changes in these policies, which sought to respond to rapidly changing conditions in the world economy, were not sufficiently dynamic.

Third, inducing the business community to cooperate in the implementation of government policies that seek to diversify the profile of Mexico's foreign economic relations remains an unresolved issue. Paradoxically, the search for fresh approaches to reestablish self-sustained economic growth, as well as increasing difficulties within the U.S. economy, may provide business in developing countries the incentive for renewed efforts to achieve diversification. In particular, if protectionism continues to grow in the United States, it does not fall within the interest of Mexican businesses to target increased exports of nonoil products to that market alone. In fact, it may well be that their changing perceptions of opportunities available within foreign markets will prove more effective than the Mexican government's political-security considerations of recent years, in leading business to diversify Mexico's profile of foreign economic relations beyond the United States.

Notes

1. Jesús Agustín Velasco, *Impacts of Mexican Oil Policy on Economic and Political Development* (Lexington, Mass., 1983); Abel Beltrán, "El síndrome del petróleo mexicano. Primeros síntomas, medidas preventivas y pronósticos," *Comercio Exterior* 30:6 (1980), pp. 556–569; Gabriel Székely, "Recent Findings and Research Suggestions on Oil and Mexico's Development Process," *Latin American Research Review* 20:3 (1985), pp. 235–246.

2. México, Secretaría de Patrimonio y Fomento Industrial, *Programa de energia. Metas a 1990 y proyecciones al año 2000* (Mexico City, 1980). See also the November 1980 issue of the monthly bulletin *Energéticos*, published by the same government agency.

3. See the text of the speech by President López Portillo, on the occasion of the forty-second anniversary of the nationalization of the oil industry, in *Excelsior*, 19 March 1980. Also, Secretaría de Patrimonio y Fomento Industrial, *Plan nacional de desarrollo industrial, 1979–1982* (Mexico City, 1979), p. 40.

4. Gabriel Székely, *La economía política del petróleo en México, 1976–1982* (Mexico City, 1983).

5. Warner Baer and Malcom Gillis (eds.), *Export Diversification and the New Protectionism: The Experiences of Latin America* (Champaign, Ill., 1981). The editors of this volume argue in their introduction that these conditions are as important as effective foreign exchange and interest rate policies to promote export success.

6. For an excellent discussion of the relationship among trade, economic development, and national security, see Ronald I. Meltzer, "Contemporary Security Dimensions and International Trade Relations," in *Economic Issues and National Security*, edited by Klaus Knorr and Frank N. Tager (Kansas City, 1977), pp. 200–230; William Cline, *Exports of Manufactures from Developing Countries* (Washington, D.C., 1984); and his essay, "Can the East Asian Model of Development Be Generalized?," *World Development* 10:2 (1982), pp. 81–90. The problem of protectionism in industrial countries is addressed in the recent study of Shailendra Anjaria, Naheed Kirmara, and Arne Petersen, *Trade Policy Issues and Development* (Washington, D.C.,1985).

7. Hanns Maull, *Oil and Influence: The Oil Weapon Examined* (London, 1975); International Economic Studies Institute, *Raw Materials and Foreign Policy* (Washington, D.C., 1976); U.S. Senate Committee on Interior and Insular Affairs, *Geopolitics of Energy*, prepared by Melvin Conant and Fern Gold, (Washington, D.C., 1977); *Energy and Security*, edited by Joseph Nye and David Deese (Cambridge, Mass., 1981).

8. México, Secretaría de Patrimonio y Fomento Industrial, *Programa de*

energía. Metas a 1990 y proyecciones al año 2000 (Mexico City, 1980). See also the November 1980 issue of the monthly bulletin, *Energéticos,* published by the same government agency.

9. Raymond Vernon, "Trade and Investment in Mexico–United States Relations," in *U.S.-Mexico Relations. Economic and Social Aspects,* edited by Clark Reynolds and Carlos Tello (Stanford, Calif., 1983), pp. 167–180.

10. International Energy Agency, *Quarterly Oil and Gas Statistics* (Paris, various issues).

11. Pemex, *Memoria de labores* (Mexico City, various issues).

12. Daniel Levy and Gabriel Székely, *Mexico: Paradoxes of Stability and Change,* 2d ed. (Boulder, 1987), pp. 232–244; G. Székely, "México y el petróleo, 1981–1985. Crónica de amargas lecciones," *La Jornada,* 1 Sept. 1985.

13. Crude oil exports in June 1985 fell to 786,000 b/d, as reported by Pemex's director general in his *Informe anual* (Mexico City, 1986), p. 9.

14. U.S. Department of Energy, *Weekly Petroleum Status Report* (Washington, D.C., various issues)]

15. The best on-record discussion of Pemex's diversification goals and policies is found in México, Cámara de Diputados, Comité de Enérgeticos, "Reunión de trabajo con los directivos de Pemex encabezados por el Lic. Mario R. Beteta, Director General" (Mexico City, 11 Oct. 1985).

16. Alirio Parra, "OPEC in a Longer-Term Perspective,"*OPEC Review* 8(4), Winter 1984, pp. 6,7.

17. International Energy Agency, *Quarterly Oil and Gas Statistics* (Paris: First Quarter, 1987), p. 127.

18. Székely, *La economía;* Angelina Alonso and Roberto López, *El Sindicato de Trabajadores Petroleros y sus relaciones con PEMEX y el estado, 1970–1985* (Mexico City, 1986).

19. Pemex, *Anuario estadístico, 1986* (Mexico City, 1986), pp. 49, 59. A good study of the petrochemical industry in Mexico is Michele Snoeck's *La industria petroquímica básica en Máxico, 1970–1982* (Mexico City, 1986).

20. Pemex's interests in Petronor and Repsol are extensively reported in the monthly *PEMEX Bulletin* (Washington, D.C., Nov. 1987), pp. 1–3.

21. Pemex, *Third Evaluation Meeting. Four Years of Oil Management, 1983–1986* (Mexico City, 1987), p. 47.

22. S. Martínez G., "En 5 años, divisas por 15 mil millones de Dls.," *Excelsior,* 10 Sept. 1987, p. 1; *PEMEX Bulletin* (Washington, D.C., Nov. 1987), p. 3.

23. Noe Cruz, "PEMEX cede la petroquímica secundaria por ahorrar en importaciones y subsidios," *El Financiero,* 23 Sept. 1986, p. 23.

24. International Monetary Fund, *Direction of Trade Statistics* (Washington, D.C., various issues).

25. U.S. International Trade Commission, *Imports under Items 806.30 and 807.00 of the Tariff Schedules of the United States, 1982–1985* (Washington, D.C., Dec. 1986), p. 54; and U.S. General Accounting Office, *International Trade: Commerce Department Conference on Mexico's Maquiladora Program* (Washington, D.C., April 1987), p. 2.

26. Gabriel Székely and Donald Wyman, "Japan's Ascendance in U.S. Economic Relations with Mexico," *SAIS Review* 8(1) 1988, pp. 171–188.

27. *Survey of Current Business,* Aug. 1987, p. 85.

28. See I. M. Destler and John Odell, *The Politics of Antiprotection* (Washington, D.C., 1988).

29. Intense negotiations to encourage freer bilateral trade flows were initiated in January 1988, covering steel, textiles, agriculture, and service industries. See Office of the U.S. Trade Representative, "Framework of Principles and Procedures for Consultations Regarding Trade and Investment Relations" (Washington, D.C., 5 Nov. 1987).

30. This section is based on my paper "Canada and Mexico: Preliminary Notes on Their Energy Policies in the 1980s," in *Policy Issues and Perspectives on North American Natural Gas Trade*, edited by Henry Goldberg (Stanford, Calif., 1984), pp. 155–176.

31. The total investment amounted to U.S. $80 million. Pemex's relations with Spain's Petronor are the subject of a candid discussion between Pemex executives and the Energy Committee of Mexico's Congress, which took place and was made public on 11 Oct. 1985. See also Petronor, *Plan Estratégico, 1983–1992* (Bilbao, 1983).

32. France's proved uranium reserves amount to 56,200 tons, or 4 percent of reserves in the West. Australia holds 21 percent of the western world's total uranium reserves; South Africa, 13 percent; Canada, 12 percent; Brazil, 11 percent; and the United States, 9 percent (France, Ministere du Redeploiement Industriel et du Commerce Exterieur, *Les Chiffres Clés de L'Energie* [Paris: 1984], p. 104).

33. José Andrés Oteyza, "México y el mercado internacional del petróleo," *Energéticos* 5(6), 1981, pp. 27–28.

34. International Energy Agency, *Quarterly Oil and Gas Statistics* (Paris, 1986), p. 106.

35. This assessment is based on personal interviews conducted with British and French oil executives early in 1985.

Conclusion:
A Cost-Benefit Analysis of the
Oil Sector in Mexican Society

George Baker
PROFMEX, Berkeley, California

As Mexico moves toward a long-range, codevelopment strategy with the United States, few tasks are more urgent than a complete reappraisal of the role of the petroleum sector in Mexican society. This question is a broader one than the eternal question that has been posed on various occasions since the expropriation: How does Mexico improve the industrial, labor, marketing, and financial efficiency of the state oil industry in Mexico?[1]

Since the advent of the presidential administration of Miguel de la Madrid in 1982, Mexicans have seen dramatic changes in the administrative framework of Petróleos Mexicanos (Pemex), the state oil, gas, and petrochemical supply agency.[2] A characteristic of these changes has been their implementation by overnight presidential decree, not by discussions in the congress or in other public forums. The best example is the radical curtailment of the economic and political power of the Pemex labor union: In January 1984, a decree was issued that required government contracts for goods and services be awarded on the basis of public bidding and that subcontracting of awarded contracts was prohibited. The union, accustomed to receiving automatic awards of Pemex contracts, many of which would be performed by others, received a double blow. This setback, however, was mild compared to the devastation that took place five years later. In 1989, de la Madrid's successor ordered, first, in January, the incarceration of the top management team of the union and its replacement by progovernment elements; second, in July, the gutting of the prounion clauses of the Pemex-union labor contract; and, third, in August, the partial deregulation of a third of the previously state-reserved petrochemicals (a measure the deposed union leadership had loudly opposed).

Such changes made many Mexicans believe that a secret plan for the complete reorganization of the oil sector was in place, awaiting for its implementation only the right market and political conditions. Both admirers and critics of government policy believed that the long axis of such a plan was the reprivatization of the state petroleum industry. Clearly, in 1986 and 1989 the state moved toward privatization in the area of petrochemicals, but the agenda for other parts of the industry remains unclear. In 1991, Mexicans wanted to know if the government intended to put the oil industry on the table for discussion in a possible Free Trade Agreement (FTA) with the United States: the Mexican government categorically denied such intentions, but, owing to the multitiered meanings of government communications (what a Pemex official calls the "double language" of the state), most policy analysts believed that the FTA would be a convenient vehicle by which private capital would be invited into previously excluded areas of the financially failing oil sector.[3] Such a plan may or may not be in place, but the history of public sector planning, as we shall see below, suggests that an independent effort should be undertaken that would take as its frame of reference not merely management questions affecting Pemex, but overall questions affecting the society's commitment to a state oil sector.

An interdisciplinary, multi-institutional project should be undertaken toward the goal of providing for senior management in Pemex and other ministries of the Mexican government a carefully reasoned evaluation of the range of options for the oil sector in the next ten to twenty-five years. This effort should be a diagnostic evaluation of the cost-benefit environment, not only of Pemex activities, but of the total area of policy action by the state in matters relating to hydrocarbons.

Several basic questions must be asked in the beginning, questions such as: Is it possible to distinguish management issues in Pemex from management issues in the Mexican public sector at large? Does the government of Pemex differ in any material way from the government of Mexican society? Such questions pose difficulties beyond the reach of the present exercise, the narrow purpose of which is to provide a shopping list of ideas for further research, analysis, and reflection.

The general question that we want to raise is, What are the costs as well as the benefits associated with the status quo? We may take as a preliminary example of a cost the problem of planning in both Pemex and the public sector. This topic will also illustrate the difficulty of separating Pemex from the public sector for purposes of organizational and management analysis. Since the time of De la Madrid (1982–1988), Pemex has been required to issue five-year plans annually (e.g., 1983–1988, 1984–1989, 1985–1990, etc.). A careful reading of successive plans shows that in many respects they contain little in common. Why? The answer seems to be that the planning cycle in the public sector in Mexico is not six years (the presidential cycle) but one year; that is, at the end of each fiscal year there is an immense struggle over who gets what percentage of the budget. In Mexico, the struggle is not carried out between the Marines and the Air Force (as it might be in the U.S. Department of Defense) but between the invisible management teams (ITMs) that make up the real party politics in Mexico. Each year the ITMs struggle to put their people into public offices in the principal cabinet ministries in the federal government, and each year there is an invisible struggle between the competing ITMs over the allocation of the federal budget. Every fifth year there is a showdown between the ITMs, and the team controlling the most political and budgetary assets in the public sector wins the right to name the next president of Mexico. In such a rough-and-tumble political environment, budgets for both operations as well as capital projects are vulnerable targets for resizing. Because Pemex is one of the principal government agencies in which the struggle by competing ITMs takes place, no budget in Pemex has much validity beyond one year. In the oil business, to say that long-range planning does not extend beyond a year is to say that planning exists in name only.[4] Surely, the cost of having no credible planning process is high. The example of the absence of real planning illustrates the problem of a hidden cost of the status quo: the cost, however, is one that Mexican society pays in all of its public sector institutions, not just in the case of Pemex.[5]

We may now turn to examples dealing specifically with the oil sector. In his State of the Union address on 1 November 1990, President Salinas was cheered by congress when he reaffirmed the message that "the nation will maintain its ownership and full dominion over hydrocarbon resources," and that the "state will continue to exercise fully its exclusive responsibilities for the development of strategic areas in accordance with Article 28 of the Constitution." That the president should receive wide moral and political support for his basic policy for the oil sector is one of the benefits of the present institutional and juridical arrangements. In other words, the exclusive control of the oil sector provides the benefits of an outlet for nationalism and a vehicle by which citizens can express their loyalty to the person and office of the president of Mexico. If, by contrast, the oil sector were in private hands, then other outlets and symbols of nationalism would have to be developed.

A second advantage of the classical model of public administration (CMPA) in Mexico is the enhancement of national security. The classical model requires that the real locus of decision making be hidden from public view, while the decoy locus is given full exposure in the media, in the two houses of the federal congress, and in Pemex's tables of organization. The beneficent outcome for the Mexican state of having this model is threefold: First, no foreigner can gain access to the inner corridors of decision making, with the result that policymaking remains enigmatically, but surely, in Mexican hands.[6] A second benefit is that not even Mexican nationals (i.e., the middle, educated class) can penetrate the system any better than can the foreign investor or government. The result is that the tenure of the political class of Mexico goes unchallenged. Finally, having the real locus of authority buried means that no cost accountability rules can be applied to any individual decision maker.[7]

Let us turn to an example of the hidden costs of the present oil sector regime. In the oil boom, it was widely said that the state oil industry was the investment lever that produced future prosperity. Further, it was said that the oil sector was the virtual engine of economic growth for the country at large. In retrospect, it appears that these beliefs were both empirically and philosophically wrong. The philosophical error consisted in treating petroleum products as if they were final goods instead of intermediate goods. Gasoline has value to a motorist, not for being a combustible fuel with a certain number of calories and other physical properties, but because the motorist has a car in working order and a destination. Without having anywhere to go, the gasoline is a useless expense. Generalizing from this example, one concludes that it is a great philosophical mistake to view the oil industry as anything more than a vehicle for achieving one's real purposes. It doesn't work, therefore, to have the intermediate oil sector enshrined as if it were a final strategic goal or area in itself. From this perspective, it is lamentable that the president's freedom of maneuver in policy matters regarding petroleum is so narrowly framed. It would be one thing if the president could say, "Fellow Mexicans, our goal is to raise the average standard of living in Mexico to that of Eastern Europe within the next ten years—and our petroleum policy is designed to help us achieve this goal"; but it is a completely different matter to have, as the centerpiece of national policy, the continued state monopoly of the oil sector. The mistake, then, lies in confusing a means for an end.

The generic question that is suggested by this set of examples concerns the long-range options for the oil sector, options that would retain some of the advantages of the current system while shedding some of the disadvantages. The question cannot be answered satisfactorily merely by exercises intended to show how present arrangements might be made more efficient. The question demands that the blackboard be erased, and that future options be explored independently of present constitutional, regulatory, or policy constraints.

In order that it might serve as a base upon which other arrangements might be sought, our proposed study will begin by considering, if only in a preliminary way, the advantages and disadvantages of the present institutional arrangements.

Before beginning our preliminary overview of issues, we should pause at the concept of advantage. What is an advantage? An advantage is normally thought of as that which promotes the interests of an individual or group. An advantage for one implies, or at least suggests, a disadvantage for another. To speak of the advantages (or disadvantages) of alternative roles for the oil sector in Mexican society is an abstract, ambiguous goal: under the heading of "Mexican society" a multitude of contradictory conceptions could come to mind. If there is no single "Mexican society," it follows that there cannot be a single "role" of the oil sector.

Despite this disclaimer, there is a strong connection between the stability and continuity of the political system since 1938 and the management philosophy governing the oil sector. Expressed differently, the political system and the state oil sector are not independent variables: the one arises from and reinforces the other.[8] The oil sector is governed by an extremely conservative criterion, one that links national sovereignty, identity, and nationalism with the appearance of a publicly owned, vertically integrated supply agency (i.e., Petróleos Mexicanos).

Since the purpose of this exercise is neither partisan nor ideological, we have no interest in proposing "improvements" in the Mexican system of government in its broad outlines. Further, our starting point for thinking about what is, or is not, an advantage must be the acceptance—even immutability—of the general outline of Mexico's political culture. The target areas for our constructive criticism, then, refer to administrative policy and patterns of institutionality, and exclude larger questions, for example, whether it would be advantageous for Mexico to have a more democratic, open system of government. Such questions are important, but our intention is to ignore them as much as possible for the purpose of this exercise.

Our final caveat is this: a careful sociological or political analysis would distinguish between what is unique to the oil sector and what is common to the political or corporate culture of the Mexican government or Mexican society as a whole. This preliminary attempt to set forth an outline for discussion of long-range options for the oil sector[9] makes no effort to enforce this distinction; in consequence, some of what we shall call disadvantages of the present arrangements in the oil sector will be found in other sectors of government or society. Not for this reason, however, should they be ignored in the oil sector.

Advantages of the Present Arrangements, by Beneficiary

The advantages of the present arrangements in the oil sector are many. They benefit certain institutions in Mexican political society, above all, the institutions of the Office of the President and the Central Bank.

Other beneficiaries include oil union leaders, the automobile industry in Mexico, Pemex suppliers, and Mexican residential and industrial consumers of petroleum products. A preliminary list of advantages, grouped by beneficiary, would include the following.

The Official Party of the Mexican Political System

1. The first advantage is a strong, centrally controlled, union labor presence in the provinces that is responsive to the will of the president and that strengthens presidentialism in Mexico.[10]

2. The party serves as a symbol of national unity and sovereignty that is understandable by the common citizen.

3. Oil sector bureaucracies are an institutional training ground for upwardly mobile political leaders.[11]

4. Oil serves as the ace in the hand in U.S.-Mexican negotiations regarding virtually any topic, such as the Free Trade Agreement.

5. There is a centralization of fiscal authority and control over foreign-exchange earnings associated with exports of crude oil and petroleum products.

6. Domestic energy prices can be controlled through subsidies.

7. Pemex exists as a principal media icon in Mexico society and serves, in this capacity, as one of the major instruments of government in the Mexican state.[12] Mexican society is constantly, if subliminally, informed that in the petroleum sector the ship of state is well captained—and, by implication, political opposition to the status quo in any area of public policy is unnecessary.[13]

Opposition Parties

1. This is the obverse of point (2) above: since oil is the symbol of all Mexicans, all Mexicans—especially leaders of opposition parties—feel free to claim their interpretation of petroleum policies as the one most faithful to the legacy of Cárdenas and the Mexican Revolution. The present arrangements in effect give the opposition a free podium and microphone with which to criticize official policies and strategies.

National Economic Policy

1. The price of gasoline is used as a key indicator (second in importance only to the dollar exchange rate for the Mexican peso) of the stability of government economic policy. Containing the rise in the price of gasoline is an easy—if questionable, on ecological grounds—anti-inflationary measure.

2. Subsidies in the price of petroleum products can be readily granted and regulated to specific industries, regions, or consumer groups.[14]

3. Even though the general experience of Third World countries possessing substantial petroleum reserves is that, despite all the good intentions to the contrary, the economy, standard of living, and environmental quality all suffer as a consequence of the volatility of the oil market, there is no logical reason for this to be so. The economic growth of the United States in the twentieth century is attributable in part to an oil market and regulatory environment that promoted the development of the transportation and industrial sectors. This potential exists for Mexico: Mexican oil reserves should be an economic asset, not a curse.

Labor Union Leaders

1. Neither the oil union's own statutes nor the regulations of Pemex, the Labor Ministry, or the Federal Labor Law require transparent financial accountability of union funds. As a result, neither financial statements nor balance sheets are published for distribution to the members. This system allows for great freedom of maneuver in the allocation of assets by national and local labor leaders.

2. Corporate culture in the oil union—implicitly supported by Pemex (in the language of the labor contract as well as in practice)—gives leaders an extraordinary degree of control over the union workers.

Industry Groups

1. The Mexican automobile industry has been favored by the availability of cheap gasoline and little regulation. (Only in 1990 were catalytic converters required for new cars, and the use of unleaded gasoline as a motor fuel has barely begun.)

2. Propane distributors have long enjoyed a virtual monopoly on the residential market by successfully opposing the use of natural gas.

Full-Time Pemex Union Employees

1. The full-time union employee of Pemex (*de planta*) enjoys the economic status of the elite blue-collar job in Mexico; unique benefits include the right to retire at age fifty-five, the right to bequeath his employment in Pemex to a son or daughter, and the right to recommend a family member for Pemex employment.

2. The full-time worker earns about three times as much as his part-time colleague when future benefits such as retirement are converted to present values.

3. There is a historic pride in the folklore of the role of the petroleum

worker in the expropriation of the oil industry; Mexican society is thereby served by having certain professions identified with nationalistic causes.[15]

Yet these advantages, like the disadvantages, have not been described or quantified with any degree of precision. As a result, the cost of these advantages is not known, nor, therefore, are the parameters of alternative (i.e., cheaper) cost environments studied and discussed.

Disadvantages of the Present Arrangements, by Topic

Disadvantages of the present arrangements are also numerous. In this preliminary overview, we will expand on the disadvantages, not because there is hard evidence that indicates that, on balance, disadvantages outweigh advantages, but because such issues will need to be addressed in any long-term reassessment of the future role of the oil sector in Mexican society.

The list of disadvantages is not meant to be exhaustive, either in the list of general categories or in the list of items under each category. We have identified major disadvantages in a half-dozen areas, presented below.

Present Arrangements Encourage a False Sense of Collective Self-worth

1. The emphasis on the uniqueness of petroleum as a measure of economic independence is wholly misplaced. Countries such as Japan and Korea achieve their trade surpluses because of their zeal and innovative approach to serving international markets, not because of inert, subsoil assets.[16]

2. Having Pemex as the "national champion" of Mexican interests in international markets diminishes the public importance given to private sector exporters of goods and services, the agricultural exporters of the state of Sinaloa, for instance. The Mexican public, told countless times that Pemex is the most important "business" in Mexico, looks at normal businesses, even highly successful ones, with disdain; yet, Pemex is not a business at all in the managerial or accounting senses of the term.

The Lack of Institutionalization of Discussion of Petroleum Policy

1. In Mexico, public policy precedes—not follows—public discussion, not only in the oil sector but in all areas of government. It can be no surprise, therefore, that no institutional mechanisms for public discussion of petroleum policy exist. The absence of such mechanisms, however, represents a cost for Mexican society. Opposition to presidential initiatives in the oil sector is based mainly on ideological and

electoral considerations, not on economic or managerial ones. One result is that constructive criticism is taken as political maneuvering—in other words, trivialized.[17] Real debate, to the extent that it exists at all, is conducted in private.[18]

2. Even though outside criticism of the oil sector is regarded largely as the product of partisan, ideological pressure, it cannot entirely be ignored by the state. It is commonly said that the Salinas administration could not afford to publicly consider risk contracts with foreign oil companies because of the political advantage that opposition parties would thereby gain. This is another way of saying that the president of Mexico has inadequate room for maneuver in regard to policymaking in the petroleum industry.[19]

3. As a second result of the polarization and politicization of petroleum policy, policymakers and academics in Mexico are afraid to voice their views honestly in public out of fear that their "declarations" might be mistaken as having political, not economic or managerial, motives.[20] Unfortunately, the consequence is that there is a great silence around petroleum policy by persons who could render valuable contributions to a discussion of petroleum policy. The state, therefore, loses (perhaps needlessly) the input of persons whose observations and suggestions could have great benefit to the institution and the society.

4. In contrast to the lack of meaningful discussions of petroleum policy in Mexico, there is a large number of people on the public payroll in oil-related staff jobs.[21] Although every major ministry in Mexico has at least a small unit watching Pemex and the international oil market, there is no positive, cumulative effect from this redundant investment in human and institutional resources.[22] On the contrary, current practices breed institutional isolation and mutual suspicion. A common view is that the corporate cultures in Pemex and the Energy Ministry (Semip) virtually require noncooperative, antagonistic relationships.[23]

5. Academic input into petroleum policy is weak, almost nonexistent. Since the death of Miguel S. Wionczek in 1988 and the disbandment of his research center at El Colegio de México (and the loss of his invaluable archives), Pemex has given little or no support to the work of energy studies programs in Mexico.[24] To judge by the abridged content of the 1989 statistical yearbook, the possibility of academic input into petroleum policymaking will become more remote. The contents and new format of the publication represent a giant step backward (toward nontransparency) by its failure to provide the minimum of administrative and financial information concerning Pemex operations. As a result, energy analysts in Mexico are forced to rely primarily on mere newspaper clippings for information on Pemex operations and government

policy. While there may be a "special relationship" between the president of Mexico and the oil union, there certainly is no such relationship between Pemex and Mexican academic institutions.

6. Owing to the absence of pertinent quantitative and qualitative data and the lack of a forum in which petroleum policy and institutional practices can be discussed seriously, Pemex and the Mexican state are vulnerable to criticism in the public media, not only in Mexico, but in the United States, by persons who have nothing constructive to say.[25] Reporting on Pemex in the local Mexican press often lacks intellectual integrity:[26] Official publications report only innocuous statistics, while other, nonofficial publications like *Proceso* make a business publishing articles dealing principally with alleged acts of corruption by Pemex or union officials. The nature of the present "placement" of the oil sector in Mexican society is the principal cause of this lack of substantive, intellectual debate about oil sector issues.

Deteriorating Public Confidence or Trust in Government Institutions and Policies

1. While members of congress and the general public might applaud the president's posture regarding the juridical-constitutional framework for the oil sector, the public's impression of the management of Pemex itself is not positive.[27]

2. The public's impression is that Pemex employment in union positions is commercially brokered by union officials, thereby throwing doubt over the real value of labor organizations in Mexican society in general.

3. The uneven quality of some Pemex products, such as gasoline and certain petrochemicals,[28] gives rise to the belief that there is no operational auditing for quality in Pemex. Are there quality-control auditing units in Pemex that employ random-sampling methods? If so, they do not seem to have sufficient authority even to appear in organizational charts.

4. The point that government price subsidies for petroleum products were responsible for environmentally dangerous patterns of overconsumption has been emphasized in the public media.

5. Not emphasized, however, is the fallacious character of the premise that economic growth (GDP) needs to be accompanied by increased energy consumption; that is, the notion that, for each additional dollar of GDP, so many additional kilocalories of petroleum will have to be consumed.

The Valley of Mexico has long since passed the point, environmentally speaking, at which growth can be thought of as having a positive correlation with the consumption of petroleum. Once the cost of the health and environmental burdens and accompanying productivity losses associated with the burning of a liter of gasoline or fuel oil are taken into account, the true cost of petroleum products probably far exceeds the corresponding export price of crude oil; in the Valley of Mexico, therefore, it is likely that there is a negative coefficient between petroleum-product consumption and economic development.[29]

Low Morale and Esprit de Corps in Pemex

1. With the exception of the Díaz Serrano period (1977–1981), morale in Pemex among the rank and file has been low since the late 1940s, owing to diverse causes.[30] One reason is that union authorities, thanks to the so-called exclusionary clause (Articles 34 and 35), have overwhelming power to intimidate and control union workers. Another reason is that, since mid-1981, no chief executive officer of Pemex has had professional qualifications in the oil industry. Having nonindustry appointees in the top Pemex job means that workers (union as well as nonunion) do not look to this individual, either in his person or office, for real leadership. On the contrary, this individual is seen as a mere go-between or message center, through whose office pass instructions from other ministries such as Hacienda, SPP, Semip, SRE, Secofi, Bank of Mexico, and the Office of the President.

2. Long-standing support by Pemex management and the state of antidemocratic rule by union bosses has led to an attitude of defeatism among unionized workers.

3. The unpredictability of the work schedule in Pemex is a nightmare for many employees, who complain that they have no guaranteed private life that is not subject to interruption by supervisors who make capricious demands on their time outside of normal working hours (7:30 a.m.–3:30 p.m.). At Pemex's headquarters, top-level managers arrive at work at 10:00 a.m., while middle managers arrive at 9:00 a.m. Pemex staffers complain that staff meetings have been called as late as 2:00 a.m. merely to satisfy the whim of their boss.[31]

4. The performance review process for politically appointed officials in Pemex is either weak or nonexistent. There have been cases in which appointees at the vice-presidential or division manager levels develop cult-of-personality traits,[32] and in consequence create around them a group of courtesans made up of yes-men and yes-women.[33]

5. Career managers in Pemex are also discouraged by the personnel rotation system that exists at the upper levels of Pemex. They know that

the director general and the deputy directors regard their positions as political appointments, the term of office of which at most will be six years. In fact, rumors of personnel changes are continuous, leaving the permanent, career staff with the uneasy feeling that their superiors have but a transient interest in their jobs and subordinates. Career staffers view political appointees as being interested primarily in receiving the economic rewards of Pemex employment.

Dissent and open questioning are discouraged. There is no culture of rewarding employees who take the initiative in their jobs; on the contrary, such employees risk sudden job transfers as punishment. Professionals who challenge the conclusions of their politically appointed superiors—even on technical matters—risk harassment and the threat of a loss of pay and employment.[34]

Another aspect of this uneasiness is the impression by career professionals in Pemex that the intellectual integrity of their work is not trusted by the political appointees to the top jobs. Career professionals point to the practice of awarding major consulting contracts to foreign firms such as McKinsey & Company, SRI International, and Chem Systems; they believe that such corporate xenophilia (in Mexico called *malinchismo*) arises from a distrust in the ability of Pemex professionals to give timely and impartial analysis of topics of top management interest.

6. Mexican public institutions are not guided by the principle that the public has a right to information.[35] As a result, there is no working distinction between public and confidential information: Mexican public institutions—and Pemex leads on this score—tend to treat *all* information as if it were confidential. The result is that analysts—both within and outside of Pemex—exhaust themselves on the task of finding out information of minor importance. There is insufficient energy available afterward for serious analytical work.

There is, then, virtually no sharing of information and insights inside Pemex among upstream, downstream, and staff organizations. The E&P Department (Producción Primaria) is the most hermetic unit in Pemex, and behaves as if it were philosophically opposed to collaborating with Pemex's Planning Department. As one result, the internal studies of the two departments often share little in common, as if they belonged to different organizations.

7. The present institutional arrangements make the corporate culture of Pemex that of a cost center, not that of a profit center. While the Mexican treasury may make "profits" from the export of crude oil, this fact does not make the driving force of Pemex that of a profit-seeking organization. As a result, neither managers nor workers are motivated to

seek greater levels of efficiency or cost-reduction steps. The legendary "inefficiency" of Pemex arises as a by-product of the lack of a profit motive (or its equivalent) at the level of the manager or worker.[36]

Controversial Management and Engineering Practices in Pemex and Other Agencies

1. Pemex is described as a business in the Mexican press and in official publications, but, befitting the mentality of a state monopoly, it is a business without any sales agents. True, there are sales clerks who take orders for Pemex's crude oil, natural gas, and refined products, including petrochemicals, but a sales clerk does no selling. No one in the Republic of Mexico or anywhere else has had a salesperson make an office call saying, "I'm from Petróleos Mexicanos. Here's a color brochure and price list of our products. How can we serve you?"[37]

2. Reservoir management policy in Pemex should be a matter for public discussion, at least to judge by the standards of a number of other state oil-exporting countries. At what rate are the Campeche and Reforma fields being produced in relation to the rate that would yield maximum cumulative production? The lack of discussion and data on this crucial topic promotes speculation that the fields are being run at their "surge capacity," which is not sustainable without water damage to the fields.[38]

3. A more general formulation of this problem concerns the evaluation of the time frame that should correspond to a given public investment. Regarding natural resources, the implicit interest rate applicable to a public investment should ordinarily be low enough to justify the criterion of maximum cumulative recovery of a resource. When, in the case of Pemex, top managers are in office six years or less, there is unavoidable pressure toward taking a much shorter time frame and a correspondingly higher implicit interest rate. It is commonly said that in Díaz Serrano's time at Pemex (1977–1981), there was so much pressure to achieve production goals that the criterion of maximum, cumulative production from a well was routinely sacrificed in favor of greater current output. Such policies, when they exist, favor the present generation at the expense of future generations.

4. The official oil reserve picture as reported by Pemex is not credible to a number of (anonymous) Pemex production engineers. The basic logic can be shown using round numbers: Separate the 70 bn bbl (billion barrels) of hydrocarbon reserves in 1981 into two groups, Reforma-Campeche and Chicontepec. (Regarding Chicontepec, no one seriously believes that with today's prices, technology, and investment requirements, the oil resources in this region can be developed commercially.)[39]

If Chicontepec has roughly 15 bn bbl of hydrocarbons, then Reforma-Campeche (and other fields) has 55 bn bbl. The recovery rate that was assigned to Reforma-Campeche for the oil in place was 40 percent, meaning that approximately 137.5 bn bbl of petroleum were believed to be in the ground, of which 40 percent would be recovered. Since 1981, however, the working estimate for the effective recovery rate has been lowered to 25–30 percent, owing largely to the absence of effective methods of secondary (to say nothing of tertiary) recovery. If the original oil in place was 137.5 bn bbl, and if, since 1981, about 15 bn bbls of oil and gas equivalent have been produced, then 25–30 percent of 122.5 (137.5–15) is between 31 and 37 bn bbl.[40] If petroleum production continues in the range of 1 bn bbl/year, then the adjusted reserve to production ratio is in the range of thirty-two to thirty-eight years, not fifty-four years as the official figure indicates.

5. The lower reserve outlook is troublesome in the light of (1) the rapid growth of domestic demand for petroleum products and (2) the absence of a vigorous program of exploration and development that would discover and develop new reserves. A 1989 internal Pemex study suggested that, should domestic demand continue to rise—and absent new production—Mexican oil exports could fall to zero by 1997. Other studies suggest other, more distant, dates at which Pemex will become a net importer of crude oil. *Any* date in the next twenty-five years, however, is a serious setback given Mexico's need for an easy-to-sell export product for foreign markets.[41]

6. The outlook for natural gas is dim. A 1989 internal study of Pemex suggested that more fuel oil should be burned to save on natural gas; but such a proposal is completely counterintuitive from an environmental perspective. Despite high production (in the area of 3.5 bcfd [billion cubic feet/day]) and reserves (73 tcf) in 1990, very little natural gas actually reaches the marketplace; an unreasonably high percentage is consumed in Pemex's petrochemical and refinery operations.

It makes little sense, except on ideological grounds, to send natural gas through a pipeline from the state of Tabasco to industrial users in Monterrey, which is just a short distance from Texas gas fields. On ecological grounds, the major South-North pipeline should be turned off in favor of making the gas available to the Valley of Mexico; the North, meanwhile, would be supplied from Texas as well as from new dry gas fields in Mexico near the U.S.-Mexico border.

Some U.S. geologists believe that substantial deposits of nonassociated natural gas lie on the Mexican side of the border as extensions of U.S.-side fields. Because of the bottlenecks in Pemex's budgetary process for capital spending in exploration and production, the development of such fields is beyond Pemex's reach or interest. Pemex is basically a southeastern oil company; what happens (or fails to happen) in the North is of secondary concern.

7. Many people believed that the 18 March refinery in metropolitan Mexico City, which was closed in 1991, should have shut down years ago on environmental grounds, with additions to the Tula refinery making up the difference. As of 1990, the refinery had not had a major overhaul in twenty-five years, and, by all measures, its presence in the major metropolitan area of Mexico was an anachronism.

8. The absence of an effective smog emissions test program for cars and trucks in the Valley of Mexico is likely based on the realistic assumption that 85–95 percent of the tested vehicles would fail such a test, if, for example, California standards were used.[42] Not having effective smog emissions tests (and enforcement) for vehicles means, in effect, that virtually nothing is being done to correct the rapidly deteriorating air quality of the Valley of Mexico.[43]

9. Some critics say that professional training levels are inadequate and conducive to serious inefficiencies in Pemex's exploration and development programs. For example, one U.S. Pemex supplier estimated the number of wells drilled in a year by a single Pemex rig was 2.5, while in the United States the comparable figure would be 6.5. In the view of this supplier, Pemex's problem in the upstream area arises from inadequate physical and human infrastructure—from mud systems to professional training.[44]

Pemex Sends Negative Signals to Some Prospective Foreign Investors

1. The partial deregulation of the petrochemical industry by the Salinas administration in July 1989 did not produce the expected level of interest among foreign investors.[45] Why? Various explanations were offered. One widely held view was that the basic industry arrangement in Mexico is too laden with risk to be of interest to the foreign investor. Further, the regulatory maze is too complicated and restrictive.[46]

With the opening in 1990 and 1991 of discussions of a Free Trade Agreement (FTA) between Mexico, the United States and possibly Canada, officials from U.S. chemical trade organizations argued in private to the International Trade Commission (ITC) that unless the Mexican state dropped its restrictions against the private manufacture of any petrochemical in Mexico, the U.S. organizations would lobby against an FTA with Mexico.[47]

The restrictions consist in the state having a monopoly over certain (twenty in 1990) commercially strategic petrochemicals (called "basic" in Pemex's ideolect), the regulation that requires that a foreign investor find a 60 percent Mexican partner for other petrochemicals, and no requirements for a third group of petrochemicals. This system restricts the market flexibility of the privately operated plant; in many cases, the marginal cost of producing "forbidden" petrochemicals would be small, with correspondingly good returns on investments.

The alternative offered by the Salinas administration is to allow foreign firms to invest in turnkey plants (using their technology) that Pemex would subsequently operate. The investor would be paid, with interest, in product shipped from the plant.[48]

The basic arrangement also requires the foreign investor to be overwhelmingly dependent on Pemex for the (1) quality, (2) price, and (3) delivery schedule of feedstock, with no guarantees that Pemex's future pricing policies would be competitive by international standards. In other words, the success or failure of a new investment could hinge, not on the standards of excellence maintained by management in the areas of production, sales, and administration, but on unpredictable swings in Pemex's pricing policies for natural gas and other energy and petrochemical products.[49]

Oil Sector Communications and a Possible Free Trade Agreement

1. During the negotiations and posturings related to a possible Free Trade Agreement (FTA) between the United States and Mexico (and which also might include Canada), an overwhelming amount of attention was placed on the matter of the oil sector: Would Mexico open up the oil sector (including petrochemicals) to U.S. investors? Large quantities of ink were spilled on both sides of the border speculating on this question. The Mexican government officially said "absolutely not," but unofficially there were hints and rumors that the matter was quietly "on the table," as the jargon of the day put it.

Such speculations—and the mood that they created—resulted only in mutual suspicions and an unwillingness on both sides to communicate. (Mexicans invoked the term *constitución* with such frequency that the attentive English-speaking listener was forced to conclude that the cognate translation, constitution, was hardly adequate: By *constitución* Mexicans mean the recapitulation of the whole of Mexico's past, not just the document signed on 5 February 1917.)[50] On the U.S. side, the unwillingness to communicate took the form of "classified" (noncirculating) documents submitted to the International Trade Commission (ITC) by representatives of the American chemical industry. One of these documents, completed in August 1990, was a "statement of principles." One would have thought such a statement would be an open document setting forth ideas and points for discussion.

A similar cat-and-mouse game of information hiding took place on the

Mexican side: in early 1991, a study board from the U.S. government was told on the eve of its departure for two weeks of interviews in Mexico City that its key appointments in Pemex and the Petrochemical Commission had been canceled. Observers explained that, in view of the upcoming negotiations, the Mexican government had instructed officials, "Don't make any statements for the record about anything that could be linked to the negotiations."[51] The attitude of the Mexican government was that free trade with the United States did not begin with a free exchange of ideas, data, and impressions.

Conclusion

We have two questions and two preliminary conclusions:

Question: If it is true that the average standard of living of Mexican citizens living in Mexico was lower in 1990 than it was in 1900 (taking quality of life, including environmental quality and infrastructure adequacy into account), the question must be raised as to the extent to which the regulatory framework for the oil sector speaks to the need to improve the standards of living of the mass of the Mexican people. Our impression is that the regulatory framework completely bypasses such concerns.

Question: Is there any basis for believing that the profound philosophical and political gulf (what Mexicans call the lack of *confianza*) between business and government in Mexico will change, even in the long run? If the answer is in the negative—and most data point in that direction—there can be no expectation that the Mexican government will ever seek to promote real efforts at quantifying unit costs of its products and services. If the government can't—or won't, and it amounts to the same thing—tell the public how much it costs to bring a liter of gasoline to the pump, then it cannot expect the private sector to be forthcoming. As an example of the notorious lack of *confianza* and data, the Chemical Manufacturing Association (ANIQ) in Mexico City conspicuously published in its 1990 statistical yearbook the amount of capitalization of each member company—as if to suggest the seriousness of the investment commitment to Mexico by the company; the amount, however, was given in pesos of the (unspecified) year in which the company was founded.[52] An investment of 100 million pesos in 1975 was the equivalent of $8 million, but in 1990 it was the equivalent of less than $34,000. With both sides hiding real data (or, worse, not collecting it in the first place), neither side will be able to convince the other of any measure of industrial, financial, or marketing efficiencies. With neither side showing progress that is statistically credible, substantive cooperation between Pemex and industry is likely to remain an unrealistic expectation.

Our first conclusion is that the Mexican constitution-framers of 1917 anticipated a budgetary framework of possibilities for the future that has not materialized. In opting—precipitiously, historians of the period tell us—for expropriation in 1938, President Lázaro Cárdenas believed that the Mexican state would have sufficient investment capital to fund Mexico's future needs in the areas of exploration and production of oil, gas, and petrochemicals. It is nothing against General Cárdenas's reputation as a nationalist and nation-builder that he should have been wrong on this score.

We may take the petrochemical sector as an example. In 1990–1991, common estimates of the future needs of the state petrochemical sector were in the area of $5 billion; according to industry observers in Mexico, without an investment of this magnitude Mexico would have to spend $10–12 billion on imports of those products that were reserved to the state. No one in Pemex or elsewhere in the Mexican government has suggested for a moment that Pemex's petrochemical/natural gas division will receive a capital budget of anything near $5 billion. From where, then, will the investment money come? Not from private banks, which are gun-shy of oil-keyed loans to Mexico; nor from the private sector prepaying for the output of these plants in order to fund their construction.[53] The private sector continues to worry about the arbitrariness of the Mexican concept of "basic" petrochemicals.[54] Evidently, what needs to take place in Mexico is a complete rethinking of the regulatory environment *in ways that match regulations with funding capabilities.*

Our second overall impression is that Mexico has both over- and underinvested in the oil sector. At the symbolic level, at the level of metaphor, Mexico has overinvested in the oil sector: the weight of the historical and ideological baggage is too hard to pull.[55] Mexico's investment in the oil metaphor has produced a blind eye toward alternative symbols, institutions and patterns and strategies of economic development. The explanation for this overinvestment is to be found in political, not industrial, concerns on the part of the Mexican state. The question we wish to raise is this: Are there alternative, less costly, and more efficient approaches to managing the oil sector in Mexican society?[56]

At the level of fixed assets, Pemex's record is mixed, but, in general, there has been a pattern of underinvestment,[57] above all in the area of environmental protection.[58] In some areas, notably in refinery technology, unit-cost accounting, and environmental protection, Pemex suffers serious problems of underinvestment.[59] Unleaded gasoline was produced for the first time for the national market only in 1990. There are parts of the oil crescent of Mexico, which extends from Ciudad Madero in the North to Ciudad del Carmen in the South, where severe environmental damage has occurred from Pemex operations.

The development of future options for the petroleum sector in Mexican society should reduce or eliminate most of the notable disadvantages (those listed here as well as others) of present patterns and institutions. In today's Mexico, there are professionals both in industry and in government who are acutely aware of the inadequacies of present regulatory precepts and management and budgetary practices. Unfortunately, owing to the close identification in the public's mind between petroleum and presidential policy, it would be risky for for highly qualified persons in Mexico to participate publicly in a serious reassessment of the oil sector. Not for this reason, however, should public and corporate policymakers in Mexico and abroad lose heart: the quality of international listening to the pulse of the Mexican oil sector has improved since 1980–1981, when international bankers stumbled over each other in search of oil-keyed loans.

As psychotherapists, parents, and good managers know, serious listening has the power to change. How far the Salinas administration, its successors—and their critics—succeed in taking up this challenge of reshaping the state oil sector to conform to the realities of capital budgeting in the years ahead will be determined, in good measure, by the quality of informed listening on the part of foreign governments and international management.

Notes

This chapter seeks to provide a preliminary diagnostic outline for future collaborative research and consultations in Mexico's petroleum sector. It is compiled from field interviews in Mexico City and elsewhere, in industry as well as in the public and academic sectors, during 1985–1991.

1. Fabio Barbosa, "Informe sobre la reconversión de la industria petrolera en México" (Mexico City, 1991, typescript). The history of the successive government diagnostic studies of the oil sector has not been written in detail. The earliest such study took place before the expropriation, in 1930–1931, during the Calles period. Cárdenas ordered a diagnostic reappraisal in the aftermath of the expropriation, as did Miguel Alemán in 1945. Other such reappraisals were conducted during the presidencies of Luis Echeverría (1970–1976), José López Portillo (1976–1982), and Miguel de la Madrid (1982–1988). Additional discussion is in Isidro Morales, chapters 7 and 8, "La expansión 'hacia afuera' de la industrial nacionalizada (1974–1982)," and "El rostro del 'Nuevo Pemex,'" in Lorenzo Meyer and Isidro Morales, *Petróleo y nación: política petrolera en México (1900–1987)* (Mexico City: Fondo de Cultura Económica, 1990), pp. 174–238.

Institute of Latin American Studies

31 Tavistock Square

London WC1H 9HA

2. Chapter 11, "Prospect," of George Baker, *Mexico's Petroleum Sector* (Tulsa: PennWell, 1984), pp. 163–174, provides a discussion of the critique of the public oil sector carried out by the De la Madrid transition team in 1982.

3. To speak of Pemex's finances as a distinct entity is something of a paradox, even an oxymoron. The bulk of Pemex's income is taken away by the state under a dubious concept of "Tax on the Production of Hydrocarbons [DEH]," but the concept of a tax is stretched when applied by the state to a state-owned enterprise. Pemex turns its substantial foreign exchange revenue over to the treasury with great fanfare as if to suggest indirectly that such is the benefit to the Mexican people of the 1938 expropriation. Pemex, which has no control over its own budgets, is eternally in financial straits because the Government set it up that way.

4. Private sector investors in the petrochemical industry seem to intuitively feel that Pemex's statements of its plans to provide "basic" petrochemical feedstocks for future domestic demand cannot be relied upon, at least for investment purposes.

5. Government of Mexico, Secretaría de Energía, Minas e Industrial Paraestatal, *Programa nacional de modernización energética, 1990–1994* (Mexico City, January 1990). In the Mexico of President Carlos Salinas much is made of the idea of modernization, by which is meant the strengthening of infrastructure. Goals, such as enhanced productivity and energy savings, are enunciated, but only in qualitative terms, without budgets.

6. This advantage for the Mexican state produces a nightmare for the prospective foreign investor who wants to meet the person in Pemex (or elsewhere in the Mexican government) who has the power to decide the fate of his proposed project.

7. From 1983–1988, Jorge Díaz Serrano, the highly acclaimed head of Pemex during the oil boom of 1977–1981, served five years in a federal penitentiary for "deciding" to divert $34 million of public funds to private hands. Informed public opinion in Mexico is divided as to his guilt: Most persons believe that his conviction (by a nonjury trial) was symbolic: he would serve as the sacrificial lamb to expiate the excesses of the former presidential sexennium. Others believe that he was guilty as charged, but with an explanation: he was obeying orders from above (i.e., the Mexican White House). Beyond such bizarre cases (another such case was the decision to expropriate the foreign oil companies in 1938), little documentation exists as to the authorship of any specific decision in Mexico's public sector.

8. To suggest that the political system arose from the oil sector may seem whimsical. The fiscal existence of the Spanish Crown was based in large measure on the theory that subsoil wealth belonged to the state which, in turn, granted economic concession to entrepreneurs. The Mexican state defined by the Constitution of 1917 adopts this type of mercantilistic framework in which the state has wealth, not by virtue of the productivity and international competitiveness of its citizens and businesses, but by virtue of being the literal owner of precious metals and metal-equivalent substances.

9. In fact, we are not pointing out long-range options; rather, we are suggesting that there are strengths and weaknesses in the status quo that should be borne in mind by persons seeking to think about options.

10. Having a union labor monopoly in Pemex overcomes a serious problem of the 1920s and 1930s when, as the research of Jonathan Brown and others amply demonstrates, competing labor unions in the oil sector competed for power in ways that caused violence and economic disruption to the economy at large. Having multiple labor unions in the oil sector also meant that the sector was vulnerable to manipulation by ex-presidents and other high political figures who wanted to gain leverage in the political system (said of Calles in relation to the Cárdenas administration).

11. For example, former president Miguel de la Madrid (1982–1988) served briefly as vice-president for finance for Pemex. President Carlos Salinas had a substantial assignment in the oil sector when he was in the Ministry of Planning and Programming: he devised the new regulations regarding bidding in state industries, the not-so-hidden purpose of which was to break the virtual monopoly enjoyed by the oil union in Pemex contracts. President José López Portillo gained working experience related to the oil sector while at the Electric Power Commission (CFE) and at the Treasury Department.

12. A media icon is an intermediate product (were it a petrochemical chain) or a virtual reality (were it a mainframe computer) that exists as a temporary, but indispensable, reality in the process of governing Mexico. It is a projection onto the screen of public awareness of images that buttress the political status quo in Mexico. The projection process is accomplished not only by statements but by actions and their subsequent media handling. For this reason, a media icon seems to be a richer, if more elusive, phenomenon than that referred to by the term "party line" as used by Sovietologists.

13. Who could reasonably argue with a government whose vision and capabilities could be described in the following terms: "With such accomplishments [an itemization of record outputs of petrochemicals], Pemex continues its efforts to modernize and broaden its petrochemical infrastructure in conformity with the policy guidelines of the Federal Government, toward the end of optimally responding to the challenges of industrial development in our country" (taken from a Pemex press release, 326/90, dated 8 Nov. 1990)?

14. Such subsidies may come to be limited by the rules of GATT, which Mexico joined in 1986.

15. The cost of this "service," however, has not been estimated.

16. At a press conference at the Foreign Press Club in Mexico City on 1 March 1991, a reporter asked, "Isn't it true that the U.S. Government is seeking to take possession of the wealth of Mexico?" The speaker replied, "In what do you consider the wealth of Mexico to consist?" "Why, in our subsoil resources," was the response. The speaker answered, "You are thinking in colonial terms, when New Spain was valued by the Spanish Crown as a place from which to extract gold and silver; today such a conception of the economic role of Mexico in the modern world is an anachronism."

17. A sociologist of education might well ask: Where, in Mexico's system of public education, are children of the next generation of leaders taught how to listen to and accept criticism? In both the private as well as the public sector, there is a tendency to regard criticism as inherently negative, that is, as a political act committed by one or another competing *equipo* (clique). The oil sector, then, only dramatizes a tendency that is found throughout Mexican society.

18. In Mexico of the 1980s, the prominent critic of oil sector policies was Ing. Heberto Castillo, a civil engineer who educated himself about oil industry issues. Coincidentally, Castillo is also a prominent member of the Opposition, the effect of which is that his constructive criticism can safely be ignored by government policymakers. There is, at present, no way to bring the ideas and analysis of persons like Castillo into the policymaking process.

19. La Quina limited the president's maneuvering room in the petrochemical subsector to less than "a millimeter." It took La Quina's incarceration for the president to have the freedom to privatize much of the state petrochemical industry.

20. A former Pemex employee told me on 7 Nov. 1990 that Pemex officials had strenuously objected to his being interviewed in the press by a reporter who was writing a story on labor issues in Pemex. Officials said such "declarations" were inappropriate, and that, for the welfare of Pemex and, indeed, the physical safety of the worker, it was imperative that he be relocated out of Mexico City immediately.

21. A good deal of redundancy exists; for example, the Petroleum Institute [IMP], the Foreign Ministry [SRE], and the Energy Ministry [Semip] all have employees whose job it is to cut articles from the Mexican press about current developments in Pemex and the international oil market.

22. One Pemex analyst ironically asked, "What percentage of Mexico's PIB (gross domestic product) goes into cutting out clippings from the Mexican press on Pemex?"

23. The ongoing fight between Pemex chief Jorge Díaz Serrano and Energy Minister José Andrés de Oteyza in 1980–1981 resulted in a commercial catastrophe for Pemex and the nation when the oil market changed in June of 1981.

24. One such program had not even received a copy of Pemex's 1989 statistical yearbook a month after it had been released.

25. A good example of Pemex mud-slinging abroad is found in the writings of Christopher Whalen, cited in *El Financiero* (29 Oct. 1990, p. 44) under the *amarrillista* title of "Pese a contar con reservas por más de 50 mil mdb de combustible, Pemex, al borde del colapso." In the original article, published in the widely read business publication *Barron's* (22 Oct. 1990), Whalen stated that Pemex's commercial deficit in 1989 was a billion dollars, where, in fact, it was $238 million. Of the half-dozen figures cited by Whalen for Pemex's trade in refined products, all but one were incorrect.

26. One should not be a purist about "intellectual integrity": at stake is survival. In 1990, one leading Mexican newspaper declined to publish an op ed piece on Pemex that took the form of a fictional report from Pemex as if to its shareholders. The editor told the reporter that "our relations with Pemex are not very cordial right now, owing to the stories that we have been running lately. We don't want any more trouble from them."

27. The scandals of corruption in Pemex (as well as elsewhere in the public sector) during the Oil Boom have had a lasting effect on public perceptions. Rumors of corruption continue to circulate: in February 1991, a sales representative for a U.S. oil field equipment supplier reported that his company was not getting orders from Pemex's purchasing department because he had not been authorized to offer the necessary kickback, which was calculated as a percentage

of the value of the order.

28. According to one report, the use of MBTE in Pemex refineries in the making of better burning gasoline is not going well. Pemex does not publish information regarding the quality of its gasoline (e.g., octane, lead content, vapor pressure). Occasionally, price increases in gasoline will be announced along with the notice that "gasoline quality has been improved"—but in which respect or by how much is never said.

29. The program to take cars out of circulation in Mexico City one day of the work week is an implicit recognition of the negative effect of gasoline consumption on the valley's productivity and standard of living; no one has suggested that productivity in the Federal District has dropped by 20 percent thanks to taking private automobiles out of circulation one day Monday through Friday.

30. Partially counterbalancing the loss of self-esteem among the rank and file as a result of government co-optation of union leadership is a pride of guild membership. At least one Mexican scholar believes that, among the oil union membership, pride outweighed fear up until the calamitous events of 1989: the incarceration of the union leadership and the sharp reversal in the collective bargaining agreement.

31. Pemex is sometimes described as the "employer of last resort" for officials from other government agencies who lose their jobs from political in-fighting. As one staffer put it, "Pemex often is forced to hire the 'politically unemployed.'"

32. One politically appointed official, who came to Pemex during the administration of Miguel de la Madrid, developed a wide reputation for management-by-monologue. This able, if controversial, official was said to be of the kind who did not brook independent thought by his subordinates.

33. Sexual harassment (by U.S. standards) was part of life in most Pemex offices for low-level secretarial jobs during the period of union patronage that ended in early 1989. Since then, conditions have improved, in part because such low-level jobs were not replaced when vacancies occurred and in part because the new union leadership did not insist on sexual favors as the coin of Pemex hiring. The term *amiga* (or *amiguita*) is used to refer to women who date married senior managers. One career professional related how in his department a foreign client was scheduled to have a late dinner (*cena*) with a corporate vice-president; the vice-president passed the task to a top manager, who, in turn, passed it on to the career professional. "About 11 p.m. the manager joined us at the restaurant, intoxicated and in the company of one of his *amigas*." The way in which this professional told this story showed clearly that his superior had a reputation for such behavior, and that there was no personnel review process that could correct it.

34. One career professional related that in 1990 he was told that owing to ongoing disagreements with a corporate vice-president he should resign from Pemex, failing which he would see the benefits from his paycheck disappear. These benefits included various classes of overtime (TEA and TEO), as well as performance bonuses, which together made up over half of his salary. When he protested, saying that it was against the Federal Labor Law, the person acting for the VP said, viciously, "It may be against anything you like, but that's what's going to happen to you." The professional's take-home pay subsequently was cut in half; only by luck did he find a position in another department in Pemex.

Another Pemex engineer, at the time a member of the oil union, had the misfortune to be quoted in the Mexican press in early 1989 about Pemex's new anti-union policies. The following day he was taken off his job in Mexico City and driven to Guadalajara: He was told that "it would be best if you were not in Mexico City for a period." Despite his having a permanent position, within a year (and without any sort of personnel hearings or review) he was without a job in Pemex.

35. There is no Freedom of Information Act in Mexico. Pemex's public information policy is vulnerable to the whims of political managers who, without explanation or discussion, cease reporting data from one year to the next; for example, Pemex's statistical yearbook for 1989 (issued in 1990) was about a third the size of the volumes of the previous fifteen years. In the view of some Pemex career professionals the only justification for such a wholesale cutting back in data reporting was to satisfy the issuing official's personal desire to have a monopoly on data that could be used to analyze Pemex's internal policies (in areas such as wages and personnel).

36. The absence of profit-mindedness came about in large part because of the absence of a real cost accounting system, a deficiency that, one hopes, the consultations of McKinsey & Company (1988–1991) will go a long way to correct. There are three inherent weaknesses in the firm's advice to Pemex: (1) The firm lacks a foundation of understanding of the history and politics of the oil sector in Mexico, (2) the haughty, gachupine style of the young, MBA managers sent by McKinsey results in resentments and noncooperation from Pemex career professionals, who (3) that feel the money spent on outside expertise should be invested in developing the internal capabilities that such foreign firms supposedly possess.

37. A cost-benefit critique of each of the major departments *(sub-direcciones)* of Pemex needs to be carried out. The Commercial Department has the counterintuitive mission of both purchasing and sales; these two quite different business functions are administratively joined for no reason that would withstand a management audit in the United States. In 1988 and 1989 Pemex created a series of off-shore companies ostensibly for the purpose of marketing crude oil, but, as of early 1991, no data indicating that benefits have accrued to Pemex or the state from this arrangement had been released.

38. Carlos Castillo Tejero (discussion of Chicontepec reserves), *Revista de ingenería mexicana* (Mexico City, June 1990), makes an interesting distinction between the recoverability of reserves (assuming the criterion of maximum cumulative production) and the effective availability of reserves (which depends on the actual rate at which oil is being produced).

39. Ibid.

40. Few countries bother with a single statistic that includes both oil and gas. These rough calculations correspond to the estimate of Carlos Castillo Tejero, whose work is cited by Noé Cruz Serrano, "Las reservas probadas de petróleo crudo, 50% más bajas de lo que reportan las autoridades," *El Financiero* (Mexico City), 14 Nov. 1990, p. 14. We rigorously applied this methodology for reconstructing reserves for the producing zones and fields in an unpublished study completed in July 1989.

41. Perhaps not having oil export revenue would be a healthy development for

the Mexican economy in that it would force the rapid emergence of alternative, nonoil exports.

42. Officially, each car in the Valley of Mexico is required to be tested, not once, but twice yearly. In practice, however, there are huge loopholes in the enforcement of the testing program. Government vehicles are used routinely in Mexico City without the smog emissions certificate; further, many vehicle owners—taxis are the most notorious example—find ways to obtain the smog certificate without actually having their vehicles inspected.

43. The responsibility for the nonenforcement of smog requirements does not lie with Pemex, however, but with the Department of the Federal District (DDF).

44. Mariano Bauer, "Energía, petróleo y desarrollo: el rumbo del futuro," in *Mexico a cincuenta años de la expropiación petrolera*, edited by Agustín Herrera Reyes and Lorea San Martín Tejeda (Mexico City: UNAM, 1989), pp. 543–550, discusses the need for investments in human capital as a dimension of investments in the energy sector.

45. Pemex estimated in 1989 that $6–$9 billion of new investments will be needed in the petrochemical sector during the upcoming six years; as of late 1990, however, less than $500 million of new commitments had been obtained. One petrochemical industry official in Mexico City commented in February 1991 that the absence of private sector investments had more to do with a downturn in world petrochemical prices than with regulatory constraints in Mexico; other officials, however, insisted that only with the complete dismantling of the restrictions on foreign investments would foreign capital be interested in Mexico as a site for new installed capacity.

46. Another senior official of a U.S. chemical company said (in private) that his company had looked at the possibility of investing from time to time but "could never find anything that wasn't in some way or another crooked." In February 1991, an experienced industry consultant in Mexico City advised foreign companies against talking with "technical people" in Pemex as their first step in developing an investment project: Instead, he insisted, a company should make contact with a member of the presidential family and indicate that equity participation would be made available on any deal cut with Pemex.

47. Dolia Estévez, "Petroquímica privatizada, pide EU," *El Financiero* (Mexico City), 5 Feb. 1991, p. 1. The ISAC (Industry Sector Advisory Committee) Number 3 issued a confidential "Statement of Principles" to the ITC in 1990 in which opposition to the constitutional and regulatory framework for petrochemicals was expressed.

48. As of early 1991, only two companies, Mexico-based Cydsa and Celanese-Hoechst, had responded favorably to this mechanism by prepaying about $30 million. No one in Pemex or the State Petrochemical Commission (CPM) admits to knowing the interest rate that the advance payment will earn.

49. The prospective investor in petrochemicals who is told that all of his feedstocks will have to be bought from Pemex (or imported) may feel anxiety in making an analogy with the government's former monopoly on newsprint: A Mexican newspaper either adhered to the basic outline of government news policy or risked having its cellulose feedstock deliveries interrupted. What is the coin in which noninterruption will be paid?, an investor might ask.

50. In spring 1991, Mexican officials told Americans from all walks of

government: "We want to modernize, we want to create an investment climate that inspires the confidence of both Mexican and American investors (as well as others), but don't force us to change at a rate faster than Mexican society can assimilate without political repercussions." The meaning of such comments clearly was metaconstitutional.

51. Explicit instructions were unnecessary, given the capacity of the Mexican government official for self-censure. In the two weeks prior to the team's visit (February 1991), a highly respected careerist in the energy sector was removed from his job as number 2 man in the Energy Ministry (Semip) for having been quoted (erroneously) in the press as having made a statement not in line with the public policy of the government. The punishment—immediate loss of employment—was sufficient to intimidate everyone else: The government's message was, "If you value your job, don't you dare speak to anyone in a way that could be interpreted that (1) you are in effect negotiating on matters that might be included in FTA discussions, or (2) you have views independent of those of official policies." In Mexico, getting fired from a politically appointed job normally means that one is out of the government, at least for the remainder of the presidential term. Given that, in Mexico, government careerists seldom seek (or find) jobs in the private sector, the economic cost to a public official of losing his job is much greater than in the United States. The nature of the basic political system, then, promotes a high degree of intellectual conformism and party self-discipline throughout all levels of government, not just in the oil sector.

52. Such "data" have only the appearance of an analytic value. Their inclusion in the association's yearbook was strictly for adornment; of course, no real quantified information, such as annual sales, assets, liabilities, and staffing levels, is provided at all.

53. The private sector reasons that if it is to build or pay for a plant, then it should have the right to own and operate it.

54. In 1986, the Mexican state reduced the number of strategic petrochemicals whose production was reserved to Pemex from seventy to thirty-four; in 1989, this number was reduced to twenty. Why not reduce that number to zero? asked many prospective foreign investors in 1990, who were still unwilling to make substantial commitments to investing in new petrochemical capacity in Mexico, owing to the policy of prohibiting vertical integration in Mexico.

55. Not for nothing did a Mexican observer of oil policy exclaim in early 1991, "We need a new constitution!"

56. This idea is discussed in outline in "No ha recibido Eximbank la solicitud del crédito para México," *El Economista* (Mexico City), 11 Dec. 1990.

57. Also entering into the causes of underinvestment is the nebulous area of investment efficiency: Some critics say that of every $1.00 of nominal investment by Pemex (and the public sector in general) only 60¢ finally becomes a fixed asset. In contrast, the private sector is credited with a 90 percent investment efficiency performance. Laura Randall discusses "The Efficiency of Pemex" in *The Political Economy of Mexican Oil* (Praeger, 1989), pp. 5–35.

58. An example of overinvestment was the 48-inch natural gas pipeline built in 1977–1978, the nominal export capacity of which was 2.0 billion cubic feet/day. Critics of the proposed line argued in 1976 that sizing back the diameter to 36 inches would reduce investment costs from over $5 billion to $1.5 billion. As

events turned out, the pipeline was never used for export volumes above 400 million cf/d.

59. Industry critics observe that Pemex's new refinery at Salina Cruz, in the State of Oaxaca, was built on the coast with an eye toward exports, thereby replicating the capital investment philosophy of the private companies in Mexico prior to the expropriation in 1938. Why, some ask, is there no refinery in the state of Jalisco that would serve Mexico's second most populous city, Guadalajara?

Contributors

Ruth Adler
La Trobe University, Bundoora, Victoria, Australia

S. Lief Adleson
Instituto Nacional de Antropología e Historia, Mexico City

George Baker
PROFMEX, Berkeley, California

Fabio Barbosa Cano
Universidad Nacional Autónoma de México, Mexico City

Jonathan C. Brown
University of Texas at Austin

Alan Knight
Oxford University

Lorenzo Meyer
El Colegio de México, Mexico City

Isidro Morales
El Colegio de México, Mexico City

Alberto J. Olvera
Centro de Investigaciones Históricas, Universidad Veracruzano

George Philip
London School of Economics and Political Science

Gabriel Székely
University of California, San Diego

Index